T0212904

Lecture Notes in Computer Science   9447

Commenced Publication in 1973
Founding and Former Series Editors:
Gerhard Goos, Juris Hartmanis, and Jan van Leeuwen

More information about this series at http://www.springer.com/series/7408

Khaled El-Fakih · Gerassimos Barlas
Nina Yevtushenko (Eds.)

Testing Software and Systems

27th IFIP WG 6.1 International Conference, ICTSS 2015
Sharjah and Dubai, United Arab Emirates, November 23–25, 2015
Proceedings

 Springer

Editors
Khaled El-Fakih
Department of Computer Science
  and Engineering
College of Engineering
American University of Sharjah
Sharjah
United Arab Emirates

Nina Yevtushenko
Department of Information Technologies
Tomsk State University
Tomsk
Russia

Gerassimos Barlas
Department of Computer Science
  and Engineering
College of Engineering
American University of Sharjah
Sharjah
United Arab Emirates

ISSN 0302-9743   ISSN 1611-3349 (electronic)
Lecture Notes in Computer Science
ISBN 978-3-319-25944-4   ISBN 978-3-319-25945-1 (eBook)
DOI 10.1007/978-3-319-25945-1

Library of Congress Control Number: 2015952759

LNCS Sublibrary: SL2 – Programming and Software Engineering

Springer Cham Heidelberg New York Dordrecht London

Printed on acid-free paper

Springer International Publishing AG Switzerland is part of Springer Science+Business Media
(www.springer.com)

Preface

This volume contains the proceedings of the 27th International Conference on Testing Software and Systems, ICTSS 2015. The conference was held in Sharjah and Dubai, United Arab Emirates, during November 23–25, 2015.

The conference has a long history. In the past five years, ICTSS was held in Madrid (Spain), Istanbul (Turkey), Aalborg (Denmark), Paris (France), and Natal (Brazil). During the 2007–2009 period, the event was held as a joint conference of the International Conference on Testing of Communicating Systems (TESTCOM) and FATES, in Tallinn (Estonia), Tokyo (Japan), and Eindhoven (The Netherlands). Before that, between 2000 and 2006, TESTCOM was held in Ottawa (Canada), Berlin (Germany), Sophia Antipolis (France), Oxford (UK), Montreal (Canada), and New York City (USA). During the 1997–1999 period, the conference was called the International Workshop on Testing of Communicating Systems (IWTCS) and was held in Cheju Island (Korea), Tomsk (Russia), and Budapest (Hungary). Between 1988 and 1996 the conference was known as the International Workshop for Protocol Test Systems (IWPTS). Nine workshops took place in Vancouver (Canada), Berlin (Germany), McLean (USA), Leidschendam (The Netherlands), Montréal (Canada), Pau (France), Tokyo (Japan), Evry (France), and Darmstadt (Germany).

We received 42 submissions, and after a careful reviewing process by the Program Committee only 14 full and four short papers were selected for presentation at the conference. The accepted papers together with the abstracts of the two invited presentations by Gregor von Bochmann from the University of Ottawa (Canada) and Teruo Higashino from Osaka University (Japan) comprise the contents of the proceedings.

We are grateful to the authors of submitted papers, the invited speakers, the additional reviewers, and the Steering and Program Committee members for their valuable contributions and particularly to Rob Hierons, Steering Committee Chair, for his help and guidance. We acknowledge the use of EasyChair for the conference management. We also thank the IFIP and Springer, the American University of Sharjah, and Tomsk State University for their support.

November 2015

Khaled El-Fakih
Gerassimos Barlas
Nina Yevtushenko

Organization

General Chairs

Khaled El-Fakih   American University of Sharjah, UAE
Gerassimos Barlas   American University of Sharjah, UAE
Nina Yevtushenko   Tomsk State University, Russia

Steering Committee

Ana R. Cavalli   Telecom SudParis, France
Rob Hierons   Brunel University, UK (Chair)
Mercedes G. Merayo   Universidad Complutense de Madrid, Spain
Edgardo Montes de Oca   Montimage, France
Brian Nielsen   Aalborg University, Denmark
Andreas Ulrich   Siemens AG, Germany
Carsten Weise   IVU Traffic Technologies, Germany
Cemal Yilmaz   Sabanci University, Turkey
Husnu Yenigun   Sabanci University, Turkey

Program Committee

Rui Abreu   University of Porto, Portugal
Gerassimos Barlas   American University of Sharjah, UAE
Gregor V. Bochmann   University of Ottawa, Canada
Kirill Bogdanov   University of Sheffield, UK
John Derrick   University of Sheffield, UK
Khaled El-Fakih   American University of Sharjah, UAE
Vahid Garousi   Hacettepe University, Turkey
Sudipto Ghosh   Colorado State University, USA
Jens Grabowski   Georg-August-Universität Göttingen, Germany
Roland Groz   Grenoble INP-LIG, France
Dieter Hogrefe   Georg-August-Universität Göttingen, Germany
Thierry Jéron   Inria Rennes-Bretagne Atlantique, France
Guy-Vincent Jourdan   University of Ottawa, Canada
Ferhat Khendek   Concordia University, Canada
Moez Krichen   Al-Baha University, KSA
Hartmut Koenig   BTU Cottbus, Germany
Victor Kuliamin   Russian Academy of Sciences, Russia
Pascale Le Gall   Université d'Evry, France
Bruno Legeard   Smartesting, France
Stephane Maag   Telecom SudParis, France

Patricia Machado	Federal University of Campina Grand, Brazil
Wissam Mallouli	Montimage, France
Nashat Mansour	Lebanese American University, Lebanon
Wes Masri	American University of Beirut, Lebanon
Mercedes Merayo	Universidad Complutense de Madrid, Spain
Tejeddine Mouelhi	itrust, Luxembourg
Brian Nielsen	Aalborg University, Denmark
Manuel Nunez	Universidad Complutense de Madrid, Spain
Jan Peleska	TZI, Universität Bremen, Germany
Alexander K. Petrenko	Russian Academy of Sciences, Russia
Adenilso Simao	ICMC/USP, Brazil
Kenji Suzuki	Kennisbron Co., Ltd, Japan
Uraz Turker	Brunel University, UK
Hasan Ural	University of Ottawa, Canada
Farn Wang	National Taiwan University, Taiwan
Neil Walkinshaw	University of Leicester, UK
Stephan Weissleder	Thales Deutschland, Germany
Franz Wotawa	Technische Universität Graz, Austria
Hirozumi Yamaguchi	Osaka University, Japan
Keiichi Yasumoto	NAIST, Japan
Hüsnü Yenigün	Sabanci University, Turkey
Nina Yevtushenko	Tomsk State University, Russia
Cemal Yilmaz	Sabanci University, Turkey
Fatiha Zaidi	Université Paris-Sud, France

Additional Reviewers

A. Armstrong
Antonio García-Domínguez
Patrick Harms
Mike Papadakis
Masaki Suzuki

Local Organization

Khaled El-Fakih	American University of Sharjah, UAE
Gerassimos Barlas	American University of Sharjah, UAE
Abdulrahman Al-Ali	American University of Sharjah, UAE

Publicity Chairs

| Moez Krichen | Al-Baha University, KSA |
| Uraz Turker | Brunel University, UK |

Invited Talks
(Abstracts)

Testing Software Systems – A Perspective

Gregor V. Bochmann

School of Electrical Engineering and Computer Science,
University of Ottawa, Canada

Abstract. The talk will begin with a review of general testing concepts, such as white-box and black-box testing, different realizations of oracles (including a formal behavior specification), fault models and fault coverage issues, and testing architectures. This will set the framework for the following discussion which has two parts: (a) a discussion of the history of the ICTSS conference and the issues discussed during the early times since around 1985, and (b) an overview of two ongoing research projects: (1) on testing implementations against partial-order specifications, and (2) on reverse engineering of Rich Internet Applications for vulnerability testing.

The first ICTSS conference was held in Vancouver (Canada) in 1988 and was called International Workshop on Protocol Test Systems. The main question discussed at that time was how to test a protocol implementation to ensure that it satisfies all requirements of a given protocol specification (a form of black-box testing). The main issues were the modeling language used for the specification, fault models, and algorithms for obtaining test suites with given fault coverage. At the same time, standardization committees of ISO and ITU developed guidelines for architectures for protocol testing and a language (TTCN) for specifying test cases. Later, the scope of ICTSS was broadened to cover the testing of many other kinds of software systems.

In the second part of the talk, we will first discuss issues that arise in testing systems against a behavior specification that defines a partial order for the interactions of the implementation. Different partial-order specification languages will be considered. Then another ongoing research project on crawling Rich Internet Applications (RIAs) is discussed. Through the testing of a given implementation, a model of the RIA is developed (this is a kind of black-box testing, but without a reference specification). The purpose here is to obtain a "complete" model of the application such that each state (i.e. each page at the user interface) of the application can be subsequently checked for security vulnerabilities or accessibility requirements. Since the state space of these applications is usually huge, we propose (a) different algorithms for obtaining the most important information relatively fast, (b) concurrent exploration by multiple crawlers, and (c) some methods for avoiding the exploration of "equivalent" and "redundant" states.

Formal Modeling and Testing for Designing Future IoT Based Systems

Teruo Higashino

Graduate School of Information Science and Technology,
Osaka University, Japan

Abstract. Recently, sensing technology and IoT (Internet of Things) have much attention for designing and developing affluent and smart social systems. In this talk, we focus on the design and development of future IoT based systems such as ITS (Self-driving vehicles and collision avoidance), smart grid (power control), crowd sensing systems from human beings with mobile devices, and so on. We discuss about considerations for developing resilient IoT based systems such as (i) mobility influence, (ii) real-time data processing, (iii) treatment of a huge amount of geospatial data, and so on, and provide frameworks for their formal modeling and testing.

The reliability and performance of most ITS and crowd sensing systems are strongly affected from vehicular and human mobility. In the first part of this talk, we summarize recent Vehicle-to-Vehicle (V2V) and Vehicle-to-Infrastructure (V2I) wireless communication mechanisms and crowd sensing systems, and discuss about their mobility influence. Then, we introduce frameworks for their formal modeling and testing in order to improve their reliability.

In urban areas, since multiple wireless communication devices often coexist, they interfere each other. In such cases, geospatial monitoring and passive testing are useful in order to observe that a set of desirable properties called "invariants" holds. In the second part of this talk, we summarize recent research about geospatial monitoring and passive testing, and show how their formal modeling and testing frameworks can be used.

In the third part of this talk, we focus on real-time data processing and treatment of geospatial data. In smart grid systems, real-time feedbacks are essential for stable power supply. In crowd sensing systems, a huge amount of geospatial sensing data need to be treated. General cloud servers might not be able to be used for storing such a huge amount of data and providing real-time feedbacks. We introduce recent research about edge computing (fog computing), and provide frameworks for their formal modeling and testing.

Contents

Model and System Testing

Real-Time Systems

Short Papers

Model Based Testing

Checking Experiments for Finite State Machines with Symbolic Inputs

Alexandre Petrenko[1(✉)] and Adenilso Simao[2]

[1] CRIM, Centre de Recherche Informatique de Montréal, 405 Ogilvy Avenue,
Suite 101, Montréal, Québec H3N 1M3, Canada
petrenko@crim.ca
[2] Instituto de Ciencias Matematicas e de Computacao,
Universidade de Sao Paulo, Sao Carlos, Sao Paulo, Brazil
adenilso@icmc.usp.br

Abstract. There exists a significant body of work in the theory of checking experiments devoted to test generation from FSM which guarantees complete fault coverage for a given fault model. Practical applications require nevertheless methods for fault-model driven test generation from Extended FSMs (EFSM). Traditional approaches for EFSM focus on model coverage, which provides no characterization of faults that can be detected by the generated tests. Only few approaches use fault models, and we are not aware of any result in the theory of checking experiments for extended FSMs. In this paper, we lift the theory of checking experiments to EFSMs, which are Mealy machines with predicates defined over input variables treated as symbolic inputs. Considering this kind of EFSM, we propose a test generation method that produces a symbolic checking experiment, adapting the well-known HSI method. We then present conditions under which arbitrary instances of a symbolic checking experiment can be used for testing black-box implementations, while guaranteeing complete fault coverage.

Keywords: Finite state machines · Extended finite state machines · Symbolic automata · Conformance testing · Checking experiments · Fault model based test generation

1 Introduction

Research in Model Based Testing (MBT) is currently advancing rapidly trying to match the growing demand from industry for more effective and better scalable test development technologies. Since the cost for leaving undetected faults in software grows with its complexity, code and model coverage by tests is often considered insufficient and the guaranteed fault detection becomes the ultimate goal. Accordingly, research in MBT has been addressing fault modeling and fault model driven test generation problems, see, e.g., [2, 38]. Fault models usually refer to test models which formalize reference specifications and/or requirements. State-oriented test models seem to be most popular models among test engineers. Finite state machines (FSM) and input output transition systems (IOTS) are state-oriented models; test generation methods have traditionally been developed separately for these models, even though, as has already been

K. El-Fakih et al. (Eds.): ICTSS 2015, LNCS 9447, pp. 3–18, 2015.
DOI: 10.1007/978-3-319-25945-1_1

demonstrated, many ideas, especially for fault model based test generation, developed for testing from FSM can successfully be used for testing from IOTS [31].

There exists a significant body of work devoted to the development of methods for test generation from a given FSM to guarantee the complete fault coverage, once a fault model is defined. The pioneering work of Moore [21] and Hennie [13] led to the development of the theory of checking experiments, where faults are modeled by a universe of FSMs with a given number of states, see, e.g., [4, 6, 10, 33]. Checking experiments have already been lifted to FSMs more general than the classical (completely specified and deterministic) Mealy machine, such as partially defined and nondeterministic state machines, see, e.g., [27]. However, practical applications require more extensions to the classical FSM model. These are commonly known as the Extended Finite State Machine (EFSM) models. Various flavors of EFSMs are used in Harel's statecharts [12], SysML/UML [9], Simulink/Stateflow [32], SDL [11] and other modelling languages. Extensions are often suggested without a formal semantics; this creates a big hurdle for fault-model based test generation. Whenever the semantics of a particular specification language is defined by the tool which supports it, fault models become specific to the tool provider and may not be adequate for implementations coming from other suppliers. General testing approaches usually rely on formally defined extensions of Mealy machine, see, e.g., [26, 36].

Most of the existing work on test generation from EFSM concentrates on the model coverage, see, e.g., [3, 14, 18, 28], which provides no characterization of faults that can be detected by the generated tests. There are some techniques for test generation from EFSM which use certain fault models [26, 36] and limited state/configuration identification sequences [5, 19, 26]. The work of [16] uses checking experiment methods, but requires first to determine input/output equivalence classes from a given specification EFSM and choose concrete inputs. To the best of our knowledge, there is no result in lifting the theory of checking experiments to extended FSMs. This observation is one of the main motivations of this work.

Another motivation comes from research on symbolic automata and transducers, which is driven by several practical problems. The work of [34] mentions applications ranging from modern regex analysis to advanced web security analysis where the so-called sanitizers, string transformation routines are extensively used as the first line of defense against cross site scripting attacks. A large class of sanitizers can be described and analyzed by using symbolic finite state transducers. Symbolic finite automata are introduced as an extension of classical finite state automata that allows transitions to be labeled with predicates. Automata with predicates instead of concrete symbols are also used in [37] and discussed in [23] in the context of natural language processing. The work on learning symbolic automata [20] has also to be mentioned here, since the automata learning shares certain aspects with the testing problem in the following sense. If a black box passes a checking experiment, then under well-defined conditions it is recognized as some automaton. Hence it is important to investigate checking experiments for symbolic automata.

The community focusing on testing from IOTS has also considered extensions to symbolic representation of transition systems which avoid enumerations of its components, see, e.g. [8, 29], but these approaches are not fault model driven, they use one or another test purpose. More references on symbolic approaches in testing could be found, e.g., in [1, 17].

In this paper, we attempt to lift the theory of checking experiments to a special type of EFSM, which extends the deterministic Mealy machine with predicates defined over input variables, considered as its symbolic inputs. We propose a test generation method that produces a symbolic checking experiment, adapting the well-known HSI method [39]. We then investigate under which conditions instances of a symbolic checking experiment can be used for testing black-box implementations, guaranteeing the full fault coverage.

The paper is organized as follows. In Sect. 2, we define the model of FSM with symbolic inputs. In Sect. 3, we study the relations between SIFSMs. Symbolic and concrete checking experiments are introduced in Sect. 4, where we also investigate fault detection capability of concrete tests obtained from symbolic checking experiments. Section 5 summarizes our contributions and presents future work.

2 Definitions and Notations

2.1 Preliminaries

We define an (input) alphabet as a set of guards over variables of well-defined types. Let G denote the universe of guards that are predicates over variables in a fixed set V for which a decision theory, e.g., an SMT solver, exists, excluding the predicates that are always false. G^* will denote the universe of input sequences.

Let D_V denote the set of all the valuations v of the input variables in the set V, called *concrete* inputs. A set of concrete inputs is called a *symbolic* input; both, concrete and symbolic, inputs are represented by guards in G. Henceforth, we use set-theoretical operations on symbolic inputs. In particular, we write $v \in g$, when concrete input v satisfies g. We define some relations between input sequences in G^*.

Definition 1. Given two input sequences $\alpha, \beta \in G^*$ of the same length k, $\alpha = g_1...g_k$, $\beta = g'_1...g'_k$, we let $\alpha \cap \beta = g_1 \cap g'_1...g_k \cap g'_k$ denote the sequence of intersections of inputs in sequences α and β; α and β are *compatible*, if for all $i = 1, ..., k, g_i \cap g'_i \neq \varnothing$. We say that α is a *reduction* of β, denoted $\alpha \subseteq \beta$, if $\alpha = \alpha \cap \beta$. If α is a sequence of concrete inputs as well as a reduction of β then it is called an *instance* of β; given a finite set of input sequences $E \subseteq G^*$, a set of concrete input sequences I is called an *instance* of the set E, if I contains at least one instance for each input sequence in E.

2.2 Symbolic Input FSM

We define a model, called a symbolic input finite state machine (SIFSM), which operates in discrete time as a synchronous machine reading values of input variables and setting up the values of output variables. Output variables are assumed to have a finite number of valuations and form a finite output alphabet. On the other hand, there may exist an infinite set of input valuations. SIFSM uses guards on transitions which are executed one at a time.

Definition 2. A *symbolic input* finite state machine S (or machine, for short) is a 7-tuple $(S, s_0, V, O, F, \delta, \lambda)$, where

- S is a finite set of states with the initial state s_0,
- V is a finite set of input variables over which guards in G are defined,
- O is a finite set of outputs,
- $F \subseteq S \times G$ is a finite specification domain,
- $\delta : F \rightarrow S$ is a transition function, and
- $\lambda : F \rightarrow O$ is an output function.

Examples of SIFSM are given in Fig. 1. Examples of realistic systems which can be specified as SIFSM could be found in [15, 28]. In the first work, the Ceiling speed monitoring following the public ETCS system specification [7] is modelled, it has two input and two output variables. In the second work, an HVAC controller specified in Simulink/Stateflow is considered, it has nine input variables, Boolean and naturals, the most complex transition guard comprises 13 terms.

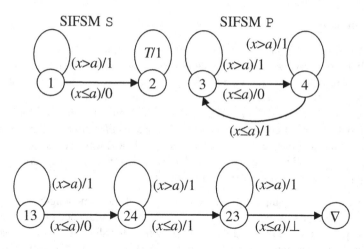

Fig. 1. SIFSMs S, P, and the distinguishing machine S $\oplus$ P.

The semantics of SIFSM is defined by a Mealy state machine with a possibly infinite input set, where the state and output sets remain finite.

Given $(s, g) \in F$, we say that input g is *defined* in state $s \in S$. Then, $G(s) = \{g \in G \mid (s, g) \in F\}$ contains all inputs defined at s. The machine S is *deterministic*, if for any $(s, g), (s, g') \in F$, it holds that $g \cap g' = \emptyset$. State s of the machine S is *input-complete*, if for each input valuation v, at least one of its guards evaluates to True, i.e., $\{v \in g \mid g \in G(s)\} = D_V$. The machine S is *input-complete*, if each state is input-complete. The machine S is *normalized*, if for all $(s, g), (s, g') \in F$, $\delta(s, g) = \delta(s, g')$ implies that $\lambda(s, g) \neq \lambda(s, g')$; in other words, the machine has at most one transition with a given output for each ordered pair of states. Any machine that is not normalized can always be converted into a normalized one by merging transitions with the same start and end states as well as the same output and forming the disjunction of their guards. This is a unique compact form of a SIFSM. We will consider only normalized deterministic input-complete specification machines.

An input sequence $\alpha \in G^*$, $\alpha = g_1...g_k$, is *defined* in state $s \in S$, if each input in α is defined in a corresponding state, i.e., if there exist states $s_1, ..., s_k, s_{k+1}$, where $s_1 = s$, such that $(s_i, g_i) \in F$ and $\delta(s_i, g_i) = s_{i+1}$ for each $1 \leq i \leq k$. Let $\Psi_S(s)$ denote the set of input sequences defined in state s, and Ψ_S denote sequences defined in the initial state of S. Moreover, $\Omega_S(s)$ denotes the set $\Psi_S(s)$ closed under the reduction relation, called the set of input sequences *admissible* in state s, i.e., $\Omega_S(s) = \{\alpha \in G^* \mid \beta \in \Psi_S(s)$, $\alpha \subseteq \beta\}$, and Ω_S denotes sequences admissible in the initial state of S. Notice that for an input-complete machine S any concrete input sequence is admissible in every state, i.e., $D_V^* = \Omega_S(s)$, for each $s \in S$. We lift the transition and output functions from inputs to admissible input sequences, including the empty sequence ε, as usual: for $s \in S$, $\delta(s, \varepsilon) = s$ and $\lambda(s, \varepsilon) = \varepsilon$; and for input sequence $\alpha \in \Omega_S(s)$ and input $g \in \Omega_S(\delta(s, \alpha))$, $\delta(s, \alpha g) = \delta(\delta(s, \alpha), g')$ and $\lambda(s, \alpha g) = \lambda(s, \alpha)\lambda(\delta(s, \alpha), g')$, if $g' \in G_S((\delta(s, \alpha))$ and $g \subseteq g'$.

Considering the input alphabet G, we further extend the transition and output functions to the set of all possible input sequences in G^*. The extended transition function describes the set of all possible states which a deterministic machine from a given state can reach in response to input sequence and the extended output reaction function gives the set of all possible corresponding output sequences; these sets are singletons if the input sequence is admissible for the starting state. We define the function $\Delta : S \times G^* \rightarrow 2^S$ as follows. Given $s \in S$ and $\alpha \in G^*$, we let $\Delta(s, \alpha)$ be $\{\delta(s, \beta) \mid \beta \subseteq \alpha, \beta \in \Omega_S(s)\}$. Obviously, for any $\alpha \in \Omega_S(s)$, $\Delta(s, \alpha) = \{\delta(s, \alpha)\}$. Similarly, we define the function $\Lambda : S \times G^* \rightarrow 2^{O^*}$. For $s \in S$ and $\alpha \in G^*$, we define $\Lambda(s, \alpha) = \{\lambda(s, \beta) \mid \beta \subseteq \alpha, \beta \in \Omega_S(s)\}$. We call the functions Δ and Λ the *extended* transition and output functions. For any $\alpha \in \Omega_S(s)$, $\Lambda(s, \alpha) = \{\lambda(s, \alpha)\}$. Given a set of symbolic input sequences $\Phi \subseteq G^*$, the SIFSM S is said to be a Φ-*converter* if for each $\alpha \in \Phi$, $|\Lambda(s_0, \alpha)| = 1$.

Given input sequence α, we use *pref(α)* to denote the set of all prefixes of α. Similar, *pref(A)* denotes the set of prefixes of sequences in A. The set A is prefix-closed if *pref(A) = A*.

3   Relations Between SIFSMs

In this section, we extend the classical equivalence and distinguishability relations to SIFSMs and introduce new types of distinguishability which have no counterparts in the classical deterministic Mealy machine. We define a designated symbolic machine which can be used to check the distinguishability of symbolic input finite state machines.

In this paper, we focus our attention on deterministic systems, in which different output sequences produced by two states in response to the same symbolic input sequence indicate that the two states can be distinguished by the input sequence.

Definition 3. Given states $s, s' \in S$ of S, states $s, s' \in S$ are *distinguishable*, denoted $s \not\approx s'$, if there exist compatible input sequences $\alpha \in \Psi_S(s)$ and $\beta \in \Psi_S(s')$, such that $\lambda(s, (\alpha \cap \beta)) \neq \lambda(s', (\alpha \cap \beta))$; the sequence $\alpha \cap \beta$ is called a *separating* sequence for distinguishable states s and s'.

Since the machine is deterministic, its reacts to a given admissible input sequence as it does to any of its reduction. We have therefore the following corollary.

Corollary 1. Any instance of a separating sequence is a separating sequence.

The importance of this property of separating sequences becomes evident in the context of testing, as we discussed later.

Given a prefix-closed set of input sequences $E \subseteq G^*$, we let $s \not\simeq_E s'$ to denote the fact that the set E contains a separating sequence. If E contains no separating sequence then states s and s' are said to be E-*equivalent*, denoted $s \simeq_E s'$, and if $E = G^*$, then the states are *equivalent*, denoted $s \simeq s'$. The machine is *reduced* if it has no equivalent states. We further assume that the specification machine S is reduced.

As usual, we define equivalence and distinguishability of machines as the corresponding relation between their initial states.

To decide distinguishability we define a designated machine, where, instead of composing transitions caused by the same input as in the case of FSMs [27], we compose transitions with compatible inputs. The machine has the common behavior of the given machines, as the classical automata product (even lifted to symbolic automata [34]), but in addition it signals when they disagree on output and enters a sink state.

Definition 4. Given two SIFSMs S = $(S, s_0, V, O, F_S, \delta_S, \lambda_S)$ and P = $(P, p_0, V, O, F_P, \delta_P, \lambda_P)$ over the same set of input variables V, a SIFSM C = $(C \cup \{\nabla\}, c_0, V, O \cup \{\perp\}, F_C, \delta_C, \lambda_C)$, where ∇ is a designated sink state, $\perp$ is a designated output, is the *distinguishing machine* for S and P denoted S $\oplus$ P, if

- $c_0 = (s_0, p_0)$
- $F_C \subseteq C \times G$ such that for $(s, p) \in C$, $g \cap g' \in G_C(s, p)$, if $g \in G_S(s)$, $g' \in G_P(p)$, and $g \cap g' \neq \varnothing$
- For $(s, p) \in S \times P$ and $g \cap g' \in G_C(s, p)$, $\delta_C((s, p), g \cap g') = (\delta_S(s, g), \delta_P(p, g'))$ and $\lambda_C((s, p), g \cap g') = \lambda_S(\delta(s, g))$, $(\delta_S(s, g), \delta_P(p, g')) \in S \times P$ if $\lambda_S(s, g) = \lambda_P(p, g')$ otherwise, i.e., if $\lambda_S(s, g) \neq \lambda_P(p, g')$, then $\delta_C((s, p), g \cap g') = \nabla$, and $\lambda_C((s, p), g \cap g') = \perp$.

We further assume that the distinguishing machine is normalized by merging, if needed, transitions with the designated output $\perp$ from the same state. By the definition, any input sequence reaching the sink state of the distinguishing machine is a separating sequence for the given machines; the distinguishing machine could be used to decide the equivalence of two distinct machines as well as states in the same machine. To illustrate the above we consider the SIFSMs in Fig. 1, where x is an input variable, a is a constant, 0, 1 and 2 are outputs and T stands for True.

The machines S and P are distinguishable, as the distinguishing machine S $\oplus$ P shows. The shortest separating sequence is $(x \leq a)(x \leq a)(x \leq a)$. Indeed, in response to it S produces 011, while P produces 010.

In this example, we have that the separating sequence is admissible in both machines, as required; however, it is defined only in one of them, namely, $(x \leq a)$ $(x \leq a)(x \leq a) \in \Psi_P$, though $(x \leq a)(x \leq a)(x \leq a) \notin \Psi_S$. This sequence is a reduction of the symbolic sequence $(x \leq a)(T)(T)$ defined in the machine S. Considering the relations between separating and defined sequences we further refine the distinguishability relation.

Definition 5. Given distinguishable states s, $s' \in S$ of S, s' is *strongly*-distinguishable from s if there exists a separating sequence defined in state s, i.e., $\alpha \in \Psi_S(s)$; if state s' is not strongly-distinguishable from state s, then s' is said to be *weakly*-distinguishable from state s.

For two arbitrary states, they could be equivalent, one can be strongly-distinguishable from another, both can be strongly-distinguishable from each other, or both can be weakly-distinguishable from each other. In the last case, they are just distinguishable. Notice that the strongly-distinguishability relationship is not symmetric.

In our example, the machine S is strongly-distinguishable from P, because the separating sequence $(x \leq a)(x \leq a)(x \leq a)$ is defined in P. The machine P, in turn, is weakly-distinguishable from S, since all the separating sequences in the distinguishing machine are not defined in S.

As follows from Corollary 1, if the machines are distinguishable, they are distinguished by any instance of a separating sequence; this is also the case when one machine is strongly-distinguishable from another machine and by the definition the separating sequence is defined in the latter. However, an arbitrary instance of such a sequence may not distinguish a machine that is weakly-distinguishable from another. This difference becomes crucial in conformance testing, when one machine represents a specification and another an implementation under test (IUT). To test the latter, only concrete input sequences would be used, when the IUT is treated as a black box. In the example, assuming that the machine P is the specification and S is the IUT, any instance of the separating sequence $(x \leq a)(x \leq a)(x \leq a)$ can be used to detect non-conformance of the IUT S, as it is not equivalent to P, moreover, S is strongly-distinguishable from P. On the other hand, if the machines swap their roles then since P is weakly-distinguishable from S, then non-conformance of the IUT P cannot be detected by an arbitrary instance of the separating sequence $(x \leq a)(x \leq a)$ $(x \leq a)$.

We formulate a condition under which a SIFSM is either equivalent to or strongly-distinguishable from another SIFSM. It is based on the property of one machine being a converter for all symbolic input sequences defined in another machine. Intuitively, the condition $|\Lambda(m_0, \alpha)| = 1$ corresponds to the case when the two machines are equivalent as well as to the case when they produce different output sequences in response to α.

Theorem 1. Given a (specification) machine S and an (implementation) machine M, if M is a Ψ_S-converter then M is either equivalent to or strongly-distinguishable from S.

Proof. Assume that M is a Ψ_S-converter, i.e., $|\Lambda(m_0, \alpha)| = 1$ for each $\alpha \in \Psi_S$. As S is deterministic, we have that $|\Lambda(s_0, \alpha)| = 1$ for each $\alpha \in \Psi_S$. Assume also that M is not strongly-distinguishable from S. Thus, for each $\alpha \in \Psi_S$, $\Lambda(m_0, \alpha) \supseteq \Lambda(s_0, \alpha)$. It implies that for each $\alpha \in \Psi_S$, $\Lambda(m_0, \alpha) = \Lambda(s_0, \alpha)$, since $|\Lambda(m_0, \alpha)| = |\Lambda(s_0, \alpha)| = 1$. Hence, there is no separating sequence for S and M, i.e., they are equivalent. $\blacklozenge$

Clearly, the sufficient condition is not a necessary one. Consider the machine P in Fig. 1 as an IUT and assume that both transitions from state 4 have the output 0. The modified machine is strongly-distinguishable from S, but it has $|\Lambda(m_0, (x \leq a)(T))| = 2$.

4 Symbolic and Concrete Checking Experiments

In this section, we define symbolic checking experiments following a usual framework for defining complete test suite for a given machine, conformance relation, and fault domain [25]. In this case, we are dealing with specification and implementation SIFSMs in a fault domain containing only normalized deterministic input-complete machines; the conformance relation is the machine equivalence. Complete test suite is considered as checking experiment, which could be symbolic or concrete. In the context of symbolic execution and constraint solving, symbolic experiments are of interest for white box testing, while concrete ones for back box testing, where all test data should be concrete. Another specific feature of testing from SIFSM is that a non-equivalent implementation machine in a fault domain can either be weakly- or strongly-distinguishable, which as we show later has a significant impact on fault detection capability of concrete checking experiments.

Let $\mathfrak{J}(V, m)$ be the universe of SIFSMs over the input variables V with at most m states. A subset of $\mathfrak{J}(V, m)$ is called a *fault domain* for a specification machine S = $(S, s_0, V, O, F, \delta, \lambda)$; it includes SIFSMs which model all possible implementations of S. A set of input sequences $E \subseteq \Omega_S$ is a *checking* experiment for S in a fault domain $\Sigma \subseteq \mathfrak{J}(V, m)$ iff S $\simeq_E$ M implies S $\simeq$ M, for each M $\in \Sigma$.

We now define main ingredients of symbolic checking experiments, following the classical approach of state identification.

A *symbolic state cover* C for the machine S is a set which contains the empty sequence and for each state $s \in S$ a single defined input sequence $\alpha \in \Psi_S$, such that $\delta(s_0, \alpha) = s$. A *symbolic transition cover* T for the machine S is a set $\{\alpha g \mid \alpha \in C, g \in G\ (\delta(s_0, \alpha))\}$, where C is a symbolic state cover.

Given state $s \in S$ of the reduced machine S, a finite set $E \subseteq \Omega_S(s)$ is a *state identifier for s*, denoted $Id(s)$, if $s \not\simeq_E s'$ for each $s' \neq s$. State identifiers in a set H = $\{Id(s) \mid s \in S\}$ are *harmonized* if for each pair of distinguishable states s and s', there exists a separating sequence $\alpha \in pref(Id(s)) \cap pref(Id(s'))$. A straightforward way of constructing HSIs is to determine a distinguishing machine for each pair of states and include the found sequence in the identifiers of the states in the pair.

Given a symbolic state cover C, a symbolic transition cover T and a set of harmonized state identifiers H = $\{Id(s) \mid s \in S\}$, a symbolic *HSI experiment* is $\{\alpha\gamma \mid \alpha \in (C \cup T), \gamma \in Id(\delta(s_0, \alpha))\}$.

As an example, we construct a symbolic checking experiment for S in Fig. 1. The state cover is $\{\varepsilon, (x \leq a)\}$, the transition cover is $\{(x > a), (x \leq a), (x \leq a)(T)\}$. The symbolic input $(x \leq a)$ separates states, so $Id(1) = Id(2) = (x \leq a)$. Then the HSI experiment becomes $\{(x > a)(x \leq a), (x \leq a)(x \leq a), (x \leq a)(T)(x \leq a)\}$, which could be simplified to $\{(x > a)(x \leq a), (x \leq a)(T)(x \leq a)\}$.

Recall that we assume that a specification SIFSM S = $(S, s_0, V, O, F, \delta, \lambda)$ is reduced, normalized, deterministic, and input-complete.

Theorem 2. Let S be a specification SIFSM, an HSI experiment is a checking experiment for S in the fault domain $\Im(V, n)$.

Before proving Theorem 2, we demonstrate some auxiliary results.

Lemma 3. Let $S = (S, s_0, V, O, F, \delta_S, \lambda_S)$ be a specification SIFSM, E be an HSI experiment for S and $M = (M, m_0, V, O, F_M, \delta_M, \lambda_M)$ be a SIFSM from the fault domain $\Im(V, n)$. If $M \simeq_E S$ then M has n states.

Proof. Let s and s' be two states of S. There exist $\alpha, \alpha' \in C$, such that $\delta_S(s_0, \alpha) = s$ and $\delta_S(s_0, \alpha') = s'$. There also exists $\gamma \in pref(Id(s)) \cap pref(Id(s'))$, such that $\alpha\gamma, \alpha'\gamma \in E$ and $\Lambda(s, \gamma) \neq \Lambda(s', \gamma)$; thus, $\Lambda(\Delta(s_0, \alpha), \gamma) \neq \Lambda(\Delta(s_0, \alpha'), \gamma)$. As $S \simeq_E M$, we have that $\Lambda(s_0, \alpha\gamma) = \Lambda(m_0, \alpha\gamma)$ and $\Lambda(s_0, \alpha'\gamma) = \Lambda(m_0, \alpha'\gamma)$. Hence, $\Lambda(\Delta(s_0, \alpha), \gamma) = \Lambda(\Delta(m_0, \alpha), \gamma)$ and $\Lambda(\Delta(s_0, \alpha'), \gamma) = \Lambda(\Delta(m_0, \alpha'), \gamma)$. Thus, $\Lambda(\Delta(m_0, \alpha), \gamma) \neq \Lambda(\Delta(m_0, \alpha'), \gamma)$ and, therefore, $\Delta(m_0, \alpha) \neq \Delta(m_0, \alpha')$. We conclude that for each pair of states of S, there exists at least a pair of states of M which are distinct. Therefore, M has at least n states. As $M \in \Im(V, n)$, M has at most n states. Thus, M has n states. ♦

Lemma 4. Let $S = (S, s_0, V, O, F_S, \delta_S, \lambda_S)$ be a specification SIFSM, E be an HSI experiment for S and $M = (M, m_0, V, O, F_M, \delta_M, \lambda_M)$ be a SIFSM from the fault domain $\Im(V, n)$. If $M \simeq_E S$ then there exists a bijection $f : S \leftrightarrow M$, such that for each $\alpha \in (C \cup T), f(\Delta(s_0, \alpha)) = \Delta(m_0, \alpha)$.

Proof. C contains n symbolic input sequences, one for each state of S. By Lemma 3, M has n states. Thus, we can define a bijection $f : S \leftrightarrow M$, such that for each $\alpha \in C, f(\Delta(s_0, \alpha)) = \Delta(m_0, \alpha)$. It thus remains to show that for each $\beta \in T$, we also have that $f(\Delta(s_0, \beta)) = \Delta(m_0, \beta)$. Let $\beta \in T$ and $s = \Delta(s_0, \beta)$. There exists $\alpha \in C$, such that $s = \Delta(s_0, \alpha)$. We have that $f(s) = \Delta(m_0, \alpha)$. Let $\alpha' \in C$, such that $s' = \Delta(s_0, \alpha') \neq s$. Thus, $f(s') = \Delta(m_0, \alpha')$. There also exists $\gamma \in pref(Id(s)) \cap pref(Id(s'))$, such that $\beta\gamma, \alpha'\gamma \in E$ and $\Lambda(s, \gamma) \neq \Lambda(s', \gamma)$; thus, $\Lambda(\Delta(s_0, \beta), \gamma) \neq \Lambda(\Delta(s_0, \alpha'), \gamma)$. As $S \simeq_E M$, we have that $\Lambda(s_0, \beta\gamma) = \Lambda(m_0, \beta\gamma)$ and $\Lambda(s_0, \alpha'\gamma) = \Lambda(m_0, \alpha'\gamma)$. Hence, $\Lambda(\Delta(s_0, \beta), \gamma) = \Lambda(\Delta(m_0, \beta), \gamma)$ and $\Lambda(\Delta(s_0, \alpha'), \gamma) = \Lambda(\Delta(m_0, \alpha'), \gamma)$. Thus, $\Lambda(\Delta(m_0, \beta), \gamma) \neq \Lambda(\Delta(m_0, \alpha'), \gamma)$ and, therefore, $\Delta(m_0, \beta) \neq \Delta(m_0, \alpha') = f(s')$ and $\Delta(m_0, \beta) \neq f(s')$. It follows that $f(s) = \Delta(m_0, \beta)$ and, thus, $f(\Delta(s_0, \beta)) = \Delta(m_0, \beta)$. ♦

Corollary 2. If $M \simeq_E S$ then for any $\alpha, \beta \in \Psi_S$, if $\Delta(s_0, \alpha) = \Delta(s_0, \beta)$ then $\Delta(m_0, \alpha) = \Delta(m_0, \beta)$.

Proof. Let $M \simeq_E S$ and $\alpha, \beta \in \Psi_S, \Delta(s_0, \alpha) = \Delta(s_0, \beta)$. First, we prove by induction on the prefixes of α that there exists a sequence $\varphi \in C$, such that $\Delta(s_0, \alpha) = \Delta(s_0, \varphi)$ and $\Delta(m_0, \alpha) = \Delta(m_0, \varphi)$.

For the base case, we have $\alpha = \varepsilon$. As $\varepsilon \in C$, the property holds for $\varphi = \alpha = \varepsilon$, since obviously $\Delta(s_0, \alpha) = \Delta(s_0, \varphi)$ and $\Delta(m_0, \alpha) = \Delta(m_0, \varphi)$.

For the inductive case, assume that $\alpha = \alpha'g$ and there exists $\varphi' \in C$, with $\Delta(s_0, \alpha') = \Delta(s_0, \varphi')$ and $\Delta(m_0, \alpha') = \Delta(m_0, \varphi')$. We have that $\varphi'g \in T$. As C is a state cover for S, there exists $\varphi \in C$, such that $\Delta(s_0, \varphi'g) = \Delta(s_0, \varphi)$; hence $\Delta(s_0, \alpha) = \Delta(s_0, \varphi)$. Thus, due to the properties for the bijection f, it follows that $f(\Delta(s_0, \varphi'g)) = \Delta(m_0, \varphi'g)$ and $f(\Delta(s_0, \varphi)) = \Delta(m_0, \varphi)$. It then follows that $\Delta(m_0, \alpha) = \Delta(m_0, \varphi'g) = f(\Delta(s_0, \varphi'g)) = f(\Delta(s_0, \varphi)) = \Delta(m_0, \varphi)$, hence $\Delta(m_0, \alpha) = \Delta(m_0, \varphi)$, concluding the induction proof.

In the same vein, we can prove that there exists a sequence $\varphi' \in C$, such that $\Delta(s_0, \beta) = \Delta(s_0, \varphi')$ and $\Delta(m_0, \beta) = \Delta(m_0, \varphi')$. As $\Delta(s_0, \alpha) = \Delta(s_0, \beta)$ and C contains only one sequence that reaches each state, we have that $\varphi = \varphi'$. Thus, $\Delta(m_0, \beta) = \Delta(m_0, \varphi) = \Delta(m_0, \varphi') = \Delta(m_0, \alpha)$, i.e., $\Delta(m_0, \beta) = \Delta(m_0, \alpha)$. ♦

Now we are ready to prove Theorem 2.

Proof of Theorem 2. Let $M = (M, m_0, V, O, F_M, \delta_M, \lambda_M)$ be a SIFSM from the fault domain $\mathfrak{J}(V, n)$, such that $M \simeq_E S$. We prove by contradiction that $M \simeq S$. Assume that $M \not\simeq S$. Let β be the shortest symbolic input sequence such that $M \simeq_{\{\beta\}} S$ and there exists $g \in G^*$ such that βg is a separating sequence, i.e., $M \not\simeq_{\{\beta g\}} S$. Thus, $\Lambda(\Delta(m_0, \beta), g) \neq \Lambda(\Delta(s_0, \beta), g)$.

Since E is an HSI experiment $\{\alpha\gamma \mid \alpha \in (C \cup T), \gamma \in Id(\delta_S(s_0, \alpha))\}$, it contains a sequence $\varphi \in C$, such that $\Delta(s_0, \varphi) = \Delta(s_0, \beta)$. Then $\Delta(m_0, \varphi) = \Delta(m_0, \beta)$, according to Corollary 2. Since $\Lambda(\Delta(m_0, \beta), g) \neq \Lambda(\Delta(s_0, \beta), g)$, it also holds that $\Lambda(\Delta(m_0, \varphi), g) \neq \Lambda(\Delta(s_0, \varphi), g)$. The HSI experiment contains a transition cover of S then there exists a symbolic input g', such that $(\Delta(s_0, \varphi), g') \in F_S$, $g \subseteq g'$, and $\varphi g' \in E$. $M \simeq_E S$ implies that $M \simeq_{\{\varphi g'\}} S$. We have that $\Delta(m_0, \varphi) = \Delta(m_0, \beta)$, then $\Lambda(\Delta(m_0, \beta), g') = \Lambda(\Delta(s_0, \beta), g')$. This contradicts the assumption that $\Lambda(\Delta(m_0, \beta), g) \neq \Lambda(\Delta(s_0, \beta), g)$, as $g \subseteq g'$. ♦

For simplicity, we have considered symbolic experiments for the fault domain $\mathfrak{J}(V, n)$. Nevertheless, based on the previous results, e.g., [30, 33], the case of a wider fault domain $\mathfrak{J}(V, m)$, where $m > n$ can also be considered.

Symbolic experiments could be used in the context of white-box testing when symbolic execution of code/model of an implementation SIFSM is possible; however, they cannot be executed against an implementation SIFSM considered as a black box. We further assume that only instances of symbolic experiments can be executed against any implementation SIFSM in a given fault domain.

Consider first the case, when an SIFSM S has a finite number of concrete inputs, in other words, it is a compact representation of a Mealy FSM S' over the finite input set D_V. Then the set of all possible instances of a symbolic checking experiment is finite and is in fact a concrete checking experiment for the SIFSM S. The latter is also a classical checking experiment for the FSM S'.

Theorem 3. Given a specification machine S with a finite input set D_V, let E be a symbolic checking experiment for S in $\mathfrak{J}(V, n)$. Let also E' be the set of all possible instances of E and S' be the FSM obtained by unfolding S. Then, E' is a concrete checking experiment for S and S' in $\mathfrak{J}(V, n)$.

Proof. As E is a symbolic checking experiment for S in $\mathfrak{J}(V, n)$, for each M in $\mathfrak{J}(V, n)$, E contains a separating sequence α distinguishing S and M. Thus, there exists an instance of α which distinguishes S and M and E' contains this instance; hence E' distinguishes S and any SIFSM in $\mathfrak{J}(V, n)$ which is distinguished by E. As E is a symbolic checking experiment for S in $\mathfrak{J}(V, n)$, it follows that E' is a checking experiment for S in $\mathfrak{J}(V, n)$. As S' is equivalent to S, we have that E' is also a checking experiment for S' in $\mathfrak{J}(V, n)$. ♦

The theorem suggests that checking experiments for SIFSMs with a finite set of concrete inputs can be constructed directly from a given specification machine without first unfolding it into a classical Mealy machine and using one of the existing methods for checking experiment generation. It might also be computationally simpler to first determine all the ingredients of a checking experiment in the symbolic form and then generate all the concrete instances of symbolic sequences one by one.

Next we consider the case when the input variables do not yield a finite set of concrete inputs and we investigate faults detectable by concrete experiments. Since we can execute only a finite number of concrete input sequences, it is interesting to know in which cases the set of single instances of each sequence in a symbolic checking experiment remains a checking experiment for a given fault domain. In the following, we identify several such cases.

Let E be a symbolic checking experiment for S in $\mathfrak{J}(V, n)$ and let Σ be a subset of $\mathfrak{J}(V, n)$. We say that E is *safely-instantiable* for Σ if any instance of E is a concrete checking experiment for S in Σ. We will use $\mathfrak{J}(V, n, \Psi_S)$ to denote the subset of $\mathfrak{J}(V, n)$, which consists of Ψ_S-converters.

Theorem 4. Let E be a symbolic checking experiment for S in $\mathfrak{J}(V, n)$. Then, E is safely-instantiable for $\mathfrak{J}(V, n, \Psi_S)$.

Proof. Let $M \in \mathfrak{J}(V, n, \Psi_S)$; thus, for each $\alpha \in \Psi_S$, $|\Lambda(m_0, \alpha)| = 1$. According to Theorem 1, the machine M is either equivalent to or strongly-distinguishable from S. Let C be an instance of E. Assume that M is not equivalent to S; thus, M is strongly-distinguishable from S. As E is a symbolic checking experiment for S in $\mathfrak{J}(V, n)$ and $\mathfrak{J}(V, n, \Psi_S) \subseteq \mathfrak{J}(V, n)$, there exists a symbolic separating sequence $\alpha \in E$, such that $M \not\approx_{\{\alpha\}} S$; by Corollary 1, any instance of the sequence α is also a separating sequence. Thus, the result follows. ♦

Theorem 4 says that any concrete experiment derived from a symbolic checking experiment is also a checking experiment for the machine S in the fault domain $\mathfrak{J}(V, n, \Psi_S)$. In other words, a complete concrete test suite can be obtained from a symbolic checking experiment. The question arises as to which structural faults in the implementation machines preserve their property of being Ψ_S-converters. Addressing this question, we follow the same approach for describing faults as in the classical deterministic Mealy machines, see, e.g., [2, 24]. Implementation faults are usually modeled by mutants of a given machine. Elements of transitions, namely, output and end state, are subjects for mutations, which yield output faults, transfer faults and transition faults combining the first two types of faults.

It is not difficult to see that all possible mutants of the specification SIFSM S with output faults are Ψ_S-converters, i.e., they are in the fault domain $\mathfrak{J}(V, n, \Psi_S)$.

As to transition faults, they should not violate the property of Ψ_S-converters, namely, a mutant with transition faults should react to any symbolic input sequence defined the specification with a single output sequence. It turns out that mutants with transition faults remain to be Ψ_S-converters under the following conditions.

Assume that the specification SIFSM S has a fixed set of guards in each and every state, i.e., $G(s) = G(s') = G_S$ for all states $s, s' \in S$. Let G_M denote the set of guards of an implementation SIFSM M with the same property.

Theorem 5. Given a specification SIFSM S with the set of guards G_S then $\{M \in \mathfrak{I}(V, n) \mid G_M = G_S\} \subseteq \mathfrak{I}(V, n, \Psi_S)$.

Proof. Let $M \in \mathfrak{I}(V, n)$, such that $G_M = G_S$. Indeed, $G_M = G_S$ implies $\Psi_M = \Psi_S$. As $\mathfrak{I}(V, n)$ includes only deterministic machines, we have that $|\Lambda(m_0, \alpha)| = 1$ for each $\alpha \in \Psi_M$; therefore $|\Lambda(m_0, \alpha)| = 1$ for each $\alpha \in \Psi_S$. Thus, $M \in \mathfrak{I}(V, n, \Psi_S)$. ♦

We identify another sufficient condition considering the case when the set of defined input sequences of each implementation machine in a fault domain is a superset of that of the specification machine. Intuitively, an implementation machine is assumed to preserve in each state guards of the specification or merge some of them.

Theorem 6. Given a specification SIFSM S, it holds that $\{M \in \mathfrak{I}(V, n) \mid \forall \alpha \in \Psi_S, \forall g \in G_S(\delta(s_0, \alpha)), \exists\, g' \in G_M(\delta(m_0, \alpha)), g \subseteq g'\} \subseteq \mathfrak{I}(V, n, \Psi_S)$.

Proof. Let $M \in \mathfrak{I}(V, n)$, such that for each $\alpha \in \Psi_S$ and each $g \in G_S(\delta(s_0, \alpha))$, there exists $g' \in G_M(\delta(m_0, \alpha))$ such that $g \subseteq g'$. We prove by induction that for each $\alpha \in \Psi_S$, $|\Lambda(m_0, \alpha)| = 1$.

For the basis step, we have that $\Lambda(m_0, \varepsilon) = \{\varepsilon\}$, i.e., $|\Lambda(m_0, \varepsilon)| = 1$. For the induction step, assume that $\alpha = \beta g \in \Psi_S$ and $|\Lambda(m_0, \beta)| = 1$. Let also $g \in G_S(\delta(s_0, \beta))$, $g' \in G_M(\delta(m_0, \beta))$, such that $g \subseteq g'$. We can see that $|\Lambda(\delta(m_0, \beta), g')| = 1$; thus $|\Lambda(\delta(m_0, \beta), g)| = 1$. Consequently, $|\Lambda(m_0, \beta g)| = 1$, i.e., $|\Lambda(m_0, \alpha)| = 1$; therefore, $|\Lambda(m_0, \alpha)| = 1$ for each $\alpha \in \Psi_S$. Thus, $M \in \mathfrak{I}(V, n, \Psi_S)$. ♦

This theorem addresses a specific fault model of symbolic implementation machines representing the mutation by merging transitions along with their guards which is not possible in classical FSM, since an implementation FSM should have all the inputs of a specification FSM. In case of SIFSMs, implementation machines have all the input variables of a specification machine, but not necessarily its guards.

Consider SIFSMs in Fig. 1. The machine S can be considered a mutant of the specification machine P, where transitions with guards $(x \leq a)$ and $(x > a)$ are merged into a transition with the guard T. On the other hand, when the machine S serves as a specification and the machine P is an implementation this mutant has a specific fault of splitting a guard used in the specification SIFSM. To detect such a fault, one has use to use at least two instances of a symbolic input sequence from the checking experiment. Since P is treated as a black box testing, and the way a guard is split is unknown, two concrete tests suffice if they properly "guess" it.

5   Conclusions

We investigated possibilities for lifting the checking experiments theory developed for the classical (Mealy) finite state machine model to its extension, where input alphabet is finite, but consists of predicates defined over input variables with large or even infinite domains. We call it FSM with symbolic inputs, SIFSM. On one hand, this model can be considered as a special type of Extended FSMs (EFSMs) [26], without context variables and operations on variables; on another hand, as symbolic automaton or symbolic transducer [23, 35]. The recent grow of interest towards symbolic models could be explained by advances in constraint solving technology, as SMT solvers become efficient [22].

We lifted the machine equivalence and distinguishability relations to SIFSM and identified new distinguishability relations which have no counterparts in classical deterministic Mealy machines. Then, we defined symbolic checking experiments for deterministic SIFSMs and demonstrated that they could be obtained by mimicking, e.g., a classical HSI method for constructing checking experiments of FSMs (other types of state identification facilities, such as W and Wp, might also be used). Since symbolic experiments could be used for white-box testing, but not for black-box testing, which requires concrete test values, we focused on investigating fault domains for which any concrete instance of a symbolic checking experiment remains a checking experiment.

As expected, in the most general setting, an arbitrary instance of a symbolic checking experiment may not be a checking experiment in the same fault domain. Nevertheless, we found some sufficient conditions for the specification and implementation machines under which any instance of a symbolic checking experiment is also a checking experiment in well-defined fault domains. Under these conditions, non-trivial faults modeled by the identified fault domains are detectable by concrete tests obtained from abstract (symbolic) tests in a symbolic checking experiment. These faults include transition merging, which is only relevant to implementations of SIFSM and not to classical Mealy machines.

The novelty of the results comes from the fact that while FSM checking experiments are known for about 60 years, EFSMs for about 30 years, there are no published results on checking experiments for EFSM which cannot be unfolded into FSM. To the best of our knowledge, it is the first attempt to advance the checking experiment theory to FSMs with a symbolic extension.

While the problem of handling more general EFSMs remains open, we believe that the presented results open a new line of research in checking experiments for symbolic state machines and transition systems.

Our current work concerns, on one hand, relaxing the sufficient conditions of safe-instantiability, and on the other hand, extending the SIFSM model with operations on output variables, thus lifting the checking experiments theory to a wider class of extended finite state machines. We also plan to investigate other fault models for which symbolic checking experiments could be used as efficiently as for the faults satisfying the formulated sufficient conditions.

Acknowledgements. The first author acknowledges financial support of NSERC via Discovery grant RGPIN/194381-2012. The second author had financial support of Brazilian Funding Agencies, CNPq, Capes and grant 2015/17753-7, São Paulo Research Foundation (FAPESP).

References

1. Anand, S., Burke, E.K., Chen, T.Y., Clark, J., Cohen, M.B., Grieskamp, W., Harman, M., Harrold, M.J., McMinn, P.: An orchestrated survey of methodologies for automated software test case generation. J. Syst. Softw. **86**(8), 1978–2001 (2013)
2. Bochmann, G.V., Das, A., Dssouli, R., Dubuc, M., Ghedamsi, A., Luo, G.: Fault models in testing. In: Proceedings of the IFIP TC6/WG6. 1 Fourth International Workshop on Protocol Test Systems, IV, pp. 17–30. North-Holland Publishing Co. (1991)
3. Cheng, K.T., Krishnakumar, A.S.: Automatic functional test generation using the extended finite state machine model. In: Proceedings of the 30th Design Automation Conference, pp. 86–91 (1993)
4. Chow, T.S.: Testing software design modeled by finite-state machines. IEEE Trans. Software Eng. **4**(3), 178–187 (1978)
5. Chun, W., Amer, P.D.L.: Test case generation for protocols specified in Estelle. In: Proceedings of the IFIP TC6/WG6. 1 Third International Conference on Formal Description Techniques for Distributed Systems and Communication Protocols: Formal Description Techniques, III, pp. 191–206. North-Holland Publishing Co. (1990)
6. Dorofeeva, R., Yevtushenko, N., El-Fakih, K. and Cavalli, A.: Experimental evaluation of FSM-based testing methods. In: Third IEEE International Conference Software Engineering and Formal Methods, pp. 23–32. IEEE Computer Society (2005)
7. European Railway Agency: ERTMS—System Requirements Specification—UNISIG SUBSET-026, May 2014. http://www.era.europa.eu/Document-Register/Pages/Set-2-System-Requirements-Specification.aspx
8. Frantzen, L., Tretmans, J., Willemse, T.A.: Test generation based on symbolic specifications. In: Grabowski, J., Nielsen, B. (eds.) FATES 2004. LNCS, vol. 3395, pp. 1–15. Springer, Heidelberg (2005)
9. Friedenthal, S., Moore, A., Steiner, R.: A Practical Guide to SysML: the Systems Modeling Language. Morgan Kaufmann, San Francisco (2014)
10. Fujiwara, S., von Bochmann, G., Khendek, F., Amalou, M., Ghedamsi, A.: Test selection based on finite state models. IEEE Trans. Softw. Eng. **17**(6), 591–603 (1991)
11. Glässer, U., Gotzhein, R., Prinz, A.: The formal semantics of SDL-2000: status and perspectives. Comput. Netw. **42**(3), 343–358 (2003)
12. Harel, D., Naamad, A.: The STATEMATE semantics of statecharts. ACM Trans. Softw. Eng. Methodol. **5**(4), 293–333 (1996)
13. Hennie, F.C.: Fault-detecting experiments for sequential circuits. In: Proceedings of the Fifth Annual Symposium on Circuit Theory and Logical Design, pp. 95–110 (1965)
14. Hong, H.S., Lee, I., Sokolsky, O., Ural, H.: A temporal logic based theory of test coverage and generation. In: Katoen, J.-P., Stevens, P. (eds.) TACAS 2002. LNCS, vol. 2280, pp. 327–341. Springer, Heidelberg (2002)
15. Huang, W.-l., Peleska, J.: Exhaustive model-based equivalence class testing. In: Yenigün, H., Yilmaz, C., Ulrich, A. (eds.) ICTSS 2013. LNCS, vol. 8254, pp. 49–64. Springer, Heidelberg (2013)
16. Huang, W., Peleska, J.: Complete model-based equivalence class testing. Int. J. Softw. Tools Technol. Transf. (2014). doi:10.1007/s10009-014-0356-8
17. Jéron, T., Veanes, M., Wolff, B. (eds.) Symbolic methods in testing. Report from Dagstuhl Seminar 13021 (2013)
18. Kalaji, A.S., Hierons, R.M., Swift, S.: Generating feasible transition paths for testing from an extended finite state machine (EFSM). In: International Conference on Software Testing, Verification and Validation, pp. 230–239. IEEE Computer Society, Silver Spring (2009)

19. Li, X., Higashino, T., Higuchi, M., Taniguchi, K.: Automatic generation of extended UIO sequences for communication protocols in an EFSM model. In: Mizuno, T., Higashino, T., Shiratori, N. (eds.) Protocol Test Systems. IFIP, pp. 225–240. Springer, New York (1994)
20. Maler, O., Mens, I.-E.: Learning regular languages over large alphabets. In: Ábrahám, E., Havelund, K. (eds.) TACAS 2014 (ETAPS). LNCS, vol. 8413, pp. 485–499. Springer, Heidelberg (2014)
21. Moore, E.F.: Gedanken-experiments on sequential machines. Automata Studies, pp. 129–153. Princeton University Press, Princeton (1956)
22. de Moura, L., Bjørner, N.S.: Z3: an efficient SMT solver. In: Ramakrishnan, C.R., Rehof, J. (eds.) TACAS 2008. LNCS, vol. 4963, pp. 337–340. Springer, Heidelberg (2008)
23. van Noord, G., Gerdemann, D.: Finite state transducers with predicates and identities. Grammars 4(3), 263–286 (2001)
24. Petrenko, A., Yevtushenko, N.: Test suite generation for a given type of implementation errors. In: Proceedings of the IFIP XII International Conference Protocol Specification, Testing, and Verification, pp. 229–243 (1992)
25. Petrenko, A., Yevtushenko, N., von Bochmann, G.: Fault models for testing in context. In: Formal Description Techniques IX—Theory, Application and Tools, pp. 163–177. Chapman & Hall, London (1996)
26. Petrenko, A., Boroday, S., Groz, R.: Confirming configurations in EFSM testing. IEEE Trans. Softw. Eng. 30(1), 29–42 (2004)
27. Petrenko, A., Yevtushenko, N.: Conformance tests as checking experiments for partial nondeterministic FSM. In: Grieskamp, W., Weise, C. (eds.) FATES 2005. LNCS, vol. 3997, pp. 118–133. Springer, Heidelberg (2006)
28. Petrenko, A., Dury, A., Ramesh, S., Mohalik, S.: A method and tool for test optimization for automotive controllers. In: Proceedings of the 9th Workshop on Advances in Model Based Testing (A-MOST 2013) of the 6th IEEE International Conference on Software Testing, Verification and Validation (ICST 2013), Luxembourg (2013)
29. Rusu, V., du Bousquet, L., Jéron, T.: An approach to symbolic test generation. In: Grieskamp, W., Santen, T., Stoddart, B. (eds.) IFM 2000. LNCS, vol. 1945, pp. 338–357. Springer, Heidelberg (2000)
30. Simao, A., Petrenko, A., Yevtushenko, N.: Generating Reduced Tests for FSMs with Extra States. In: Núñez, M., Baker, P., Merayo, M.G. (eds.) TESTCOM 2009. LNCS, vol. 5826, pp. 129–145. Springer, Heidelberg (2009)
31. Simao, A., Petrenko, A.: Generating complete and finite test suite for ioco: is it possible? In: Proceedings of MBT 2014, Electronic Proceedings in Theoretical Computer Science, vol. 141, pp. 56–70 (2014)
32. Tiwari, A.: Formal semantics and analysis methods for Simulink Stateflow models. Technical report, SRI International (2002)
33. Vasilevskii, M.P.: Failure diagnosis of automata. Cybernetics 9(4), 653–665 (1973). Plenum Publishing Corporation, New York
34. Veanes, Margus: Applications of symbolic finite automata. In: Konstantinidis, S. (ed.) CIAA 2013. LNCS, vol. 7982, pp. 16–23. Springer, Heidelberg (2013)
35. Veanes, M., Hooimeijer, P., Livshits, B., Molnar, D., Bjorner, N.: Symbolic finite state transducers: algorithms and applications. In: Proceedings of the 39th ACM Symposium on Principles of programming languages, pp. 137–150 (2012)
36. Wang, C.J., Liu, M.T.: Generating test cases for EFSM with given fault model. In: Proceedings of Twelfth Conference of the IEEE Computer and Communications Societies, pp. 774–781 (1993)

37. Watson, B.W.: Implementing and using finite automata toolkits. In: Extended Finite State Models of Language, pp. 19–36. Cambridge University Press, New York (1999)
38. Yannakakis, M., Lee, D.: Testing finite state machines: fault detection. J. Comput. Syst. Sci. **50**(2), 209–227 (1995)
39. Yevtushenko, N., Petrenko, A.: Synthesis of test experiments in some classes of automata. Autom. Control Comput. Sci. **24**(4), 50–55 (1990)

Using Multiple Adaptive Distinguishing Sequences for Checking Sequence Generation

Canan Güniçen[1], Guy-Vincent Jourdan[2], and Hüsnü Yenigün[1($\boxtimes$)]

[1] Sabanci University, Istanbul, Turkey
{canangunicen,yenigun}@sabanciuniv.edu
[2] University of Ottawa, Ottawa, ON, Canada
gvj@eecs.uottawa.ca

Abstract. A new method for constructing a checking sequence for finite state machine based testing is introduced. Unlike previous methods, which are based on state recognition using a single state identification sequence, our approach makes use of multiple state identification sequences. Using multiple state identification sequences provides an opportunity to construct shorter checking sequences, choosing greedily the state identification sequence that best suits our goal at different points during the construction of the checking sequence. We present the results of an experimental study showing that our approach produces shorter checking sequences than the previously published methods.

1 Introduction

Testing is an important part of the system development but it is expensive and error prone when performed manually. Therefore, there has been a significant interest in automating testing from formal specifications. Finite State Machines (FSM) are such a formal model used for specification. Deriving test sequences from FSM models, has been an attractive topic for various application domains such as sequential circuits [9], lexical analysis [1], software design [5], communication protocols [3,6,19,22,24,25], object-oriented systems [2], and web services [13,30]. Such techniques have also been shown to be effective in important industrial projects [11].

In order to determine whether an implementation N has the same behaviour as the specification M, a test sequence is derived from M and applied to N. Although, in general, observing the expected behaviour from N under a test sequence does not mean that N is a correct implementation of M, it is possible to construct a test sequence with such a guarantee under some conditions on M and N. A test sequence with such a full fault coverage is called *a checking sequence* (CS) [5,23].

There are many techniques that automatically generate a CS. In principle, a CS consists of three types of components: *initialization, state identification,* and *transition verification*. As the transition verification components are also based on identifying the starting and ending states of the transitions, a CS incorporates many applications of input sequences to identify the states of the underlying

© IFIP International Federation for Information Processing 2015
K. El-Fakih et al. (Eds.): ICTSS 2015, LNCS 9447, pp. 19–34, 2015.
DOI: 10.1007/978-3-319-25945-1_2

FSM. For the state identification, we focus on the use of *Distinguishing Sequences* (DS) and in particular *Adaptive Distinguishing Sequences* (ADS) in this paper. An (A)DS does not necessarily exist for an FSM, however when it exists, it allows constructing a CS of polynomial length. Therefore many researchers have considered (A)DS based CS construction methods.

There exists a line of work to reduce the length of CS as it determines the duration and hence the cost of testing, In these works, the goal is to generate a shorter CS, by putting the pieces that need to exist in a CS together in a better way [4,10,15,16,26,28,29]. All of these papers focus mainly on generating as good a CS as possible for a given (A)DS, without elaborating on the choice of that (A)DS.

As a different perspective, the use of shorter ADSs is also suggested to reduce the length of a CS [27]. However an ADS provides a state identification sequence which may be short for a state but long for another state. It is thus natural to consider using several ADSs in the construction of a CS, is order to have access to a short state identification sequences for each of the states. This is the topic of this paper, in which we demonstrate that under some conditions, it is possible to use several ADSs when constructing a CS, and we experimentally show that this usually results in shorter CS than the most efficient method known so far, especially for larger FSMs. To the best of our knowledge, the only other paper in which using several DSs was considered was [17]. However, in that paper the goal was to overcome some problems linked to distributed, multi port systems and not to create shorter CSs. Dorofeeva et al. also consider using multiple state identification sequences [8], but the CS construction method used in [8] is not an ADS based approach and requires the assumption that a reliable reset exists in the implementation.

In this paper, after introducing our notation and giving preliminary definitions in Sect. 2, we explain the motivation behind and the additional issues that need to be addressed when using multiple ADSs in CS construction in Sect. 3. A sufficient condition for a sequence to be a CS when a set of ADSs is used is given in Sect. 4. In Sect. 5, we first explain how we modify an existing CS generation method to use the new sufficient condition, and then present an experimental study that we performed to assess the potential improvement that can be obtained in the length of CS when multiple ADSs are used.

2   Preliminaries

A *deterministic finite state machine* (FSM) is specified by a tuple $M = (S, s_1, X, Y, \delta, \lambda)$, where S is a finite set of states, s_1 is the initial state, X is a finite set of input symbols, and Y is a finite set of output symbols. $\delta : S \times X \to S$ is a transition function, and $\lambda : S \times X \to Y$ is an output function. Throughout the paper, we use the constants n, p, and q to refer to the cardinalities $|S|$, $|X|$, and $|Y|$, respectively.

For a state $s \in S$, an input (symbol) $x \in X$, and an output (symbol) $y \in Y$, having $\delta(s, x) = s'$ and $\lambda(s, x) = y$ corresponds to a transition from the state s

to the state s' under the input x and producing the output y. We denote this transition by using the notation $(s, s'; x/y)$, where s is called the *starting state*, x is called the *input*, s' is called the *ending state*, and y is called the *output* of the transition.

An FSM M is *completely specified* if the functions δ and λ are defined for each $s \in S$ and for each input symbol $x \in X$. Otherwise M is called *partially specified*. In this paper, we consider only completely specified FSMs.

An FSM can be depicted as a directed graph as shown in Fig. 1. Here, $S = \{s_1, s_2, s_3\}$, $X = \{a, b, c\}$, and $Y = \{0, 1\}$. Each transition $(s_i, s_j; x/y)$ of the FSM is shown as an edge from s_i to s_j labeled by x/y. An FSM M is called *strongly connected* if the underlying directed graph is strongly connected.

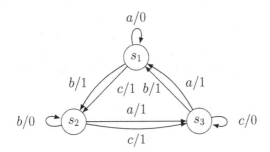

Fig. 1. The FSM M_0

The functions δ and λ are extended to input sequences as explained below, where ε denotes the empty sequence. For a state $s \in S$, an input sequence $\alpha \in X^*$, and an input symbol $x \in X$, $\bar{\delta}(s, \varepsilon) = s$, $\bar{\lambda}(s, \varepsilon) = \varepsilon$, $\bar{\delta}(s, x\alpha) = \bar{\delta}(\delta(s, x), \alpha)$, and $\bar{\lambda}(s, x\alpha) = \lambda(s, x)\bar{\lambda}(\delta(s, x), \alpha)$. Throughout the paper, we will keep using the symbols δ and λ for $\bar{\delta}$ and $\bar{\lambda}$, respectively. We also use the notation $(s_i, s_j; \alpha/\beta)$ to denote a (compound) transition from a state s_i to a state s_j with an input sequence α and an output sequence β. Note that, even though there might be more than one input symbol in α, we still call $(s_i, s_j; \alpha/\beta)$ a transition.

Two states s_i and s_j of M are said to be *equivalent* if, for every input sequence $\alpha \in X^*$, $\lambda(s_i, \alpha) = \lambda(s_j, \alpha)$. If for an input sequence α, $\lambda(s_i, \alpha) \neq \lambda(s_j, \alpha)$, then α is said to *distinguish* s_i and s_j. For example, the input sequence a distinguishes states s_1 and s_2 of M_0 given in Fig. 1.

Two FSMs M and M' are said to be *equivalent* if the initial states of M and M' are equivalent. An FSM M is said to be *minimal* if there is no FSM with fewer states than M that is equivalent to M. For an FSM M, it is possible to compute a minimal equivalent FSM in $O(pn \lg n)$ time [18].

In this paper, we consider only deterministic, completely specified, minimal, and strongly connected finite state machines.

An *Adaptive Distinguishing Sequence* (ADS) of an FSM M is a decision tree. An ADS A for an FSM with n states, is a rooted decision tree with n leaves, where the leaves are labeled by distinct states of M, internal nodes are labeled with input symbols, the edges emanating from a node are labeled with distinct output symbols. The concatenation of the labels of the internal nodes on a path from the root to the leaf labeled by a state s_i is denoted by A^i. Note that A^i is an input sequence and it is called the *State Distinguishing Sequence* (SDS) of s_i in A. Let Y^i be the concatenation of the output labels on the edges along the same root to leaf path. In this case, we also have $\lambda(s_i, A^i) = Y^i$. Since the output symbols on the edges originating from the same node are distinct, for any other state s_j, we have $\lambda(s_i, A^i) \neq \lambda(s_j, A^i)$. An ADS does not necessarily exist for an FSM, however the existence of an ADS can be decided in $O(pn \lg n)$ time, and if one exists, and ADS can be constructed in $O(pn^2)$ time [20].

The fault model considered in FSM based testing in the literature is in general given as follows. Let $\Phi(M)$ be the set of all FSMs with the set of input symbols X, with the set of output symbols Y, and with at most n states. An implementation N of an FSM M is assumed to belong to the set of FSMs $\Phi(M)$. A *checking sequence* (CS) for M is an input sequence that can distinguish M from any faulty $N \in \Phi(M)$, that is from any N which is not isomorphic to M.

3   An Illustration of the Approach

In this section, we illustrate the use of multiple ADSs for CS generation. We first provide an example to explain the advantage that using more than one ADS could provide. We then show by a counter example that one cannot simply use several ADSs while building a CS, and that some additional steps are required.

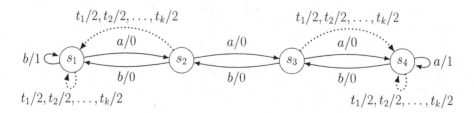

Fig. 2. The FSM M_1

3.1   A Motivational Example

The FSM M_1 depicted in Fig. 2 has two inputs a and b that produce sometimes 0, sometimes 1 as output (solide edges in the picture), as well as a series of k inputs $t_1, t_2, \ldots, t_k$ that always produce 2 as output (dotted edges in the picture). M_1 has several ADS trees, for example A_a such that $A_a^1 = A_a^2 = aaa$, $A_a^3 = aa$ and $A_a^4 = a$, and A_b such that $A_b^1 = b$, $A_b^2 = bb$, and $A_b^3 = A_b^4 = bbb$.

Although there are a number of different checking sequence construction methods published in the literature, all of them will require applying at least once the SDS of the end-state of each transition after going over that transition. In our example, it means that the SDS of s_1 will have to be applied at least $2k + 2$ times and the SDS of s_4 will also have to be applied at least $2k + 2$ times. If one chooses to use a single ADS during the construction, say A_a (resp. A_b), the number of inputs required for the SDS of s_1 is 3 (resp. 1) and the number of inputs required for the SDS of s_4 is 1 (resp. 3). It means that no matter which ADS is chosen, about half the time (and at least $2k + 2$ times) the longest possible SDS will have to be applied.

If, in contrast, we can use $both$ A_a and A_b when building the checking sequence, then we could use the shortest possible SDS each time, namely $A_b^1 = b$ for the transitions ending on s_1 and $A_a^4 = a$ for the transitions ending on s_4, which would result in a significant decrease in the size of the generated DS, especially if k is large. We note that there are also other possible benefits coming from this choice, including more opportunities for $overlap$ as well as additional choices for the ending state reached after application of the SDS in order to reduce subsequent transfer sequences. As we will see, there are however additional constraints that must be satisfied when using multiple ADSs.

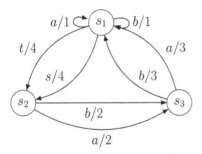

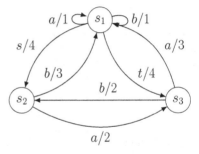

Fig. 3. The FSM M_2 with two ADS trees: a and b.

Fig. 4. This FSM is not isomorphic to the M_2 but produces the same output response to $aasaaabbtbbb$

3.2   Challenges When Using Multiple ADSs

In addition to the obvious problem that using multiple ADS trees requires each of these trees to be applied to every state of the FSM, another issue is what we call *Cross Verification*. In order to explain the problem, let us suppose that A_j^i and A_k^i are two SDSs for a state s_i, and they are applied to the implementation at nodes n and n', and the expected outputs are observed. When one considers the application of A_j^i and A_k^i independently, both n and n' are recognized as the state s_i. However, we cannot directly infer from the application of A_j^i and A_k^i that n and n' are actually the same implementation states. A faulty implementation may have two different states, and we might be applying A_j^i and A_k^i at those states. Therefore, one needs to make sure that n and n' are actually the same implementation states as well. This requires some additional information to be extracted based on the observations from the implementation.

To explain the need for cross verification, suppose that we are given the FSM M_2 in Fig. 3. We can split M_2 into two subgraphs as shown in Figs. 5 and 6, such that each subgraph has all the states of the original FSM and a subset of the edges. The union of the subgraph is the original graph. Then we generate checking sequences for each subgraph, using a different ADS tree each time. We use two simple ADS trees a and b for subgraphs shown in Figs. 5 and 6, respectively. Then, we generate the checking sequences for each graph as $CS_1 = aasaaa$ and $CS_2 = bbtbbb$. Since both sequences start and end in state s_1, we can simply concatenate them to attempt to create a checking sequence for original FSM M_1, e.g. $CS_3 = aasaaabbtbbb$. Unfortunately, the resulting sequence is not a checking sequence: the FSM shown in Fig. 4 produces the same output sequence as the response to CS_3 with the FSM of Fig. 3, although it is not isomorphic to the FSM shown in Fig. 3.

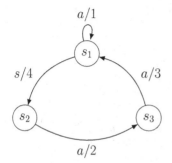
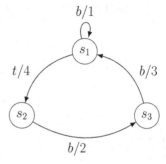

Fig. 5. A subgraph of the FSM M_2: *aasaaa* is a CS

Fig. 6. Another subgraph of the FSM M_2: *bbtbbb* is a CS

The problem is that although each subgraph is independently correctly verified by its own checking sequence, the states that are identified in each subgraph do not correspond to each other (in some sense, states s_2 and s_3 are swapped between the two subgraphs in this example). What we need to do, in addition to the above, is to force the fact that the node recognized by each application of the ADS in different subgraphs correspond to one another. One simple solution is to create a spanning tree on top of the original graph, and add the recognition of the spanning tree in each of the subgraphs. This way, we know that the nodes in different subgraphs correspond to the same implementation states as well. For example, if we add the spanning tree shown in Fig. 7, the checking sequence for subgraph in Fig. 5 doesn't change since the tree is included in it, while the checking sequence for the second subgraph in Fig. 6 becomes $CS_2 = bbtbbbsbab$, and the combined checking sequence is $aasaaabbtbbbsbab$, which does not produce the expected output sequence on the FSM of Fig. 4.

In our algorithm, we overcome this problem by differentiating between the concepts of "d-recognition" and "d-recognition by an ADS A_j". We declare a

Fig. 7. Spanning tree of the FSM M_2

node d-recognized if it is d-recognized by A_j for all j's. This requirement forces an observation of the application of each ADS A^j on the same implementation state. Such a set of observations provides information that the states recognized by different ADSs are the same implementation states. Therefore, we cross verify the node by all ADSs.

4   A Sufficient Condition for Checking Sequences Using Multiple ADS

For an input sequence $\omega = x_1 x_2 \ldots x_k$, let us consider the application of ω to an implementation FSM $N = (Q, q_1, X, Y, \delta_N, \lambda_N)$. The sequence α is designed as a test sequence to be applied at the state q_1 of N that corresponds to the initial state s_1 of M. N is initially assumed to be at this particular state[1]. However, since we do not know if N is really at this particular state, let us refer to this unknown state of N as node n_1. When $x_1 x_2 \ldots x_k$ is applied at n_1, N will go through a sequence of states that we refer here by the node sequence $n_2 n_3 \ldots n_{k+1}$. Based on this sequence of nodes, we define the path P_ω as $(n_1, n_2; x_1/y_1)(n_2, n_3; x_2/y_2) \ldots (n_k, n_{k+1}; x_k/y_k)$, which is the sequence of transitions of N executed by the application of ω. Note that n_i's are the unknown states of N that are traversed and y_i's are the outputs produced by N during the application of ω. If $y_1 y_2 \ldots y_k \neq \lambda(s_1, \omega)$, N is obviously a faulty implementation. Therefore, from now on we assume that $y_1 y_2 \ldots y_k = \lambda(s_1, \omega)$, and under this assumption we provide below a sufficient condition for ω to be checking sequence for M.

For the definitions below, let ω be an input sequence, R be an equivalence relation on the set of nodes of P_ω, and $\mathcal{A} = \{A_1, A_2, \ldots, A_k\}$ be a set of ADSs.

Note that each node n_i is a state in N. Based on the observations that we have in P_ω, under some conditions, it is possible to infer that two different nodes n_i and n_j are actually the same state in N. We use the following equivalence relation on the nodes of P_ω to denote the set of nodes that are the same implementation state.

Definition 1. *An equivalence relation R on the nodes of P_ω is said to be an i–equivalence if for any two nodes n_1, n_2 in P_ω, $(n_1, n_2) \in R$ implies n_1 and n_2 are the same (implementation) state in N.*

P_ω itself, when viewed as a linear sequence of application of input symbols in ω, presents explicit observations on N. For example, having a subpath

---

[1] A homing sequence or a synchronizing sequence, possibly followed by a transfer sequence is used to (supposedly) bring N to this particular state.

$(n_i, n_j; \alpha/\beta)$ in P_ω, we have an explicit observation of the application of the input sequence α at node n_i. We call this compound transition $(n_i, n_j; \alpha/\beta)$ in N an *observation*. Based on the additional information of the equivalence of the nodes in P_ω, it is actually possible to *infer* some new observations that are not explicitly displayed in P_ω.

Definition 2. *An observation* $(n, n'; \alpha/\beta)$ *is an R–induced observation in* P_ω

i. *if* $(n, n'; \alpha/\beta)$ *is a subpath in* P_ω, *or*
ii. *if there exist two R–induced observations* $(n, n_1; \alpha_1/\beta_1)$ *and* $(n_2, n'; \alpha_2/\beta_2)$ *in* P_ω *such that* $(n_1, n_2) \in R$ *and* $\alpha/\beta = \alpha_1\alpha_2/\beta_1\beta_2$.

An input/output sequence α/β *is said to be R–observed in* P_ω *at* n *if there exists* n' *such that* $(n, n'; \alpha/\beta)$ *is an R–induced observation in* P_ω.

Note that R–observing an input/output sequence α/β at a node n is not necessarily an explicit observation in N. In other words, we do not necessarily have an explicit application of the input sequence α at the state of N represented by the node n in P_ω. However, when R is an i–equivalence relation, it is guaranteed that if we were to apply α at the state of N represented by the node n, we would have observed β. This claim is formalized below.

Lemma 1. *Let R be an i-equivalence relation, n be a node in P_ω, and α/β be an input/output sequence R–observed at n. Let s be the implementation state corresponding to n and λ_N be the output function of the implementation N. Then $\lambda_N(s, \alpha) = \beta$.*

Proof. The proof is immediate by induction on the length of α, since in Definition 2 the nodes n_1 and n_2 are necessarily the same state in N (when R is an i–equivalence relation), and α_1 and α_2 are shorter than α.   □

An ADS A_i of the specification M is understood to be an ADS for the implementation N as well, when we have the observations for the applications of all SDSs A_i^j $(s_j \in S)$ of A_i on N. However, these observations do not have to be explicit observations, we can also use inferred observations.

Definition 3. *An ADS A_i is an R–valid ADS in P_ω if for all $s_j \in S$ there exists a node n in P_ω such that $A_i^j/\lambda(s_j, A_i^j)$ is R–observed in P_ω at n.*

When an ADS A_i of M is understood to be an ADS of N as well, we can use the observations of the applications of SDSs of A_i to recognize the states of N as states in M. Definition 4 below is a generalization of d–recognition and t–recognition in the literature (see e.g. [28]) by considering that different ADSs can be used for such recognitions.

Definition 4. *For a node n of P_ω and an ADS A_i, n is R–A_i–recognized as state s_j if A_i is an R–valid ADS in P_ω, and*

i. $A_i^j/\lambda(s_j, A_i^j)$ *is R–observed at n, or*

ii. there exist nodes n', n'', n''' of P_ω, an ADS $A_\ell \in \mathcal{A}$, a state $s_r \in S$, and an input/output sequence α/β such that n' and n'' are R–A_ℓ–recognized as s_r, n''' is R–A_i–recognized as s_j, and $(n', n; \alpha/\beta)$ and $(n'', n'''; \alpha)$ are R–induced observations in P_ω.

One issue that needs to be addressed when we have multiple ADSs is the following. Suppose that a node n is R–A_i–recognized as state s_j in P_ω. Let n' be another node in P_ω which is R–A_k–recognized as state s_j as well, but by using another ADS A_k. We cannot directly deduce that n and n' are the same implementation states. Stated in a different way, if a node n is R–A_i–recognized as state s_j in P_ω for some ADS $A_i \in \mathcal{A}$, it is not necessarily R–A_k–recognized as state s_j in P_ω directly for another ADS $A_k \in \mathcal{A}$. We need to have an observation of the application of A_k^j at n as well. Therefore, we have the following definition to make sure that a node is actually recognized as the same state s_j by all the ADSs in $\mathcal{A}$.

Definition 5. *A node n of P_ω is R–$\mathcal{A}$–recognized as state s_j if for all $A_i \in \mathcal{A}$, n is R–A_i–recognized as state s_j.*

Now we can generalize the notion of "transition verification" to the case of multiple ADSs.

Definition 6. *A transition $(s, s'; x/y)$ of M is R–$\mathcal{A}$–verified in P_ω, if there exists a subpath $(n, n'; x/y)$ in P_ω such that n is R–$\mathcal{A}$–recognized as state s and n' is R–$\mathcal{A}$–recognized as state s'.*

Note that, the identity relation $\mathcal{I}$ on the nodes in P_ω is obviously an i–equivalence relation. When one uses the identity relation $\mathcal{I}$ as the relation R, and $\mathcal{A}$ is a singleton set, then any induced observation in P_ω must actually be a subpath of P_ω. Also under this restriction, Definition 4 is equivalent to the usual state recognitions definitions (i.e. d–recognition and t–recognition given e.g. in [14]) in the literature. Therefore the following holds for this restricted case:

Theorem 1 (Adapted from Theorem 2 in [14]). *When $\mathcal{A}$ is a singleton set, an input sequence ω is a checking sequence if all transitions of M are $\mathcal{I}$–$\mathcal{A}$–verified in P_ω.*

Generalizing Theorem 1 to the case where $\mathcal{A}$ is not singleton is easy.

Theorem 2. *Let $\mathcal{A}$ be a set of ADSs, and ω be an input sequence. If all transitions of M are $\mathcal{I}$–$\mathcal{A}$–verified in P_ω, then ω is a checking sequence.*

Proof. For each transition $(s, s'; x/y)$, by Definition 6, there exists subpath $(n, n'; x/y)$ such that n and n' are $\mathcal{I}$–$\mathcal{A}$–recognized as s and s', respectively. Based on Definition 5, n and n' are $\mathcal{I}$–A_i–recognized as s and s', by all $A_i \in \mathcal{A}$. Let us consider a particular ADS $A_1 \in \mathcal{A}$. The nodes n and n' are $\mathcal{I}$–$\{A_1\}$–recognized, and hence the transition $(s, s'; x/y)$ is $\mathcal{I}$–$\{A_1\}$–verified. Using Theorem 1, ω is a checking sequence. □

Finally we generalize the sufficiency condition to use an arbitrary i–equivalence relation R as follows.

Theorem 3. *Let $\mathcal{A}$ be a set of ADSs, and ω be an input sequence, and R be an i–equivalence relation. If all transitions of M are R–$\mathcal{A}$–verified in P_ω, then ω is a checking sequence.*

Proof. For each transition $(s, s'; x/y)$, by Definition 6, there exists subpath $(n, n'; x/y)$ such that n and n' are R–$\mathcal{A}$–recognized as s and s', respectively. Lemma 1 implies that n and n' are also $\mathcal{I}$–$\mathcal{A}$–recognized as s and s'. By Theorem 2, ω is a checking sequence.   □

Theorem 3 provides a sufficient condition for a sequence to be a checking sequence. It can be used to verify if an input sequence ω is a checking sequence, provided that we are given an i–equivalence relation R. Lemma 2 explains how one can obtain such a relation by starting from the trivial i–equivalence relation $\mathcal{I}$, the identity relation.

Lemma 2. *Let R be an i–equivalence relation, n_1 and n_2 be two nodes in P_ω such that $(n_1, n_2) \notin R$, and $A_i \in \mathcal{A}$ be an ADS such that both n_1 and n_2 are R–A_i–recognized as s_j. Consider the equivalence relation R' obtained from R by merging the equivalence classes of n_1 and n_2 in R. Then R' is an i–equivalence relation.*

Proof. Recall that Definition 4 implies that if n_1 and n_2 are R–A_i–recognized as s_j, then A_i is R–valid, meaning there are n different responses R–observed for the application of A_i. If s_1 and s_2 are the implementation states corresponding to the nodes n_1 and n_2, due to the fact that R is an i–equivalence relation Lemma 1 tells us that $\lambda_N(s_1, A_i^j) = \lambda_N(s_2, A_i^j)$. This is only possible when s_1 and s_2 are the same implementation states.   □

Starting from the finest i–equivalence relation $\mathcal{I}$, one can use Lemma 2 repeatedly to obtain coarser i–equivalence relations. By using a coarser i–equivalence relation R, more R induced observations will be obtained. These new inferred observations provide an opportunity to identify new i-equivalent nodes in P_ω, hence to obtain an even coarser i–equivalence relation.

5   Experimental Study

In this section, we present an experimental study that we performed to assess the potential improvement on the length of the checking sequences that one can obtain by using multiple ADSs for checking sequence construction.

5.1   Checking Sequence Generation

In order to construct a checking sequence, we use a modified version of the algorithm given in [26]. The method given in [26] starts from an empty sequence $\omega = \varepsilon$, and ω is iteratively extended until it becomes a checking sequence by the sufficiency condition provided by Theorem 1. We can note here that Theorem 3 is a general sufficiency condition. Although other checking sequence construction methods can be adapted to use Theorem 3, we consider the method given in [26], since it is the most recent and a successful checking sequence construction method reported in the literature.

We modify the method to use the sufficiency condition provided by Theorem 3. Although Lemma 2 requires R–valid ADSs to be used when extending R, we found that delaying the extension of R until R–valid ADSs are obtained is not efficient in terms of the length of the checking sequences obtained. Instead, we construct a sequence first by using Lemma 2 without requiring R–valid ADSs. Then, in a second phase, we extend the sequence further to force the validity of all the ADSs that have been used in the first phase.

Consider the linear path P_ω and an i-equivalence relation R. We keep track of a graph G_ω where each equivalence class in R on the nodes of P_ω is represented by a node in G_ω. An edge $(n_i, n_{i+1}; x/y)$ in P_ω is represented by an edge $([n_i], [n_{i+1}]; x/y)$ in G_ω, where $[n_i]$ and $[n_{i+1}]$ are the nodes in G_ω corresponding to the equivalence classes of n_i and n_{i+1} in R. By merging the equivalence classes of R into a single node in G_ω, R–induced observations are directly represented by paths in G_ω.

Similarly to the method in [26], while extending ω in each iteration, we prefer a shortest input sequence α to be appended to ω that can (i) recognize a state by some ADS, or (ii) perform a transition verification, or (iii) transfer to another state at which we can perform a state recognition/transition verification. The details of the method can be found in [12]. Here we simply emphasize that while deciding how to extend ω, we have more alternative to chose from than the method given in [26]. First, we are using multiple ADSs and hence we need to have more state recognitions (possibly by using different SDSs). Second, if we note n_c the last node in P_ω, in [26] an extension of ω by an input sequence α is considered if there exists a node n in P_ω such that $(n, n_c; \alpha'/\beta')$ is a subpath in (actually a suffix of) P_ω, and $\alpha\alpha'$ is an SDS for the state corresponding to node n. There is a linear view used for backtracking (in order to search for overlapping opportunities) which is performed on P_ω. However in our case, due to the merging of equivalence classes of the nodes of P_ω into a single node in G_ω, when searching for overlapping opportunities, we backtrack from $[n_c]$ in G_ω, hence we do not have a single suffix, but a tree of suffixes to chose from.

5.2   Selecting a Subset of ADSs

In Sects. 4 and 5.1 we explained how we generate a checking sequence when a set $\mathcal{A}$ of ADSs is given. While constructing a checking sequence, having more ADSs in $\mathcal{A}$ increases the alternatives for shorter state recognitions, hence presents an opportunity to reduce the length of the checking sequence. However, having more ADSs in $\mathcal{A}$ also has an increasing effect on the length of the checking sequence, due to the need for the cross verification and the need to validate each ADS. Therefore, in the experiments we perform, we select a subset $\mathcal{A}^\star$ of the a given set $\mathcal{A}$ of ADSs to minimize the length of the checking sequence. The selection process is based on a greedy heuristic and it is independent on how the set $\mathcal{A}$ is constructed. Therefore, we first explain our heuristic approach to select $\mathcal{A}^\star$ in this section. The construction of the set $\mathcal{A}$ of ADSs is explained in Sect. 5.3.

Let $CS(M, \mathcal{A})$ be the checking sequence constructed by using the method explained in this paper, for an FSM M using a set $\mathcal{A}$ of ADSs. From a given set of ADSs $\mathcal{A} = \{A_1, A_2, \ldots, A_k\}$, we start by generating a checking sequence $CS(M, \mathcal{A}')$ for each $\mathcal{A}' \subseteq \mathcal{A}$ such that $|\mathcal{A}'| = 2$. The subset $\mathcal{A}'$ giving the shortest checking sequence $CS(M, \mathcal{A}')$ is considered as the initial subset $\mathcal{A}^\star$. We then iteratively attempt to improve the length of the checking sequence by adding an ADS $A \in (\mathcal{A} \setminus \mathcal{A}^\star)$ into $\mathcal{A}^\star$. If there exists an ADS $A \in (\mathcal{A} \setminus \mathcal{A}^\star)$ such that $CS(M, \mathcal{A}^\star \cup \{A\})$ is shorter than $CS(M, \mathcal{A}^\star)$, we chose the ADS $A \in (\mathcal{A} \setminus \mathcal{A}^\star)$ such that $CS(M, \mathcal{A}^\star \cup \{A\})$ is the shortest, and update $\mathcal{A}^\star$ as $\mathcal{A}^\star = \mathcal{A}^\star \cup \{A\}$. The iterations terminate when we cannot add any ADS into $\mathcal{A}^\star$.

5.3   Generating a Set of ADSs

The motivation of using multiple ADSs to construct a checking sequence is that, while recognizing a state s_i within a checking sequence, one can use an ADS A_j such that the SDS A_j^i is shorter. Therefore, it makes sense to have an ADS A_i in $\mathcal{A}$ where the SDS A_i^i for the state s_i is as short as possible.

For an FSM with n states, we start by generating an ADS A_i for each state s_i. Therefore, we initially have at most (as some of ADSs may turn out to be the same) n ADSs in $\mathcal{A}$, and we rely on the heuristic given in Sect. 5.2 to select a subset $\mathcal{A}^\star$. While generating the ADS A_i for the state s_i, we aim for the minimization of the length of the SDS A_i^i.

Minimizing the length of the SDS of a state is introduced as MINSDS problem and it is proven to be NP–hard in [27]. Therefore a minimal length SDS A_i^i is generated by considering an Answer Set Programming [21] formulation of the MINSDS problem as explained in [12]. Given an SDS A_i^i, we construct an ADS A_i such that the SDS of state s_i in A_i is A_i^i. The details of this process can also be seen in [12], but the main idea is the following. A_i^i is a path in the ADS A_i that will be constructed. Let α be a prefix of A_i^i, S' be the set of states not distinguished from each other by α, distinguished from s_i by α, but not distinguished from s_i by any proper prefix of α. One can then use the standard ADS construction algorithm given in [20] to construct an ADS for the states reached from S' by α. These ADSs are used to form an ADS A_i from SDS A_i^i.

5.4   Random FSM Generation

The FSMs used in the experiments are generated using the random FSM generation tool reported in [7]. For the experiments, 10 sets of FSMs are used. Each

Table 1. Average percentage improvement in the length of checking sequences

n	$p = 5$	$p = 9$	$p = 13$
10	5,39	7,82	10,37
20	4,5	8,1	9,54
30	4,91	8,38	10,17
40	5,16	8,16	9,96
50	5,15	7,26	9,44
60	6,43	7,1	8,34
70	6,23	7,46	7,78
80	6,61	7,49	8,08
90	6,32	6,94	7,52
100	5,98	6,52	6,98

Table 2. Number of FSMs where $|C(M, \mathcal{A}^\star)| < |C_1|$

n	$p = 5$	$p = 9$	$p = 13$
10	61	69	78
20	61	78	82
30	66	84	92
40	74	83	93
50	78	83	93
60	95	87	94
70	95	96	97
80	100	100	100
90	100	100	100
100	100	100	100

set of FSMs contains 100 FSMs having a number of states $n \in \{10, 20, \ldots, 100\}$, hence a total of 1,000 FSMs are used in the experiments. Each FSM has 5 input symbols and 5 output symbols. Under this settings, a random FSM M is generated by randomly assigning $\delta(s, x)$ and $\lambda(s, x)$ for each state s and for each input symbol x. If after this random assignment of the next states and outputs for the transition, M is a strongly connected FSM with an ADS (in which case M is minimal as well), then it is included in the set of FSMs to be used.

5.5   Experimental Results

For an FSM M, let $\mathcal{A}$ be the set of ADSs computed as explained in Sect. 5.3. We first find the shortest checking sequence that can be generated by using a single ADS among the set $\mathcal{A}$ of ADSs. For this purpose, we compute $CS(M, \{A\})$ for each $A \in \mathcal{A}$, and find the minimum length checking sequence. Let C_1 be this minimum length checking sequence when a single ADS is used. For the same FSM M, we also compute the set $\mathcal{A}^\star$ of ADSs as explained in Sect. 5.2, and compute the checking sequence $C^\star = CS(M, \mathcal{A}^\star)$. The percentage improvement in the length of the checking sequence for M by using multiple ADSs is then computed as $100 \times (|C_1| - |C^\star|)/|C_1|$. Note that, this improvement can be negative, when using two or more ADSs does not give a shorter checking sequence than C_1.

For each $n \in \{10, 20, \ldots, 100\}$, there are 100 randomly generated FSMs with n states and with $p = 5$ input symbols as explained in Sect. 5.4. We present the average percentage improvement over 100 FSMs in Table 1. The number of FSMs in which we have a positive improvement in the length of checking sequence by using multiple ADSs is given in Table 2.

If we consider a fixed number of states for an FSM, it is expected to have a better improvement in the length of checking sequences by using multiple ADSs when there are more transitions. This is because, having the same number of states keeps the cost of cross verification constant but the savings due to the use of shorter SDSs in the transition verifications increases. In order to test this hypothesis, for each FSM M that we randomly generate, we construct an FSM M' (resp. M'') by adding 4 (resp. 8) more inputs onto M. The next state and the output symbols for the transitions of the additional input symbols are randomly assigned. Note however that M' and M'' still use the same set $\mathcal{A}$ of ADSs constructed for M. We present the experimental results for the set of FSMs with $p = 9$ inputs and $p = 13$ inputs in Tables 1 and 2 as well.

We would like to emphasize that C_1 is not a CS constructed by using a random ADS in $\mathcal{A}$, but it is constructed by using the ADS that is the best among all the ADSs in $\mathcal{A}$. Therefore the improvement figures in Table 1 are obtained against a very good ADS. We also see that, by keeping the number of states constant and increasing the number of transitions, the improvement obtained by using multiple ADSs increase as well, as hypothesized by the motivation of this work. Note that when $|C_1| < |C(M, \mathcal{A}^\star)|$, one can obviously use C_1 instead of $C(M, \mathcal{A}^\star)$. This approach would make the average improvement figures in Table 1 a little bit higher, since we will never have a negative improvement in this case. However the experimental results given here does not take this opportunity, and always insist on using two or more ADSs.

As the number of states increases, the percentage of FSMs in which there is an improvement in the length of the checking sequence increases, but the average improvement in the length of the checking sequence decreases. Our investigations show that, with increasing number of states, our approach starts using more ADSs in $\mathcal{A}^\star$, which pushes the cost of cross verification to higher values. For $p = 5$, our method used an average of 3 ADSs in $\mathcal{A}^\star$ for $n = 10$, whereas this average is 9 ADSs for $n = 100$. As explained in Sect. 5.1, our CS generation method consists of two phases, where in the second phase the sequence is basically extended to cross verify ADSs. We observe that the average length of extension in phase 2 is only 3% of the overall length of the checking sequence for $n = 10$. This percentage contribution increases with the number of states and reaches to 47% for $n = 100$.

6   Concluding Remarks

We presented a sufficient condition that can be used for constructing a CS using multiple ADSs. We also presented a modification of an existing CS construction method to adopt the new sufficient condition. We performed experiments to assess the potential reduction in the length of a CS that can be obtained by using multiple ADS. The experiments indicate that as the number of states increases, using multiple ADSs almost certainly decreases the length of the checking sequence, but the average improvement decreases. The investigations point to the fact that the cost of cross verification increases with the number of states.

One approach to keep the cost of cross verification limited might be to construct ADSs that has the same SDS for the states. If two ADSs A_i and A_j have the same SDS for a state s_k, then by applying this SDS at a node n, one would recognize n as s_k both by A_i and A_j, cross verifying A_i and A_j at node n immediately. This requires a more careful design of the set $\mathcal{A}$ of ADSs to be used in our method. Another potential improvement can come from the way the subset $\mathcal{A}^\star$ is selected. Currently, our greedy approach for selecting $\mathcal{A}^\star$ terminates when it is not possible to extend $\mathcal{A}^\star$ by adding another ADS from $\mathcal{A}$, but it does not actually mean that one cannot reduce the size of the checking sequence by using another subset of $\mathcal{A}$ with a larger cardinality than $\mathcal{A}^\star$.

As a final remark, we want to point out the fact that our improvement figures in Table 1 are obtained by comparing $CS(M, \mathcal{A}^\star)$ with $C_1 = CS(M, \{A\})$, where A is the "best" ADS in $\mathcal{A}$. Note that, while constructing C_1, there is no need for the cross verification since there is only one ADS, but the "induced observation" idea of Definition 2 is still being used. It might be interesting to compare the length of C_1 by a checking sequence which is constructed by using the method given in [26] based on the same ADS A.

Acknowledgment. The authors would like to thank Robert M. Hierons and Hasan Ural for their useful input on an early version of this work.

References

1. Aho, A.V., Sethi, R., Ullman, J.D.: Compilers, Principles, Techniques, and Tools. Addison-Wesley series in computer science. Addison-Wesley Pub. Co., Reading (1986)
2. Binder, R.V.: Testing Object-Oriented Systems: Models, Patterns, and Tools. Addison-Wesley, Reading (1999)
3. Brinksma, E.: A theory for the derivation of tests. In: Proceedings of Protocol Specification, Testing, and Verification VIII, Atlantic City, North-Holland, pp. 63–74 (1988)
4. Chen, J., Hierons, R.M., Ural, H., Yenigun, H.: Eliminating redundant tests in a checking sequence. In: Khendek, F., Dssouli, R. (eds.) TestCom 2005. LNCS, vol. 3502, pp. 146–158. Springer, Heidelberg (2005)
5. Chow, T.S.: Testing software design modelled by finite state machines. IEEE Trans. Softw. Eng. **4**, 178–187 (1978)
6. Dahbura, A.T., Sabnani, K.K., Uyar, M.Ü.: Formal methods for generating protocol conformance test sequences. Proc. IEEE **78**(8), 1317–1326 (1990)
7. Dincturk, E.: A Two phase approach for checking sequence generation. Master's thesis, Sabanci University, Turkey (2009)
8. Dorofeeva, R., El-Fakih, K., Yevtushenko, N.: An improved conformance testing method. In: Wang, F. (ed.) FORTE 2005. LNCS, vol. 3731, pp. 204–218. Springer, Heidelberg (2005)
9. Friedman, A.D., Menon, P.R.: Fault Detection in Digital Circuits. Computer Applications in Electrical Engineering Series. Prentice-Hall, Prentice (1971)
10. Gonenc, G.: A method for the design of fault detection experiments. IEEE Trans. Comput. **19**, 551–558 (1970)
11. Grieskamp, W., Kicillof, N., Stobie, K., Braberman, V.A.: Model-based quality assurance of protocol documentation: tools and methodology. Softw. Test. Verification Reliab. **21**(1), 55–71 (2011)

12. Güniçen, C.: Checking sequence construction using multiple adaptive distinguishing sequences. Master's thesis, Sabanci University, Turkey (2015)
13. Haydar, M., Petrenko, A., Sahraoui, H.A.: Formal verification of web applications modeled by communicating automata. In: de Frutos-Escrig, D., Núñez, M. (eds.) FORTE 2004. LNCS, vol. 3235, pp. 115–132. Springer, Heidelberg (2004)
14. Hierons, R.M., Jourdan, G.V., Ural, H., Yenigün, H.: Using adaptive distinguishing sequences in checking sequence constructions. In: Proceedings of the 2008 ACM symposium on Applied computing, pp. 682–687. ACM (2008)
15. Hierons, R.M., Ural, H.: Reduced length checking sequences. IEEE Trans. Comput. **51**(9), 1111–1117 (2002)
16. Hierons, R.M., Ural, H.: Optimizing the length of checking sequences. IEEE Trans. Comput. **55**, 618–629 (2006)
17. Hierons, R.M., Ural, H.: Checking sequences for distributed test architectures. Distrib. Comput. **21**(3), 223–238 (2008)
18. Hopcroft, J.E.: An $n \log n$ algorithm for minimizing states in a finite automaton. Technical report STAN-CS-71-190, Stanford University (1971)
19. Lee, D., Sabnani, K.K., Kristol, D.M., Paul, S.: Conformance testing of protocols specified as communicating finite state machines-a guided random walk based approach. IEEE Trans. Commun. **44**(5), 631–640 (1996)
20. Lee, D., Yannakakis, M.: Testing finite-state machines: state identification and verification. IEEE Trans. Comput. **43**(3), 306–320 (1994)
21. Cabalar, P.: Answer set; programming? In: Balduccini, M., Son, T.C. (eds.) Logic Programming, Knowledge Representation, and Nonmonotonic Reasoning. LNCS, vol. 6565, pp. 334–343. Springer, Heidelberg (2011)
22. Low, S.H.: Probabilistic conformance testing of protocols with unobservable transitions. In: Proceedings 1993 International Conference on Network Protocols, pp. 368–375 (1993)
23. Moore, E.P.: Gedanken-experiments. In: Shannon, C., McCarthy, J. (eds.) Automata Studies. Princeton University Press, Princeton (1956)
24. Sabnani, K., Dahbura, A.: A protocol test generation procedure. Comput. Netw. **15**(4), 285–297 (1988)
25. Sidhu, D.P., Leung, T.K.: Formal methods for protocol testing: a detailed study. IEEE Trans. Softw. Eng. **15**(4), 413–426 (1989)
26. Simão, A.S., Petrenko, A.: Generating checking sequences for partial reduced finite state machines. In: Suzuki, K., Higashino, T., Ulrich, A., Hasegawa, T. (eds.) TestCom/FATES 2008. LNCS, vol. 5047, pp. 153–168. Springer, Heidelberg (2008)
27. Türker, U.C., Yenigün, H.: Hardness and inapproximability of minimizing adaptive distinguishing sequences. Formal Methods Syst. Des. **44**(3), 264–294 (2014)
28. Ural, H., Wu, X., Zhang, F.: On minimizing the lengths of checking sequences. IEEE Trans. Comput. **46**(1), 93–99 (1997)
29. Ural, H., Zhu, K.: Optimal length test sequence generation using distinguishing sequences. IEEE/ACM Trans. Netw. **1**(3), 358–371 (1993)
30. Utting, M., Pretschner, A., Legeard, B.: A taxonomy of model-based testing approaches. Softw. Test. Verification Reliab. **22**(5), 297–312 (2012)

Model-Based Testing from Input Output Symbolic Transition Systems Enriched by Program Calls and Contracts

Imen Boudhiba[1], Christophe Gaston[2], Pascale Le Gall[1(✉)], and Virgile Prevosto[2]

[1] Laboratoire MAS, CentraleSupelec, 92195 Châtenay-Malabry, France
{imen.boudhiba,pascale.legall}@centralesupelec.fr
[2] CEA LIST, Point Courrier 174, 91191 Gif-sur-Yvette, France
{virgile.prevosto,christophe.gaston}@cea.fr

Abstract. An Input Output Symbolic Transition System (IOSTS) specifies all expected sequences of input and output messages of a reactive system. Symbolic execution over this IOSTS then allows to generate a set of test cases that can exercise the various possible behaviors of the system it represents. In this paper, we extend the IOSTS framework with explicit program calls, possibly equipped with contracts specifying what the program is supposed to do. This approach bridges the gap between a model-based approach in which user-defined programs are abstracted away and a code-based approach in which small pieces of code are separately considered regardless of the way they are combined. First, we extend symbolic execution techniques for IOSTS with programs, in order to re-use classical test case generation algorithms. Second, we explore how constraints coming from IOSTS symbolic execution can be used to infer contracts for programs used in the IOSTS.

Keywords: Input output symbolic transition systems · Program contracts · Model-based testing · Symbolic execution · Feasibility

1 Introduction

Symbolic transition systems, such as Input Output Symbolic Transition Systems (IOSTS) [11] are a classical reference modeling framework for model-based testing of reactive systems. They provide a convenient abstraction of the behaviors of such systems by modeling system state evolution using variable assignments. The symbolic execution tree of an IOSTS characterizes the different classes of numeric executions. Each path defines a sequence of symbolic inputs and outputs, and a path condition which is a formula constraining the values exchanged (inputs or outputs) with the environment of the system. It is possible to use

Work described in this paper has been partially funded by the ITEA project OpenETCS and the BGLE project Sesam-Grids.

K. El-Fakih et al. (Eds.): ICTSS 2015, LNCS 9447, pp. 35–51, 2015.
DOI: 10.1007/978-3-319-25945-1_3

such paths as reference symbolic behaviors to be tested (i.e. as *test purposes*). In [11], we have proposed a framework to analyze IOSTS both to extract such test purposes and to solve the oracle problem thanks to a fully on-line algorithm. However, this kind of framework is limited by the symbolic treatment of functions. Indeed, IOSTS variables are assigned by terms built on functions. In order to be able to reason on the symbolic values assigned to variables, the symbolic execution engine is equipped with constraint solving techniques able to analyze those functions. As long as one deals with basic arithmetic or boolean functions, it is generally tractable, but as soon as one deals with user-defined or ad-hoc functions, solving techniques may fail to scale, or even, due to undecidability results, such techniques may not exist. Analyzing such functions (later referred as "programs") may require both to deal with sophisticated data structures and to explore their (arbitrarily complex) control graph.

In this paper we propose an approach to overcome this limitation by abstracting program behaviors by means of *contracts* [18]. A contract for a program consists in a collection of couples, also called *behaviors*, formed of a pre-condition that specifies constraints that the caller must enforce at the call site, and a post-condition which is a property guaranteed at the program return. We enrich the basic IOSTS framework to deal with program calls equipped with contracts. We show how to extend symbolic execution mechanisms to reason about IOSTS equipped with program calls by analyzing those calls through their contracts. Thus, we avoid analyzing the actual behavior of the program and replace it by abstract constraints on its formal parameters. Our framework allows computing symbolic paths that can be used as test purposes. It may happen that guards and contracts are incompatible so that some symbolic paths are infeasible (*i.e.* they have no associated trace). In practice it means that there exists no program that can both satisfy its associated contracts and compute values allowing to follow the whole symbolic path. We show how to use symbolic techniques to check that a given set of symbolic paths is consistent with respect to program calls.

Moreover, since guards occurring on transitions of an IOSTS interact with contracts associated to programs, we present an approach to extract new contracts for each of the program exercised. Such contracts reflect constraints on the program that make the path feasible. As such, they represent new contracts that can be used at the unitary level, to evaluate the correctness of actual program used to implement the system under test.

The remaining of the paper is organized as follows. In Sect. 2, we give basic definitions about many-typed first order logic. Section 3 presents programs and their contracts. In Sect. 4, we introduce IOSTS with programs. Section 5 defines symbolic execution of an IOSTS with programs and the associated feasibility condition. Finally, usage of symbolic execution for testing purposes, including contract inference for unitary testing is introduced in Sect. 6.

2   Preliminaries

For two sets A and B, B^A denotes the set of mappings $f : A \to B$ from A to B and id_A is the identity mapping on A. For a mapping $f : A \to B$, $f[a_i \mapsto b_i]_{i \in 1..n}$

is the mapping associating b_i to a_i for all i in $1..n$ and $f(a)$ to a not belonging to $\{a_i \mid i \in 1..n\}$. By convention, $[a_i \mapsto b_i]_{i \in 1..n}$ stands for $id_A[a_i \mapsto b_i]_{i \in 1..n}$. For two mappings $f : A_1 \to B$ and $g : A_2 \to B$ with $A_1 \cap A_2 = \emptyset$, $f \cup g : A_1 \cup A_2 \to B$ is the mapping defined by: $\forall a \in A_1, (f \cup g)(a) = f(a)$ and $\forall a \in A_2, (f \cup g)(a) = g(a)$. A^* (resp. A^+) denotes the set of words on A provided with the concatenation operator '.' and the empty word ε (resp. deprived of the empty word ε). For an ordered list $l = (a_1, \ldots, a_n)$ of n elements of A, $\{\!\{l\}\!\}$ denotes the set $\{a_1, \ldots, a_n\}$ of elements occurring in l.

We use classical multi-typed first order logic to handle data. A *data signature* is a pair (S, F) where S is a set of so-called *types* and F is a set of *functions* provided with a profile $s_1...s_{n-1} \to s_n$ with each $s_i \in S$. For $V = \coprod_{s \in S} V_s$ a set of variables typed in S, the set $T_F(V) = \coprod_{s \in S} T_F(V)_s$ of so-called functional terms over V is defined as usual over (S, F). Moreover, each set V_s contains an identified subset, denoted V_s^{fro}, whose elements are called *frozen variables* and we denote $V^{fro} = \coprod_{s \in S} V_s^{fro}$ the subset of V of all frozen variables. The set $Sen_F(V)$ of *formulas* is built over Boolean constants $\top$ and $\bot$, equalities $t = t'$ for t and t' terms in $T_F(V)$ of same type and usual Boolean connectives ($\wedge$, $\vee$, $\neg$, ...). *Substitutions* over V are applications $\sigma : V \to T_F(V)$ that preserve types and are such that all elements of V^{fro} are frozen for σ (i.e. $\forall v \in V^{fro}, \sigma(v) = v$). Thus, as frozen variables cannot be substituted, they may be considered as new special constants. Substitutions can be canonically extended to $T_F(V)$. For a term t in $T_F(V)$, for a formula φ in $Sen_F(V)$, $Occ(t)$ and $Occ(\varphi)$ will denote the set of variables occurring in respectively t and φ.

A F-*model* is a set of typed variables $M = \coprod_{s \in S} M_s$ provided with a function $\overline{f} : M_{s_1} \times \cdots \times M_{s_{n-1}} \to M_{s_n}$ for each $f : s_1 \cdots s_{n-1} \to s_n$ in F. An *interpretation* is an application $\nu : M^V$ that preserves types and can be canonically extended to $T_F(V)$. The satisfaction of a formula φ in $Sen_F(V)$ by an interpretation $\nu \in M^V$, denoted $M \models_\nu \varphi$, is defined as usual by considering the meaning of the equality predicate, Boolean constants and connectives. A formula φ in $Sen_F(V)$ is valid if and only if for all interpretations $\nu : V \to M$, $M \models_\nu \varphi$. In the sequel, data signature (S, F) and F-model M are supposed given.

3   Programs and Contracts

Programs. User-defined functions, called *programs*, are identifiers provided with an interface specifying their formal parameters used to store input and output data. We only consider here programs with no side effect and one output variable.

Definition 1 (Program). *Let* $X = \coprod_{s \in S} X_s$ *be a set of typed variables. A program over X is an identifier p provided with:*

- *a list* $InOut(p) = (x_1, \cdots, x_{n+1}) \in X^{n+1}$, *called the* interface *of p, with $n \geq 1$ and $\forall i \neq j, x_i \neq x_j$. $In(p)$ (resp. $Out(p)$) denotes the list $(x_1 \cdots x_n)$ (resp. (x_{n+1})) of input (resp. output) formal parameters of p.*
- *and a mapping* $Sem : M^{\{\!\{In(p)\}\!\}} \to M^{\{\!\{InOut(p)\}\!\}}$, *called the* semantics *of p, verifying the so-called* semantic condition:
  $\forall \nu \in M^{\{\!\{In(p)\}\!\}}, \forall x_j \in \{\!\{In(p)\}\!\}, Sem(\nu)(x_j) = \nu(x_j).$

Depending on the values associated to $In(p)$ through the interpretation ν, *Sem* associates a value to the formal parameter x_{n+1} in $Out(p)$. The semantic condition ensures that a program call has no effect on its input formal parameters. By extrapolation, given a list $l = (x_1, \cdots, x_{n+1})$, $In(l)$ and $Out(l)$ will resp. denote $(x_1, \cdots, x_n)$ and (x_{n+1}).

A *signature* Σ is a tuple (S, F, X, P) where (S, F) is a data signature and P is a set of programs defined over the set of typed variables X.

Let $V = \coprod_{s \in S} V$ be a set of typed variables. The set $T_\Sigma(V) = \coprod_{s \in S} T_\Sigma(V)_s$ of *typed terms* over V contains:

- all functional terms of $T_F(V)$
- all elements $p(t_1, \cdots, t_n)$ with $p \in P$ of interface $(x_1, \cdots, x_{n+1})$, $\forall 1 \leq i \leq n$, $x_i \in X_{s_i}$, and $t_i \in T_F(V)_{s_i}$. If $x_{n+1} \in V_s$, $p(t_1, \cdots, t_n) \in T_\Sigma(V)_s$.

Any interpretation $\nu : V \to M$ can be canonically extended on $T_\Sigma(V)$ as follows: for any program p in P defined by its interface $(x_1 \cdots x_{n+1})$ and its semantics Sem_p, let us consider $\mu_\nu^p : \{\!\!\{In(p)\}\!\!\} \to M$ an interpretation such that $\forall 1 \leq i \leq n$, $\mu_\nu^p(x_i) = \nu(t_i)$, we have $\nu(p(t_1, \cdots, t_n)) = Sem_p(\mu_\nu^p)(x_{n+1})$.

Contracts. Contracts specify what programs are expected to compute, as opposed to how they compute their result. They have been introduced in the pioneering work of Floyd [10] and Hoare [12], and form a key ingredient of the Eiffel programming language [18]. In short, a contract describes what a program requires from its caller (the pre-condition) and what it guarantees when it returns (the post-condition). We use here a slightly refined notion where a contract can be split in a set of behaviors [2,5]. In this setting, pre-condition of a behavior indicates a possible case in which the program may be executed. As before, when a behavior is active, its post-condition must hold at the end of the execution.

Most of the times, pre and post conditions of a program are simply formulas in resp. $Sen_F(\{\!\!\{In(p)\}\!\!\})$ and $Sen_F(\{\!\!\{InOut(p)\}\!\!\})$. However, contracts can involve other variables representing the global state of the system. The latter will be frozen variables whose associated values are conditioned by axioms and cannot be modified. These variables will be useful for inferring contracts from symbolic execution tree, as shown in Sect. 6.2.

Definition 2 (Program Contract). *Let $l = (x_1, \ldots, x_{n+1})$ be a list of variables with $\forall i \leq n + 1, x_i \in X$. Let W be a subset of frozen variables verifying $X \cap W = \emptyset$. A program contract for l and W is a set:*

$$\{(Pre_1, Post_1), \ldots, (Pre_k, Post_k)\}$$

such that $\forall\, i \leq k$, $Pre_i \in Sen_F(\{\!\!\{In(l)\}\!\!\} \cup W)$ and $Post_i \in Sen_F(\{\!\!\{l\}\!\!\} \cup W)$.
A program contract is said to be:

- disjoint *if for all $i, j \leq k$ with $i \neq j$, the formula $\neg(Pre_i \wedge Pre_j)$ is valid.*
- complete *if the formula $\bigvee_{i \leq k} Pre_i$ is valid.*

Disjointness requires that at most one behavior of the contract is applicable for any considered input data, *i.e.* the pre-conditions are mutually exclusive. For simplicity purpose, we only consider disjoint contracts in this paper. Completeness indicates that for any input at least one behavior is applicable. In practice, programs are often partially defined over their input domain. We thus allow incomplete contracts, rejecting input data outside the scope of preconditions.

Example 1. Let us consider a program *Price* of interface (x_1, x_2) where x_1 is of type *Drink*, an enumerated type with two values $\{0, 1\}$ and x_2 is of type *Integer*. x_1 is the input parameter indicating the selected beverage and x_2 is the output parameter corresponding to its price. An example of contract for *Price* is $C_r = \{(Pre_1, Post_1), (Pre_2, Post_2)\}$ (both disjoint and complete), with:

- Pre_1 : $x_1 = 0$, $Post_1$: $x_2 \geq 100 \wedge x_2 \leq 200$
- Pre_2 : $x_1 = 1$, $Post_2$: $x_2 \geq 200 \wedge x_2 \leq 300$

Definition 3 (Contract Satisfaction). *Let $l = (x_1, \cdots, x_{n+1})$ be an interface, W a set of frozen variables provided with $Ax \subseteq Sen_F(W)$ and C a contract for l and W. Let us consider an interpretation $\nu \in M^W$ such that $M \models_\nu Ax$ and a mapping $Sem : M^{\{In(l)\}} \to M^{\{l\}}$ satisfying the semantic condition.*
Sem satisfies C up to ν, denoted $Sem \models_\nu C$, if and only if:

$$\forall (Pre, Post) \in C, \forall \mu \in M^{\{In(l)\}}, M \models_{\nu \cup \mu} Pre \Rightarrow M \models_{\nu \cup Sem(\mu)} Post$$

$Sem_\nu(C) = \{Sem : M^{\{In(l)\}} \to M^{\{l\}} \mid Sem \models_\nu C\}$ *denotes the set of semantics satisfying C up to ν.*

For each interface l, we consider the trivial contract $C_{\emptyset,l} = \{\}$, simply denoted $C_\emptyset$, defined on l that does not restrict behaviors of programs, that is $p \in Sem(C_\emptyset)$ for all programs p of interface l. Similarly, we consider the contract $C_{\top,l} = \{(\top, \top)\}$, simply denoted $C_\top$, defined on l that requires that the program is defined for every well-typed input data tuple.

Given a signature $\Sigma = (S, F, X, P)$, a set of frozen variables W with its set of axioms $Ax \subseteq Sen_F(W)$, and an interpretation $\nu \in M^W$ verifying $M \models_\nu Ax$, we consider families $\mathbb{C} = (C_p)_{p \in P}$ of contracts indexed by P, in particular $\mathbb{C}_\emptyset = (C_\emptyset)_{p \in P}$ and $\mathbb{C}_\top = (C_\top)_{p \in P}$. $Mod_\nu(\mathbb{C})$ is the set of all families $Sem = (Sem_p)_{p \in P}$ such that $\forall p \in P, Sem_p \models_\nu C_p$. Sem is then called a *P-model.*

4   IOSTS

Input Output Symbolic Transition Systems (IOSTS) represent behaviors of reactive systems as sequences of emissions or receptions of values through communication channels conditioned by guards expressed on some attribute values. An *IOSTS-signature* Γ is a couple (A, Ch), where $A = \coprod_{s \in S} A_s$ is a set of types variables, called *attribute variables*, such that for all s in S, $A_s \cap X_s = \emptyset$ and where Ch is a set of *communication channel names*.

An IOSTS communicates with its environment through communication actions. The set of *symbolic actions* over Γ, denoted $Act(\Gamma)$, is $I(\Gamma) \cup O(\Gamma) \cup \{\tau\}$ where: $I(\Gamma) = \{c?x | x \in A, c \in Ch\}$ is the set of inputs, $O(\Gamma) = \{c!t | t \in T_\Sigma(A), c \in Ch\}$ is the set of outputs and τ is an internal action.

Values of attribute variables can be modified in two ways: by receiving a value from the environment or by assigning a value from some internal process.

Definition 4 (IOSTS). *An IOSTS (Q, q_0, Tr) over Σ and $\Gamma = (A, Ch)$ is a triple where Q is a set of states, $q_0 \in Q$ is the initial state and $Tr \subseteq Q \times Sen_F(A) \times Act(\Gamma) \times T_\Sigma(A)^A \times Q$ is a set of transitions tr of the form (q, ψ, act, ρ, q') where:*

- *q and q' are resp. the source (source(tr)) and target state (target(tr)) of tr,*
- *$\psi \in Sen_F(A)$ is a guard*
- *$act \in Act(\Gamma)$ is a communication action;*
- *$\rho \in T_\Sigma(A)^A$ is a substitution associating a term to attribute variables;*

Remark 1. We can always consider an IOSTS in which guards only contain conjunctions. If not, for a transition tr of guard ψ, it suffices to use a disjunctive normal form $\bigvee_{i=1}^{n} \psi_i$ equivalent to ψ and to split the transition into n transitions having the same source, target and communication action as tr and ψ_i as guard.

Example 2 (Drink vending machine). We consider a very simple drink vending machine. Its behavior is specified by the IOSTS in Fig. 1. An initialization step $(q \rightarrow q_0)$ sets the amount to zero. Then, in q_0, the machine waits for an amount (x) of *coins* introduced by the user, and updates the amount m. The user then chooses his/her beverage (0 or 1 for "Tea" or "Coffee"). The choice is stored in variable B. In the transition $q_2 \rightarrow q_3$, the program *Price* computes the price of the chosen drink. Two cases are possible here. If the introduced amount is lower than the price $(m < p)$, then a message "Add" appears on the screen and the machine returns to q_0. Otherwise $(m \geq p)$, the drink is delivered, the amount is reinitialized to zero and the machine goes back to q_0. Note that transitions outgoing from q_3 constrain the value (p) computed by *Price* $(p \geq 150 \land p \leq 200)$.

For a transition $tr = (q, \psi, act, \rho, q') \in Tr$ and a P-model $\mathcal{Sem}$, the semantics of tr, denoted as $Run(tr, \mathcal{Sem}) \subseteq M^A \times Act^M(\Gamma) \times M^A$, is defined as the set of triple (ν_i, act_M, ν_f) verifying:

- if act is of the form $c!t$ *(resp. τ)*, then $M \models_{\nu_i} \psi$, $\nu_f = \nu_i \circ \rho$ and $act_M = c!\nu_i(t)$ *(resp. $act_M = \tau$)*
- if act is of the form $c?x$, then $M \models_{\nu_i} \psi$, there exists ν_a such that $\nu_a(z) = \nu_i(z)$ for every $z \neq x$, $\nu_f = \nu_a \circ \rho$ and $act_M = c?\nu_a(x)$,

Note that the definition of semantics of transitions is very classical and does not explicitly refers to $\mathcal{Sem}$. In fact, semantics of programs are taken into account when defining ν_f from the extensions of ν_i or ν_a to $T_\Sigma(A)$ as defined in Sect. 3.

For a run $r = (\nu_i, act_M, \nu_f)$, we note $source(r)$, $act(r)$ and $target(r)$ resp. for ν_i, act_M and ν_f. ν_i and ν_f are the interpretation of attribute variables resp.

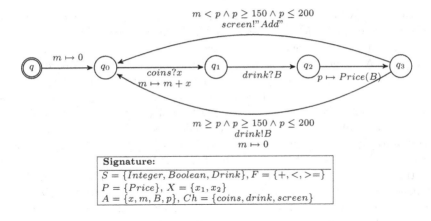

Fig. 1. IOSTS of the drink vending machine.

before and after executing the transition. Let us observe that, given a transition tr and an interpretation ν_i, the set $Run(tr, Sem)$ does not necessarily contain a run of the form (ν_i, act_M, ν_f) due to the fact that ν_i may not satisfy ψ.

The set of paths of an IOSTS $\mathbb{G} = (Q, q_0, Tr)$, denoted $Path(\mathbb{G})$, are all finite sequences $tr_1.\cdots.tr_n$ of transitions with $source(tr_1) = q_0$ and $\forall i, 1 \leq i < n$, $target(tr_i) = source(tr_{i+1})$. The set of runs of a path $pa = tr_1.\cdots.tr_n$ in $Path(\mathbb{G})$, denoted as $Run(pa, Sem)$, are sequences $r_1.\cdots.r_n$ such that $\forall i \leq n$, $r_i \in Run(tr_i, Sem)$ and $\forall i < n$, $target(r_i) = source(r_{i+1})$. Similarly, the set of traces $Traces(pa, Sem)$ of pa is the set of sequences $act(r_1).\cdots.act(r_n)$ for all $r_1.\cdots.r_n \in Run(pa, Sem)$, $act(r)$ being equal to ε if $act(r) = \tau$.

In general, it is not guaranteed that there exists at least a run for a given path pa, as it depends on the semantics associated to programs involved in pa.

Definition 5 (Path Feasibility Condition). *Let* $\mathbb{G} = (Q, q_0, Tr)$ *be an IOSTS over* $\Gamma = (A, Ch)$ *and* pa *a path of* $\mathbb{G}$. pa *is a feasible path if and only if:*

$$\exists\, Sem \in Mod(\mathbb{C}_\emptyset), Traces(pa, Sem) \neq \emptyset$$

Let W *be a set of frozen variables provided with* $Ax \subseteq Sen_F(W)$ *and* $\nu \in M^W$ *an interpretation satisfying* $M \models_\nu Ax$. *Let us consider* $\mathbb{C} = (C_p)_{p \in P}$ *a family of contracts indexed by* P. pa *is a feasible path up to* $(\nu, \mathbb{C})$ *if and only if:*

$$\exists Sem \in Mod_\nu(\mathbb{C}), Traces(pa, Sem) \neq \emptyset$$

5   Symbolic Execution and Path Feasibility Condition

Symbolic execution consists in executing an IOSTS for symbolic values (taken from a dedicated set of frozen variables $Fr = \coprod_{s \in S} Fr_s$) rather than numerical ones, and computing constraints on those values for all possible IOSTS executions. The main novelties with respect to [11] are twofold: substitutions occurring in transitions may include program calls and a renaming mechanism ensures that a given frozen variable can not appear in two distinct paths.

To store information concerning an execution, we use structures called symbolic states. A *symbolic state* is a tuple of the form $(q, \pi, \lambda, \kappa)$ where $q \in Q$, $\pi \in Sen_F(Fr)$, $\lambda : A \to T_F(Fr)$ is an application preserving types and $\kappa \subset P \times T_F(Fr)^* \times Fr$. For a symbolic state $\eta = (q, \pi, \lambda, \kappa)$, q (or $q(\eta)$) denotes the state reached after an execution leading to η, π (or $\pi(\eta)$) is a constraint on variables in Fr called *path condition* that should be satisfied for the execution to reach η, λ (or $\lambda(\eta)$) denotes terms over variables in Fr that are assigned to variables of A and κ (or $\kappa(\eta)$) denotes the set of tuples of the form $(p, (t_1, \cdots, t_n), x)$ indicating that a program call has been performed for the program p with the arguments $(t_1, \cdots, t_n)$ and that its result is stored in the variable x in Fr.

In our approach we do not have the code of programs. Instead, we reason on their contracts. Since the input formal parameters associated to a call are represented symbolically by functional terms $t_1, \cdots, t_n$, different pre-conditions may hold depending on the way those terms will be interpreted. At the symbolic execution level, we thus consider a sub-case for each of those pre-conditions. More precisely, the symbolic execution of a transition tr from a given symbolic state η will consist in a set of symbolic transitions, one for each possible combination of pre-conditions for all program calls occurring in tr. We now introduce some notations aiming at tracing program calls: for a substitution $\rho : A \to T_\Sigma(A)$ and for $p \in P$, $Res(p, \rho)$ is the set of variables $y \in A$ such that $\rho(y)$ is of the form $p(t_1, \cdots, t_n)$ and for such an y, $Arg(y, \rho)$ is then $(t_1, \cdots, t_n)$ and $Prog(y, \rho) = p$. We also denote $Res(\rho)$ for $\bigcup_{p \in P} Res(p, \rho)$.

Definition 6 (Symbolic Execution of Transitions). *Let* $\mathbb{G} = (Q, q_0, Tr)$ *be an IOSTS over* Σ *and* $\Gamma = (A, Ch)$, $tr = (q, \psi, act, \rho, q') \in Tr$ *be a transition and* $\eta = (q, \pi, \lambda, \kappa)$ *be a symbolic state over* $\mathbb{G}$.

If act is of the form $c?x$, $\lambda_i = \lambda[x \mapsto f]$, f *fresh in* Fr. *Otherwise,* $\lambda_i = \lambda$.

λ' *is the substitution such that for all* $y \in Res(\rho)$, $\lambda'(y)$ *is a fresh variable of* Fr *and for all* $y \in A \setminus Res(\rho)$, $\lambda'(y) = \lambda_i \circ \rho(y)$.

The symbolic execution $SE(tr, \eta)$ *of tr from* η *is the set defined as follows:*

- *if* $Res(\rho) = \emptyset$ *then* $SE(tr, \eta) = \{(\eta, \lambda_i(act), \eta')\}$ *with* $\eta' = (q', \pi \wedge \lambda(\psi), \lambda', \kappa)$.
- *if* $Res(\rho) \neq \emptyset$, *we consider all mappings* $Beh : Res(\rho) \to \bigcup_{p \in P} C_p$ *such that for* $y \in Res(p, \rho)$, $Beh(y) = (Pre_y, Post_y) \in C_p$. *For* $y \in Res(p, \rho)$ *with* $InOut(p) = (x_1, \cdots, x_n, x_{n+1})$ *and* $Arg(y, \rho) = (t_1, \cdots, t_n)$, *we have* $(\eta, \lambda_i(act), \eta') \in SE(tr, \eta)$ *with*
  - η' *the symbolic state* $(q', \pi \wedge \lambda(\psi) \wedge \bigwedge_{y \in Res(\rho)} \Delta(y), \lambda', \kappa')$
  - $\Delta(y) = (Pre_y \wedge Post_y)[x_1 \mapsto \lambda_i(t_1) \cdots x_n \mapsto \lambda_i(t_n), x_{n+1} \mapsto \lambda'(x)]$
  - κ' *the set* $\kappa \cup \bigcup_{y \in Res(\rho)} \{(Prog(y, \rho), (\lambda_i(t_1), \cdots, \lambda_i(t_n)), \lambda'(y))\}$

Elements of $SE(tr, \eta)$ *are called* symbolic transitions. *We denote* $Fr(\eta')$ *the set of all fresh variables of* Fr *occurring in its definition.*

Example 3. In order to illustrate Definition 6, let us consider a transition tr of the form $(q, \psi, c?x, \rho, q')$ with $\rho = [y \mapsto p_1(t_1, t_2), z \mapsto t_1' + t_2']$ with p_1 a program and t_1, t_2, t'_1, t'_2 functional terms. Let us observe that $Res(p_1, \rho) = \{y\}$, $Arg(y, p_1) = (t_1, t_2)$, $Prog(y, \rho) = p_1$ and $Res(\rho) = \{y\}$.

Let $\eta = (q, \pi, \lambda, \kappa)$ be a symbolic state. Let us suppose that the program p_1 is provided with an interface (x_1, x_2, x_3) and with a behavior $(Pre_1, Post_1)$. Then $SE(tr, \eta)$ contains the symbolic transition $(\eta, c?f_1, \eta')$ with f_1 a fresh variable of Fr and η' the symbolic state defined as:

$$(\ q', \pi \wedge \lambda(\psi) \wedge (Pre_1 \wedge Post_1)[x_1 \mapsto \lambda[x \mapsto f_1](t_1), x_2 \mapsto \lambda[x \mapsto f_1](t_2), x_3 \mapsto f_2]$$
$$[x \mapsto f_1, y \mapsto f_2, z \mapsto \lambda[x \mapsto f_1](t'_1 + t'_2)],$$
$$\kappa \cup \{(p_1, (\lambda[x \mapsto f_1](t_1), \lambda[x \mapsto f_1](t_2)), f_2)\})$$

$Fr(\eta')$ is then $\{f_1, f_2\}$.

Definition 7 (IOSTS Symbolic Execution). *Given an IOSTS $\mathbb{G}$, the symbolic execution $SE(\mathbb{G}) = (Init, ST)$ of $\mathbb{G}$ is minimally defined by:*

- $Init = (q_0, Ax, \lambda_0)$ *with* $\forall x \in A, \lambda_0(x) \in Fr$ *and* $\forall x \neq y \in A, \lambda_0(x) \neq \lambda_0(y)$,
- *for* $tr \in Tr$ *and* η *symbolic state with* $source(tr) = q(\eta)$, $SE(tr, \eta) \subseteq ST$.
- *for any distinct* $SE(tr_1, \eta_1)$ $SE(tr_2, \eta_2)$ *that are defined,* $Fr(SE(tr_1, \eta_1)) \cap Fr(SE(tr_2, \eta_2)) = \emptyset$.

Definition 8 (Paths and Distinguished Paths). *The set $Paths(SE(\mathbb{G}))$ of paths of $SE(\mathbb{G})$ is the set of all sequences $tr_1 \cdots tr_n$ with $\forall i \in 1..n, tr_i \in ST$ such that $source(tr_1) = Init$ and for any $j < n$, $q(target(tr_j)) = q(source(tr_{j+1}))$.*

For a non-empty sequence $\delta = tr_1 \cdots tr_n$, we note $End(\delta) = target(tr_n)$ and $Fr(\delta) = \cup_{i \in 1..n} Fr(target(tr_i))$. By convention, $End(\varepsilon) = Init$ and $Fr(\varepsilon) = \emptyset$.

Given a finite subset Δ of $Paths(SE(\mathbb{G}))$, $DPaths(\Delta)$ is a set of paths δ^* such that there exists an unique path δ in Δ such that δ and δ^* are isomorphic up to a renaming of variables of Fr and such that for two distinct paths δ_1^* and δ_2^* in $DPaths(\Delta)$, $Fr(\delta_1^*) \cap Fr(\delta_2^*) = \emptyset$.

We say that $DPaths(\Delta)$ is a set of distinguished *paths issued from $SE(\mathbb{G})$.*

Generally speaking, a set Δ of $Paths(SE(\mathbb{G}))$ represents a tree whose transitions issued from the root $Init$ can be shared by several paths of Δ while $DPaths(\Delta)$ consists in applying a variable renaming mechanism in order to duplicate shared transitions to completely separate paths. Distinguished paths can still share common variables, namely those in W.

Example 4. The drink vending machine of Fig. 1 has two possible paths from q to q_0 with exactly one cycle on q_0. They share a transition with a call to program $Price$ defined by its contract C_r as seen in Example 1. We thus get 4 distinguished paths shown in Fig. 2. Associated path conditions are the following:

$$pc_1 : B_1 = 0 \wedge p_1 \geq 100 \wedge p_1 \leq 200 \wedge v_1 < p_1 \wedge p_1 \geq 150 \wedge p_1 \leq 200$$
$$pc_2 : B_2 = 0 \wedge p_2 \geq 100 \wedge p_2 \leq 200 \wedge v_2 \geq p_2 \wedge p_2 \geq 150 \wedge p_2 \leq 200$$
$$pc_3 : B_3 = 1 \wedge p_3 \geq 200 \wedge p_3 \leq 300 \wedge v_3 < p_3 \wedge p_3 \geq 150 \wedge p_3 \leq 200$$
$$pc_4 : B_4 = 1 \wedge p_4 \geq 200 \wedge p_4 \leq 300 \wedge v_4 \geq p_4 \wedge p_4 \geq 150 \wedge p_4 \leq 200$$

$Init_1$	$Init_2$	$Init_3$	$Init_4$
$\downarrow \tau$	$\downarrow \tau$	$\downarrow \tau$	$\downarrow \tau$
η_1^1	η_1^2	η_1^3	η_1^4
$\downarrow coins?v_1$	$\downarrow coins?v_2$	$\downarrow coins?v_3$	$\downarrow coins?v_4$
η_2^1	η_2^2	η_2^3	η_2^4
$\downarrow drink?B_1$	$\downarrow drink?B_2$	$\downarrow drink?B_3$	$\downarrow drink?B_4$
η_3^1	η_3^2	η_3^3	η_3^4
$\downarrow \tau$	$\downarrow \tau$	$\downarrow \tau$	$\downarrow \tau$
η_4^1	η_4^2	η_4^3	η_4^4
$\downarrow screen!"Add"$	$\downarrow drink!B_2$	$\downarrow screen!"Add"$	$\downarrow drink!B_4$
η_5^1	η_5^2	η_5^3	η_5^4

Fig. 2. Symbolic paths.

A path condition is a formula over the frozen variables built by accumulating constraints from the guards of the IOSTS transitions and from constraints of called programs contracts. The path is infeasible if its path condition is not satisfiable. In addition, this feasibility depends on the fact that if a program is called twice with the same arguments, it returns the same value (semantic condition of Definition 1). Since this is not enforced by the path condition alone, we consider another set of constraints accounting for this condition:

Definition 9 (Feasibility of a Set of Paths). *Let $\mathbb{G}$ be an IOSTS over $\Gamma = (A, Ch)$ and let Δ^* be a set of distinguished paths issued from $SE(\mathbb{G})$.*

For any program p of interface $(x_1, \cdots, x_n, x_{n+1})$, for $(p, (t_1, \cdots, t_n), f)$ and $(p, (t_1', \cdots, t_n'), f')$ two distinct elements of $\cup_{\delta^* \in \Delta^*} \kappa(End(\delta^*))$ we introduce the deterministic program condition *relating to these two program calls as the formula $\phi_{\{f,f'\}}$ defined by $\bigwedge_{i=1}^n t_i = t_i' \Rightarrow f = f'$.*

The deterministic program condition *related to Δ^* is then $\Phi_p = \bigwedge \phi_{\{f,f'\}}$, for all f and f' appearing as return variable of a call of p in Δ^*.*

Finally, the feasibility condition of Δ^* is

$$\bigwedge_{\delta^* \in \Delta^*} \pi(End(\delta^*)) \wedge \bigwedge_{p \in P} \Phi_p$$

If this feasibility condition holds, it is possible to implement the programs occurring in the IOSTS so that all paths of Δ^* will complete successfully. Note that the contracts of the programs are taken into account in the path condition, and have thus an impact on the paths that are feasible or not.

Example 5. In the context of the drink vending machine, we now want to check the feasibility condition of the distinguished paths associated to the paths described in Example 4 according to two distinct contracts for *Price*, denoted resp. C_w and C_r (in Example 1). Both C_w and C_r include two behaviors resulting in 4 distinguished paths. Path conditions are given in Table 1.

– With the contract C_w, no distinguished path is feasible because of contradictions between guards of the IOSTS transitions and post-conditions of C_w.

– With the contract C_r, all distinguished paths are feasible. *Price* can return anything between 150 and 200 for an argument equal to 0 and must return 200 for an argument equal to 1.

Table 1. Feasibility according to different contracts

$C_w : \{(x_1 = 0, x_2 \geq 0 \wedge x_2 \leq 100), (x_1 = 1, x_2 \geq 250)\}$	$C_r : \{(x_1 = 0, x_2 \geq 100 \wedge x_2 \leq 200), (x_1 = 1, x_2 \geq 200 \wedge x_2 \leq 300)\}$
$pc_1 : B_1 = 0 \wedge p_1 \geq 0 \wedge p_1 \leq 100 \wedge v_1 < p_1 \wedge p_1 \geq 150 \wedge p_1 \leq 200$	$pc_1 : B_1 = 0 \wedge p_1 \geq 100 \wedge p_1 \leq 200 \wedge v_1 < p_1 \wedge p_1 \geq 150 \wedge p_1 \leq 200$
$pc_2 : B_2 = 0 \wedge p_2 \geq 0 \wedge p_2 \leq 100 \wedge v_2 \geq p_2 \wedge p_2 \geq 150 \wedge p_2 \leq 200$	$pc_2 : B_2 = 0 \wedge p_2 \geq 100 \wedge p_2 \leq 200 \wedge v_2 \geq p_2 \wedge p_2 \geq 150 \wedge p_2 \leq 200$
$pc_3 : B_3 = 1 \wedge p_3 \geq 250 \wedge v_3 < p_3 \wedge p_3 \geq 150 \wedge p_3 \leq 200$	$pc_3 : B_3 = 1 \wedge p_3 \geq 200 \wedge p_3 \leq 300 \wedge v_3 < p_3 \wedge p_3 \geq 150 \wedge p_3 \leq 200$
$pc_4 : B_4 = 1 \wedge p_4 \geq 250 \wedge v_4 \geq p_4 \wedge p_4 \geq 150 \wedge p_4 \leq 200$	$pc_4 : B_4 = 1 \wedge p_4 \geq 200 \wedge p_4 \leq 300 \wedge v_4 \geq p_4 \wedge p_4 \geq 150 \wedge p_4 \leq 200$
$\phi_{\{p_1,p_2\}} : B_1 = B_2 \Rightarrow p_1 = p_2$	$\phi_{\{p_1,p_2\}} : B_1 = B_2 \Rightarrow p_1 = p_2$
$\phi_{\{p_1,p_3\}} : B_1 = B_3 \Rightarrow p_1 = p_3$	$\phi_{\{p_1,p_3\}} : B_1 = B_3 \Rightarrow p_1 = p_3$
$\phi_{\{p_1,p_4\}} : B_1 = B_4 \Rightarrow p_1 = p_4$	$\phi_{\{p_1,p_4\}} : B_1 = B_4 \Rightarrow p_1 = p_4$
$\phi_{\{p_2,p_3\}} : B_2 = B_3 \Rightarrow p_2 = p_3$	$\phi_{\{p_2,p_3\}} : B_2 = B_3 \Rightarrow p_2 = p_3$
$\phi_{\{p_2,p_4\}} : B_2 = B_4 \Rightarrow p_2 = p_4$	$\phi_{\{p_2,p_4\}} : B_2 = B_4 \Rightarrow p_2 = p_4$
$\phi_{\{p_3,p_4\}} : B_3 = B_4 \Rightarrow p_3 = p_4$	$\phi_{\{p_3,p_4\}} : B_3 = B_4 \Rightarrow p_3 = p_4$
Feasibility: No	Feasibility: Yes

6 Testing

6.1 Model-Based Testing of IOSTS with Program Calls and Contracts

In a previous work [11], we have proposed an online testing algorithm to test Systems Under Test (SUT) with respect to a basic IOSTS (without program calls). The algorithm is based on the *ioco* conformance relation [21] and on the use of test purposes (TP) to select some behaviors to be tested. A TP is a finite sub-tree of the symbolic execution structure (SES) derived from the IOSTS of reference so that any execution trace constructed by interacting with SUT and leading to a leaf of TP will be considered as covering TP. The testing process is implemented as a simultaneous traversal of both SES and TP. Verdicts depend on whether the observed execution trace does or does not belong to TP and SES: $WeakPASS$ when the execution trace covers TP and belongs to at least one path of SES which does not end at a leaf of TP, $PASS$ when the execution trace covers TP and does not belong to another path of SES, $INCONC$ (for inconclusive) when the execution trace belongs to SES but does not cover TP, $FAIL$ when the execution trace does not cover TP and goes outside SES.

In Sect. 5, we have associated to any IOSTS with contracts a symbolic tree structure in order to be able to use it both as the SES input of the algorithm given in [11] and as a carrier to extract a finite sub-tree to play the role of TP. We can use the work described in [11] with the following slight modifications:

- Unlike [11], we allow unobservable τ transitions. Under the assumption that there does not exist a cycle of τ transitions, we can replace any sequence of consecutive τ transitions by a transition carrying the input/output action just located at the end of the τ sequence. Furthermore, in [11], quiescence conditions are expressed by enriching the reference IOSTS with transitions carrying the special label δ denoting the intended absence of reaction. Because the presence of τ transitions makes such a direct enrichment tricky, it becomes more appropriate to perform this enrichment at the level of the τ-reduced symbolic execution itself. Once the operations of τ-reduction and δ-enrichment are applied to the symbolic execution of the IOSTS with contracts, we can then apply the algorithm of [11] for free.
- In [11], path conditions for paths that are part of test purposes are satisfiable by construction. In our setting, we have to take into account the notion of feasibility, i.e., the existence or not of programs that meet their associated contracts and that are compatible with considered paths. Indeed, if the considered set of distinguished paths constituting the test purpose is unfeasible, then the application of algorithm is meaningless. In other words, the feasibility of the targeted set of paths plays the role of a testing hypothesis.

6.2 Contracts Inference

As we have seen in Sect. 5, the feasibility condition checks whether a given program contract preserves the feasibility of a symbolic path or not. In this section, we focus on the inference of contracts based on path conditions. Such contracts can then be used to define unit tests for the programs. More precisely, we start with an IOSTS $\mathbb{G}$ calling programs without associated contract. We then show that we can infer contracts such that feasible paths of $\mathbb{G}$ are guaranteed to verify the feasibility condition of the IOSTS augmented with contracts. The generated contract for a program p contains one behavior per call to p in $SE(\mathbb{G})$. For that, we use the parts of the final condition of the path on which the call occurs that are related to the return variable and to the arguments.

Given a formula F, we define inductively the set $Rel_F(X)$ of variables related to a set X of variables, as the smallest set satisfying the following conditions

- $X \subset Rel_F(X)$
- $Occ(t_1 = t_2) \cap Rel_{t_1=t_2}(X) \neq \emptyset \Rightarrow Occ(t_1 = t_2) \subset Rel_{t_1=t_2}(X)$
- $Rel_{F_1}(X) \cup Rel_{F_2}(X) = Rel_{F_1 \wedge F_2}(X) = Rel_{F_1 \vee F_2}(X)$
- $Rel_F(X) = Rel_{\neg F}(X)$

Similarly, for a formula F and a set of variables X, $Clean_X(F)$ is defined as follows. As noted in Remark 1, we can assume that the path condition only has conjunctions, and is in negation-normal form.

- $Clean_X(\top) = \top$ and $Clean_X(\bot) = \bot$
- $Clean_X(t_1 = t_2) = t_1 = t_2$ if $Occ(t_1 = t_2) \cap X \neq \emptyset$
- $Clean_X(t_1 = t_2) = \top$ if $Occ(t_1 = t_2) \cap X = \emptyset$
- $Clean_X(\neg t_1 = t_2) = \neg t_1 = t_2$ if $Occ(t_1 = t_2) \cap X \neq \emptyset$
- $Clean_X(\neg t_1 = t_2) = \top$ if $Occ(t_1 = t_2) \cap X = \emptyset$
- $Clean_X(F_1 \wedge F_2) = Clean_X(F_1) \wedge Clean_X(F_2)$

Remark 2. If F is satisfiable, then $Clean_X(F)$ is also satisfiable, as we only remove atomic propositions from the conjunction.

Definition 10 (Contract Inference). *Let $\mathbb{G}$ be an IOSTS , Δ^* a set of distinguished paths from $SE(\mathbb{G})$. We note $\kappa(\Delta^*) = \cup_{\delta^* \in \Delta^*} \kappa(End(\delta^*))$.*

For any f such that $(p, (t_1, \cdots, t_n), f) \in \kappa(\Delta^*)$, with $In(p) = (x_1, ..., x_n)$ and $Out(p) = x_{n+1}$, we define a behavior $(Pre_f, Post_f)$ for p, as well as a set of frozen variables G_f and axioms Ax_f.

We pose $\phi = \pi(End(\delta^*))$ the final condition for the path containing the call and $Y = Occ(t_1, \cdots, t_n) \cup \{f\}$ the variables occurring in the call. Then

- G_f *is* $Rel_\phi(Y)$
- Ax_f *is* $Clean_{Rel_\phi(Y)}(\phi)$
- Pre_f *is* $\bigwedge_{i=1}^{n} x_i = t_i$
- $Post_f$ *is* $x_{n+1} = f$

Finally, the inferred contracts for Δ^* are defined as follows.

- G *is* $\bigcup_{(p,(t_1, \cdots, t_n), f) \in \kappa(\Delta^*)} G_f$
- Ax *is* $\bigwedge_{(p,(t_1, \cdots, t_n), f) \in \kappa(\Delta^*)} Ax_f$
- $\forall p \in P, C_p = ((Pre_f, Post_f))_{(p,(t_1, \cdots, t_n), f) \in \kappa(\Delta^*)}$

Example 6. Let us consider here a symbolic path δ^* of our drink vending machine's specification (Fig. 3) that calls twice the program *Price* of interface (x_1, x_2). The first call leads to the appearance of a message "Add" on the screen and the second call permits the drink delivery, such that:

$$\pi(End(\delta^*)) : v_1 < p_1 \wedge p_1 \geq 150 \wedge p_1 \leq 200 \wedge (v_1 + v_2) \geq p_2 \wedge p_2 \geq 150 \wedge p_2 \leq 200$$

From the path condition $\phi = \pi(End(\delta^*))$, two behaviors will be generated according to Definition 10. For p_1 the result of the first call $(Price, (B_1), p_1)$ we have:

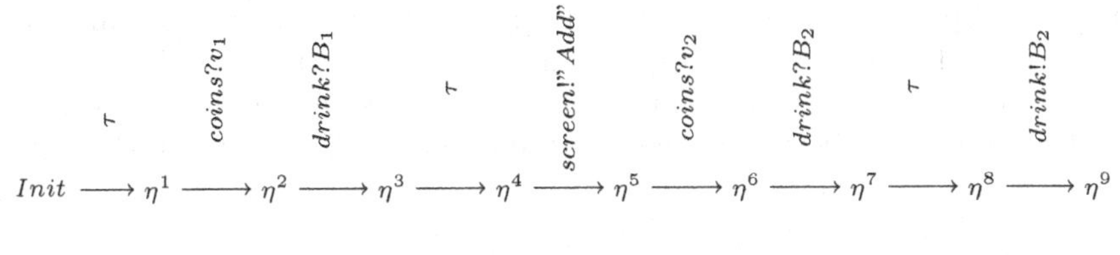

$$Init \xrightarrow{\tau} \eta^1 \xrightarrow{coins?v_1} \eta^2 \xrightarrow{drink?B_1} \eta^3 \xrightarrow{\tau} \eta^4 \xrightarrow{screen!"Add"} \eta^5 \xrightarrow{coins?v_2} \eta^6 \xrightarrow{drink?B_2} \eta^7 \xrightarrow{\tau} \eta^8 \xrightarrow{drink!B_2} \eta^9$$

Fig. 3. Symbolic path.

$$Y \quad : \{B_1, p_1\}$$
$$G_{p_1} \quad : \{B_1, p_1, v_1, p_2, v_2\}$$
$$Ax_{p_1} \quad : v_1 < p_1 \wedge p_1 \geq 150 \wedge p_1 \leq 200 \wedge (v_1 + v_2) \geq p_2 \wedge p_2 \geq 150 \wedge p_2 \leq 200$$
$$Pre_{p_1} \quad : x_1 = B_1$$
$$Post_{p_1} \quad : x_2 = p_1$$

For p_2 the result of the second call $(Price, (B_2), p_2)$ we have:

$$Y \quad : \{B_2, p_2\}$$
$$G_{p_2} \quad : \{B_2, p_2, v_1, p_1, v_2\}$$
$$Ax_{p_2} \quad : v_1 < p_1 \wedge p_1 \geq 150 \wedge p_1 \leq 200 \wedge (v_1 + v_2) \geq p_2 \wedge p_2 \geq 150 \wedge p_2 \leq 200$$
$$Pre_{p_2} \quad : x_1 = B_2$$
$$Post_{p_2} \quad : x_2 = p_2$$

Finally, the inferred contract for our program $Price$ in δ^* is defined by: $G = G_{p_1} \cup G_{p_2}$, $Ax = Ax_{p_1} \wedge Ax_{p_2}$ and $C = ((Pre_{p_1}, Post_{p_1}), (Pre_{p_2}, Post_{p_2}))$

We can now define the IOSTS $\mathbb{G}'$ with the same signature and transitions than $\mathbb{G}$ and equipped with the inferred contracts for the programs in P. Then, for every path δ^* in Δ^* that is feasible, there exist paths $\underline{\delta^*}$ in $\mathbb{G}'$ similar to δ^* except that the path conditions π are augmented with axioms and behaviors. For each $(p, (t_1, ..., t_n), f) \in \kappa(End(\delta^*))$, Ax_f is satisfiable by Remark 2 and the behavior $(Pre_f, Post_f)$ becomes trivially true: one of the behaviors of p makes the corresponding transition feasible. Since this is true for any call in δ^*, there exists thus a path in $\underline{\delta^*}$ that is feasible. This leads to the following theorem.

Theorem 1 (Feasibility Preservation). *Let $\mathbb{G}$ be an IOSTS, Δ^* a set of feasible distinguished symbolic paths of $\mathbb{G}$. $\mathbb{G}'$ is the IOSTS obtained by adding to G the inferred contracts of Definition 10. For any path δ^* in Δ^*, there exists a symbolic path $\delta^{*'}$ for $\mathbb{G}'$ having the same transitions as δ^* and which is feasible.*

7   Related Work

In the context of reactive systems verification, IOSTS and symbolic execution have been used in many works [1,11,14] for different purposes. They use IOSTS with atomic actions and substitutions whereas, in our case, we enrich IOSTS with programs specified by contracts. Our purpose is to define an integration framework and analyze in one hand the impact of programs contracts on a whole system and in the other hand elicit accurate contracts for our programs.

Our work is quite close to [13], that augments a SOA's BPEL business model with pre- and post-condition contracts defining essential component traits, and derive a suite of feasible test cases, taking into account contracts that are provided for some of the opaque components of their system. On the other hand, they do not infer contracts from the constraints expressed directly in the BPEL model as is done in Sect. 6.2.

The use of symbolic execution and path feasibility analysis are studied in [3,22] but this is limited to the analysis of programs themselves and does not take in consideration as we do the impact of the program calls on the feasibility of the system as a whole. Similarly, symbolic execution techniques over the code have been used to infer program annotations. More specifically, such approaches concentrate on generating invariants. This is for instance the case in the KeY verification framework [20], for the DySy tool [7], or for the iDiscovery tool [24]. Those invariants are meant to help the formal verification of the code against its specification, while we are aiming at generating a specification that the programs must meet in order to be usable in the context of the system under test.

The problem of inferring contracts for programs has been studied differently in other works that do not rely on symbolic execution. In particular, [6] derives pre-conditions from assertions already present in the code using abstract interpretation. [23] uses dynamic analysis to augment simple programmer-written contracts with candidate post-conditions that describes precisely what the code is doing, building upon techniques developed initially in the Daikon tool [9] for proposing likely invariants. This kind of inference is dual to ours, in the sense that we infer contracts in a top-down approach, in order to express what conditions individual components should fulfill inside a broader system, while the works mentioned above are bottom-up, encapsulating the behavior of actual code in contracts in order to check whether callers can use this particular implementation. The same can be said of works that aim at generating transition systems modeling the behavior of programs, either as message sequence charts as in [16], or as scenarios expressed under the form of live sequence charts, as in [17].

8   Conclusion

In this work, we extended the IOSTS framework with programs which are specified with contracts and we adapted symbolic execution techniques to deal with them. This gives rise to two main results. First, we study how contracts impact path conditions and describe the feasibility condition of the entire symbolic execution tree. Second, we show that path conditions can be used to infer contracts for programs in order to specify what these programs should do in the context of the system under test. Such contracts can then be used for unitary testing purposes, while feasibility preservation theorem gives some guarantees that program calls will not get in the way during integration testing.

The contribution of this paper is mainly theoretical, only illustrated by a toy example by lack of space. In [4], we provide a more realistic example involving a program call for giving the money change by considering three possible values for coins and the state of the coin reserve of the vending machine.

Implementation of the technique presented in this paper is currently under development in the Diversity [8] symbolic execution tool and the Frama-C [15] C code analysis framework using the ACSL specification language [2] as target for contract inference.

This work is in its early stages, nevertheless it provides a promising framework to explore integration testing for systems whose user scenarios are described using some IOSTS extensions (e.g. UML Sequence Diagrams [19]) and whose unitary bricks are program calls.

References

1. B. Bannour. Symbolic analysis of scenario based timed models for component-based systems: Compositionality results for testing. PhD thesis, Ecole Centrale Paris, CEA, 2012
2. Baudin, P., Filliâtre, J.-C., Hubert, T., Marché, C., Monate, B., Moy, Y., Prevosto, V.: ACSL: ANSI/ISO C Specification Language, v1.9, March 2015
3. Bjørner, N., Tillmann, N., Voronkov, A.: Path feasibility analysis for string-manipulating programs. In: Kowalewski, S., Philippou, A. (eds.) TACAS 2009. LNCS, vol. 5505, pp. 307–321. Springer, Heidelberg (2009)
4. Boudhiba, I., Gaston, C., Le Gall, P., Prevosto, V.: Input ouput symbolic transitions systems enriched by program calls and contracts : a detailed example of a vending machine. Technical report hal-01191890, MAS Laboratory, CentraleSupelec (2015)
5. Chalin, P., Kiniry, J.R., Leavens, G.T., Poll, E.: Beyond assertions: advanced specification and verification with JML and ESC/Java2. In: de Boer, F.S., Bonsangue, M.M., Graf, S., de Roever, W.-P. (eds.) FMCO 2005. LNCS, vol. 4111, pp. 342–363. Springer, Heidelberg (2006)
6. Cousot, P., Cousot, R., Logozzo, F.: Precondition inference from intermittent assertions and application to contracts on collections. In: Jhala, R., Schmidt, D. (eds.) VMCAI 2011. LNCS, vol. 6538, pp. 150–168. Springer, Heidelberg (2011)
7. Csallner, C., Tillmann, N., Smaragdakis, Y.: Dysy: Dynamic symbolic execution for invariant inference. In Proceedings of ICSE (2008)
8. Deltour, J., Faivre, A., Gaudin, E., Lapitre, A.: Model-based testing: an approach with SDL/RTDS and DIVERSITY. In: Amyot, D., Fonseca i Casas, P., Mussbacher, G. (eds.) SAM 2014. LNCS, vol. 8769, pp. 198–206. Springer, Heidelberg (2014)
9. Ernst, M.D., Cockrell, J., Griswold, W.G., Notkin, D.: Dynamically discovering likely program invariants to support program evolution. Trans. Soft. Eng. **27**, 99–123 (2001)
10. Floyd, R.W.: Assigning meanings to programs. In: Proceedings AMS Symposium on Applied Mathematics, vol. 19 (1967)
11. Gaston, C., Le Gall, P., Rapin, N., Touil, A.: Symbolic execution techniques for test purpose definition. In: Uyar, M.Ü., Duale, A.Y., Fecko, M.A. (eds.) TestCom 2006. LNCS, vol. 3964, pp. 1–18. Springer, Heidelberg (2006)
12. Hoare, C.A.R.: An axiomatic basis for computer programming. Commun. ACM **12**(10), 576–583 (1969)
13. Jehan, S. Pill, I., Wotawa, F.: Functional SOA testing based on constraints. In: Automation of Software Test (2013)
14. King, J.C.: Symbolic execution and program testing. Comm. ACM **17**, 385–395 (1976)
15. Kirchner, F., Kosmatov, N., Prevosto, V., Signoles, J., Yakobowski, B.: Frama-C: a software analysis perspective. Formal Aspects Comput. **27**, 573–609 (2015)
16. Kumar, S., Khoo, S.-C., Roychoudhury, A., Lo, D.: Inferring class level specifications for distributed systems. In: Proceedings ICSE (2012)
17. Lo, D., Maoz, S.: Scenario-based and value-based specification mining: better together. Autom. Softw. Eng. **19**, 423–458 (2012)
18. Meyer, B.: Applying "design by contract". IEEE Comput. **25**(10), 40–51 (1992)
19. Object Management Group. OMG Unified Modeling Language™ (OMG UML), version 2.5 edition (2013)

20. Schmitt, P.H., Weiß, B.: Inferring invariants by symbolic execution. In: VERIFY Workshop. CEUR Workshop Proceedings, vol. 259 (2007)
21. Tretmans, J.: Conformance testing with labelled transition systems: implementation relations and test generation. Comput. Netw. ISDN Syst. **29**, 49–79 (1996)
22. Wang, Y., Xing, Y., Zhang, X.: A method of path feasibility judgment based on symbolic execution and range analysis. Int. J. Future Gener. Commun. Networking **7**, 205–212 (2014)
23. Wei, Y., Furia, C.A., Kazmin, N., Meyer, B.: Inferring better contracts. In: Proc ICSE (2011)
24. Zhang, L., Yang, G., Rungta, N., Person, S., Khurshid, S.: Invariant discovery guided by symbolic execution. In: The Java PathFinder Workshop (2013)

Test Derivation Methods

Graph Methods for Generating Test Cases with Universal and Existential Constraints

Sylvain Hallé[✉], Edmond La Chance,
and Sébastien Gaboury

Laboratoire d'informatique formelle, Département d'informatique et de
mathématique, Université du Québec à Chicoutimi, Chicoutimi, Canada
shalle@acm.org

Abstract. We introduce a generalization of the t-way test case generation problem, where parameter t is replaced by a set Φ of Boolean conditions on attribute values. We then present two reductions of this problem to graphs; first, to graph colouring, where we link the minimal number of tests to the chromatic number of some graph; second, to hypergraph vertex covering. This latter formalization allows us to handle problems with constraints of two kinds: those that must be true for every generated test case, and those that must be true for at least one test case. Experimental results show that the proposed solution produces test suites of slightly smaller sizes than a range of existing tools, while being more general: to the best of our knowledge, our work is the first to allow existential constraints over test cases.

1 Introduction

In recent years, combinatorial testing has gathered increasing interest as a testing technique that can exercise interactions between parameters in an efficient way. Various testing tools, such as PICT [9], have been developed to produce a series of test cases that cover all interactions of t parameters through a test suite containing as few tests as possible. Various approaches attempt to expand the problem by providing *constraints* on what values each parameter can take; for example, one may require that when $a = 0$, then $b \neq 0$, thereby limiting the number of valid test cases that are available. A variety of tools support constraints of such kind, which must be fulfilled by *every* test case returned by the tool.

However, the problem of generating test cases where a set of conditions has to be fulfilled *at least once* by some test has seldom been studied. In this paper, we introduce the concept of Φ-way covering, a generalization of classical t-way test case generation where each Boolean condition in an arbitrary set must be validated by at least one test case. Section 2 formally defines Φ-way covering, and shows a number of testing scenarios where existential (rather than universal) constraints are required, and which cannot be handled by current combinatorial test generators.

© IFIP International Federation for Information Processing 2015
K. El-Fakih et al. (Eds.): ICTSS 2015, LNCS 9447, pp. 55–70, 2015.
DOI: 10.1007/978-3-319-25945-1_4

In Sect. 3, we show how Φ-way test case generation can be reduced to finding a colouring of some graph, and link the minimal number of tests to its chromatic number. However, this reduction is shown to work only when the resulting graph satisfies a property called *maximal satisfiability*. Therefore, in Sect. 4, we construct a second reduction, this time to the problem of hypergraph vertex covering, which drops the maximal satisfiability requirement and works for arbitrary conditions. Moreover, this second construction also allows us to handle universal constraints that are supported by existing combinatorial testing tools and algorithms.

We have implemented a test-generation tool that uses our graph-based approaches to produce a set of test cases for parameters with arbitrary domains. Experimental results, presented in Sect. 5, show that a straightforward application of existing graph heuristics, without any further optimization, already produces test suites whose size is comparable to the output of existing tools, and in particular shares the same asymptotic complexity, both in terms of the number of attributes and the number of values. Moreover, this is obtained while our proposed solutions solve a more general problem than existing tools, as they allow both universal and (most importantly) *existential* conditions on test cases.

2 Φ-way Covering

In this section, we introduce the problem of Φ-way test covering and describe a number of testing scenarios where such form of test covering naturally arises.

2.1   Formalization

Let $D_0, D_1, \ldots D_{n-1}$ be domains (sets of possible values) for n different parameters $p_0, \ldots, p_{n-1}$. Let $\Phi = \{\varphi_0, \ldots, \varphi_{m-1}\}$ be a set of m Boolean formulæ whose ground terms are of the form $p_i = d$, for p_i one of the parameters and $d \in D_i$. A Φ-way covering is a set $\Sigma \in 2^{D_0 \times \cdots \times D_{n-1}}$, such that for every $\varphi_i \in \Phi$, there exists an assignment of values $\sigma \in \Sigma$ that makes φ_i evaluate to true (which we shall note $\sigma \models \varphi_i$).

One can see how this problem is a generalization of classical t-way test case generation. Given parameters $p_0, \ldots, p_{n-1}$ with domains $D_0, D_1, \ldots D_{n-1}$, we can construct Φ as the smallest set such that for every set of t parameters $p_1, \ldots, p_t$ and values $d_1, \ldots, d_t$ in their respective domains, the formula $p_1 = d_1 \wedge \cdots \wedge p_t = d_t$ is in Φ. Since the resulting Φ-way covering ensures that every formula in Φ is true, it follows that every combination of values for t parameters is present in the set. As an example, Table 1 gives the set of constraints representing the 2-way covering of the set of parameters a, b and c, each having two possible values.

However, we can show that Φ-way covering is a strict generalization of t-way test case generation, as finding *one* solution to the problem is in the same complexity class as finding the *best* solution for a t-way test case generation problem [11].

Table 1. The set of Boolean constraints representing the 2-way coverage of three 2-valued parameters named a, b, c.

$$\{a = 0 \wedge b = 0, a = 0 \wedge b = 1, a = 1 \wedge b = 0, a = 1 \wedge b = 1,$$
$$a = 0 \wedge c = 0, a = 0 \wedge c = 1, a = 1 \wedge c = 0, a = 1 \wedge c = 1,$$
$$b = 0 \wedge c = 0, b = 0 \wedge c = 1, b = 1 \wedge c = 0, b = 1 \wedge c = 1\}$$

Theorem 1. *Finding a solution to the Φ-way Covering problem is NP-complete.*

Proof. Given a set Σ, verifying that each $\varphi_i \in \Phi$ is satisfied at least once amounts to evaluating it with every $\sigma \in \Sigma$, which is done in polynomial time; hence the problem is in NP. Solving Φ-way covering when Φ consists of a single Boolean expression φ is nothing but solving the satisfiability problem (SAT) for φ; hence the problem is NP-hard.

2.2 A Case for Φ-way Covering

While t-way test case generation has proved useful in many scenarios, it was shown how in some situations, constraints must be added to the original t-way requirement to correctly handle the problem at hand. Current tools and algorithms have focused up to now on *universal* constraints, which must hold true on every test case of the test suite. For example, in some situations, a combination of values for two parameters might be mutually exclusive: one can imagine a function which can send its output either to stdout or to a file; it does not make sense, in such a case, to set the output parameter to stdout, and to have a non-empty value for parameter filename. This constraint must apply to every test case produced by an algorithm.

However, the question of *existential* constraints, as is the case in the Φ-way covering presented above, has been studied much less often. Yet, in the following, we show three test case scenarios where such constraints are required —that is, the same functionality cannot be obtained, or expressed differently, using only universal constraints.

Example 1: Completing an Existing Test Suite. As a first example, suppose we have an existing test suite, which does not cover all t-combinations of values. One would like to extend that test suite, keeping existing test cases but adding the minimum number of new tests so that 100 % coverage of all t-combinations is achieved.[1] Imagine for example parameters a, b and c, each with domain $\{0,1\}$, and a test suite T composed of only two tests: $\{(a = 0, b = 0, c = 0), (a = 0, b = 0, c = 1)\}$.

To find an extension to that test suite, it suffices to first generate the set Φ of conditions corresponding to t-way coverage as described above (for example, for

---

[1] Note how this is different from finding the minimum number of tests from scratch, as the existing test cases may not be part of an optimal solution, yet must be kept.

$t = 2$, we obtain the set in Table 1). We then create one existential condition for each test in T; in the present case, this would lead to the addition of conditions $a = 0 \land b = 0 \land c = 0$ and $a = 0 \land b = 0 \land c = 1$ to Φ. We then solve the Φ-way covering problem. By construction, any minimal solution for this problem is the smallest way to obtain t-way covering while preserving the existing tests. With a graph theory approach, completing a test suite is faster than producing one from scratch because the generated graph is smaller.

Example 2: Equivalence Classes. In some cases, the original requirement of t-way coverage might prove needlessly strict. Φ-way coverage allows one to relax these conditions, while still looking for an optimal test suite. Consider for example parameters a, b and c with domains $\{0, \ldots, 9\}$, $\{0, 1\}$ and $\{0, 1\}$, respectively. Suppose that some values of a are equivalent in its relationship with b; for example, all values of $a < 5$ behave in the same way when $b = 0$. In other words, when $b = 0$ and c has some arbitrary values, all values of $a < 5$ exercise the same functionality, and do not need to be tested separately.

It is not possible to express such a fact using standard t-way test covering algorithms, which will produce an overly strong (and large) test suite, as they will try to cover all combinations of values for a, b, and c. Moreover, it is not possible either to recover from this issue by writing universal constraints, unless one forces the selection of one value for a when $b = 0$, which in turn might prevent the resulting test suite from being optimal. Finally, one can imagine more complex dependencies on parameter values where imposing fixed values to parameters in an optimal way amounts to nothing but hard-coding the solution by hand inside the constraints.

On the other hand, this situation is nicely handled in Φ-way covering. When generating the set Φ of constraints for t-way covering, it suffices to replace all conditions $a = x \land b = 0 \land c = x'$ (where $x_i < 5$ and some fixed value x') by the *single* condition $a < 5 \land b = 0 \land c = x'$, and then to solve the resulting Φ-way problem.

The reader shall remark that the same thing can be achieved by replacing the values 0 to 4 in the domain of a by a symbolic value meaning "$a < 5$", and to solve the corresponding t-way problem. Indeed, all combinations of values of parameters a and c are still considered distinct; these combinations will be missed if values 0 to 4 are amalgamated into a single symbol.

Example 3: MC/DC Testing. The modified condition/decision coverage [6] (MC/DC) is a code coverage criterion for test cases which, among other things, requires that each condition in a decision takes on every possible outcome, and that each condition in a decision is shown to independently affect the outcome of the decision.

The question of performing both t-way testing and MC/DC testing in a single test suite has only been recently studied [13]. Current approaches have measured the amount of MC/DC coverage provided by a t-way test suite, without providing any specific adaptation of existing algorithms for MC/DC coverage (and vice versa). Therefore, any good MC/DC coverage obtained by a t-way test suite is, for the moment, unintentional.

However, this can be handled with Φ-way covering. One first generates the set Φ of conditions required for t-way coverage, as was described earlier. To obtain MC/DC coverage, one simply adds to Φ the conditions corresponding to MC/DC. By construction, any solution to the resulting problem will make sure that each of the t-way conditions is met by at least one test case, and that each of the MC/DC conditions will also be met by at least one test case. Note that this may result in more test cases than for any problem taken separately; however, any minimal solution of the combined problem is guaranteed to be optimal.

3   Reduction to Graph Colouring

Assuming a few restrictions on the set of conditions Φ, we shall now show how the problem of generating Φ-way test cases can be reduced to a well-known graph problem.

3.1   Construction

Given a set of Boolean formulas Φ, the conjunctive closure of Φ is the smallest set $\Phi' \supseteq \Phi$ such that if $\varphi, \varphi' \in \Phi'$, then $\varphi \wedge \varphi' \in \Phi'$.[2] A set Φ is said to be *maximally satisfiable* if every formula in its conjunctive closure is satisfiable.

We shall now devise a construction that reduces the problem of Φ-way covering to the problem of graph colouring. Let $G = \langle V, E \rangle$ be a graph such that $V = \Phi$, and E is such that there is an edge between two vertices φ, φ' if and only if $\varphi \wedge \varphi'$ is unsatisfiable. Let C be a set of vertex "colours" and $\kappa : V \rightarrow C$ a function assigning a colour to every vertex of the graph. For $k = |C|$, the function κ is called a k-colouring if it is surjective and moreover, any two adjacent vertices are not assigned the same colour. We will define $V_c \subseteq V$ as the set of vertices that are assigned colour c by κ (and by extension, the set of all Boolean expressions assigned to these vertices). Figure 1 shows an example of such a colouring, for the set of constraints given in Table 1.

Theorem 2. *Let Φ be a set of formulæ, G be the graph constructed from Φ as described above and κ be a k-colouring of G. If V_c is maximally satisfiable for every $c \in C$, then there exists a Φ-way covering Σ such that $|\Sigma| = k$.*

Proof. Define Φ_c as the conjunction of all expressions in V_c. One can construct a test case from V_c by choosing any satisfying assignment of variables of Φ_c. Such an assignment exists, since V_c is maximally satisfiable. Let Σ be the set of all test cases constructed in such a way, for every colour $c \in C$. Since every vertex is given a colour, taken together, the test cases in Σ satisfy every condition of Φ at least once, and hence constitute a Φ-way covering.

---

[2] Although Φ' is potentially infinite, it can be restricted to a finite subset by avoiding constructing expressions of the form $\varphi \wedge \varphi$, which are equivalent to φ.

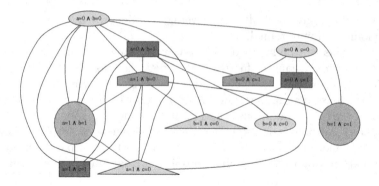

Fig. 1. The graph constructed from the constraints given in Table 1, and a possible 5-colouring.

This result shows that a *minimal* Φ-way coverage can be computed by converting the problem into the classical graph colouring problem, provided that the resulting colouring produces maximally satisfiable sets of vertices. This is not always true in the general case; Fig. 2 shows a graph whose colouring is not maximally satisfiable. One can see that for every pair of vertices, it is possible to find values for a and b that satisfy both conditions; this is why no vertex is connected to any other. Hence it is possible to assign the same colour to every vertex; however, one can see that the conjunction of the condition of all three nodes is a contradiction —in other words, it is not possible to form a test case out of it.

Fig. 2. A graph whose colouring is not maximally satisfiable.

However, we can show that a colouring is always maximally satisfiable if we impose restrictions on Φ.

Theorem 3. *Let Φ be a set of Boolean formulæ $\{\varphi_1, \ldots, \varphi_n\}$, where each φ_i is a conjunction of atomic propositions of the form $p_j = d$. If $\varphi_i \wedge \varphi_j$ is satisfiable for any pair of formulæ $\varphi_i, \varphi_j \in \Phi$, then Φ is maximally satisfiable.*

Proof. Suppose the contrary. Then there exists a set $S \subseteq 2^{[1,n]}$ of indices such that $\bigwedge_{i \in S} \varphi_i$ is unsatisfiable. Since every φ_i is a conjunction of parameter-value equalities, this entails that there exist two assertions $p_j = d$ and $p_j = d'$ such that $d \neq d'$. Let $k, k' \in [1, n]$ such that the first assertion occurs in φ_k and the second occurs in $\varphi_{k'}$. Then $\varphi_k \wedge \varphi_{k'}$ is unsatisfiable, which contradicts the hypothesis.

3.2   Complexity Results

This result has a couple of important consequences. First, we can show that any classical t-way covering problem generates a graph that satisfies the hypotheses of Theorem 3.

Corollary 1. *Let $G = \langle V, E \rangle$ be a graph generated from a t-way problem instance and let $\kappa : V \to C$ be a colouring of G as defined above. For any colour $c \in C$, V_c is maximally satisfiable.*

Proof. Since every vertex in V_c is a conjunction of expressions of the form $p_j = d$, the result follows from Theorem 3.

Hence finding a set of k test cases, if it exists, can be solved by converting the problem to k-colouring. Second, and perhaps most importantly, the previous construction provides us with a means of calculating the *exact* lower bound to the number of tests required to achieve t-way coverage. This bound is nothing but the *chromatic number* of the graph. Moreover, it is possible to compute this optimal size without even generating the solution, by constructing the *chromatic polynomial* of the graph; the chromatic number (and hence the smallest number of tests cases required) is the smallest integer that is not a root of this polynomial.

The current best known algorithm can find a k-colouring in time $O(2^n \cdot n)$, where n represents the number of constraints. Given the chromatic number can be known directly through the method described above, this gives us the same complexity for generating a minimal set of test cases. In the absence of the known value, one can fall back on simple dichotomic search, as the desired value k lies between 1 and $C(t, n) \times |D|^t$, the total number of combinations for values of t parameters.

3.3   Heuristics for Graph Colouring

One main advantage of reducing the test case generation problem to an existing mathematical problem is that one can then tap directly into a number of optimizations specific to that problem, rather than trying to solve it from scratch. This is precisely the case for graph colouring, which has been the subject of extensive study for decades. In particular, a number of methods for computing an approximate solution, called *heuristics*, can be used to produce a test suite whose size can be bounded in terms of the size of the optimal solution.

The most well known heuristic for graph colouring is DSATUR from Brélaz [2]. This heuristic is partially built on the observation that more often than not, vertices with a bigger degree generally end up with a colour of their own instead of being assigned an existing colour. The algorithm starts out by selecting the biggest degree vertex, colouring it, and then it colours the neighborhood of that vertex using the DSAT (Degree Saturation) measure. When the DSAT of two vertices is the same, the degree is used for tie-breaker. The DSAT of all vertices is updated at every colouring of a vertex. The DSAT of a vertex is an integer representing how many adjacent colours are in the neighborhood.

The DSATUR heuristic is unfortunately not great for combinatorial testing because in the generated graph files, every graph node has the same degree. Therefore, the heuristic cannot really work like it is supposed to.

The depth-first search (DFS) greedy heuristic is perhaps the most simple heuristic of all. The graph is simply explored in a typical depth-first-search fashion and the colours are assigned turn by turn. The quality of the solution depends exclusively on the sequence of the vertices. In fact, the DFS algorithm can be modified into an exact backtracking algorithm. For instance, if the backtracking algorithm is called with the task of finding a 13-colour permutation and the current colour count is 14, it does not make any sense to keep colouring the graph. The algorithm needs to backtrack and change it's permutation until it can colour the whole graph with the proper number of colours. This backtracking algorithm is almost impossible to use in practice for combinatorial testing because the graphs are too big.

Since trying every path leads to the exact solution, sampling the paths by using randomness is also a good way to go and leads to better solutions than greedy algorithms. The random DFS heuristic works in this way. For each vertex exploration, the neighborhood will be explored in a random way a number of times. When the k random explorations fail, the algorithm falls back to regular neighborhood exploration, until it can return or go to the next vertex. This is done because of course, true random exploration could slow the algorithm to a stall.

Since adding randomness to the DFS exploration scheme turns out to be very cheap and not increasing the time complexity, this heuristic is usually ran hundreds of times and the best result is used.

4   Reduction to Hypergraph Vertex Cover

As we have seen in the previous section, the graph colouring approach can only be applied when the set of assertions resulting from the initial constraints is maximally satisfiable. Yet, there exist situations where this additional hypothesis does not hold. In this section, we present an alternate method that attempts to alleviate this problem.

This method is a reduction of the Φ-way covering problem to finding a vertex covering of some hypergraph. As a reminder, a *hypergraph* is a tuple $G = \langle V, E \rangle$, where V is a set of vertices and $E \subseteq 2^{2^V}$ is a set of edges. A hypergraph generalizes a classical graph by having edges that may link more than two vertices. A *vertex covering* of some hypergraph $G = \langle V, E \rangle$ is a set of vertices $V' \subseteq V$, such that for every edge $e = \{v_0, v_1, \ldots, v_k\} \in E$, we have that $e \cap V' \neq \emptyset$. Hence every hyperedge of the graph is adjacent to at least one vertex in V'.

4.1   Construction

Given parameters $p_0, \ldots, p_{n-1}$ with domains $D_0, D_1, \ldots D_{n-1}$, let Φ be a set of Boolean constraints whose ground terms are parameter-value equalities. Define

$V = D_0 \times D_1 \times \cdots \times D_{n-1}$ as the set of all possible combinations of values for each parameter. The set of hyperedges E is then constructed such that $e = \{v_0, v_1, \ldots, v_k\} \in E$ if and only if there exists some $\varphi \in \Phi$, such that $v_i \in e$ if and only if $v_i \models \varphi$. In other words, each condition $\varphi \in \Phi$ is associated to exactly one hyperedge, linking all vertices giving values for parameters that make that condition evaluate to true.

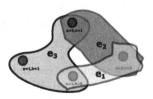

Fig. 3. The hypergraph constructed from the constraints $\Phi = \{a = 0, b = 0, a \neq 0 \vee b \neq 0\}$. Numbers are used to label segments belonging to the same hyperedge.

Figure 3 gives an example of such a construction, for the simple set of conditions $\Phi = \{a = 0, b = 0, a \neq 0 \vee b \neq 0\}$, assuming that parameters a and b have the same domain $D = \{0, 1\}$. One can see that the hyperedge labelled "1" links all vertices with values satisfying the first condition $(a = 0)$; similarly, the hyperedge labelled "2" links all vertices with values satisfying the second condition $(b = 0)$. Finally, the hyperedge labelled "3" links all vertices with values satisfying the last condition $(a \neq 0 \vee b \neq 0)$; this last edge links three vertices.

We shall now demonstrate how one can extract a Φ-way covering out of a vertex cover.

Theorem 4. *Let $p_0, \ldots, p_{n-1}$ be parameters with domains $D_0, D_1, \ldots D_{n-1}$, and Φ be a set of Boolean constraints whose ground terms are parameter-value equalities. Let $G = \langle V, E \rangle$ be the hypergraph constructed from a set of conditions Φ as described above, and let V' be a vertex covering for G. There exists a set $\Sigma \subseteq D_0 \times D_1 \times \cdots \times D_{n-1}$ that is a Φ-way covering; moreover, this set is of size $|V'|$.*

Proof. It suffices to show that $\Sigma = V'$ is the set we are looking for. By construction, every hyperedge of G is adjacent to some $v \in V'$. By construction, this entails that for every $\varphi \in \Phi$, there exists a combination of parameter values v such that $v \models \varphi$, hence V' is a Φ-way covering.

In Fig. 3, vertices forming a possible covering of size 2 have been identified in yellow. One can see how every hyperedge is indeed adjacent to some yellow vertex. Moreover, it is easy to see that no covering of size 1 could achieve the same result. Hence, finding the the minimal Φ-way covering amounts to finding the minimal vertex covering of the hypergraph G constructed from Φ.

Universal Constraints. Contrary to the graph colouring reduction described in Sect. 3, the reduction to hypergraph vertex cover works for *arbitrary* existential conditions, thus dropping the requirement for maximal satisfiability that was necessary in the former. Moreover, universal conditions (which must be true for every test case) can also be taken into account in a very straightforward way. Given a set Φ' of such constraints, it suffices to remove from V any vertex for which one of the constraints in Φ' evaluates to false. Since each vertex completely defines the values of all parameters, such an evaluation is always possible, and the fate of every vertex can always be determined. The computation of a vertex cover can then proceed on the pruned graph.

By construction, all vertices in the graph that remains fulfill all the conditions in Φ'. In addition, the vertex cover guarantees that each hyperedge (i.e. each existential condition) is covered at least once. Hence this construction allows us to handle both arbitrary universal and arbitrary existential conditions at the same time.

4.2   Complexity Results

We have already shown that finding a vertex covering of a given size k is NP-complete. However, finding the *minimal* value such that a covering exists is a much harder problem in the general case. Providing the latest complexity results for this problem is out of the scope of this paper, as abundant literature on the subject can easily be found. It is known, for example, that if d is the maximal cardinality of hyperedges and n is the size of the hypergraph, there exists an algorithm that finds a covering of size k in time $d^k n^{O(1)}$ [4].

Upper bounds have also been demonstrated for approximation algorithms. For example, one can construct a maximal matching by greedily adding edges and then let the vertex cover contain all endpoints of each edge in the matching. It can be shown that this algorithm produces a vertex covering at most d times larger than the optimal solution. For $d = 2$, a slightly lower factor of $2 - o(1)$ has been demonstrated [5,7].

Hypergraph colouring is equivalent to another problem called *hitting set*. Given a set of sets of elements $E = \{e_1, \dots e_n\}$, a hitting set is a subset V that intersects with every $e_i \in E$. When E is the set of hyperedges of G, a hitting set is precisely a set of vertices covering every edge of the hypergraph.

These results can be transferred directly to Φ-way and t-way covering. Given uniform domains of size $|D|$ for each parameter, classical t-way covering for a set of n parameters generates a hypergraph with $|D|^n$ vertices whose edges are of uniform cardinality $k = |D|^{n-t}$. Applying a result from Khot and Regev [8] which assumes the so-called *unique games conjecture*, this entails that finding the minimal number of tests is hard to approximate within any constant factor better than k.

5   Experimental Results

We implemented both approaches into an open source and mixed-language combinatorial test case generator, which is publicly available.[3] First, a PHP script takes as input a file in the PICT format, giving the name of each parameter and its possible values. Since our tool also handles universal and existential constraints, we extended the PICT format to allow the expression of these conditions. They either begin by the reserved word Once or Always, and can express any Boolean combination of elementary condition on the file's declared parameters. Figure 4 shows a sample input file.

```
a : 0, 1, 2
b : 0, 1
c : 2, 3, 4, 5

Once a != b
Always !(a > b) || c == 2
Once a < b
```

Fig. 4. An extended PICT input file for our test case generator.

The script returns a file in the Graphviz format (DOT) representing either the graph for which a colouring needs to be found, or the hypergraph for which a covering must be computed. Then, a C++ implementation of both graph algorithms reads this file and applies the corresponding heuristics, and outputs the resulting colouring or vertex cover, which can then be directly reinterpreted as a set of test cases, as explained earlier.

To assess the interest of the approach, we designed a benchmark pitting our implementation against four other tools: QICT [9], AllPairs[4], Jenny[5] and TCases[6]. These where the only tools listed on the Pairwise Testing website[7] that were both free and usable from the command-line. They vary in their support of features outside standard t-way covering, as is illustrated in Fig. 5. AllPairs and QICT only work for 2-way covering without constraints. Jenny supports $t > 2$, and allows the user to specify forbidden tuples, a restricted form of universal constraints, while TCases supports arbitrary universal constraints. Finally, our graph colouring approach handles existential constraints, while the hypergraph vertex cover handles both universal and existential constraints.

The task of exhaustively comparing our proposed implementation with a large sample of existing tools is clearly out of the scope of this paper, especially given that most of these tools are comparable only for the simplest case

---

[3] https://bitbucket.org/sylvainhalle/gcases.

[4] http://www.mcdowella.demon.co.uk/allPairs.html.

[5] http://burtleburtle.net/bob/math/jenny.html.

[6] https://code.google.com/p/tcases/.

[7] www.pairwise.org/tools.asp.

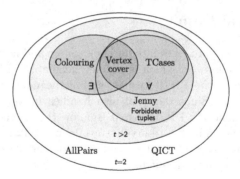

Fig. 5. Support of various features by the testing tools included in our study.

($t = 2$ with no constraints). Nevertheless, we carried four sets of experiments, and measured the size of the resulting test suites for all tools that could solve the problem.

Simplest Case: $t = 2$. In the first set of experiments, we considered only pairwise testing with no constraints, and computed the impact on the size of the test suite by varying the values of $|D|$ (the size of the domain) and n (the number of parameters). The results are plotted in Fig. 6b for increasing values of $|D|$, and in Fig. 6a for increasing values of n. One can see that graph colouring performs comparably to QICT, AllPairs and Jenny, with TCases producing slightly larger test suites. The hypergraph vertex covering provides the best results with respect to n, but shows a steeper increase than other tools with respect to $|D|$.

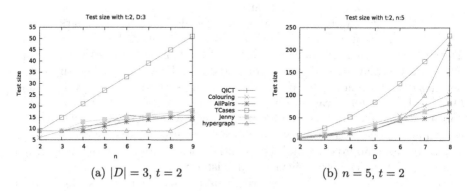

(a) $|D| = 3$, $t = 2$ (b) $n = 5$, $t = 2$

Fig. 6. Test suite size output by various tools, for a varying number of parameters when $t = 2$.

Beyond Pairwise: $t > 2$. The same trend continues when the strength of the test suite is extended beyond pairwise testing. This time, AllPairs and QICT are no longer able to solve these problems, and only Jenny, TCases and our two graph solutions remain. As Fig. 7a and b show, our tool produces test suites that are again of size smaller than TCases', and identical to Jenny's.

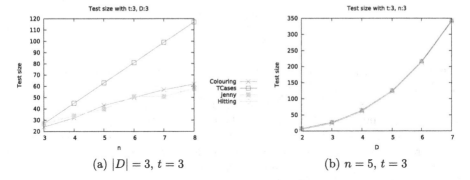

(a) $|D| = 3$, $t = 3$ (b) $n = 5$, $t = 3$

Fig. 7. Test suite size output by various tools, for a varying number of parameters when $t > 2$.

Universal Constraints. We complexify the tests even further by introducing universal constraints. This time, only TCases and our hypergraph vertex covering can handle such a problem. We experimented both approaches with $t = 2$, and with the universal constraint $\neg(p_3 = 1 \wedge p_4 = 1)$. The results are given in Table 2. As one can see, the graph-based approach provides smaller test suites of a factor of roughly $2\times$ with respect to TCases's algorithm.

Table 2. Test suite size output by various tools, for a varying number of parameters when $t = 2$.

n	Hypergraph	TCases
5	60	158
6	60	203
7	118	254

Existential Constraints. In this last category, only the hypergraph approach subsists. We experimented it with $t = 2$, and with the existential constraint $\neg(p_3 = 1 \wedge p_4 = 1)$. The results are given in Table 3.

6   Related Work

As far as we could check, the problem of generating t-way test cases has never been generalized to account for a set of arbitrary Boolean conditions that must

Table 3. Test suite size output by the hypergraph approach, for a varying number of parameters when $t = 2$.

n	Hypergraph
5	65
6	66
7	110

each apply in at least one test. Given some condition φ, Φ-way covering requires that there exists at least one test in T that satisfies φ, i.e. $\exists t \in T : t \models \varphi$. On the contrary, tools like TCases, PICT, Jenny and VPTag[8] to write conditions that must be true for some attribute to be allowed to take a given value, using some form of if-then construct or by specifying forbidden value combinations. A constraint ψ in these tools must be true for all test cases, i.e. $\forall t \in T : t \models \psi$.

This is in fact the exact logical dual of Φ-way covering. It follows easily that it is impossible to find φ and ψ that make both expressions equivalent for any arbitrary set T. As we have seen, the introduction of Φ-way coverage allows us to express and solve some problem instances that current approaches cannot.

The use of graph colouring for t-way test case generation was first suggested by Cheng et al. [3]. However, there are several differences between this related approach and the one suggested here. First, while the approach allows one to pick sets of parameters for which coverage is required, it is assumed that *all* combinations of their values must be present in the resulting solution. Our construction is more flexible and allows us to express arbitrary tuples of values of irregular length (e.g. a = 0 ∧ b = 0, a = 1). Moreover, graph colouring is used by Cheng et al. only to pick a subset of parameters on which an initial t-way must then be generated by some other means; that solution is then "blown up" to include coverings for the remaining parameters; as a consequence, the minimality of the resulting covering is not ensured.

Recently, an optimization of the IPOG algorithm's vertical growth phase was suggested [12]. This optimization relies on a "conflict graph", whose colouring allows the algorithm to identify the next best missing tuples to add to the test suite. However, to the best of our knowledge, the present paper is the first time the smallest covering array is expressed directly in terms of the minimal colouring of some graph.

The use of hypergraphs for test case generation appears to be even less common. They have been used to reason about orthogonal arrays [10], although not directly to compute an optimal set of test cases.

7   Conclusion

We have shown how Φ-way covering, a generalization of t-way test case generation, can be reduced to the classical graph colouring problem, thereby providing

---

[8] http://sourceforge.net/projects/vptag/. VPTag is limited to the case where $t = 2$, while our approach generalizes to other values of t.

(in theory) a way to compute the minimal number of test cases required by any problem instance. This result applies, provided an additional hypothesis on the shape of possible solutions —a hypothesis fulfilled by any classical t-way covering problem. Moreover, in our second modelling, which relies on a translation to the hypergraph vertex covering problem, the Φ-way covering offers the possibility to express conditions in a fashion that goes outside the expressiveness of existing solutions based on dependencies, allowing both universal and existential constraints of arbitrary nature on test cases. Experimental results have shown that, compared to a set of existing test generation tools, both our approaches generate test suites of comparable size, while being strictly more general in terms of expressiveness.

These promising experimental results warrant future work on the approach. First, additional graph colouring and vertex covering heuristics could be implemented and evaluated experimentally. Second, improvements on the efficiency of the generation of the graph from a given problem instance are currently being worked on. Finally, a third graph-based reduction, merging the two approaches presented in this paper, is also planned. It is hoped that, in the longer term, the use of our graph-based algorithms shall provide a drop-in replacement for the existing methods used in current tools and systems.

References

1. 8th IEEE International Conference on Software Testing, Verification and Validation, ICST 2015, Graz, Austria, 13–17 April 2015. IEEE (2015). http://ieeexplore. ieee.org/xpl/mostRecentIssue.jsp?punumber=7102553
2. Brélaz, D.: New methods to color the vertices of a graph. Commun. ACM **22**(4), 251–256 (1979)
3. Cheng, C.T., Dumitrescu, A., Schroeder, P.J.: Generating small combinatorial test suites to cover input-output relationships. In: QSIC. pp. 76–82. IEEE Computer Society (2003)
4. Flum, J., Grohe, M.: Parameterized Complexity Theory. Springer, Heidelberg (2006)
5. Halperin, E.: Improved approximation algorithms for the vertex cover problem in graphs and hypergraphs. SIAM J. Comput. **31**(5), 1608–1623 (2002)
6. Hayhurst, K.J., Veerhusen, D.S., Chilenski, J.J., Rierson, L.K.: A practical tutorial on modified condition/decision coverage. Technical report NASA/TM-2001-210876, NASA (2001). http://shemesh.larc.nasa.gov/fm/papers/ Hayhurst-2001-tm210876-MCDC.pdf
7. Karakostas, G.: A better approximation ratio for the vertex cover problem. In: Caires, L., Italiano, G.F., Monteiro, L., Palamidessi, C., Yung, M. (eds.) ICALP 2005. LNCS, vol. 3580, pp. 1043–1050. Springer, Heidelberg (2005)
8. Khot, S., Regev, O.: Vertex cover might be hard to approximate to within $2 - \epsilon$. J. Comput. Syst. Sci. **74**(3), 335–349 (2008)
9. McCaffrey, J.: Pairwise testing with QICT. MSDN Mag. **29**(12), 28–35 (2009)
10. Raaphorst, S., Moura, L., Stevens, B.: A construction for strength-3 covering arrays from linear feedback shift register sequences. Des. Codes Cryptogr. **73**(3), 949–968 (2014). http://dx.doi.org/10.1007/s10623-013-9835-2

11. Tai, K., Lei, Y.: A test generation strategy for pairwise testing. IEEE Trans. Softw. Eng. **28**(1), 109–111 (2002). http://doi.ieeecomputersociety.org/10.1109/32.979992
12. Vilkomir, S., Anderson, D.: Improving IPOG's vertical growth based on a graph coloring scheme. In: 8th IEEE International Conference on Software Testing, Verification and Validation Workshops, ICSTW 2015, Graz, Austria, 13–17 April 2015, pp. 1–8 (2015) [1]. http://ieeexplore.ieee.org/xpl/mostRecentIssue.jsp? punumber=7102553
13. Vilkomir, S., Anderson, D.: Relationship between pair-wise and MC/DC testing: initial experimental results. In: 8th IEEE International Conference on Software Testing, Verification and Validation Workshops, ICSTW 2015, Graz, Austria, 13–17 April 2015 [1]. http://ieeexplore.ieee.org/xpl/mostRecentIssue.jsp? punumber=7102553

Reducing the Cost of Grammar-Based Testing Using Pattern Coverage

Cleverton Hentz[1]([✉]), Jurgen J. Vinju[2,3,4], and Anamaria M. Moreira[5]

[1] Federal University of Rio Grande do Norte, Natal, Brazil
chentz@ppgsc.ufrn.br
[2] Centrum Wiskunde & Informatica, Amsterdam, The Netherlands
[3] Eindhoven University of Technology, Eindhoven, The Netherlands
jurgen.vinju@cwi.nl
[4] INRIA Lille Nord Europe, Villeneuve-d'Ascq, France
[5] Federal University of Rio de Janeiro, Rio de Janeiro, Brazil
anamaria@dcc.ufrj.br

Abstract. In grammar-based testing, context-free grammars may be used to generate relevant test inputs for language processors, or meta programs, such as programming language compilers, refactoring tools, and implementations of software quality metrics. This technique can be used to test these meta programs, but the amount of sentences, and syntax trees thereof, which needs to be generated to obtain reasonable coverage of the input language is exponential.

Pattern matching is a programming language feature used often when writing meta programs. Pattern matching helps because it automates the frequently occurring task of detecting shapes in, and extracting information from syntax trees. However, meta programs which contain many patterns are difficult to test using only randomly generated sentences from grammar rules. The reason is that statistically it is uncommon to directly generate sentences which accidentally match the patterns in the code.

To solve this problem, in this paper we extract information from the patterns in the code of meta programs to guide the sentence generation process. We introduce a new coverage criterion, called Pattern Coverage, which focuses on providing a test strategy to reduce the amount of test necessary cases, while covering the relevant parts of the meta program. An initial experimental evaluation is presented and the result is compared with traditional grammar-based testing.

Keywords: Software test · Meta program · Pattern matching · Grammar-based testing

1 Introduction

Meta programs are tools which read sentences of software languages, such as programming languages, and produce any kind of output [9]. Examples of meta

© IFIP International Federation for Information Processing 2015
K. El-Fakih et al. (Eds.): ICTSS 2015, LNCS 9447, pp. 71–85, 2015.
DOI: 10.1007/978-3-319-25945-1_5

programs are compilers, interpreters, refactoring tools, static analysis tools, and source code metrics tools. The amount and diversity of such tools are growing as processing power and large memory become available to the machines on which software is being developed, but verifying such tools is quite a challenge. Even simple metric tools are known to contain many bugs [24].

Meta programs for real programming languages are complex and hard to prove or test because the languages are big (more than 400 context-free grammar rules is quite normal) and their semantics is often unclear. Apart from some notable exceptions [23], proofs of correctness of meta programs are not to be expected. Therefore we wish to quickly find common errors in meta programs by exercising their code based on test generation.

Grammar-based testing is a preferred approach for testing meta programs [5,20]. The input syntax of most meta programs can be modeled precisely using context-free grammars (CFG). From such CFG specifications we can define sets of input sentences which satisfy different coverage criteria of the input language. However, the amount of sentences necessary to cover an entire language is intractable. For Java, for example, if we consider only sentences generated by derivation tree up to height 7 the amount of sentences that can be generated is around 46.26×10^9. If we increase this value to 10, the amount goes to around 9.43×10^{43}. But, even if we can run a Java processor on such corpus of inputs in reasonable time, chances are the corpus will still not lead to good coverage of the code of the processor itself as some constructs will only appear deeper in the grammar.

The reason for the bad coverage is that a context-free grammar describes all possible inputs for a meta program, but it does not specify precisely which part of the language is used by the given meta program or how different parts of the language are distributed over the meta program. A random distribution over an input grammar will therefore typically not generate an effective test set for a given meta program. The grammars of real programming languages have hundreds of (recursive) rules, generating a super-exponential amount of syntactically correct inputs. Due to the size of such grammars, statistically it is hard to generate exactly the right combination to cover a meta program with a limited (feasible) set of test cases. To further aggravate this problem, some important semantic information, which is dealt with in the meta program, is often missing from context-free grammar descriptions.

Pattern matching is an interesting feature which is often used during the development of meta programs. With it, it is simpler to describe specific situations over the input language, simplifying the implementation of this kind of programs. Many meta programming languages (specialized languages for the development of meta programs) and libraries are based on expressive forms of pattern matching (Haskell [15], Scala [28], TOM [3], ASF+SDF [6], Maude [8], StrategoXT [7], ELAN [4] and Rascal [18,19]).

The challenge we address is: given a grammar which describes syntactically correct inputs, to generate a minimal amount of inputs which will cover the meta program. Our contribution is the notion of pattern coverage which links grammar coverage to conditional coverage in meta programs which use pattern matching.

We propose the use of patterns as reference for the definition of test data and a pattern-based coverage criterion which defines a set of test data requirements from a set of language patterns. These patterns may be extracted from different sources: from language or meta program specifications, from the patterns used in the code of the meta program, or even from a non pattern-based meta program from which some mining of patterns has been carried out.

The main contributions of this paper are then:

- the definition of the *Pattern Coverage* criterion;
- an initial algorithm for generating sentences for *Pattern Coverage*;
- an empirical evaluation of the relation between *Pattern Coverage* and existing notions of grammar coverage.

We conduced the evaluation using two meta programs that implement the Cyclomatic Complexity algorithm [25] for Java and Pico [12] languages. To evaluate and compare the pattern coverage criterion we used the mutation technique [11] to evaluate the generated test sets. As result of pattern coverage use we could observe a reduction on the test set size and the preservation of the quality level for the pattern coverage test set.

The remainder of this article is organized as follows. Section 2 presents the basic theoretical foundation used to the work presentation. Section 3 define the pattern coverage criterion and present the test data generation algorithm. The Sect. 4 present the evaluation process and the results obtained during the process. Related work is discussed in Sect. 5, followed by concluding remarks in Sect. 6.

2   Background

In this section we briefly introduce and discuss the theoretical background on which this paper is based. First, in Sect. 2.1, some grammar-based testing concepts are introduced and discussed. Then, we define pattern matching, the mechanism used to simplify the structure of meta programs and that our proposal uses to make meta program testing more efficient.

2.1   Grammar-Based Testing

There are many different criteria for software testing in the literature. They may be classified in different (often orthogonal) ways, depending on: the stage of the software development in which they are to be applied (e.g., unit, system or regression testing), the reference artifact used for test design (e.g., white and black box testing), the kind of abstraction used to extract requirements from the reference artifact (e.g., graphs, logical expressions or grammars).

As pointed out in [1], the most important classification when it comes to define or chose a criterion is the used abstraction. As our focus here are meta programs, and the classical way of dealing with criteria-based test design for meta programs is through *grammar-based coverage criteria*, where tests are derived from grammar descriptions of the software or of some software artifact. As these criteria are defined in terms of grammar components, in the following, we present the definition of the most commonly used type of grammar (*Context-Free Grammar (CFG)*) where those components are introduced.

Definition 1 (Context-Free Grammar). *A Context-Free Grammar G is a 4-tuple* (N, S, T, P) *such that:*

1. N *is a finite set of* nonterminals;
2. T *is a finite set of* terminals;
3. P *is a finite subset of* $N \times (T \cup N)^*$ *called* production rules
4. $S \in N$ *is a start symbol.*

Every grammar G defines a language (set of sentences), which is noted $L(G)$. The sentences of the language are the sequences of terminals of G which can be derived from the initial symbol S by sequences of production rule applications (*derivations*)[1].

The grammar-based test design process starts with the application of the chosen criterion to the grammar to define a set of *test requirements*. These test requirements specify properties that need to be satisfied by the set of test cases (*test set*), and a test requirement is said to be *satisfied* if at least one of the test cases of the test set satisfies the specified property.

The typical grammar-based test criteria are defined in terms of terminals, production rules or language sentences or derivations.

Definition 2 (Grammar-based Coverage Criteria). *For a grammar* $G = (N, S, T, P)$,

- Terminal Coverage *(TSC): for each terminal symbol* $t \in T$ *there exists exactly one test requirement: t occurs in the sentence, or, simply, t. So,* $TSC = \{t \in T\}$ *is the set of test requirements to cover this criterion;*
- Production Coverage *(PDC): for each production rule* $\rho \in P$ *there exists exactly one test requirement:* ρ *is used in the derivation of the sentence, or, simply,* ρ. *So,* $PDC = \{\rho \in P\}$ *is the set of test requirements to cover this criterion;*
- Derivation Coverage *(DC): for a grammar* G, *each derivation represented by* $s \in L(G)$ *one test requirement. So, the set* $DC = \{s \in L(G)\}$ *represents all test requirements to cover this criterion.*

While Terminal Coverage and Production Coverage usually require a small amount of test cases (test sentences) to be attained, Derivation Coverage is obviously impossible to achieve in most cases. A variant is often used [21,27], then, which is to limit the length of the considered strings or derivations to some fixed limit and define as requirements the subset of $L(G)$ up to length n.

---

[1] In the absence of grammar ambiguity, there is a one-to-one correspondence between sentences and derivation. We assume here non ambiguous grammars to simplify presentation.

There are some tools that use those coverage criteria to generate test cases, for example the YouGen [14], XTextGen [13] and LGen [27] tools. These tools basically receive a context-free grammar as input and some additional restrictions and generate a set of test cases (language sentences). These restrictions are necessary to limit the size of the resulting set, since, in general, the language associated to the input grammar is infinite.

2.2   Pattern Matching Mechanism

Pattern matching is a programming language feature. It is common to implement meta programs using pattern matching because it facilitates the description of interesting cases over the object language and dubs as a de-structuring variable binding mechanism.

Formally, the pattern matching problem is, given two terms s and l, determine if there is a substitution σ, such that $\sigma(l) = s$ [2]. The substitution itself, if it exists, represents the binding of variables which can be used by the program after the match.

Table 1 depicts a number of pattern types as used in the Rascal language [18]. Each line shows a value on the right and a pattern on the left of the match := operator.

A most basic form of pattern, the congruence pattern, is an arbitrarily nested expression using only constructors and open variables. On table item 2, a pattern is used as a condition to the if statement. The congruence match succeeds because the value builds and **add** term, which the pattern matches literally. Then the children of the **add** term, **var("x")** and **var("y")** can be matched to the unconditional variables **l** and **r** respectively. The **l** and **r** variables may now be used in the program as normal variables, for example by printing them.

A more advanced pattern is the deep match on table item 3. It can be arbitrarily combined with any other match operator; in this case a typed variable. The current pattern will recursively traverse the matched value and succeed if a value of type **str** is found anywhere or fail otherwise. Such a pattern is *non-unitary* in the sense that it could match a single value in many ways (twice in

Table 1. Example of some pattern-based instructions in Rascal.

N.	Instruction	Description
1	`int x := 3;`	Typed pattern, the **x** variable is bound to value 3.
2	`if (add(l, r) := add(var("x"), var("y")))` `   println(l + "," r);`	Constructor pattern, the identifier **add** is the constructor and the variables **l** and **r** are bound to values **var("x")** and **var("b")**, respectively.
3	`for (/str x := add(var("x"), var("y")))` `   println(x);`	Deep matching pattern, the matching can happen on any level of the term.

this example). Using the `for` loop the programmer can iterate over all possible
bindings of x, namely "x" and "y".

3   Testing Meta Programs Using Pattern Coverage

Our proposal to deal with the original problem is to use the pattern information
related to a meta program and with it generate a test set that will be used in the
test process. This strategy may be applied on white-box testing, if the patterns
are derived from the program, or black-box testing, if they are extracted from
some more abstract model or specification of the meta program.

During this section, we will use a meta program (presented on Listing 1.1)
as example to illustrate the concepts introduced on the section. This example
is a typical implementation for the Cyclomatic Complexity (CC) [25] algorithm.
The implementation of CC is coded in Rascal and was used by Landman [22] to
calculate and analyze the correlation between the CC and source lines of code
on a large corpus of Java code. For the purpose of the current paper this code
is assumed to be correct. The `visit` statement generates a recursive traversal
and each `case` represents a pattern to detect in the traversed tree, and after
the colon (:) an action to perform when it matches (increasing a counter). Most
of the cases define simple patterns which identify a particular node type, but
two are more interesting, filtering only infix expressions with either && or || as
operators. The same code was used into our evaluation process and it will be
detailed on Sect. 4.

Our first step to address the test of meta programs is to define a coverage
criterion that formalizes the requirements for a set of test cases. On Sect. 3.1
we introduce this criterion. After that, we introduce on Sect. 3.2 a prototype of
algorithm to generate a test set that contains test cases to satisfy those requirements.

Listing 1.1. .]Example of a pattern-based meta program written in Rascal [22].

```
1 int calcCC(Statement impl) {
2   int result = 1;
3   visit (impl) {
4     case \if(_,_) : result += 1;
5     case \if(_,_,_) : result += 1;
6     case \case(_) : result += 1;
7     case \do(_,_) : result += 1;
8     case \while(_,_) : result += 1;
9     case \for(_,_,_) : result += 1;
10    case \for(_,_,_,_) : result += 1;
11    case \foreach(_,_,_) : result += 1;
12    case \catch(_,_): result += 1;
13    case \conditional(_,_,_): result += 1;
14    case \infix(_,"&&",_) : result += 1;
15    case \infix(_,"||",_) : result += 1;
16  }
17  return result; }
```

3.1 A Pattern-Based Coverage Criterion

Our proposal is, given some pattern information corresponding to a meta program, to generate test cases exercising these patterns, i.e., to generate sentences that match them. To systematize this strategy, we define a new coverage criterion:

Definition 3 (Pattern Coverage). *For a pattern-based meta program m, and $\mathcal{P}_m$, the set with all instances of patterns of m, the test requirement set TR contains each element of the pattern set $\mathcal{P}_m$. Satisfaction of each of these requirements is attained by any subject which matches the corresponding pattern.*

To illustrate the pattern coverage definition, we can apply the definition to the CC implementation on Listing 1.1. For the given code the pattern set produced by collecting patterns is $\mathcal{P}_m = \{$`Statement impl`, `\if(_,_)`, `\if(_,_,_)`, ..., `infix(_,"||",_)`$\}$ Since in Rascal functions are dispatched by patterns, the formal parameter `Statement impl` is also considered a pattern, namely matching only abstract syntax trees of type `Statement`. The set $TR = \mathcal{P}_m$, and to cover TR the test data must include the set of java statements that match the corresponding patterns. For example, the pattern `\if(_,_)` would be covered by a program including the statement "`if (true) {}`", and an input which covers also the patterns for the Boolean operators would be "`if (true && false || true) { }`".

3.2 A Simple Algorithm to Generate Pattern Covering Test Sets

We propose an effective algorithm to generate test cases from grammars which cover a selected set of patterns extracted from the meta program under test. In this algorithm, we assume one constructor in a pattern corresponds to one labeled production rule of a context-free grammar. This initial algorithm guarantees full pattern coverage but not minimality of the set of test inputs. We shall see in the evaluation that the expected amount of tests generated is already so small that optimization in this direction is not necessarily an interesting avenue.

Given the set of pattern requirements corresponding to the meta program under test, the algorithm takes the following steps, for each pattern instance on the set:

1. Identify the open variables and their type (nonterminal);
2. Create a term for each identified variable for the given type using standard grammar-based test input generation;
3. Substitute the variable by the generated term in the pattern;
4. From the start symbol of the input grammar generate a sentence in the language including the previously generated term;
5. Add the result sentence to the test set.

On the first step, the algorithm identifies the open variables inside the term and generate terms to bind with them (step 2). Next step is apply a substitution of variable by the generated term (step 3). With this, we have a term that matches the original patterns, but it is only part of a full input program. So, we generate a sentence using the input grammar (step 4). It is created from the start symbol and needs to reach the same nonterminal associated with the partial term that was generated on the last step. This step could be easily automated by adapting the traditional grammar-based testing algorithms. Finally, the resulting sentence is added to the test set (step 5).

Listing 1.2. Example of a Java sentence produced by the generation algorithm.

```
1 public class id0 {
2   static {
3     if (true)
4         return ;
5   }
6 }
```

To illustrate the algorithm execution, we use the implementation of CC on Listing 1.1 as example. The test requirement \if(_,_) is a pattern of type constructor and it has two open variables named as _. According to step 1 in the algorithm these two variable are detected and their nonterminal symbols are identified. The next step is to create a subterm for each of them: the first is a Java Boolean expression and the second a Java statement. For example these terms could be `true` and `return ;`. On step 3 the variables are substituted by these terms and the result is a new subterm, in our example, if (true) `return ;`. The last step to produce the test data is to generate a sentence from the grammar start symbol including the previous subterm as an instance of its corresponding nonterminal. The Listing 1.2 shows a possible resulting Java sentence generated by this algorithm for the test requirement \if(_,_).

In this paper we propose the use of patterns as reference for the definition of test data and a pattern-based coverage criterion which defines a set of test data requirements from a set of language patterns. These patterns may be extracted from different sources: from language or meta program specifications, from the patterns used in the code of the meta program, or even from a non pattern-based meta program from which some mining of patterns has been carried out.

The algorithm presented here was used in the evaluation process described in Sect. 4.

4   Evaluation

To evaluate our claim of effectiveness, we compare our new method of generating test inputs for meta programs to the state-of-art grammar-based testing methods in this section. Our evaluation is scoped to Rascal meta programs, which we assume to be representative for all meta programs which strongly depend on pattern matching.

The evaluations questions are:

RQ1: How efficient and effective are standard grammar-based testing techniques efficient for testing of Rascal meta programs?

RQ2: Is pattern-based testing more efficient and more effective than grammar-based testing for testing Rascal meta programs?

4.1 Evaluation Method

We use two variables to measure the efficiency and effectiveness of this criterion: test set size for cover a given coverage criterion and mutation score, respectively.

The mutation score is a measure of effectiveness based on the concept of mutation testing [1,11]. Mutation testing provides a repeatable process for measuring the effectiveness of test cases and identifying disparities in (random) test sets. It involves the use of original software under test to create a variation of it that contains an artificial fault. Each fault inserted in original software produces a *mutant* and the specific fault injected is called *mutation operator*. After the application of a mutation operator the mutant is executed using the test set under evaluation, if the test indeed fails for one of the generated test cases the mutant is killed and the test set is good enough to detect that mutant operator. Otherwise, if all all tests set run without any failure, the mutant is alive and the random test case generation is deemed ineffective. For this last case there are two possibilities: the test set is indeed not good enough to trigger the mutant or the mutant is accidentally semantically equivalent to the original program. At the end, the percent of mutants killed by the test set is called *mutation score*.

The mutation process used in the evaluation is implemented in Rascal for Rascal. The set of mutation operators (Table 2) introduces bugs randomly, simulating programmers forgetting cases, making errors in patterns and making errors in the code that is triggered after a pattern is matched. Rascal is a pattern-oriented language, where patterns govern both data (binding) and control flow (conditionals) dependency. Patterns occur in the conditions of all structured control-flow statements and the parameters of functions (dynamic dispatch). Common Rascal programming errors are forgetting to update a pattern when a language has changed, accidentally overlapping patterns for which the code is then never or always executed, and writing overly restrictive patterns accidentally. The mutation operators are designed to highlight code which is executed conditionally under a pattern, in order to make observable whether and how quickly the test set can trigger code which depends on (possibly buggy) patterns.

Table 2. Table of Rascal mutation operators.

Operator code	Description
OP0	Remove pattern rewrite
OP1	Remove pattern with action
OP2	Remove `if` conditionals. Simple `if`
OP3	Remove `if` conditionals. Remove `if` code block
OP4	Remove `if` conditionals. Remove `else` code block
OP5	Remove `while` conditionals
OP6	Remove `for` conditionals

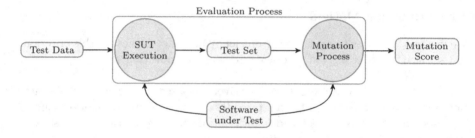

Fig. 1. An overview of evaluation process.

To evaluate the efficiency, we measure the number of test cases necessary to kill 100 % of the mutants.

The Comparison Process. To provide an answer to the second question, we then run the same process using a test set that covers the pattern coverage criterion. The result of this second experiment is then compared with to the previous experiment. The comparison process is shown in Fig. 1. The circles represent the process and the rectangles represent data. The process starts with the generation of a set of test data based on the language's context-free grammar using the algorithm in Sect. 3.2. An initial test data set is used with the software under test (Listing 1.1) to generate the expected results for this set of input. Since we use mutation testing to evaluate the test set effectivity we may use the not mutated version as the oracle. Given this generated test set and the generated oracle, the mutation process is started and each mutant is tested. This test process logs the two metrics (mutation score and number of test cases).

Selected Languages and Program Under Test. We use Java and Pico as the object languages for our experiment and a typical algorithm for computing the Cyclomatic Complexity (CC) [25] of a program for both languages (see Listing 1.1). CC is a basic but non-trivial algorithm, so this evaluation should be seen as an initial experiment and proof-of-concept. Lincke et al. [24] showed how even relatively basic and often used software metric implementations are inconsistent with each other, and thus broken, underlying the relevance of a feasible method for testing them thoroughly.

For the Java language, we used the *Java Specification Language* [17] and the ANTLR Java Grammar[2] specification as references. Since Java is a big language and therefore our initial demonstration and evaluation first focuses on a smaller language with a mini grammar: Pico [12]. The Pico language is a small educational programming language with a Rascal implementation[3]. This initial evaluation would also detect bugs in either our implementations or our evaluation methods. After this we continue with our evaluation on the Java language. Table 3 lists the sizes of the Pico and Java grammars we used.

---

[2] https://github.com/antlr/examples-v3/blob/master/java/java/Java.g.
[3] http://tutor.rascal-mpl.org/Recipes/Languages/Pico/Pico.html.

Table 3. Grammar statistics for Java and Pico used in the evaluation.

Structure	Size	
	Pico	Java
Production rules	18	272
Terminals	23	98
Nonterminals	9	142

To generate production coverage test data we used the LGen tool [27]. For both languages we generated the test data and after that ran the software under test, the cyclomatic complexity algorithms, to create the expected result and produce the complete test set.

4.2   Results for Pico Cyclomatic Complexity

For the Pico language the results obtained by the evaluation method is presented in Table 4. Using the production coverage test set we reach 100 % of mutation score. It means that all mutations generated by mutation process have been killed by the test set. The pattern coverage test set we also killed all mutants, but in this case with a lower number of test cases. This results provides an initial evaluation about the pattern coverage's efficiency but without enough confidence on it because its small scale and low complexity of the Pico language.

Table 4. Results obtained by the evaluation using the Pico language.

Coverage criterion	Test set size	Mutation score
Production coverage	10	100 %
Pattern coverage	2	100 %

4.3   Results for Java Cyclomatic Complexity

The results obtained from Java case are shown in Table 5. In this case, we observe a reduction over on the number of test cases using the pattern coverage criterion. This is related to the amount of patterns used on program 1.1. Furthermore, the mutation score for this coverage criterion shows an increase in relation to the production coverage criterion.

4.4   Discussion and Threats to Validity

Even given the small size and complexity, from the Pico experiment we learn that pattern coverage may reduce the amount of required test cases dramatically

Table 5. Results obtained by the evaluation using the Java language.

Coverage criterion	Test set size	Mutation score
Production coverage	85	8.33 %
Pattern coverage	12	83.33 %

without sacrificing test quality. This small demonstration can not be generalized to other languages or meta programs, but it motivates to continue investigating and served as an integration test for our experimental setup.

The Java language results show that the approach will scale to full programming languages. We observe that indeed the number of test cases drops significantly without loss of test quality.

The main threat to validity of the above observations is the size and complexity of the meta program under test, which is not representative of the broader set of meta programs we wish to target. These initial results are promising nevertheless. We expect future investigation on larger meta programs to produce more specific patterns (which does not incur an overhead since pattern extraction is linear in the size of the meta program). More specific patterns will likely lead to larger but not more test cases. We hypothesize that pattern-based testing will still outperform exhaustive grammar-based testing in the number of test cases, while we need to find out experimentally what the mutation scores will show. The mutation score is influenced by the internal complexity of the meta program which may use other kinds of predicates and queries next to pattern matching to guide control flow. More complex meta programs will also require us to extend the set of mutation operators to generate representative mutations. Our future target is a group of type analysis and type inference tools for Rascal, Java and PHP which we wish to test exhaustively.

We believe that future work to extend pattern-based testing to other application domains based on schemata and patterns may be fruitful (XML processing, DOM manipulation and model driven engineering)

5   Related Work

Grammar-based testing has been used in compiler testing for many years [5,20]. Compilers are a specific kind of meta programs and could be tested using similar techniques. The YouGen tool [14] generates test data based on grammar definitions, controlling depth of derivation trees based on annotations. The major difference is about the algorithm based on enumeration and filtering of the derivation trees. This also reduces the number of test data generated, but the filtering is guided only using information from the grammar. Our approach also uses information from the program under test.

In the same direction, the XTextGen [13] generates test-data based from grammars. This tool has a different approach to generate the data. It uses Cantor pairing and mandatory multiplicity control. The generation process is split into two phases. First, an enumeration process and then a semantics-directed post-processing over the result a set of transformation. With XTextGen it should be possible, in principle, to simulate pattern-based testing as we propose in the current paper. An appropriate encoding would have to be developed to do so, which would amount to an alternative implementation of our sentence generation algorithm.

Jagannath et al. [16] propose several ways of reducing the cost of bounded exhaustive testing (the generalization of grammar-based testing) by test prioritization and by merging smaller inputs into fewer bigger inputs. Our approach also reduces the cost of exhaustive testing, by selecting the right test inputs to run, but in a completely different way.

SafeRefactor [10] also uses bounded exhaustive search for generating test programs (in AST format and for the purpose of refactoring tools). A key ingredient is programmable specialization of the generated ASTs to better fit the specific meta program under test. This framework, which was elaborated on later for scalability [26,30], could be extended with our approach to automatically feed-back patterns back into the AST generators.

With concolic testing [29] a similar effect of selecting the right test cases could be achieved as our approach can. Concolic testing is based on symbolically simulating a program for a given test input and using a SMT solver or theorem prover to generate the next input which will cover a different execution path than the previous test input did. One would need to add a theory for grammar and pattern matching to the solver and a simulation engine for the meta language for this approach to work. Our approach is different and much more lightweight, neither requiring a hard-to-obtain efficient solver nor a symbolic execution engine, just a pattern extraction tool and a grammar-based sentence generator.

6   Conclusions and Future Work

In this paper, we presented a new coverage criterion for test case design, pattern coverage) and its preliminary evaluation of effectiveness in the context of pattern-based meta programs. The evaluation considered the amount of test cases and mutation score, taking as reference traditional grammar-based testing. We conclude that our experiments indicate a significant reduction in necessary test cases to achieve coverage, while improving the quality of the tests in terms of mutation score. Further evaluation with a richer set of meta programs and mutation operators is planned in the next steps of the research.

This work is part of a more general research direction in which we are investigating lightweight techniques to more effectively test meta programs: extracting constraints from the source code of the programs under test (or their specifications) to direct a sentence generator.

Acknowledgments. This work is partly supported by CNPq grants 237049/2013-9 and 573964/2008-4 (National Institute of Science and Technology for Software Engineering—INES, www.ines.org.br).

References

1. Ammann, P., Offutt, J.: Introduction to Software Testing. Cambridge University Press, New York (2008)
2. Baader, F., Nipkow, T.: Term Rewriting and All That. Cambridge University Press, New York (1998)
3. Balland, E., Brauner, P., Kopetz, R., Moreau, P.-E., Reilles, A.: Tom: piggybacking rewriting on Java. In: Baader, F. (ed.) RTA 2007. LNCS, vol. 4533, pp. 36–47. Springer, Heidelberg (2007)
4. Borovanský, P., Kirchner, C., Kirchner, H., Moreau, P.-E., Vittek, M.: Elan: a logical framework based on computational systems. Electron. Notes Theor. Comput. Sci. **4**, 35–50 (1996)
5. Boujarwah, A.S., Saleh, K.: Compiler test case generation methods: a survey and assessment. Inf. Softw. Technol. **39**(9), 617–625 (1997)
6. den van Brand, M.G.J., van Deursen, A., Heering, J., de Jong, H.A., de Jonge, M., Kuipers, T., Klint, P., Moonen, L., Olivier, P.A., Scheerder, J., Vinju, J.J., Visser, E., Visser, J.: The ASF+SDF meta-environment: a component-based language development environment. In: Wilhelm, R. (ed.) CC 2001. LNCS, vol. 2027, p. 365. Springer, Heidelberg (2001)
7. Bravenboer, M., Kalleberg, K.T., Vermaas, R., Visser, E.: Stratego/XT 0.17. A language and toolset for program transformation. Sci. Comput. Program. **72**(1–2), 52–70 (2008). Special Issue on Second issue of experimental software and toolkits (EST)
8. Clavel, M., Durán, F., Eker, S., Lincoln, P., Martí-Oliet, N., Meseguer, J., Talcott, C.: The maude 2.0 system. In: Nieuwenhuis, R. (ed.) RTA 2003. LNCS, vol. 2706, pp. 76–87. Springer, Heidelberg (2003)
9. Czarnecki, K., Eisenecker, U.W.: Generative Programming - Methods, Tools and Applications. Addison-Wesley, Reading (2000)
10. Daniel, B., Dig, D., Garcia, K., Marinov, D.: Automated testing of refactoring engines. In: Proceedings of the the 6th Joint Meeting of the European Software Engineering Conference and the ACM SIGSOFT Symposium on The Foundations of Software Engineering, ESEC-FSE 2007, pp. 185–194. ACM, New York (2007)
11. DeMillo, R.A., Lipton, R.J., Sayward, F.G.: Hints on test data selection: help for the practicing programmer. Computer **11**(4), 34–41 (1978)
12. Deursen, A.V., Heering, J., Klint, P. (eds.): Language Prototyping: An Algebraic Specification Approach, vol. V. Scientific Publishing Co. Inc., River Edge (1996)
13. Härtel, J., Härtel, L., Lämmel, R.: Test-data generation for Xtext. In: Combemale, B., Pearce, D.J., Barais, O., Vinju, J.J. (eds.) SLE 2014. LNCS, vol. 8706, pp. 342–351. Springer, Heidelberg (2014)
14. Hoffman, D., Ly-Gagnon, D., Strooper, P., Wang, H.-Y.: Grammar-based test generation with yougen. Softw. Pract. Experience **41**, 427–447 (2011)
15. Hudak, P., Peyton Jones, S., Wadler, P.: Report on the Programming Language Haskell, A Non-strict Purely Functional Language (Version 1.2). ACM SIGPLAN Not. **27**(5), 1–164 (1992)
16. Jagannath, V., Lee, Y.Y., Daniel, B., Marinov, D.: Reducing the costs of bounded-exhaustive testing. In: Chechik, M., Wirsing, M. (eds.) FASE 2009. LNCS, vol. 5503, pp. 171–185. Springer, Heidelberg (2009)
17. Gosling, J., Joy, B., Steele, G., Bracha, G., Buckley, A.: The Java Language Specification, vol. 1, 3rd edn. Addison Wesley, Reading (2005)

18. Klint, P., van der Storm, T., Vinju, J.: Rascal: A domain specific language for source code analysis and manipulation. In: IEEE International Workshop on Source Code Analysis and Manipulation, pp. 168–177 (2009)
19. Klint, P., van der Storm, T., Vinju, J.: EASY meta-programming with rascal. In: Fernandes, J.M., Lämmel, R., Visser, J., Saraiva, J. (eds.) Generative and Transformational Techniques in Software Engineering III. LNCS, vol. 6491, pp. 222–289. Springer, Heidelberg (2011)
20. Kossatchev, A.S., Posypkin, M.A.: Survey of compiler testing methods. Program. Comput. Softw. **31**(1), 10–19 (2005)
21. Lämmel, R., Schulte, W.: Controllable combinatorial coverage in grammar-based testing. In: Uyar, M.Ü., Duale, A.Y., Fecko, M.A. (eds.) TestCom 2006. LNCS, vol. 3964, pp. 19–38. Springer, Heidelberg (2006)
22. Landman, D., Serebrenik, A., Vinju, J.: Empirical analysis of the relationship between CC and SLOC in a large corpus of Javah methods. In: 30th IEEE International Conference on Software Maintenance and Evolution, ICSME 2014 (2014)
23. Leroy, X.: A formally verified compiler back-end. J. Autom. Reason. **43**(4), 363–446 (2009)
24. Lincke, R., Lundberg, J., Löwe, W.: Comparing software metrics tools. In: Proceedings of the 2008 International Symposium on Software Testing and Analysis, ISSTA 2008, pp. 131–142. ACM, New York (2008)
25. McCabe, T.: A complexity measure. IEEE Trans. Softw. Eng., SE **2**(4), 308–320 (1976)
26. Mongiovi, M., Mendes, G., Gheyi, R., Soares, G., Ribeiro, M.: Scaling testing of refactoring engines. In: 30th IEEE International Conference on Software Maintenance and Evolution, Victoria, BC, Canada, 29 September 2014–3 October 2014, pp. 371–380 (2014)
27. Moreira, A.M., Hentz, C., de Menezes Ramalho, V.: Application of a syntax-based testing method and tool to software product lines. In: 7th Brazilian Workshop on Systematic and Automated Software Testing, SAST 2013 (2013)
28. Odersky, M., Micheloud, S., Mihaylov, N., Schinz, M., Stenman, E., Zenger, M., et al.: An overview of the scala programming language. Technical report, École Polytechnique Fédérale de Lausanne (2004)
29. Sen, K., Marinov, D., Agha, G.: Cute: a concolic unit testing engine for C. In: Proceedings of the 10th European Software Engineering Conference Held Jointly with 13th ACM SIGSOFT International Symposium on Foundations of Software Engineering, ESEC/FSE 2013, pp. 263–272. ACM, New York (2005)
30. Soares, G., Gheyi, R., Massoni, T.: Automated behavioral testing of refactoring engines. IEEE Trans. Softw. Eng. **39**(2), 147–162 (2013)

Automated Test Design for Boundaries of Product Line Variants

Stephan Weißleder[1], Florian Wartenberg[1], and Hartmut Lackner[2]([✉])

[1] Thales Transportation Systems, Schützenstraße 25, 10117 Berlin, Germany
{stephan.weissleder,florian.wartenberg}@thalesgroup.com
[2] Humboldt-Universität zu Berlin, Rudower Chaussee 25, 12489 Berlin, Germany
lackner@informatik.hu-berlin.de

Abstract. Developing product lines is usually more efficient than developing single products because of the reuse of single components. Testing, however, has to consider complete, integrated systems. To prevent testing every product on system level, the whole product line should be analyzed with the aim of selecting distinguishing product behavior and a minimum of system products to test. In this paper, we present a model-based test design approach for testing the selected behavior of products, but also their deselected behavior. A major challenge of this approach is that the deselected behavior of a product is often not part of its behavioral model. Thus, we use the variability model to transform the behavioral model so that showing the exclusion of the deselected behavior is also covered by tests. We present the approach, a corresponding prototypical implementation, and our experiences using a set of examples.

1   Introduction

Configurability is a key selling point of many systems. For instance, every possible variant of a German car is sold only once or twice on average. Correspondingly, it is infeasible to design every variant from scratch. Instead, system components are reused to a maximum extent. The reuse and variability of system components can be described in a variability model like, e.g., a feature model with features linked to system components. Although this process leads to a significant gain in development efficiency, system test efficiency is not impacted, because the whole integrated system has to be tested.

Quality assurance is one of the most important aspects in systems engineering. Low quality usually results in high costs for defect rectification. Testing is an important quality assurance technique. In many cases, however, it is considered to be very expensive. Automated test execution helps in reducing test execution time and costs. It faces, however, the issue of high costs for test design adaptation. The automation of test design is a solution to such issues.

Existing approaches are focused on covering the selected behavior of a product, i.e., they check if everything that should be in the product is really implemented. In this paper, we focus on covering the deselected behavior by checking if everything that should not be in the product variant is really not implemented. Common approaches cannot be used for this, because they are focused

© IFIP International Federation for Information Processing 2015
K. El-Fakih et al. (Eds.): ICTSS 2015, LNCS 9447, pp. 86–101, 2015.
DOI: 10.1007/978-3-319-25945-1_6

on cutting away all deselected behavior for a variant, and thus the model for the variant does not contain deselected behavior, anymore. To overcome this issue, we introduce model transformations that create new model elements describing the non-existence of deselected behavior.

The paper is structured as follows. In Sect. 2, we present the preliminaries. Section 3 describes our approach. The implementation and experiments are described in Sect. 4. Section 5 contains an analysis of the related work. In Sect. 6, we conclude and discuss our approach including threats to validity.

2 Preliminaries

This section contains the preliminaries of this paper. It describes automated test design, model-based product line (PL) engineering, and the combination of both.

2.1 Automated Test Design

Testing is a common approach to quality assurance. The idea is to systematically compare the observed system behavior with the expected one. There are various approaches and tools to automate the test execution. The biggest issue of this approach are changes. A change of requirements or customer wishes results in high effort for test design adaptation. In the worst case, test design adaptation costs outweigh the costs saved by automated test execution. In order to solve this issue, test design also needs to be automated. An often used approach for this is model-based testing [5,24]. We apply state machines of the Unified Modeling Language (UML) as the basis for automated test design [28]. UML state machines are used to express state-based system behavior. There are several corresponding test generators [9,20,27].

2.2 Model-Based Product-Line Engineering

A demand for high configurability at low costs drives engineering disciplines to increase the number of product features while keeping systems engineering costs at a reasonable level. Reusing system components helps in reducing engineering costs. A PL is a set of related products that share a common core of assets (commonalities), but can be distinguished (variabilities) [21]. Consequently, PL engineering is a technique to fulfill the wish for high configurability at low costs.

PL engineering can be supported by models like, e.g., feature models that enable facilitating the explicit design of global system variation points [15]. As a consequence, system variation points are not spread across one or multiple domain models or code fragments anymore, but instead linked to one core of variability description.

A feature model is a tree with root feature and linked feature children (see Fig. 1). A parent feature can have the following relations to its child features: (a) *Mandatory*: child feature is required, (b) *Optional*: child feature is optional, (c) *Or*: at least one of the child features must be selected, and (d) *Alternative*: exactly one of the child features must be selected. Furthermore, cross-tree

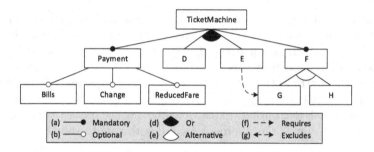

Fig. 1. A feature model for the ticket machine example.

constraints between two features A and B are possible: (f) A *requires* B: the selection of A implies the selection of B, and (g) A *excludes* B: both features A and B must not be selected for the same product.

As Czarnecki et al. presented in [11], feature models can be transformed into propositional formulas defined over a set of Boolean variables, where each variable corresponds to a feature. This allows for checking every combination of features according to its validity, i.e., if it represents a valid variant of the feature model. For instance, the boolean formula for the Ticket Machine in Fig. 1 is:

$$
\begin{aligned}
FM = \ & TM \wedge (\neg Bills \vee Payment) \wedge (\neg Change \vee Payment) \\
& \wedge (\neg ReducedFare \vee Payment) \wedge (\neg Payment \vee TM) \\
& \wedge (\neg D \vee TM) \wedge (\neg E \vee TM) \wedge (\neg F \vee TM) \\
& \wedge (\neg G \vee F) \wedge (\neg H \vee F) \wedge (\neg E \vee G) \\
& \wedge (\neg TicketMachine \vee Payment) \wedge (\neg TicketMachine \vee F) \\
& \wedge (\neg D \vee E) \wedge ((G \wedge \neg H) \vee (\neg G \wedge H))
\end{aligned}
$$

Any assignment that satisfies the formula is a valid configuration. The following formula is a valid configuration for the feature model presented in Fig. 1.

$$
\begin{aligned}
P = \{ & TicketMachine, Payment, \neg Bills, \neg Change, \\
& \neg ReducedFare, D, E, F, G, \neg H \}
\end{aligned}
$$

2.3   Automated Test Design for Product Lines

A feature model contains the system's variation points. Its elements, however, are only symbols [10]. Semantics is provided by mapping features to artifacts with semantics such as system models or source code. Such a mapping can be defined using a mapping models that contain relations from features to artifacts with semantics.

In our case, the system model is designed as a so called 150 % model containing every element that is used in at least one potential product configuration and, thus, describing all possible variants [13]. Hence our PL model comprises a 150 % system model that is a UML state machine, a feature model explicitly

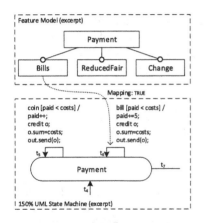

Fig. 2. Excerpt of the product line model for the TicketMachine.

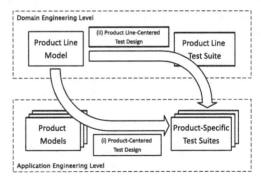

Fig. 3. Product-centered and product line-centered test design.

expressing the PL's variation points, and a feature mapping model that connects both. The current version of our work maps features to states and transitions. Each mapping has a Boolean flag that indicates whether the mapped model elements are part of the product when the feature is selected (*Mapping: TRUE*) or unselected (*Mapping: FALSE*).

In Fig. 2, we depict an excerpt of the PL model for our Ticket Machine example with feature model and UML state machine. In this excerpt, the system waits for coins or bills to be inserted until the costs for the selected tickets are covered. The dotted arrow maps the feature *Bills* to the transition t_6 in the state machine: If the Ticket Machine's configuration includes the feature *Bills*, then the mapped transition t_6 must be present in the corresponding product. If the feature is not selected, this transition is not part of the corresponding product and hence leaving the customer's only payment option to be coins as denoted in transition t_5.

Based on this, we defined two approaches to automated test design for PLs [16] as depicted in Fig. 3: (i) *product-centered* (PC) and (ii) *product line-centered* (PLC). The product-centered approach consists of selecting a representative set of products (test models) and afterwards generating test cases from each of these models. This approach is focused on satisfying a defined coverage on each test model, which also leads to an overlap of the resulting test cases. In contrast, the PLC approach directly applys the PL model for designing tests. The second approach is focused on the behavior defined at the PL level and does not focus on covering single products. Instead, there is still variability in the choice of the concrete products for which the test cases will be executed.

3   Testing Boundaries of Products

A product is configured to include a subset of the specified behavior of a PL model, the rest is excluded. Model-based testing (MBT) is focused on creating test cases based on models. Typically, MBT designs tests for performig positive testing by means of checking the included behavior for conformance. The information about parts being explicitly excluded, however, is valuable too. A test designer can make use of this information by creating tests that actively try to invoke excluded behavior. We think of this as an attempt of breaching the boundaries of a product under test (PUT), where the boundary is predefined by the PUT's configuration. A boundary is overcome if an excluded behavior is invoked and executed as specified in the PL model.

3.1 Boundary Transitions

Inside the PUT's boundaries is the PL's core and all included features declared by the configuration. Outside its boundaries lie the excluded features. Figure 4 depicts an excerpt of a ticket machine product, in which the feature *Bills* is deactivated. Here, the state "Payment" and the transitions t_4, t_5, t_7 lie within the boundaries of the product. Transition t_6 as shown in the excerpt of Fig. 2 is not part of this product. We overcome this boundary, if we make the product process a bill in this state as defined in the PL model in Fig. 2. More formally speaking, we define a product's boundary by *boundary transitions* over UML State Machines. We define a boundary transition bt, where S be the set of states and T be the set of transitions in a PL model and $t(s, s')$ be a transition from state s to s' as:

$$bt(s, s') \in T | s, s' \in S \wedge s \in productmodel$$
$$\wedge \, bt \notin productmodel$$

Hence, a boundary transition is not part of the particular product. We call a product to have an *open boundary*, if behavior from an excluded feature can be invoked at some point of the PUT's execution.

In general, it is possible to detect open boundaries by stimulating the PUT with unexpected events in every state. This resembles sneak-path-analysis and is costly [14]. Here, we propose a method to reduce test effort by stimulating the PUT with unexpected events only if its active state has at least one boundary transition. In particular, we stimulate the PUT with only those events that could possibly trigger one of its boundary transitions.

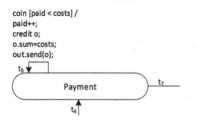

Fig. 4. Product of ticket machine excerpt without feature *Bills*.

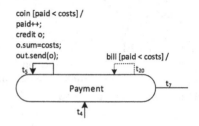

Fig. 5. Same product with additional complementary transition.

3.2 Turning Open Boundaries into Test Goals

We chose transition-based coverage criteria for selecting test goals. Our approach comprises introducing a transition for each boundary transition to which we refer to as *complementary transition*. The intention of this is to create transitions specifying that the PUT should stay in its current state and with events that are not expected to trigger product behavior. Hence, for every boundary transition, we add a complementary transition with its source state as target and source. For the presented ticket machine product without feature *Bills*, Fig. 5 shows the same excerpt of the product as in Fig. 4, but with the additional complementary transition t_{20}, which complements boundary transition t_6 of this product. The complementary transition must have no effect, since in the state "Payment" no reaction is expected for any product that does not include feature *Bills*. However, we should not add a complementary transition, if there is an explicitly specified behavior for processing the signal event when feature *Bills* is excluded as in state "Selection".

So far, we defined boundary transitions for a given product and outlined how to add complementary transitions. For PLC test design we must raise these concepts to the PL level, in order to set complementary transitions as test goals. Particularly, we define a transformation for adding complementary transitions to the PL model whenever there is a boundary transition of any product available. This enables PLC test design methods to consider complementary transition as test goals during test design. Also, PC test design methods can benefit from this approach, since the complementary transitions persist during the derivation process.

In Fig. 6, we depict the desired outcome of the transformation: we added a complementary transition t_{20} to state *Payment* for transition t_6, which is a boundary transition for any product not including the feature *Bills*. Hence, the complementary transition is mapped to feature *Bills* with the mapping's flag set to *false*, denoting the transition is only to be included when the feature *Bills* is deselected. We present the pseudo code to achieve the result shown in Fig. 6 in Algorithm 1. Let $SM(S, T)$ be a state machine, where S is the set of states and T the set of transitions. For each transition $t \in T$ we define:

- source(t) as the source state of t,
- target(t) as the target state of t,
- triggers(t) as the triggers of t,
- triggers $*(t)$ as the triggers from all transitions leaving target(t), if triggers(t) is empty, and triggers(t) otherwise. Since this is a recursive definition, triggers $*(t)$ must stop once all $t \in T$ are traversed.
- features(e) as the set of feature selections mapped to an UML element $e \in SM$. A feature selection states whether a feature must be selected or deselected to include e.
- *concurrentGuards*(t) as a conjunction of guard conditions. The conditions are collected from transitions that can be concurrently enabled with t.

First a set of transitions for storing complementary transitions during this procedure is initialized. Then for all transitions of the state machine the following

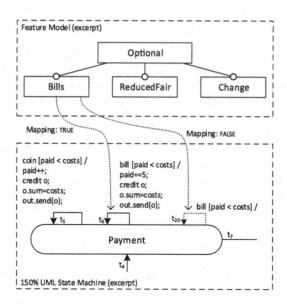

Fig. 6. PL model example: ticket machine with complementary transition.

actions are performed: the algorithm checks in lines 4–7 if current transition b is a boundary transition for some product. This is achieved by checking whether b has different feature mapping selections than its source state. The selections from b, which are not shared by its source state are stored in *difference*. When *difference* is not empty, b is a boundary transition and creation of a complementary transition begins. Otherwise, the for-loop continues with the next b.

From line 8 to 12, the complementary transition c is added to C and is initialized with source(b) as target *and* source state, and triggers $*(b)$ as triggers. The complementary transition's guard is built from the original boundary transition's guard and, to prevent non-deterministic behavior, conjoined with the negated guard conditions of concurrently enabled transitions. Lastly in this if-block, c is mapped to the negated difference of feature selections unified with the selections of b's source state, so c is included in every product when b's source state is, but b is not. Line 14 concludes the procedure by adding the set of complementary transitions C to the state machine's set of transitions T.

The outcome of this procedure when applied to the ticket machine's PL model is depicted in Fig. 7. We denote the mappings from the feature model by feature formulas in the transition's guards analog to Featured Transition System (FTS) introduced by Classen [8]. We use the following acronyms: B for *Bills*, C for *Change*, and R for *ReducedFare*. The complementary transitions added by our transformation procedure are denoted by dotted arcs (transitions t_{19}–t_{22}). Beginning from the initial state, we find the first state with at least one boundary transition to be "Selection". The boundary transition here is t_3, which is enabled when the feature *ReducedFare* is part of a product. Hence, t_{19} is added to the state machine for serving as an additional test goal to any product not including

Algorithm 1. Adds Complementary Transitions to a Region

1: **procedure** ADDCOMPLEMENTARYTRANSITIONS
2:     $C \leftarrow \emptyset$
3:     **for all** $b \in T$ **do**
4:         incoming $\leftarrow \bigcup \text{features}(s \in S | s = \text{source}(b))$
5:         difference $\leftarrow \text{features}(b) - \text{incoming}$
6:         **if** difference $\neq \emptyset$ **then**
7:             $C \leftarrow C \cup c$
8:             source$(c) \leftarrow$ source(b)
9:             target$(c) \leftarrow$ source(b)
10:             guard$(c) \leftarrow$ guard$(b) \wedge \neg(concurrentGuards(b))$
11:             triggers$(c) \leftarrow$ triggers $*(b)$
12:             features$(c) \leftarrow incoming \wedge \neg$ difference
13:         $T \leftarrow T \cup C$

ReducedFare. To achieve all-transition coverage, a test case must include sending the signal event "reducedTicket" when the feature *ReducedFare* is disabled while the state machine is supposed stay in state "Selection". Analog to this, transition t_{20} is added for boundary transition t_6 in state "Payment".

In state "TicketIssue" are three boundary transitions t_9, t_{12}, and t_{13}. Transition t_9 has no trigger, hence its target state must be checked for outgoing transitions with triggers. The transformation's check for further transitions in t_9's target state delivers t_9 to t_{13}. Since t_9 is currently under investigation it will not be checked for triggers again. Transitions t_{10} and t_{11} are untriggered and thus their target state must be evaluated for further triggers. Since their target state is also "TicketIssue", for which this check is currently performed, there are no further checks at this point. For each of the triggered transitions t_{12} and t_{13} one self-loop must be created. Each of them includes the copied trigger, negated feature constrained for the currently investigated feature *ReducedFare* and its guard constraint, the copied feature mapping (C) from the transition at the target state, and its negated guard constraint:

$$t_{12} : change\left[\neg R \wedge tRed > 0 \wedge C \right.$$
$$\left. \wedge \neg(tDay == 0 \wedge tShort == 0 \wedge tRed == 0)\right]/$$

$$t_{13} : noChange\left[\neg R \wedge tRed > 0 \wedge \neg C \right.$$
$$\left. \wedge \neg(tDay == 0 \wedge tShort == 0 \wedge tRed == 0)\right]/$$

We combine both transitions to create t_{21} with both triggers and reduced guards, where constraint C and $\neg C$ cancel each other out. Unfortunately, t_{21} is unreachable, since the condition $tRed > 0$ never holds for any product that does not include t_3. Transitions t_{22} and t_{23} are added accordingly. Finally, no further boundary transitions exists and therefore the procedure ends here.

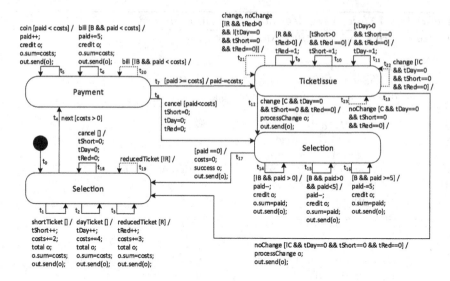

Fig. 7. PL model example: TicketMachine model with added feature formulas and complementary transitions.

4   Examples and Evaluation

In this section, we present the evaluation of the product line's test suites, with and without the presented model transformations. We assess all tests by means of fault detection capability. First, we introduce the used approach of measuring the fault detection capability of the test suite. Afterwards, we describe the used examples, the test setup, and the results.

4.1   Mutation System for PLs

Mutation analysis (also mutation testing) [12] is a fault-based testing technique with the intended purpose to assess the quality of tests by introducing faults into a system and measuring the success rate of fault detection.

The process of mutation analysis inserts defects into software by creating multiple versions of the original software, where each created version contains one deviation. Afterwards, existing test cases are used to execute the faulty versions (*mutants*) with the goal to distinguish the faulty ones (*to kill a mutant*) from the original software. The ratio of killed mutants to generated mutants is called *mutation score*. The main goal of the test designer is to maximize the mutation score. A mutation score of 100 % is seldom possible, because some deviations may lead to an unchanged system behavior, i.e. semantically equivalent mutants.

We think that mutation systems for PLs need novel mutation operators and mutation processes. The reason for this is the separation of concerns in model-based PL engineering, where variability and domain engineering are split into

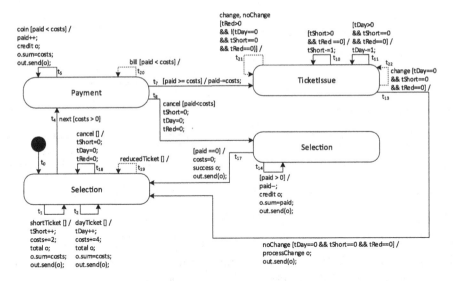

Fig. 8. Product example: state machine model of a ticket machine without Bills, Change, and ReducedFare.

different phases and models. Hence of new modeling languages used in PL engineering, more *kinds* of errors can be made on the model-level than in non-variable systems engineering. In our case, new errors occur in feature mapping models. Of course, the here defined operators are only useful, if system engineering was facilitated by feature models and feature mappings with negative variability. Otherwise, the here described errors are unlikely and hence not applicable.

Mutation processes for PLs differ from conventional mutation processes, since a mutated PL model is not executable per se. Thus, testing cannot be performed until a decision is made towards a set of products for testing. This decision depends on the PL test suite itself, since each test is applicable to just a subset of products. In Fig. 9, we depict a mutation process for assessing PL test suites, which addresses this issue. Independently from each other, we gain (a) a set of PL model mutants by applying mutation operators to the PL model and identify (b) a set of configurations describing the applicable products for testing. We apply every configuration from (b) to every mutant in (a), which returns a new set of product model mutants. Any mutant structurally equivalent to the original product model is removed and does not participate in the scoring. The model mutants are then derived to product mutants and finally, tests are executed. Our mutation scores are based on the PL model mutants, hence we established bidirectional traceability from any PL model mutant to all its associated product mutants and back again. If a product mutant is killed by a test, we backtrack its original PL model mutant and flag it as killed. The final mutation score is then calculated from the set of killed and the overall number of PL model mutants.

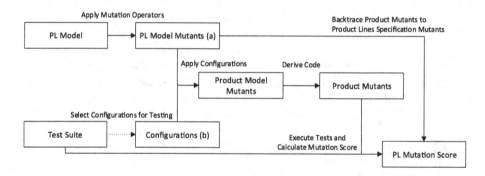

Fig. 9. Mutation process for PLs

We provide the following mutation operators for the mapping model:

- *Delete Mapping (DMP)*: Deletes a mapping from the mapping model. This enables all referenced elements that have no other mappings.
- *Delete Mapped Element (DME)*: Deletes an UML element from a mapping. This enables all referenced elements that have no other mappings.
- *Insert Mapped Element (IME)*: Adds a new UML element to the mapping. This element will only be available in products including the mapped feature.
- *Change Feature Value (CFV)*: Flips the feature value of a mapping so that the UML element is included when it has been excluded before and vice versa.
- *Swap Feature (SWF)*: Substitutes a feature from a mapping by another feature from the mapping model.

For our experiment, we perform mutation analysis with all of these operators.

4.2   Examples

We assessed the quality for three test suites, where each test suite belongs to a different case study. These case studies represent three kinds of systems: an e-commerce shop (eShop), which makes contains many signals, but only few guards, the Ticket Machine (TM) that uses less signals and in contrast more guards, and lastly, an alarm system (AS), which is offers most product variations.

In the eShop example, a customer can browse the catalog of items, or if provided, use the search function. Once the customer puts items into the cart, he can checkout and may choose from up to three different payment options, depending on the eShop's configuration. The transactions are secured by either a standard or high security server. A constraint ensures that credit card payment is only offered if the eShop also implements a high security server.

The TM example is adopted from Cichos et al. [7]. The functionality is as follows: a customer may select tickets, pay for them, receive the tickets, and collect change. The feature model has a root feature with three optional sub-features attached to it. Depending on the selected features, the machine offers reduced tickets, accepts not only coins but also bills, and/or will dispense change.

The AS example is adopted from Cichos et al. [6]. The alarm may be set off manually or automatically by a vibration detector. Both features are part of an or-group and, thus, at least one of the two features must be present in every product. In the event of an alarm, a siren or a warning light will indicate the security breach. When the vibration does not stop after a predefined period of time, the system optionally escalates the alarm by calling police authorities and/or sending photos of evidence. Additionally to its alarming functionality, the PL of the AS provides a feature for taking a photo of any operator that configures the system for security measures. We adopted the AS model by removing manual timers that were implemented as guard conditions.

4.3 Setup

We design two test suites for each example. For the first test suite we use the original models, for the second we apply our transformations first and then run the test design process. The design of each test suite is facilitated by model-based testing techniques. In particular, we used a product line-centered test design process as defined in [16], where tests are designed based on the PL model.

We apply transition coverage for test selection. A test generator then automatically designed the tests. From the tests, SPLTestbench selected products for testing and derived them from the mutated PL models into product model mutants. Since our examples lack implementations, we decided to generate code from the product model mutants and run the tests on them.

4.4 Results

In Table 1, we show the test assessment results of test suites, that were designed with the original models. In each row, we show the mutation results for all examples in the form of killed mutants/all mutants. As supposed, mutations with behavior that is not described by the test model (DME, DMP) are not detected. For the other two mutation types which alter specified behavior (IME, CFV), we receive mixed results in the range of 40 % to 100 %. In contrast, Table 2 depicts the assessment results for the test suites that were created from our transformed

Table 1. Mutation scores for regular tests

Op	TM	eShop	AS	p.Op
DMP	1/5	0/4	0/8	1/17
DME	1/8	0/14	0/21	1/43
IME	2/5	1/4	2/8	5/17
CFV	5/5	4/4	6/8	15/17
SWV	3/5	2/4	3/8	8/17
per Ex.	12/28	7/30	11/53	

Table 2. Mutation scores for tests with transformations

Op	TM	eShop	AS	p.Op
DMP	3/5	4/4	5/8	12/17
DME	3/8	4/14	8/21	15/43
IME	3/5	4/4	2/8	9/17
CFV	5/5	4/4	7/8	16/17
SWV	4/5	4/4	4/8	12/17
per Ex.	18/28	20/30	26/53	

models. Again in each row, we show the mutation results for all examples in the form of killed mutants/all mutants. We observe increased scores for every mutation operator on any of our examples.

In the last row of each table, we show the overall results for each example. Furthermore, in the last column we present the accumulated scores of every mutation operator over all examples.

5   Related Work

In recent years model-based testing (MBT) emerged as an efficient test design paradim that yields a number of improvements compared to conventional test design such as higher test coverage or earlier defect detection. There are several surveys on the effectiveness of MBT in general [5,25,29] and MBT of software product lines [18]. In contrast to this, we combine the application of model-based software product line testing with a product line-specific sneak path analysis. To our knowledge, this combination has not been covered before.

In earlier work [16], we present two approaches for product line test design automation. However, the current paper is focused on testing whether unselected features are actually excluded from the product variant. Our approach reuses the concept of *Simulated Satisfaction* of coverage criteria by transforming the test model instead of improving the applied test generation tools [26]. Hence, the herein presented approach is independent of the test design method, as long as it relies on models.

There are many studies on fault detection effectiveness of model-based test generation using mutation analysis [1,2,19,22,23]. In order to further assess our approach we extended our SPLTestBench by a mutation framework and defined mutation operators for feature models, feature mappings, and the test model.

An early evaluation of the mutation scores suggests that our generated test suites satisfying all-transitions coverage are capable of detecting many seeded faults except unspecified behavior, so-called sneak paths [3]. In safety-critical systems, an unintentional sneak path may have catastrophic consequences. Sneak path testing aims at verifying the absence of sneak paths and at showing that the software under test handles them in a correct way. Several studies showed that sneak path testing improves the fault detection capabilities [4,14,17]. However, the effort spent for sneak path testing is considerably high. Here, we present a novel, more efficient approach for detecting unspecified behavior in product line engineering: We define boundary transitions that stimulate the product under test with only those events that could possibly trigger a transition that would invoke excluded behavior. To our knowledge, this approach has not been applied in the context of software product line engineering before.

6   Conclusions, Discussion and Future Work

Conclusions: In this paper, we combined model-based test design for software product lines with boundary transition analysis. We extended our previous work on product-line centered model-based test design with model transformations that increase the fault detection capabilities of the generated test suites.

We were able to significantly increase the mutation score in each of our three examples using the proposed model transformation and for each of the proposed mutation operators. The scores increased for the eShop by 43 %, for the TicketMachine by 24 % and for the AlarmSystem by 29 %. As for the operators the numbers increased by 63 % for the DMP operator, by 33 % for the DME operator, by 24 % for the IME operator, and by 6 % for the CFV operator (which were already very high), and for the SWV operator by 23 %.

Discussions: Our results support the recommendation of Binder [3] and the conclusions drawn by Mouchawrab et al. [17] and Holt et al. [14]: Testing sneak paths (in our case as boundaries of product line variants) is an essential component of state-based testing and drastically increases fault detection capabilities. Furthermore the results indicate that sneak path testing is a necessary step in state-based testing due to the same observations made by Holt et al. [14]: (1) The proportion of sneak paths in the collected fault data was high (61,5 %), and (2) the presence of sneak paths is undetectable by conformance testing.

We were able to increase the amount of killed mutants by a significant amount through our model transformations but were not able to kill all mutants. Especially the mutation score for the DME operator is still below 50 % of killed mutants. This is partly the result of unreachable behavior, e.g. in the case when an UML element (e.g. a transition) that was mapped to a feature (and thus is now permanently enabled) has preceding elements mapped to the same feature. In that case the element is always enabled but only reachable if its preceding elements are present, which is only true if its the feature is present. A fundamental question here is if this indicates an issue of the test design or an unrealistic mutation operator, and further if the design of novel mutation operators was necessary at all.

This leads to the consideration of the threats to validity. The first point was already mentioned: The introduced mutation operators are new and depend on a model-based product line engineering. Further analysis with well-known mutation operators need to be done. This leads to the validity of our examples. We are aware that the used examples are rather small. A big case study with realistic background would be necessary to underline the advantages of our approach and also the assumed conditions like, e.g., the application of feature models.

Future Work: In our future, we plan to apply our approach to a real case study. We also want to review the defined mutation operators and compare the effects when applying well-known mutation operators.

Acknowledgments. This work is partially supported by grants from Deutsche Forschungsgemeinschaft, Graduiertenkolleg METRIK (GRK 1324).

References

1. Andrews, J.H., Briand, L.C., Labiche, Y.: Is mutation an appropriate tool for testing experiments? In: Proceedings of the 27th International Conference on Software Engineering, ICSE 2005, pp. 402–411 (2005)
2. Andrews, J.H., Briand, L.C., Labiche, Y., Namin, A.S.: Using mutation analysis for assessing and comparing testing coverage criteria. IEEE Trans. Softw. Eng. **32**(8), 608–624 (2006)
3. Binder, R.V.: Testing Object-Oriented Systems: Models, Patterns, and Tools. Addison-Wesley Longman Publishing Co., Inc., Boston (1999)
4. Briand, L.C., Penta, M.D., Labiche, Y.: Assessing and improving state-based class testing: a series of experiments. IEEE Trans. Softw. Eng. **30**(11), 770–783 (2004)
5. Broy, M., Jonsson, B., Katoen, J.P.: Model-Based Testing of Reactive Systems: Advanced Lectures. Lecture Notes in Computer Science, vol. 3472. Springer, Heidelberg (2005)
6. Cichos, H., Heinze, T.S.: Efficient reduction of model-based generated test suites through test case pair prioritization. In: Proceedings of the 7th International Workshop on Model-Driven Engineering. Verification and Validation (MoDeVVa 10), pp. 37–42. IEEE Computer Society Press, Los Alamitos (2011)
7. Cichos, H., Lochau, M., Oster, S., Schürr, A.: Reduktion von testsuiten für software-produktlinien. In: Jähnichen, S., Küpper, A., Albayrak, S. (eds.) Software Engineering 2012: Fachtagung des GI-Fachbereichs Softwaretechnik, 27. Februar - 2. März 2012 in Berlin. LNI, vol. 198, pp. 143–154. GI (2012)
8. Classen, A., Heymans, P., Schobbens, P.Y., Legay, A.: Symbolic model checking of software product lines. In: 33rd International Conference on Software Engineering, ICSE 2011, May 21–28, 2011, Waikiki, Honolulu, Hawaii, Proceedings, pp. 321–330. ACM (2011)
9. Conformiq Qtronic: Semantics and Algorithms for Test Generation: A Conformiq Software Whitepaper (2008)
10. Czarnecki, K., Antkiewicz, M.: Mapping features to models: a template approach based on superimposed variants. In: Glück, R., Lowry, M. (eds.) GPCE 2005. LNCS, vol. 3676, pp. 422–437. Springer, Heidelberg (2005)
11. Czarnecki, K., Wasowski, A.: Feature diagrams and logics: there andback again. In: Software Product Line Conference, 2007. SPLC 2007. 11th International, pp. 23–34 (2007)
12. DeMillo, R.A.: Mutation Analysis as a Tool for Software Quality Assurance. In: COMPSAC 1980 (1980)
13. Grönniger, H., Krahn, H., Pinkernell, C., Rumpe, B.: Modeling variants of automotive systems using views. In: Kühne, T., Reisig, W., Steimann, F. (eds.) Tagungsband zur Modellierung 2008 (Berlin-Adlershof, Deutschland, 12–14. März 2008). LNI, Gesellschaft für Informatik, Bonn (2008)
14. Holt, N.E., Torkar, R., Briand, L.C., Hansen, K.: State-based testing: Industrial evaluation of the cost-effectiveness of round-trip path and sneak-path strategies. In: 23rd IEEE International Symposium on Software Reliability Engineering, ISSRE 2012, Dallas, TX, USA, November 27–30, pp. 321–330. IEEE Computer Society (2012)
15. Kang, K.C., Cohen, S.G., Hess, J.A., Novak, W.E., Peterson, A.S.: Feature-Oriented Domain Analysis (FODA) Feasibility Study (1990)

16. Lackner, H., Thomas, M., Wartenberg, F., Weißleder, S.: Model-based test design of product lines: raising test design to the product line level. In: ICST 2014: International Conference on Software Testing, Verification, and Validation, pp. 51–60. IEEE Computer Society (2014)

17. Mouchawrab, S., Briand, L.C., Labiche, Y., Di Penta, M.: Assessing, comparing, and combining state machine-based testing and structural testing: a series of experiments. IEEE Trans. Softw. Eng. **37**(2), 161–187 (2011)

18. Oster, S., Wubbeke, A., Engels, G., Schürr, A.: A survey of model-based software product lines testing. In: Zander, J., Schieferdecker, I., Mosterman, P.J. (eds.) Model-Based Testing for Embedded Systems. Computational Analysis, Synthesis, and Design of Dynamic Systems, pp. 339–384. CRC Press, Boca Raton (2011)

19. Paradkar, A.: Case studies on fault detection effectiveness of model based test generation techniques. In: Proceedings of the 1st International Workshop on Advances in Model-based Testing, A-MOST 2005, pp. 1–7 (2005)

20. Peleska, J.: RT-Tester Model-Based Test Case and Test Data Generator: User Manual: Version 9.0–1.0.0 (2013)

21. Pohl, K., Böckle, G., van der Linden, F.: Software Product Line Engineering: Foundations, Principles and Techniques. Springer, Heidelberg (2005)

22. Siami Namin, A., Andrews, J.H., Murdoch, D.J.: Sufficient mutation operators for measuring test effectiveness. In: Proceedings of the 30th International Conference on Software Engineering, ICSE 2008, pp. 351–360 (2008)

23. Smith, B.H., Williams, L.: Should software testers use mutation analysis to augment a test set? J. Syst. Softw. **82**(11), 1819–1832 (2009)

24. Weißleder, S., Schlingloff, H.: An evaluation of model-based testing in embedded applications. In: ICST 2014: International Conference on Software Testing, Verification, and Validation. IEEE Computer Society (2014)

25. Utting, M., Legeard, B.: Practical Model-Based Testing: A Tools Approach, 1st edn. Morgan Kaufmann Publishers Inc., San Francisco (2006)

26. Weißleder, S.: Simulated satisfaction of coverage criteria on UML state machines. In: ICST - 3rd International Conference on Software Testing, Verification and Validation (2010)

27. Weißleder, S.: ParTeG (Partition Test Generator) (2009)

28. Weißleder, S., Schlingloff, H.: Automatic model-based test generation from UML state machines. In: Zander, J., Schieferdecker, I., Mosterman, P.J. (eds.) Model-Based Testing for Embedded Systems. Computational Analysis, Synthesis, and Design of Dynamic Systems. CRC Press, Boca Raton (2011)

29. Zander, J., Schieferdecker, I., Mosterman, P.J.: A taxonomy of model-based testing for embedded systems from multiple industry domains. In: Zander, J., Schieferdecker, I., Mosterman, P.J. (eds.) Model-based testing for embedded systems. Computational Analysis, Synthesis, and Design of Dynamic Systems. CRC Press, Boca Raton (2011)

Monitoring and Fault Localization

Guiding Testers' Hands in Monitoring Tools: Application of Testing Approaches on SIP

Xiaoping Che[1], Stephane Maag[2], Huu Nghia Nguyen[3(✉)],
and Fatiha Zaïdi[4]

[1] School of Software Engineering, Beijing Jiaotong University, Beijing, China
xpche@bjtu.edu.cn
[2] Telecom SudParis, CNRS UMR 5157,
9 rue Charles Fourier, 91011 Evry Cedex, France
stephane.maag@telecom-sudparis.eu
[3] Montimage EURL, 39 rue Bobillot, 75013 Paris, France
huunghia.nguyen@me.com
[4] Universite Paris-Sud XI, CNRS UMR 8623, Bat 650, 91405 Orsay Cedex, France
fatiha.zaidi@lri.fr

Abstract. The importance and impact of testing are becoming crucial and strategic for the deployment and use of software and systems. Several techniques have been defined all along the protocol testing process, that allow validating multiple facets of a protocol implementation in particular its *conformance* to the standardized requirements. Among these testing techniques, the ones denoted as *passive* are currently often applied. Indeed, there are non intrusive and based on network observations. In this paper, we intend to help and guide the protocol testers regarding their testing choices by considering the functional protocol properties to check, and the analysis of testing verdicts obtained by applying passive testing tools. We propose a compared analysis of the application of two efficient passive testing methodologies through the study of the Session Initiation Protocol. The results analysis demonstrates that depending on the properties to test, the way to model them, the way of testing (on-line/off-line), the available testing time resources, tradeoffs are needed. Thus, this analysis aims at guiding the testers when tackling the passive testing of communication protocols.

Keywords: Formal methods · Passive testing · Monitoring · SIP

1 Introduction

While todays communications are essential and a huge set of services is available online, computer networks continue to grow and novel communication protocols are continuously being defined and developed. De facto, protocol standards are required to allow different systems to interwork. Though these standards can be formally verified [31], the developers may produce some errors leading to faulty implementations. That is the reason why their implementations must be *tested*.

© IFIP International Federation for Information Processing 2015
K. El-Fakih et al. (Eds.): ICTSS 2015, LNCS 9447, pp. 105–123, 2015.
DOI: 10.1007/978-3-319-25945-1_7

Testing is mainly known as the process of checking that a system possesses a set of desired properties and behaviour. Its importance and impact are becoming crucial and strategic for the future deployment and use of software and systems. This can be noticed through the numerous works on testing areas provided by the research communities of course [30] but also by the industry [11] and the standardization institutes [12].

Several techniques have been defined all along the protocol testing process. The main approaches are based on formal models in order, first, to automate the different test phases but also to ease the development and improvement of network protocols. Applying formal techniques allow to validate multiple facets of a protocol implementation such as their reliability, scalability, security, and in particular its *conformance* to the standardized requirements [1]. These techniques are mainly split in two categories: *Active* and *Passive* techniques. While the active ones require a stimulation of the Implementation Under Test (IUT) and an important testing architecture, the passive ones tackled in this work are based on the observation of input and output events of an implementation under test at run-time. Basically, *passive testing* techniques are applied whenever the state of an IUT cannot be controlled by means of test sequences either because access to the interfaces of the system is unavailable or a reset of the IUT is undesired. The term "passive" means that the tests do not disturb the natural run-time of a protocol as the implementation under test is not stimulated. The *trace*, i.e. the record of the event observation, is then compared to the expected behaviour of the IUT allowing to check its conformance.

When testing the implementation of a network protocol, its behaviour is defined either by a formal model or by a set of expected functional properties. In this current work, we consider formal properties to design the expected behaviour of an implementation under test. However, based on the IUT functionalities, the architecture, the system in which it will be integrated, a tester is faced towards the testing methodology to follow, the way to extract relevant protocol properties, how to express them, which tool to apply, etc. Depending on the properties to check, the languages to model them, their expressiveness and the network monitored, the met difficulties could be diverse and the test verdicts different as well. In this paper, we therefore intend to help and guide the protocol testers regarding their testing choices by considering the functional properties to check, and the analysis of testing verdicts obtained by applying testing tools. We propose a compared analysis of the application of two efficient passive testing methodologies by taking into account not only the control parts of the protocol messages but also the data parts. Further, the two chosen techniques proceed differently: on-line versus off-line. The studied comparison is performed through the study of an IP Multimedia Subsystem (IMS) based protocol (the Session Initiation Protocol - SIP). Some traces and formal properties are used as inputs of two open source tools. The results analysis aims at guiding the testers when tackling the passive testing of communication protocols.

Our main contributions are the following:

- The study of two different passive testing approaches on a common network protocol. Based on the same traces sets and functional properties extracted from the SIP standard, the techniques/tools are applied on a real IMS test bed.
- A study of the expressiveness of the languages used to model the functional properties. This allows notably to help the testers when designing certain kinds of properties.
- The analysis and understanding of both sets of obtained test verdicts. Depending on some contexts, it allows to raise false negatives and to reduce inconclusive verdicts.
- To help guiding the protocol testers while choosing some passive testing techniques for a specific system under test.

The remainder of the paper is organized as follows. Both passive testing approaches: Datamon and Prop-tester are described in the Sect. 2. We herein also define the main concepts of protocol messages and traces. In Sect. 3, the experiments are performed on a real IMS platform from which traces are collected and formal SIP properties checked on these execution traces. The results analysis are provided in Section refDiscussion and discussions allowing to guide the testers are given. Section 5 depicts the related works on the passive testing area and we conclude in Sect. 6 with future works mentioned.

2   Basics

In this section, we introduce the general definition of messages and traces in communication protocols. Then, the syntax and semantics of Datamon and Prop-tester are briefly described with the expression equivalence of both tools.

2.1   Message and Trace

A message in a communication protocol is, using the most general possible view, a collection of data fields belonging to multiple domains. Data fields in messages are usually either *atomic* or *compound*, i.e. they are composed of multiple elements (e.g. a URI sip: name@domain.org). Due to this, we also divide the types of possible domains in *atomic*, defined as sets of numeric or string values[1], or *compound*, as follows.

Definition 1. *A compound value v of length $k > 0$, is defined by the set of pairs $\{(l_i, v_i) \mid l_i \in L \land v_i \in D_i \cup \{\epsilon\}, i = 1 \ldots k\}$, where $L = \{l_1, \ldots, l_k\}$ is a predefined set of labels and D_i are data domains, not necessarily disjoint.*

In a *compound* value, in each element (l, v), the label l represents the functionality of the piece of data contained in v. The length of each compound value is fixed, but undefined values can be allowed by using ϵ (null value). A

---

[1] Other values may also be considered atomic, but we focus here, without loss of generality, to numeric and strings only.

compound domain is then the set of all values with the same set of labels and domains defined as $\langle L, D_1, \ldots, D_k \rangle$. Notice that, D_i being domains, they can also be either *atomic* or *compound*, allowing for recursive structures to be defined. Finally, given a network protocol P, a compound domain M_p can generally be defined, where the set of labels and element domains derive from the message format defined in the protocol specification. A *message* of a protocol P is any element $m \in M_p$.

A *trace* is a sequence of messages of the same domain (i.e. using the same protocol) containing the interactions of an entity of a network, called the *point of observation* (P.O), with one or more peers during an indeterminate period of time (the life of the P.O).

Definition 2. *Given the domain of messages M_p for a protocol P. A trace is a sequence $\Gamma = m_1, m_2, \ldots$ of potentially infinite length, where $m_i \in M_p$.*

Definition 3. *Given a trace $\Gamma = m_1, m_2, \ldots$, a trace segment is any finite subsequence of Γ, that is, any sequence of messages $\rho = m_i, m_{i+1}, \ldots, m_{j-1}, m_j (j > i)$, where ρ is completely contained in Γ (same messages in the same order). The order relations $\{<, >\}$ are defined in a trace, where for $m, m' \in \rho, m < m' \Leftrightarrow pos(m) < pos(m')$ and $m > m' \Leftrightarrow pos(m) > pos(m')$ and $pos(m) = i$, the position of m in the trace ($i \in \{1, \ldots, len(\rho)\}$).*

2.2 Datamon

A syntax based on Horn clauses is used to express properties. The syntax is closely related to that of the query language Datalog, described in [2], for deductive databases, however, extended to allow for message variables and temporal relations. Both syntax and semantics are described in the current section.

Syntax. Formulas in this logic can be defined with the introduction of terms and atoms, as defined below.

Definition 4. *A term is either a constant, a variable or a selector variable. In BNF: $t ::= c \mid x \mid x.l.l \ldots l$ where c is a constant in some domain (e.g. a message in a trace), x is a variable, l represents a label, and $x.l.l \ldots l$ is called a selector variable, and represents a reference to an element inside a compound value, as defined in Definition 1.*

Definition 5. *An atom is defined as $A ::= \overbrace{p(t, \ldots, t)}^{k} \mid t = t \mid t \neq t$ where t is a term and $p(t, \ldots, t)$ is a predicate of label p and arity k. The symbols $=$ and $\neq$ represent the binary relations "equals to" and "not equals to", respectively.*

In this logic, relations between terms and atoms are stated by the definition of clauses. A *clause* is an expression of the form $A_0 \leftarrow A_1 \wedge \ldots \wedge A_n$, where A_0, called the head of the clause, has the form $A_0 = p(t_1^*, \ldots, t_k^*)$, where t_i^* is a restriction on terms for the head of the clause ($t^* = c \mid x$). $A_1 \wedge \ldots \wedge A_n$ is called the body of the clause, where A_i are atoms.

A *formula* is defined by the following BNF:

$$\phi ::= A_1 \wedge \ldots \wedge A_n \mid \phi \rightarrow \phi \mid \forall_x \phi \mid \forall_{y>x} \phi$$
$$\mid \forall_{y<x} \phi \mid \exists_x \phi \mid \exists_{y>x} \phi \mid \exists_{y<x} \phi$$

where $A_1, \ldots, A_n$ are atoms, $n \geq 1$ and x, y are variables. Some more details regarding the syntax are provided in the following:

- The $\rightarrow$ operator indicates causality in a formula, and should be read as *"if-then"* relation.
- The $\forall$ and $\exists$ quantifiers, are equivalent to its counterparts in predicate logic. However, as it will be seen on the semantics, here they only apply to messages in the trace. Then, for a trace $\rho, \forall_x$ is equivalent to $\forall(x \in \rho)$ and $\forall_{y<x}$ is equivalent to $\forall(y \in \rho; y < x)$ with the '<' indicating the order relation. These type of quantifiers are called *trace temporal quantifiers*.

Semantics. The semantics used in our work is related to the traditional Apt-Van Emdem-Kowalsky semantics for logic programs [10], from which an extended version has been provided in order to deal with messages and trace temporal quantifiers.

Based on the above described operators and quantifiers, we provide an interpretation of the formulas to evaluate them to $\top$ (*'Pass'*), $\bot$ (*'Fail'*) or '?' (*'Inconclusive'*). We formalize properties by using the syntax above described and the truth valués $\{\top, \bot, ?\}$ are provided to the interpretation of the obtained formulas on real protocol execution traces. Due to the space limitation, we will not go into details of the semantics. However, the interesting reader can refer to [17] in which all the algorithms are defined.

2.3 Prop-tester

Prop-tester was presented in [27] to verify SOAP messages exchanged between Web services. It is an online passive testing tool relying on XML Query processor. In this section we introduce briefly some of its notions and adapt them to be able to verify SIP messages. Let us start with definition of a message.

Definition 6. *Given a finite set of names $\mathcal{O}$, of labels L, and of atomic data values D, a message m takes the form: $o(l_1 = v_1, \ldots, l_n = v_n)$, where $o \in \mathcal{O}$ represents the name of the message. The composite data of the message is represented by a set $\{l_1 = v_1, \ldots, l_n = v_n\}$, rewritten as $(\bar{l} = \bar{v})$ for short, in which each field of this data structure is pointed by a label $l_i \in L$ and its value is $v_i \in D$.*

We define a *candidate event* (CE) e/ϕ as a set of messages e that satisfy some predicate ϕ that represents either functional conditions or non-functional conditions, e.g., conditions of QoS. The predicate can be omitted if it is *true*. As the SIP response messages do not contain operation names but status code numbers, we then extend our definitions with *empty operation name* and *any operation name* by ϵ and $\sim$ respectively. For example, the INVITE(*requestURI* $= x$)/($x =$ "*sip:ua2@CA.cym.com*") represents any INVITE message whose *requestURI* is "*http://sip:ua2@CA.cym.com*", while the $\sim$ (*method* $= x$)/($x \neq$ "ACK") represents the any message except ACK, and the ϵ(*statusCode* $= x$)/($x \geq 200 \wedge x <$ 300) represents any 2xx response.

Definition 7. *A property is described by the form:*

$$\mathcal{P} ::= \text{Context} \xrightarrow{d} \text{Consequence} \quad (positive)$$
$$\mathcal{P} ::= \text{Context} \xrightarrow{d} \neg\text{Consequence} \; (negative)$$

where $d > 0$ is an integer, Context *is a sequence of CEs, and* Consequence *is a set of CEs.*

This definition allows to express that *if* the Context is satisfied *then* the Consequence should or should not (depending on the formula type $\mathcal{P}$ or $\neg\mathcal{P}$) be validated after at most d messages. The Context is satisfied when all of its CEs are satisfied while the Consequence is satisfied when there exists at least one CE which is satisfied and, the Consequence is not satisfied when all of its CEs are not satisfied.

Semantics of a Prop-tester property are given by its evaluation on a trace segment. A verdict is emitted if and only if the context of property is satisfied. If there is no non-functional conditions, the verdict is either *Pass* or *Inconclusive* depending on the consequence is satisfied or not respectively. The *Fail* verdict is emitted only if the consequence is not satisfied and there exists a message which violates a non-functional condition of the consequence.

The evaluation of a property on an arbitrary (potential infinite) trace Γ is relied on its evaluation on a segment of Γ as above. In a property, a later CE may depend on a former one, consequently, the verification of a message may require the presence of its precedence. Since we can forward only read data in a continuous stream mode, we need to create buffer which contains some segment of messages stream, what we call a *window*. A created window contains firstly messages validating the context of the property and the d next messages in Γ. Once a window is created, the verification process on the window can start in parallel with the other created windows.

3   Experiments

3.1   Description of the Tools

For the experiments, traces were obtained from SIPp [13]. SIPp is an Open Source implementation of a test system conforming to the IMS, and it is also a test tool and traffic generator for the SIP protocol, provided by the Hewlett-Packard company. It includes a few basic user agent scenarios (UAC and UAS) and establishes and releases multiple calls with the INVITE and BYE methods. It can also read custom XML scenario files describing from very simple to complex call flows (e.g. subscription including SUBSCRIBE and NOTIFY events). It also supports IPv6, TLS, SIP authentication, conditional scenarios, UDP retransmissions, error robustness, call specific variable, etc. SIPp can be used to test many real SIP equipments like SIP proxies, B2BUAs and SIP media servers. The traces obtained from SIPp contain all communications between the client and the SIP core. Based on these traces and properties extracted from the SIP RFC, tests were performed using our above mentioned methodologies and tools. And all the experiments have been performed on one laptop (2.5 GHz Intel Core i5 with 4 GB RAM).

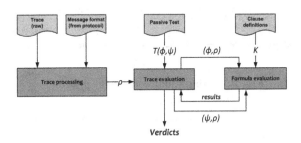

Fig. 1. Testing framework of Datamon

Datamon. The testing framework of Datamon[2] is implemented by using Java. It is composed of three main modules: (1) Filtering and conversion of collected traces; (2) Evaluation of tests; and (3) Evaluation of formulas. Figure 1 shows the way the modules interact and the inputs and outputs from each one. The trace processing module takes the raw traces collected from the network exchange, and it converts the messages from the input format. In our particular implementation, the input trace format is PDML, an XML format that can be obtained from Wireshark traces. The purpose of the module is to convert each packet in the raw trace into a data structure (a compound value) conforming to the definition of a message. This module also performs filtering of the trace in order to only take into account messages of the studied protocol.

The test evaluation module receives input of a passive test, as well as a trace from the trace processing module, and produces a verdict from the satisfaction results of the test and conditional formulas. The formula evaluation module receives a trace and a formula, along with the clause definitions and returns a set of satisfaction results for the query in the trace, as well as the messages and variable bindings obtained in the process.

---

[2] The implementation and the files used for the experiments can be found at http://www-public.it-sudparis.eu/~maag/Datamon/web/Datamon.html.

Prop-tester. The architecture of Prop-tester[3] is depicted on Fig. 2. The property to be tested is translated into an XQuery such that it returns *false* iff the property is violated, and *true* iff the property is validated. A parser[4] is constructed to parse the log file captured by SIPp tool in *pcap* format. It extracts necessary information, then writes these information into an opened pipeline between the tester and the parser, where it will be verified by an XQuery processor. The properties to be tested in XQuery form will be executed by MXQuery processor on the XML pipeline supplying by the parser. A verdict is emitted as soon as it is found.

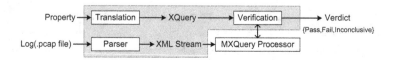

Fig. 2. Testing framework of Prop-tester

3.2 Architecture of SIP

The IMS (IP Multimedia Subsystem) is a standardized framework for delivering IP multimedia services to users in mobility. It was originally intended to deliver Internet services over GPRS connectivity. This vision was extended by 3GPP, 3GPP2 and TISPAN standardization bodies to support more access networks, such as Wireless LAN, CDMA2000 and fixed access network. The IMS aims at facilitating the access to voice or multimedia services in an access independent way to develop the fixed-mobile convergence. Further, the IMS makes now part of the LTE core network for the voice and visio over LTE.

The core of IMS network consists on the Call Session Control Functions (CSCF) that redirect requests depending on the type of service, the Home Subscriber Server (HSS), a database for the provisioning of users, and the Application Server (AS) where the different services run and interoperate. Most communications with the core network and between the services are done using the Session Initiation Protocol [28]. Figure 3 shows the core functions of the IMS framework and the inherent protocols.

The Session Initiation Protocol (SIP) is an application-layer protocol that relies on request and response messages for communication, and it is an essential part for communication within the IMS framework. Messages contain a header which provides session, service and routing information, as well as a body part (optional) to complement or extend the header information. Several RFCs have been defined to extend the protocol. These extensions are used by services of the IMS such as the Presence service [3] and the Push to-talk Over Cellular (PoC) service [4].

---

[3] The tool is freely available at https://github.com/nhnghia/prop-tester.

[4] https://github.com/nhnghia/pcap2xml.

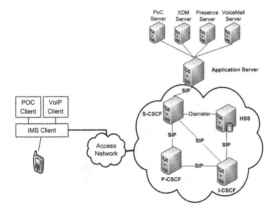

Fig. 3. Core functions of IMS framework

3.3   Properties

In the experiments, a set of properties are tested through Datamon and Prop-tester, in order to analyse their functionality and performance under different conditions.

Property 1. Initially, a simple conformance property *"For every request there must be a response"* is tested.

Table 1. For every request there must be a response

Trace	#Messages	Datamon				Prop-tester			
		#Pass	#Fail	#Inc	Time(s)	#Pass	#Fail	#Inc	Time(s)
1	500	153	0	2	1.652	153	0	2	1.103
2	1000	297	0	0	1.518	297	0	0	1.487
3	2000	575	0	0	3.071	575	0	0	2.246
4	4000	1189	0	1	7.506	1189	0	1	3.190
5	8000	2376	0	1	11.365	2376	0	1	5.480
6	16000	4796	0	1	25.942	4796	0	1	10.106
7	32000	9593	0	0	43.105	9593	0	0	18.728
8	64000	19252	0	1	88.578	19252	0	1	37.128
9	128000	38468	0	1	182.305	38468	0	1	70.390

As Table 1 shows, Datamon and Prop-tester obtain the same number of 'Pass' and non-pass verdicts. Since a finite segment of an infinite execution is being tested in our experiments, it is not possible to declare a *'Fail'* verdict in Datamon and Prop-tester, for the indeterminacy that testers do not know if it may become a *'Pass'* in the future. As a result, they treat the non-pass verdicts as *'Inconclusive'* verdicts. In this simple property, there is no essential difference between the results returned by Datamon and Prop-tester.

Property 2. Therefore, a more complex conformance property *"For successfully established sessions, every INVITE request should be responded with a 200 response"* is tested for delving deeper into the differentiation between the tools.

The results shown in Table 2 illustrate that a difference between mechanisms can result on evaluation times. Although both tools still obtain the same number of *'Pass'* and non-pass verdicts, it can be observed that Prop-tester takes much less evaluation time than Datamon, especially when handling numerous messages. As introduced in previous sections, Prop-tester introduces a predefined distance value d into its evaluation process for instantly concluding verdicts. With the help of this value, Prop-tester will omit comparisons with messages beyond this distance.

Table 2. For successfully established sessions, every INVITE request should be responded with a 200 response

Trace	#Messages	Datamon				Prop-tester			
		#Pass	#Fail	#Inc	Time(s)	#Pass	#Fail	#Inc	Time(s)
1	500	57	0	11	1.700	57	0	11	1.058
2	1000	119	0	22	4.038	119	0	22	1.385
3	2000	248	0	53	13.505	248	0	53	2.114
4	4000	459	0	123	46.358	459	0	123	2.782
5	8000	926	0	233	180.388	926	0	233	5.019
6	16000	1842	0	440	658.148	1842	0	440	8.476
7	32000	3667	0	905	2559.239	3667	0	905	14.542
8	64000	7230	0	1911	7510.563	7230	0	1911	28.735
9	128000	14511	0	3767	28187.956	14511	0	3767	56.579

Conversely, Datamon has to compare all the following messages till the end of a trace, in order to confirm the non-existence of a target message. However, the mechanism used in Prop-tester raises a question: How will Prop-tester react if target messages appear after the predefined distance d?

Property 3. Before answering to the question, a related property relevant to time *"For each INVITE request, the response should be received within 16s"* is tested for verifying the extensibility of both monitoring tools.

Time relevant properties can be seen as performance requirements which are different from the conformance requirements tested above, having the ability to test performance requirements is a crucial step for monitoring tools to extend its

Table 3. For each **INVITE** request, the response should be received within 16s

Trace	#Messages	Datamon				Prop-tester			
		#Pass	#Fail	#Inc	Time(s)	#Pass	#Fail	#Inc	Time(s)
1	500	57	11	0	1.098	57	11	0	1.043
2	1000	119	22	0	3.192	119	22	0	1.383
3	2000	248	53	0	9.841	248	53	0	1.870
4	4000	459	123	0	35.214	459	123	0	2.765
5	8000	926	233	0	131.578	926	233	0	4.533
6	16000	1842	140	0	486.181	1842	440	0	8.069
7	32000	3667	905	0	1728.003	3667	905	0	14.512
8	64000	7230	1911	0	7286.181	7230	1911	0	28.321
9	128000	14511	3767	0	30804.213	14511	3767	0	56.817

functionality. Not surprisingly, as Table 3 shows, both tools can test this performance property and they obtain the same results. Nevertheless, non-pass verdicts are concluded as '*Fail*' verdicts which is different from testing the previous conformance requirements. Because when testing such performance requirements with timing constraint, there is no indeterminacy in the trace. Definite verdicts ('*Pass*' or '*Fail*') should be emitted, rather than indefinite ones ('*Inconclusive*'). That is notably the reason why the reader will notice that the results are here similar to the ones obtained with Property 2 in the way that all '*Inconclusive*' verdicts of Property 2 are now '*Fail*'. Besides, Prop-tester still takes the lead in evaluation time.

Property 4. Back to figuring out the answer raised in Property 2, a more complicated property *"Every 2xx response for INVITE request must be responded with an ACK"* is tested.

Different from previous properties, obvious discrepancies between the verdicts returned from Datamon and Prop-tester can be observed from Table 4. Take a closer look at trace 6, all the '*Inconclusive*' verdicts reported from Prop-tester are caused by missing '**ACK**' responses. In fact, these '**ACK**' responses do exist in the trace, but appear after the predefined d in Prop-tester. Consequently Prop-tester treats these 'missing' '**ACK**' responses as '*Inconclusive*' verdicts could be considered as false negatives. The false negatives also occur in trace 7, 8 and 9 due to the same reason.

These phenomena answer to the question raised in Property 2: the mechanism used in Prop-tester would lead to inconclusive verdicts if the predefined distance d is set improperly. In contrast, owing to its rigorous mechanism for obtaining verdicts, Datamon does not have such problems but its evaluation times are still far behind Prop-tester.

Table 4. Every 2xx response for **INVITE** request must be responded with an **ACK**

Trace	#Messages	Datamon				Prop-tester			
		#Pass	#Fail	#Inc	Time(s)	#Pass	#Fail	#Inc	Time(s)
1	500	57	0	0	1.241	57	0	0	24.805
2	1000	119	0	0	3.884	119	0	0	50.570
3	2000	248	0	0	12.102	248	0	0	103.088
4	4000	459	0	0	45.365	459	0	0	199.890
5	8000	926	0	0	181.758	926	0	0	400.920
6	16000	1842	0	0	658.033	1831	0	11	796.477
7	32000	3666	0	1	2631.765	3588	0	79	1617.233
8	64000	7217	0	13	7501.719	6931	0	299	3204.401
9	128000	14493	0	18	28616.957	13868	0	643	6216.099

Property 5. Furthermore, a sophisticated conformance property *"No session can be initiated without a previous registration"* is tested for exploring the functionality of both tools in depth.

Table 5. No session can be initiated without a previous registration

Trace	#Messages	Datamon			
		#Pass	#Fail	#Inc	Time(s)
1	500	56	0	1	10.318
2	1000	114	0	5	41.272
3	2000	243	0	5	165.090
4	4000	457	0	2	660.361
5	8000	912	0	14	2531.445
6	16000	1840	0	2	10565.782
7	32000	3659	0	8	40439.623
8	64000	7225	0	5	160578.492
9	128000	14506	0	5	593073.968

Besides different mechanisms, the diverse logic used for formalizing properties in both tools affect testing results likewise. As shown in Table 5, Datamon appears its potentiality on formalizing and testing sophisticated properties which Prop-tester can not handle. Although the evaluation times seem a bit high, it has to be noticed that the low performance of evaluation is due to memory limitation of the computer we used. If a more powerful server is applied, the evaluation times will be apparently reduced to satisfying numbers.

4   Discussions and Testers' Guidance

In this section, we will first point out the drawbacks and advantages of each approach according to different evaluation criteria. Then, we will give some advices to the tester to guide him depending on his testing objectives.

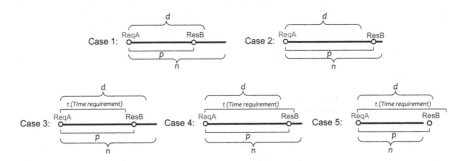

Fig. 4. Different cases, ReqA, ResB represent for a request and its response respectively.

- The two approaches are property-based passive testing techniques. The properties are checked on the real execution traces. The Datamon tool is based on definition of Horn clauses which are closely related to the query Datalog language. Such formulas are made of atoms and terms. Formulas with quantifiers and data can be defined. Prop-tester is based on *if then* clause where the quantifiers are implicit and data can also be expressed. The main difference relies on the distance used by Prop-tester. Prop-tester is clearly an on-line testing tool and it is why such a distance is needed to buffer the traces. Regarding expressiveness issue, such a distance can be a drawback. Indeed, if the distance is not explicitly stated in the requirements, the distance is an artefact used by the testing method. In this case, if the trace does not satisfy the property because of the distance, an inconclusive verdict is emitted. On the contrary, if the distance is a constraint of the requirement, a fail verdict should be emitted. Concerning the property 4 that needs to verify a triple of SIP messages with a partial order between them ($m1 \leq m2 \leq m3$), Prop-tester is not able to express it. For that purpose, a combinatorial numbers of properties has to be written, in this case 50 properties. Moreover, Prop-tester, as an online tool, is not able to express the property 5 which is a complex property that relates to a behaviour occurred in the past of the trace.
  Except this difference, we demonstrate that the properties expressed by both tools are LTL+FO equivalent because the part of the formula related to the distance is always true. The properties equivalence is not shown in this paper for lack of room. Interested readers can refer to the technical report [8].
- One interesting feature of the Prop-tester tool is that negative property can be written. We can specify what should never occur in the system. For that purpose, prop-tester negates positive property.

- Both approaches have different complexity. In Datamon, the algorithm uses a recursive procedure to evaluate formulas, coupled with a modification of SLD (Selective Linear Definite-clause) resolution algorithm [5] for evaluation of Horn clauses. In the work, it is shown that the worst-case time complexity for a formula with k quantifiers is $\mathcal{O}(n^k)$ to analyse the full trace, where n is the number of messages in the trace. Although the complexity seems high, this corresponds to the time to analyse the complete trace, and not for obtaining individual solutions, which depends on the type of quantifiers used. For instance for a property $\forall_x p(x)$, individual results are obtained in $\mathcal{O}(1)$, and for a property $\forall_x \exists_y q(x,y)$, results are obtained in the worst case in $\mathcal{O}(n)$. Finally, it can also be shown that a formula with a '$\rightarrow$' operator, where Q are quantifiers

$$\underbrace{Q \ldots Q}_{k}(\underbrace{Q \ldots Q}_{l}(A_1 \wedge \ldots \wedge A_p) \rightarrow \underbrace{Q \ldots Q}_{m}(A'_1 \wedge \ldots \wedge A'_q))$$

has a worst-case time complexity of $\mathcal{O}(n^{k+max(l,m)})$, which has advantages with respect to using formulas without the '$\rightarrow$' operator. For instance, evaluation of the formula $\forall_x(\exists_y p(x,y) \rightarrow \exists_z q(z))$ has a complexity of $\mathcal{O}(n^2)$, while the formula $\forall_x \exists_y \exists_z (p(x,y) \wedge q(z))$ has a complexity of $\mathcal{O}(n^3)$ in the worst case [17].

For Prop-tester, the complexity to verify of a property $\langle e_1, \ldots, e_k \rangle \xrightarrow{d} \{e'_1, \ldots, e'_m\}$ on a trace containing n messages is as follows. Prop-tester forwards only read data in a continuous stream mode. The verification is done on a buffer which contains some fragments of message streams, what we call a *window*. The window size is $k+d$. There are $n-k$ windows. The complexity is $\mathcal{O}((n-k)*(k+d))$. Since k and d are constant and usually highly smaller than n, the complexity would be $\mathcal{O}(n)$. In the worst case where one wants buffer the entire trace, *i.e.*, $d \geq n-k$, the complexity is $\mathcal{O}(n^2)$.

The better complexity of Prop-tester is demonstrated in the experiments that have been conducted. Prop-tester is very performant in time to evaluate the properties.

- The Datamon tool has been designed to perform off-line analysis. Indeed, execution traces are recorded and afterwards analysed while Prop-tester is mainly efficient to perform on-line analysis during the real execution of the system. To perform on-line testing, the tool needs to have good performance and as consequence to give rapid answer for the verification process. The efficiency of Prop-tester is dependent on the efficiency of the XQuery engine that it relies on.

- Concerning the conformance verdicts emitted by both tools, there exist some differences in their accuracy. To exhibit this point, we illustrate it with Fig. 4. For the case 1, the distance d of the Prop-tester tool has no impact on the verdict as d is greater than the distance p between the request and its response. As for case 2, it proves the deduction we had in the experiments. When the distance d is shorter than p, Prop-tester emits '*Inconclusive*' verdicts.

For the cases 3 to 5, when timing constraints are expressed by the properties, both tools can emit different verdicts depending on the time requirement t and the size of the trace n, as illustrated in Table 6. In case 3, it is almost the same case as case 1. The distance d does not influence on the verdict if d is greater than the distance p and the time requirement t, both tools return a '*Fail*' verdict when the timing constraint is violated. However, in case 4, when the distance d is shorter than t and p, Prop-tester will emit '*Inconclusive*' verdicts while Datamon still can detect the response and emit definite verdicts. For case 5, let us assume that the response $resB$ is present in the trace but will appear after the captured trace. For Datamon, if $resB$ appears after n, it will issue a '*Fail*' verdict even if the timing constraint is not violated. Contrarily, with Prop-tester a '*Fail*' verdict can be emitted if the time is elapsed during the d distance otherwise it will emit an '*Inconclusive*' verdict.

Table 6. Verdicts of tools under different cases, case 1 and 2 are tested through property 1, case 3 to 5 are tested through property 3.

Case	Datamon				Prop-Tester			
	#Pass	#Fail	#Inc	Time(s)	#Pass	#Fail	#Inc	Time(s)
1	1	0	0	1.382	1	0	0	2.509
2	1	0	0	1.750	0	0	1	2.562
3	0	1	0	1.022	0	1	0	2.665
4	1	0	0	0.939	0	0	1	2.485
5	0	1	0	0.939	0	0	1	2.485

We have mentioned the advantages and drawbacks of each approach and their related tools. What is important to point out is for what purpose each tool has been designed. Datamon is clearly well suited for off-line analysis of a system while Prop-tester is very efficient for on-line analysis. Regarding this main feature, the drawbacks and advantages are closely related. As already pointed out above, the expressiveness is better for Datamon. Indeed, the off-line analysis allows to express complex properties and even properties that express constraints on the past of the trace. Obviously, for an on-line analysis which analyses the stream in a forward manner and with the form of *if then clause* of Prop-tester such properties cannot be expressed. Moreover, always due to the form of its properties, properties expressing relations with several variables (more than two) cannot be expressed by Prop-tester. Furthermore, Prop-tester needs for its on-line analysis to determine a d distance. Such a distance can be seen as a constraint of the requirements and in this case, the verdicts will be impacted. Otherwise, it must not have an impact on the verdict as it represents an implementation constraint needed by the approach to limit the stream to be analysed. A very important strength of Prop-tester relies on its performance which is of very important interest to test complex system in a continuous way.

Both tools are complementary. Indeed, for a rapid analysis of the running system, the main behaviours of a system can be tested as the expressiveness is not always an issue for some tested systems. It can help to fix rapidly an erroneous system by providing rapid feedback of discrepancy between the system and what it is expected to do. Meanwhile, Datamon can be used as a background tool to carefully analyse recorded system traces and by having more complex properties that can be checked.

To conclude, Prop-tester can be used as an off-line tool and in this case, the d distance is no longer used in the expression of the property and as a consequence some limitations can be overcome. The form of the properties can also be modified in order to increase the expressiveness. Concerning Datamon, this tool is clearly not designed to be an on-line tool.

5   Related Work

Formal testing methods have been used for years to prove correctness of implementations by combining test cases evaluation with proofs of critical properties. In [14,17] the authors present a description of the state of the art and theory behind these techniques. Within this domain, and in particular for network protocols, passive testing techniques have to be used to test already deployed platforms or when direct access to the interfaces is not available. Some examples of these techniques using Finite State Machine derivations have been used in the past which are described in [21,25]. Most of these techniques consider only control portions, in [15,20,29], data portion testing is approached by evaluation of traces by use of EEFSM (Event-based Extended Finite State Machine), SEFSM (Simplified Extended Finite State Machine) and IOTS (Input-Output Transition Systems) models. They focus on testing correctness in the specification states and internal variable values. Our approach, although inspired by it, is different in the sense that we test critical properties directly on the trace without any generation or specification of state models of the tested protocol or functional properties. A study of the application of invariants to an IMS service was also presented by us in [17,18].

In [26], the authors defined a methodology for the definition and testing of time extended invariants, where data is also a fundamental principle in the definition of formulas and a *packet* (similar to a *message* in our work) is the base container data. In this approach, the satisfaction of the packets to certain *events* is evaluated, and properties are expressed as $e_1 \xrightarrow{When,n,t} e_2$, where e_1 and e_2 are events defined as a set of constraints on the data fields of packets, n is the number of packets where the event e_2 should be expected to occur after finding e_1 in the trace, and t is the amount of time where event e_2 should be found on the trace after (or before) event e_1. This work served as an inspiration for both approaches described in the current document, however we improved it by allowing the definition of formulas that test data relations and causality between multiple messages/packets.

Although closer to runtime monitoring, the authors of [7] propose a framework for defining and testing security properties on Web Services using the Nomad [9] language, based on previous works by the authors of [22]. As a work on web services, data passed to the operations of the service is taken into account for the definition of properties, and multiple events in the trace can be compared, allowing to define, for instance, properties such as "Operation *op* can only be called between operations *login* and *logout*". Nevertheless, in web services, operations are atomic, that is, the invocation of each operation can be clearly followed in the trace, which is not the case with network protocols where operations depend on many messages and sometimes on the data associated with the messages.

Further, other recent works like [23] present distributed passive testing frameworks aiming at simplifying and automating service testing. And, techniques based on "geometric approaches" [19] have been used in continuous distributed monitoring for analyzing the behaviors of communication protocols.

Besides, some researchers presented a tool for exploring online communication and analyzing clarification of requirements over the time in [16]. It supports managers and developers to identify risky requirements. Another interesting tool is PTTAC [6] which automatizes a formal framework to perform passive testing for systems where there is an asynchronous communications channel between the tester and the system. We should also cite the recent extension of PASTE [24] that performs passive testing of communication systems with temporal constraints associated to performance and delays. Though these tools are interesting, they need specific state models or do not allow to analyze data payloads.

6   Conclusion and Perspectives

In this paper, we described two passive testing approaches to test efficiently, in a non intrusive way, the main properties of a communicating protocol, the Session Initiation Protocol. The approaches and their associated freely available tools, Datamon and Prop-tester, allow to test real execution traces provided by SIPp. Both approaches are based on formal definition of desired properties to be tested. The performances and accuracy of verdicts for both tools are dependent on the expressiveness of properties and also on the techniques used, i.e. off- or on-line techniques. The approaches can be used by a tester in a complementary way. In one hand, Prop-tester can be used to have rapid testing answer on some properties to be tested and it can be launched in a continuous way to analyse the execution traces. On the other hand, Datamon, as a back-end tool, can be used to test more intensively the protocol with the definition of complex properties on the recorded traces.

As an immediate perspective line, we expect to integrate more smoothly both techniques in order to provide to testers more accurate verdicts, by reducing the number of inconclusive verdicts. Moreover, both tools can take advantage of each other and then improve for one its expressiveness and for the other its performances. Such improvements can be reached by learning from each technique. Prop-tester has been used for its first time in the testing of such communicating protocol. We expect to promote the use of such tools to other real-life protocols.

References

1. ISO/IEC 9646-1: Information technology - open systems interconnection - conformance testing methodology and framework - part 1: General concepts. Technical report, ISO, January 1994
2. Abiteboul, S., Hull, R., Vianu, V.: Datalog and Recursion, 2nd edn. Addison-Wesley, Reading (1995)
3. Open Mobile Alliance: Internet messaging and presence service features and functions. Technical report, OMA (2005)
4. Open Mobile Alliance: Push to talk over cellular requirements. Technical report, OMA (2006)
5. Apt, K., Van Emden, M.: Contributions to the theory of logic programming. J. ACM (JACM) **29**(3), 841–862 (1982)
6. Camacho-Magrinan, M.A., Merayo, M.G., Medina-Bulo, I.: PTTAC: passive testing tool for asynchronous systems. In: Proceedings of SITIS, pp. 223–229 (2014)
7. Cao, T.D., Phan-Quang, T.T., Félix, P., Castanet, R.: Automated runtime verification for web services. In: Proceedings of ICWS, pp. 76–82 (2010)
8. Che, X., Maag, S., Nguyen, H.N., Zaïdi, F.: Guiding testers' hands in monitoring tools/appendix: expression equivalence of the two approaches. Technical report RR15001-RS2M, Institut Mines-Telecom/Telecom SudParis, August 2015
9. Cuppens, F., Cuppens-Boulahia, N., Sans, T.: Nomad: a security model with non atomic actions and deadlines. In: Proceedings of CSFW, pp. 186–196 (2005)
10. Emden, M.V., Kowalski, R.: The semantics of predicate logic as a programming language. J. ACM **23**(4), 733–742 (1976)
11. ETSI/ES 201 873-1: Methods for testing and specification (MTS); the testing and test control notation version 3; part 1: TTCN-3 core language, v3.2.1. Technical report, ETSI (2007)
12. European Telecommunications Standards Institute/ETSI TS 134 123-3: Universal mobile telecommunications system (UMTS); user equipment (UE) conformance specification; part 3: abstract test suite (ATS). Technical report, ETSI, June 2013
13. Hewlett-Packard: SIPp (2004). http://sipp.sourceforge.net/
14. Hierons, R.M., Krause, P., Luttgen, G., Simons, A.J.H.: Using formal specifications to support testing. ACM Comput. Surv. **41**(2), 176 (2009)
15. Hierons, R.M., Merayo, M.G., Núñez, M.: Passive testing with asynchronous communications. In: Beyer, D., Boreale, M. (eds.) FORTE 2013 and FMOODS 2013. LNCS, vol. 7892, pp. 99–113. Springer, Heidelberg (2013)
16. Knauss, E., Damian, D.: V:Issue:lizer: exploring requirements clarification in online communication over time. In: Proceedings of ICSE, pp. 1327–1330 (2013)
17. Lalanne, F., Maag, S.: A formal data-centric approach for passive testing of communication protocols. IEEE/ACM Trans. Netw. **21**(3), 788–801 (2013)
18. Lalanne, F., Maag, S., de Oca, E.M., Cavalli, A.R., Mallouli, W., Gonguet, A.: An automated passive testing approach for the IMS PoC service. In: Proceedings of ASE, pp. 535–539 (2009)
19. Lazerson, A., et al.: Monitoring distributed streams using convex decompositions. VLDB Endow. **8**(5), 545–556 (2015)
20. Lee, D., Miller, R.: Network protocol system monitoring - a formal approach with passive testing. IEEE/ACM Trans. Netw. **14**(2), 424–437 (2006)
21. Lee, D., Netravali, A.N., Sabnani, K.K., Sugla, B., John, A.: Passive testing and applications to network management. In: Proceedings of ICNP, pp. 113–119 (1997)

22. Li, Z., Jin, Y., Han, J.: A runtime monitoring and validation framework for web service interactions. In: Proceedings of ASWEC, pp. 70–79 (2006)
23. Lopez, J., Maag, S., Morales, G.: Behavior evaluation for trust management based on formal distributed network monitoring. World Wide Web 1–19 (2015)
24. Merayo, M.G., Núñez, A.: Passive testing of communicating systems with timeouts. Inf. Softw. Technol. **64**, 19–35 (2015)
25. Miller, R.: Passive testing of networks using a CFSM specification. In: Proceedings of IPCCC, pp. 111–116 (1998)
26. Morales, G., Maag, S., Cavalli, A.R., Mallouli, W., de Oca, E.M., Wehbi, B.: Timed extended invariants for the passive testing of web services. In: Proceedings of ICWS, pp. 592–599 (2010)
27. Nguyen, H.N., Poizat, P., Zaïdi, F.: Online verification of value-passing choreographies through property-oriented passive testing. In: Proceedings of HASE, pp. 106–113 (2012)
28. Rosenberg, J., Schulzrinne, H., Camarillo, G., Johnston, A., Peterson, J., Sparks, R., Handley, M., Schooler, E.: SIP: session initiation protocol (2002)
29. Ural, H., Xu, Z.: An EFSM-based passive fault detection approach. In: Petrenko, A., Veanes, M., Tretmans, J., Grieskamp, W. (eds.) TestCom/FATES 2007. LNCS, vol. 4581, pp. 335–350. Springer, Heidelberg (2007)
30. Utting, M., Pretschner, A., Legeard, B.: A taxonomy of model-based testing approaches. Softw. Test. Verification Reliab. **22**, 297–312 (2012)
31. Woodcock, J., Larsen, P.G., Bicarregui, J., Fitzgerald, J.: Formal methods: practice and experience. ACM Comput. Surv. **41**, 19:1–19:36 (2009)

Testing for Distinguishing Repair Candidates in Spreadsheets – the Mussco Approach

Rui Abreu[1]([✉]), Simon Außerlechner[2], Birgit Hofer[2], and Franz Wotawa[2]

[1] Palo Alto Research Center, Palo Alto, CA, USA
rui@computer.org
[2] Graz University of Technology, Graz, Austria
{bhofer,wotawa}@ist.tugraz.at

Abstract. Companies and other organizations use spreadsheets regularly as basis for evaluation or decision-making. Hence, spreadsheets have a huge economical and societal impact and fault detection, localization, and correction in the domain of spreadsheet development and maintenance becomes more and more important. In this paper, we focus on supporting fault localization and correction given the spreadsheet and information about the expected cell values, which are in contradiction with the computed values. In particular, we present a constraint approach that computes potential root causes for observed behavioral deviations and also provide possible fixes. In our approach we compute possible fixes using spreadsheet mutation operators applied to the cells' equations. As the number of fixes can be large, we automatically generate distinguishing test cases to eliminate those fixes that are invalid corrections. In addition, we discuss the first results of an empirical evaluation based on a publicly available spreadsheet corpus. The approach generates on average 3.1 distinguishing test cases and reports 3.2 mutants as possible fixes.

Keywords: Fault localization · Spreadsheet debugging · Distinguishing test-cases · Spreadsheet mutations

1 Introduction

Spreadsheets are a flexible end-users programming environment. "End-user" programmers vastly outnumber professional ones: the US Bureau of Labor and Statistics estimates that more than 55 million people used spreadsheets and databases at work on a daily basis by 2012 [14]. 95 % of all U.S. companies use spreadsheets for financial reporting [19], and 50 % of all spreadsheets are the basis for decisions.

Numerous studies have shown that existing spreadsheets contain redundancies and errors at an alarmingly high rate, e.g., [6]. This high error rate can be explained with the lack of fundamental support for testing, debugging, and structured programming in the spreadsheet world. Errors in spreadsheets may entail a serious economical impact, causing yearly losses worth around 10 billion

© IFIP International Federation for Information Processing 2015
K. El-Fakih et al. (Eds.): ICTSS 2015, LNCS 9447, pp. 124–140, 2015.
DOI: 10.1007/978-3-319-25945-1_8

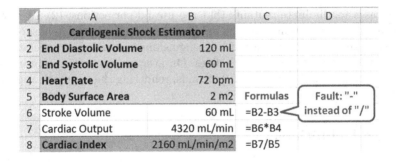

Fig. 1. The Cardiogenic shock estimator spreadsheet

dollars [18][1]. This paper improves the state-of-the-art in spreadsheet debugging by proposing an approach for correcting faults in spreadsheets.

In this paper, we make use of the running example illustrated in Fig. 1. This spreadsheet is used by physicians to estimate cardiogenic shock[2]. Cells B2 to B5 are those cells that need an input from the user. Cell B8 shows the result of the computation from which physicians derive their conclusions. Cell B6 is faulty. It computes B2/B3 instead of B2−B3. As a consequence, the value of cell B8 is outside the bounds even when the patient's input values are okay. If the physician notices that the computed value is outside the bounds, he might want to *debug* the spreadsheet.

In this paper, we use constraint-based techniques for spreadsheet debugging [3,13]. These techniques take as input a faulty spreadsheet and a test case[3] that reveals the fault in order to compute a set of diagnosis candidates (cells). The spreadsheet and the test case are converted into a constraint satisfaction problem (CSP). A constraint or SMT (satisfiability modulo theories) solver is used to obtain the set of diagnosis candidates. A major limitation of these approaches is that they yield many diagnosis candidates. To avoid this problem, we propose to integrate testing for restricting the number of diagnosis candidates. In particular, we propose to compute possible corrections of the program (using mutation techniques) and from these distinguishing test cases. A test case is a distinguishing test case if and only if there is at least one output variable where the computed value of two mutated versions of a spreadsheet differ on the same input. We have two main contributions: (1) We propose MUSSCO (Mutation Supported Spreadsheet COrrection), an approach to fault localization in spreadsheets that relies on constraint-based reasoning to provide suggestions for possible fixes by applying spreadsheet mutation operators. Since the number of such mutants can be large, our approach automatically generates distinguish-

---

[1] http://www.eusprig.org/horror-stories.htm.

[2] A cardiogenic shock is when the heart has been damaged so much that it is unable to supply enough blood to the organs.

[3] A test case specifies values for the input cells as well as the expected values for the output cells.

ing test cases to eliminate mutants that are invalid corrections. (2) We carried out an empirical evaluation using the publicly available Integer Spreadsheet Corpus. Results show that on average 3.1 distinguishing test cases are generated and 3.2 mutants are reported as possible fixes. On average, generating mutants and distinguishing test cases requires 47.9 seconds, rendering the approach applicable as a real-time application.

2 Basic Definitions

In this paper, we rely on the spreadsheet language $\mathcal{L}$ defined by Hofer *et al.* [11]. We refer the interested reader to that paper for more information about the syntax and semantics of the underlying spreadsheet language. For the sake of completeness, we state the most important concepts and definitions in the following paragraphs.

Every spreadsheet is a matrix of cells that are uniquely identifiable using their corresponding column and row number. The function φ maps the cell names from a set $CELLS$ to their corresponding position (x, y) in the matrix where x represents the column and y the row number. The functions φ_x and φ_y return the column and row number of a cell respectively. Each cell $c \in CELLS$ has a corresponding value $\nu(c)$ and an expression $\ell(c)$. The value of a cell can be either undefined ϵ, an error $\perp$, or any number, Boolean or string value. The expression of a cell $\ell(c)$ can either be empty or an expression written in the language $\mathcal{L}$. The value of a cell c is determined by its expression. If no expression is explicitly declared for a cell, the function ℓ returns ϵ while the function ν returns 0.

An area $c_1 : c_2 \subseteq CELLS$ is a set consisting of all cells that are within the area spanned by the cells c_1, c_2, i.e.:

$$c_1 : c_2 \equiv_{def} \left\{ c \in CELLS \left| \begin{array}{l} \varphi_x(c_1) \leq \varphi_x(c) \leq \varphi_x(c_2) \wedge \\ \varphi_y(c_1) \leq \varphi_y(c) \leq \varphi_y(c_2) \end{array} \right. \right\}$$

For our debugging approach, we require information about cells that occur in an expression, i.e. the referenced cells. The function $\rho : \mathcal{L} \mapsto 2^{CELLS}$ returns the set of referenced cells.

Definition 1 (Spreadsheet). *A countable set of cells $\Pi \subseteq CELLS$ is a spreadsheet if all cells in Π have a non-empty corresponding expression or are referenced in an expression, i.e., $\forall c \in \Pi : (\ell(c) \neq \epsilon) \vee (\exists c' \in \Pi : c \in \rho(\ell(c')))$.*

This definition restricts spreadsheets to be finite. For our approach, we only consider loop-free spreadsheets, i.e., spreadsheets that do not contain cycles within the computation. Therefore, we introduce the notation of data dependence between cells, and the data dependence graph.

Definition 2 (Direct dependence). *Let c_1, c_2 be cells of a spreadsheet Π. The cell c_2 directly depends on cell c_1 if and only if c_1 is used in c_2's corresponding expression, i.e., $dd(c_1, c_2) \mapsto (c_1 \in \rho(\ell(c_2)))$.*

Definition 3 (Data dependence graph). *The data dependence graph (DDG) of a spreadsheet Π is a tuple (V, A) with V being a set of vertices comprising exactly one vertex n_c for each cell $c \in \Pi$, and A being a set of arcs (n_{c_1}, n_{c_2}) for all n_{c_1}, n_{c_2} where there is a direct dependence between the corresponding cells c_1 and c_2 respectively, i.e. $A = \bigcup (n_{c_1}, n_{c_2})$ where $n_{c_1}, n_{c_2} \in V \wedge dd(c_1, c_2)$.*

From this definition, we are able to define general dependence between cells. Two cells of a spreadsheet are dependent if and only if there exists a path between the corresponding vertices in the DDG. A spreadsheet Π is feasible if and only if its DDG is acyclic. From here on, we assume that all spreadsheets we consider for debugging are feasible. Hence, we use the terms spreadsheet and feasible spreadsheet synonymously. For debugging, we have to define test cases for distinguishing faulty spreadsheets from correct spreadsheets.

Definition 4 (Input, output). *Given a feasible spreadsheet Π and its DDG (V, A), then the input cells of Π (or short: inputs) comprise all cells that have no incoming edges in the corresponding vertex of Π's DDG. The output cells of Π (or short: outputs) comprise all cells where the corresponding vertex of the DDG has no outgoing vertex.*

$$inputs(\Pi) = \{c \in \Pi | \nexists (n_{c'}, n_c) \in A\}$$
$$outputs(\Pi) = \{c \in \Pi | \nexists (n_c, n_{c'}) \in A\}$$

All formula cells of a spreadsheet that serve neither as input nor as output are called intermediate cells. With the definition of inputs and outputs, we can now define test cases.

Definition 5 (Test case). *A test case T for a spreadsheet Π is a tuple (I, O) where I is a set of pairs (c, v) specifying the values for all $c \in inputs(\Pi)$ and O is a set of pairs (c, e) specifying the expected values for some output cells. T is a failing test case for spreadsheet Π if there exists at least one cell c where the expected value e differs from the computed value $\nu(c)$ when using I on Π.*

We say that a test case is a passing test case if all computed values are equivalent to the expected values.

Definition 6 (Spreadsheet debugging problem). *A spreadsheet Π and a failing test case T form a spreadsheet debugging problem.*

Example 1. The test case T with $I = \{(\text{B2}, 120), (\text{B3}, 60), (\text{B4}, 72), (\text{B5}, 2)\}$ and $O = \{(\text{B8}, 2160)\}$ is a failing test case for the Cardiogenic shock estimator spreadsheet. This test case together with the spreadsheet forms a debugging problem.

A solution of a spreadsheet debugging problem (Π, T) is a set of cells that explain the faulty behavior. In particular, we say that an explanation Π^E is itself a spreadsheet comprising the same cells as Π but different cell expressions that make the test case T a passing test case for Π^E.

Example 2. A spreadsheet Π_1 where the expression of cell B6 is changed to B2 − B3 is obviously an explanation that makes the test case T a passing one. However, a spreadsheet Π_2 where we change the expression of B7 to 30 * B6 * B4 is an explanation as well.

3   Constraint Satisfaction Problem

A constraint satisfaction problem (CSP) is a tuple (V, D, C) where V is a set of variables with a corresponding domain from D, and C is a set of constraints [8]. Each constraint has a set of variables and specifies the relation between the variables. Abreu et al. [3] have shown how to state the spreadsheet debugging problem as a CSP. To be self-contained, we briefly explain the conversion in Algorithm Convert (Fig. 2). Details about the conversion can be found in the work of Abreu et al. [3]. Formula cells are concatenated with a variable representing the health state of that formula: A cell c is faulty, i.e. c does not behave as expected, or the constraints representing the formula must be satisfied (Line 3). The expressions of the formula cells are converted using the Algorithm ConvExp which works as follows: Constants are represented by themselves. Cell references are mapped to the corresponding variables. In case of compound expressions, the conversions of the single expressions and the constraint representing the compound expression are added to the constraint system. The values of the input cells and the expected values indicated in the test case are added to the constraint system (Line 6).

Example 3. The constraint representation of our example from Fig. 1 is: $B2 ==$ $120, B3 == 60, B4 == 72, B5 == 2, ab_{B6} \vee B6 = B2/B3, ab_{B7} \vee B7 = B6*B4,$ $ab_{B8} \vee B8 = B7/B5, B8 == 2160.$

Since spreadsheets must be finite, the Convert algorithm terminates. The computational complexity of the algorithm is $O(|CELLS| \cdot L)$ where L is the maximum length of an expression. For computing diagnoses, let SD be the obtained constraint representation for a spreadsheet Π. A diagnosis Δ is a subset of the cells contained in Π such that $SD \cup \{\neg ab_c | c \in \Pi \setminus \Delta\} \cup \{ab_c | c \in \Delta\}$ is satisfiable. We use an SMT solver for computing solutions for a given CSP. The theoretic background of using SMT solvers for CSPs is explained by Liffiton and Sakallah [15, 16].

Input: Spreadsheet Π, test case $T = (I, O)$
Output: A set of constraints representing Π and T.
1: CONS = $\emptyset$
2: **for** $c \in (\Pi \setminus inputs(\Pi))$ **do**
3:     CONS = CONS $\cup \{ab_c \vee v_c ==$ ConvExp$(\ell(c))\}$
4: **end for**
5: **for** tuples $(cell, value) \in (I \cup O)$ **do**
6:     CONS = CONS $\cup \{v_{cell} == value\}$
7: **end for**
8: **return** CONS

Fig. 2. Algorithm Convert(Π, T)

4   Mutation Creation

With the previously described fault localization technique, the user only gets the information which cells have to be changed, but not how the cells have to be changed. We are confident that the information of how cells have to be changed is important for the user. Therefore, we propose an approach that automatically creates versions, i.e. mutants, of the spreadsheet that satisfy the given test case.

Weimer *et al.* [23] introduced genetic programming for repairing C programs. Similar to them, we make assumptions how to restrict the search space. For example, we perform mutations on the cone for a given cell[4] and Weimer *et al.* make mutations on the weighted path. In addition, Weimer *et al.* assume that the programmer has written the correct statement somewhere else in the program. We assume that when a spreadsheet programmer referenced the wrong cell, the correct cell is in the surrounding of the referenced cell. However, we differ from their genetic programming approach as we do not use crossover and randomness for selecting mutations.

A primitive way to compute mutants is to clone the spreadsheet and change arbitrary operators and operands in all formulas of the cells contained in one diagnosis. If the created mutant satisfies the given test case we present the mutant to the user. Otherwise we discard the mutant and create another mutant. The problem with this approach is that too many mutants have to be computed until the first mutant passes the given test case. Therefore, we propose a more sophisticated approach which includes the mutation creation process in the CSP. Instead of only transforming cell formulas into a value-based constraint model, we also include the information how the cells could be mutated. We allow the following mutation operations:

- replace constant with reference or other constant
- replace reference with constant or other reference
- replace arithmetical (relational) operator with other arithmetical (relational) operator
- replace function with other functions of the same arity
- resize areas

We are aware that these mutation operators are not able to correct all faulty spreadsheets. In particular, the creation of completely new formulas is up to future work.

When creating mutants, we have to face two challenges: (1) The created mutant must be a feasible spreadsheet. (2) Theoretically, an infinite number of mutations can be created. To handle the first challenge, we propose the following solution: Each cell that is represented in the CSP gets an additional Integer variable with the domain $\{1, |\Pi|\}$. The constraint solver has to assign values to these variables in such a way that each cell gets a number that is higher than the numbers assigned to the cells this cell references. This constraint ensures that

---

[4] A cone for a cell c is recursively defined as the union of all cones of the cells which are referenced in c and the cell c itself.

the created mutant is still a feasible spreadsheet. To handle the second challenge, we reduce the search space by making following restrictions:

- Mutations are only indicated for cells that are contained in the cone of any erroneous output cell.
- When replacing references with constants, we do not immediately compute the concrete constant. Instead, we use the information, that there exists a constant that could eliminate the observed misbehavior. Only if we present a mutant to the user, we compute a concrete value for that constant. The reason for this delayed computation is the fact that there often exist many constants that satisfy the primary test case. During the distinguishing test case creation process, we gain additional information, which helps to reduce the number of constants.
- When changing references or resizing areas, we make use of the following assumption: If the user made a mistake when indicating the reference or area, the intended reference(s) might be in the surrounding of the originally indicated reference(s). We define the surrounding of a cell c as follows:

$$\text{SURROUND}(c) \equiv_{def} \left\{ c_1 \in CELLS \,\middle|\, \begin{array}{l} \varphi_x(c) - 2 \le \varphi_x(c_1) \le \varphi_x(c) + 2 \,\wedge \\ \varphi_y(c) - 2 \le \varphi_y(c_1) \le \varphi_y(c) + 2 \end{array} \right\}.$$

We model into our CSP that the reference to the cell is either correct or that it should be replaced by one of the cells in the surrounding. In case of an area, we define the surrounding of the area as follows:

$$\text{SURROUND}(c_1 : c_2) \equiv_{def} \left\{ c_3 \in CELLS \,\middle|\, \begin{array}{l} \varphi_x(c_1) - 2 \le \varphi_x(c_3) \le \varphi_x(c_2) + 2 \,\wedge \\ \varphi_y(c_1) - 2 \le \varphi_y(c_3) \le \varphi_y(c_2) + 2 \end{array} \right\}.$$

For areas, we allow to select/deselect any cell in the surrounding. This allows both, the shrinking and enlargement of areas and non-continuous areas.
- We allow only one mutation per cell.

These restrictions do not allow to find suited mutants for all given faulty spreadsheets. However, they allow the approach to be used in practice.

Example 4. The extended constraint representation for the cell $B6$ of our Cardiogenic shock estimator from Fig. 1 changes from $ab_{B6} \vee B6 = B2/B3$ to: $(ab_{B6} \wedge (B6 = B2 + B3 \vee B6 = B2 - B3 \vee B6 = B1/B3 \vee B6 = 5/B3 \vee \ldots)) \vee B6 = B2/B3$.

5   Computing Distinguishing Test Cases

Usually, there exists more than one possible correction. In practice, a large number of repair suggestions overwhelms the user. Consequently, there is a strong need for distinguishing such explanations. One way to distinguish explanations is to use distinguishing test cases. Nica *et al.* [17] define a distinguishing test case for two variants of a program as input values that lead to the computation of different output values for the two variants. When translating this definition to the spreadsheet domain, we have to search for constants that are assigned to inputs, which lead to different output values for the different explanations. The user (or another oracle) has to clarify which output values are correct.

Example 5. The following new input values form a distinguishing test case for the variants Π_1 and Π_2 of our running example: $\ell(\text{B2}) = 30$, $\ell(\text{B3}) = 30$, $\ell(\text{B4}) = 30$, $\ell(\text{B5}) = 1$. For these input values, Π_1 computes a value 0 for cell B8, where Π_2 would return 900.

Algorithm MUSSCO (Fig. 3) describes our overall approach. The algorithm takes a faulty spreadsheet and a failing test case as input and determines possible solutions with increasing cardinality. Since input cells are considered correct, the upper bound of the solutionSize is equal to the amount of non-input cells. In Line 1, the set TS initialized with the given failing test case. The sets eqM and udM are used to store the pairs of equivalent and undecidable mutants. The faulty spreadsheet and the given test cases are converted into constraints in Line 4. The function CONVERT slightly differs from the function described in Fig. 2: instead of only converting an expression into its constraint representation, also possible mutations are encapsulated in the constraint representation. The function GETSIZECONSTRAINT(Cons, n) creates a constraint that ensures at most n of the abnormal variables contained in Cons can be set to true (Line 5). In Line 6, the function HASSOLUTION checks if the solver can compute any mutants that satisfy the given constraint system. In Line 7, the function GETMU-TANT returns a mutant that satisfies the given constraint system. This mutant is added to the list of mutants M (Line 8) and is blocked in the constraint system (Line 9). If M contains at least two mutants that are not equivalent or undecidable (Line 11), we call the test case retrieval function GETDISTTESTCASE with these mutants as parameters (Line 12). If this function returns UNSAT, the pair m_1, m_2 is added to the set eqMut (Line 14). If the function returns UNKNOWN, the pair m_1, m_2 is added to the set undesMut (Line 17). Otherwise, the function returns a new test case. The function GETEXPECTEDOUTPUT is used to determine the expected output for the given test case (Line 19). This function asks the user (or another oracle) for the expected output. The test case is added to the set of test cases (Line 20) and to the constraint system (Line 21). The function FILTER returns the set of mutants that fail this test case (Line 22). Those mutants are removed from the set of mutants (Line 23). After retrieving all mutants for the given solutionSize, the remaining solutions M are presented to the user. If the user accepts one solution, the algorithm terminates. Otherwise, the solutionSize is incremented (Line 31).

Algorithm GETDISTTESTCASE (Fig. 4) creates distinguishing test cases. This algorithm takes as input a spreadsheet and two mutated versions of that spreadsheet. The functions GETINPUTCELLS and GETOUTPUTCELLS return the set of input and output cells for a given spreadsheet (Lines 1 and 2). In Lines 3 and 4, the mutants m_1 and m_2 are converted into their constraint representations. When creating a distinguishing test case, we have to exclude the input

Input: A spreadsheet Π, a test case T
Output: A set of possible corrections
1: solutionSize = 1; TS = $\{T\}$
2: **while** solutionSize $\leq$ ($|\Pi| - |\text{GETINPUTCELLS}(\Pi)|$) **do**
3:     $M = \{\}$; eqM $= \{\}$; udM $= \{\}$
4:     Cons = CONVERT(Π, TS)
5:     Cons = Cons $\cup$ GETSIZECONSTR(Cons, solutionSize)
6:     **while** HASSOLUTION(Cons) **do**
7:         m = GETMUTANT(Cons)
8:         $M = M \cup \{m\}$
9:         Cons = Cons $\cup \{\neg m\}$
10:         **while** $|M| \geq 2$ $((m_1, m_2) \in M : (m_1, m_2) \notin$ eqM $\wedge (m_1, m_2) \notin$ udM$)$ **do**
11:             Select m_1, m_2 from M where $(m_1, m_2) \notin$ eqM $\wedge (m_1, m_2) \notin$ udM
12:             $T' = $ GETDISTTESTCASE(Π, m_1, m_2)
13:             **if** $T' = $ UNSAT **then**
14:                 eqM = eqM $\cup \{(m_1, m_2)\}$
15:             **else**
16:                 **if** $T' = $ UNKNOWN **then**
17:                     udM = udM $\cup \{(m_1, m_2)\}$
18:                 **else**
19:                     $T' = T' \cup$ GETEXPECTEDOUTPUT(Π, T')
20:                     TS = TS $\cup \{T'\}$
21:                     Cons = Cons $\cup$ CONVERT(T')
22:                     $M' = $ FILTER(Π, T', M)
23:                     $M = M \setminus M'$
24:                 **end if**
25:             **end if**
26:         **end while**
27:     **end while**
28:     **if** User accepts any solution in M **then**
29:         **return** M
30:     **end if**
31:     solutionSize = solutionSize + 1
32: **end while**
33: **return** no solution

Fig. 3. Algorithm MUSSCO(Π, T)

cells from the spreadsheet. Therefore, we only hand over the spreadsheet without the input cells to the function CONVERT. This function slightly differs from the CONVERT function from Fig. 2, because it takes two additional parameters: (1) the particular mutant in use and (2) a constant that acts as postfix for variables. This postfix is necessary to distinguish the constraint representation of m_1 from that of m_2: Each variable in the constraint system for mutant m_1 (m_2) gets the postfix "_1" ("_2"). In Line 5, a constraint is created that ensures that the input of m_1 is equal to the input of m_2. In Line 6, a constraint is created that ensures that at least one output cell of m_1 has a different value than the same

Input: A spreadsheet Π, mutants m_1, m_2
Output: A distinguishing test case or UNSAT/UNKOWN
1: inputCells = GETINPUTCELLS(Π)
2: outputCells = GETOUTPUTCELLS(Π)
3: Cons1 =CONVERT($\Pi \setminus$ inputCells, m_1, "_1")
4: Cons2 =CONVERT($\Pi \setminus$ inputCells, m_2, "_2")
5: inputCon = $\bigwedge_{c \in inputCells} c\_1 = c\_2$
6: outputCon = $\bigvee_{c \in outputCells} c\_1 \neq c\_2$
7: Cons = Cons1 $\cup$ Cons2 $\cup$ inputCon $\cup$ outputCon
8: **return** GETSOLUTION(Cons)

Fig. 4. Algorithm GETDISTTESTCASE(Π, m_1, m_2)

output cell in m_2. The function GETSOLUTION calls the solver with these constraints (Line 8). This function either returns a distinguishing test case, UNSAT (in case of equivalent mutants) or UNKOWN (in case of undecidability).

The worst-case time complexity of the Algorithm from Fig. 3 is exponential in the number of cells ($O\left(2^{|CELLS|}\right)$). In practice, only solutions up to a certain size, i.e. single or double fault solutions, are relevant. The algorithm terminates: The outer while-loop (Line 2) is bound to the size of the spreadsheet. The while-loop in Line 6 is limited since there only exists a limited number of mutants that can be created and we do not allow to report mutants twice (Line 9). The inner-most loop (Line 10) is limited since the number of mutants in M has to be greater or equal to two and the selected pair has not already been proven to be equivalent or undecidable. In each iteration of this loop, either a new pair is added to the equivalent or undecidable set (Lines 14 and 17) or the set M shrinks (Line 23). M must shrink because the return set of the function FILTER (Line 22) contains at least on element, since the mutants m_1 and m_2 must compute different output values for the given test case.

6   Empirical Evaluation

We implemented a prototype in Java that uses Z3 [7] as solver. This prototype supports the conversion of spreadsheets with basic functionality (arithmetic and relational operators, the functions 'IF', 'SUM', 'AVERAGE', 'MIN', and 'MAX') into Z3 formula clauses.

For the evaluation, we used the publicly available Integer Spreadsheet Corpus [5]. This corpus comes with 33 different spreadsheets (12 artificially created spreadsheets and 21 real-life spreadsheets) and 229 mutants of these 33 basic spreadsheets. We excluded some spreadsheets from our evaluation, because MUSSCO was not able to generate the required mutation to correct the observed misbehavior. There are two reasons for this: (1) The correction requires more than one mutation within a single cell, which is currently not supported by our approach. (2) The required mutation operator is not implemented in MUSSCO.

In the following empirical evaluation, we only consider the 73 spreadsheets where MUSSCO was able to compute the required mutation in order to correct the fault.

The original spreadsheets used in this empirical evaluation are listed in Table 1. Because of space limitations, we only list the original version of the spreadsheets, instead of each faulty version. This table indicates for each spreadsheet the amount of input, output and formula cells. The smallest spreadsheet contains 8 formulas and the largest contains 69 formula cells. On average, a spreadsheet contains 31.2 formula cells. To express the complexity of the spreadsheets, we adapt the Halstead complexity measures [9] to the spreadsheet domain. η_1 represents the number of distinct operators that are used within a spreadsheet. η_2 is the number of distinct operands (i.e. cell references, constants) that are used within a spreadsheet. N_1 indicates the total number of operators while N_2 indicates the total number of operants. From these basic metrics, we derive the vocabulary ($\eta = \eta_1 + \eta_2$) and the spreadsheet length ($N = N_1 + N_2$). The average vocabulary is 74.4 and the average spreadsheet length is 229.1. An interesting Halstead metric is the difficulty ($D = \frac{\eta_1}{2} \times \frac{N_2}{\eta_2}$). The difficulty measure can be seen as the difficulty to understand the spreadsheet when debugging the spreadsheet. The difficulty of the investigated spreadsheets ranges from 1.0 to 8.5. The average difficulty is 4.5.

The faulty spreadsheet variants have on average 1.14 erroneous output cells. 52 mutated spreadsheets contain single faults. 20 mutated spreadsheets contain double faults, i.e. two cells with wrong formulas. One mutated spreadsheets contains three faults. The evaluation was performed using a PC with an Intel Core i7-3770K CPU and 16GB RAM. The evaluation machine runs a 64-bit Windows 7 and the Oracle Java Virtual Machine version 1.7.0_17. We set a time limit of 2000 seconds (i.e. approximately 33 min) per faulty spreadsheet for generating mutants and distinguishing test cases. The evaluation results are averaged over 100 runs.

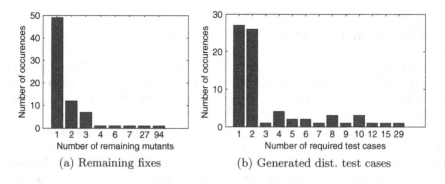

(a) Remaining fixes   (b) Generated dist. test cases

Fig. 5. Empirical results

In order to investigate a larger amount of spreadsheets, we decided to simulate the user interactions. Therefore, we use the original correct spreadsheets

Table 1. Structure and complexity of the evaluated spreadsheets

Name	Number of cells			Halstead complexity				
	In	Out	Form.	η_1	η_2	N_1	N_2	*difficulty*
amortization	16	1	16	5	33	31	67	5.4
arithmetics00	10	1	8	1	23	11	29	1.3
arithmetics01	9	1	11	2	23	14	34	2.4
arithmetics02	13	1	16	1	36	21	50	1.2
arithmetics03	19	1	35	1	64	45	99	1.1
arithmetics04	23	2	24	1	59	51	98	1.0
austrian_league	91	10	32	3	103	96	267	4.2
bank_account	45	13	27	7	76	103	187	6.4
birthdays	39	3	39	7	86	78	189	8.5
cake	101	1	69	3	155	69	238	5.2
comp_shopping	37	4	36	6	64	151	288	5.7
conditionals01	9	1	11	5	25	34	65	4.8
dice_rolling	31	3	21	4	40	99	190	3.8
fibonacci	25	1	46	1	68	16	87	2.7
matrix	51	1	13	3	23	17	67	5.9
oscars2012	60	2	22	3	76	24	104	6.5
prom_calculator	46	1	14	2	63	14	73	5.2
shares	43	12	39	4	69	37	118	6.4
shop_bedroom1	67	2	32	2	78	32	129	4.0
shop_bedroom2	70	4	64	4	109	148	338	4.6
training	34	3	53	4	93	99	223	4.5
weather	70	5	41	6	131	89	231	7.8
wimbledon2012	90	1	49	4	135	280	538	3.8
Average	**43.4**	**3.2**	**31.2**	**3.4**	**71.0**	**67.8**	**161.3**	**4.5**

as oracles to determine the output values for the generated distinguishing test cases.

Figure 5(a) shows the amount of correction suggestions that are returned to the user. For 49 spreadsheets, only the correct mutation is returned to the user. On average, 3.2 mutants are reported to the user. For one faulty spreadsheet containing two faulty cells, Mussco determines 27 correction suggestions. Moreover, applying the algorithm to a spreadsheet with three faults results in 94 correction suggestions. The evaluation shows that in case of double or triple faults, Mussco finds a higher amount of equivalent solutions.

Figure 5(b) illustrates the number of generated distinguishing test cases. For 27 spreadsheets, only a single distinguishing test case is required. For 26 spreadsheets, two distinguishing test cases are necessary. For one spreadsheet,

29 distinguishing test cases have to be generated. This spreadsheet contains a double fault. Therefore, MUSSCO creates many mutants which have to be killed by the distinguishing test cases. On average, 3.1 distinguishing test cases are required.

The average runtime is 49.1 seconds, at which the runtime is less than 10 seconds for 23 of the spreadsheets. The average runtime for single faults is 25.1 seconds. The average runtime for double and triple faults is 108.6 seconds. Most of the runtime, i.e. 95.5 % is consumed by the mutation creation process. The creation of the distinguishing test cases requires on average 1.4 % of the total run time. The remaining 3.1 % encompasses between the time required for filtering the mutants and setting up MUSSCO (read spreadsheet data in, convert spreadsheet).

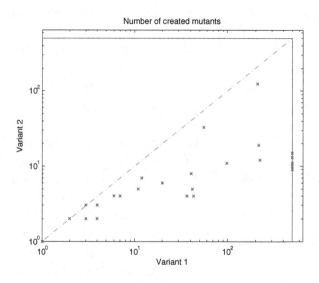

Fig. 6. Comparison of two computation variants w.r.t. the number of created mutants. Data points along the dashed line indicate that the variants generate the same number of mutants. Data points below the dashed line indicate that Variant 1 creates more mutants. The solid lines indicate the timeout.

We create a distinguishing test case as soon as we have two mutants available. Another possibility is to immediately compute all possible mutants of a particular size and afterwards generate the test cases. Does the implemented method perform better with respect to runtime? We suppose that adding more test cases to the constraint system decreases the number of mutants that are created and therefore decreases the total computation time. For clarifying our assumptions, we compare the two methods with respect to the number of generated mutants and the total computation time in the Figs. 6 and 7. Variant 1 denotes the version where we first compute all possible mutants. Variant 2 denotes the version described in Algorithm MUSSCO (Fig. 3). For six spreadsheets, Variant 1 results

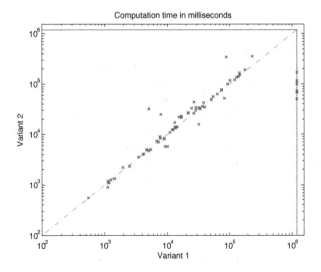

Fig. 7. Comparison of two computation variants w.r.t. the total computation time. Data points along the dash-dot line indicate that the variants perform equal w.r.t. runtime. Data points below the dashed line indicate that Variant 2 requires less computation time than Variant 1. The solid lines indicate the timeout.

in a timeout. On average, Variant 1 creates 17.2 mutants while Variant 2 creates 5.2 mutants (when comparing only those spreadsheets without timeouts). However, when comparing the computation time (see Fig. 7), the two variants only slightly differ (expect for the six spreadsheets yielding a timeout when using Variant 1). It turns out, that decreasing the number of computed mutants through more test cases, increases the computation time per mutant. Nevertheless, we favor Variant 2 over Variant 1 since the user gets earlier a first response.

7   Related Work

Our approach is based on model-based diagnosis [20], namely its application to (semi-) automatic debugging. It uses a constraint representation and a constraint solver, which pinpoints software failures. Jannach and Engler [13] presented a model-based approach that uses an extended hitting-set algorithm and user-specified or historical test cases and assertions, to calculate possible error causes in spreadsheets.

GoalDebug [1] is a spreadsheet debugger for end-users. This approach generates a list of change suggestions for formulas that would result in a user-specified output. GoalDebug relies upon a set of pre-defined change inference rules. Hofer and Wotawa [12] also proposed an approach for generating repair candidates via genetic programming. In contrast to these approaches, we encode the mutation creation into a constraint satisfaction problem. In addition, we generate distinguishing test cases to keep the number of possible fixes small.

Ruthruff *et al.* [22] and Hofer *et al.* [10] propose to use spectrum-based fault localization for spreadsheet debugging. In contrast to MUSSCO, these approaches only identify the locations of faults instead of giving repair suggestions.

Spreadsheet testing is closely related to debugging. In the WYSIWYT system, users indicate correct/incorrect output values by placing a correct/faulty token in the cell [21]. The spreadsheet analysis tools of Abraham and Ewig [2] and Ahmad *et al.* [4] reason about the units of cells to find inconsistencies in formulas. The tools differ in the rules they employ and in the degree to which they require users to provide additional input. Ahmad's tool requires users to annotate the spreadsheet cells with additional information. UCheck [2] fully automatically performs unit analysis by exploiting techniques for automated header inference.

8 Conclusions

Our spreadsheet debugging approach MUSSCO maps a spreadsheet into a set of constraints for computing potential diagnosis candidates. The approach makes use of mutations, i.e., small changes of formulas used in the spreadsheets, to create diagnosis candidates. These diagnosis candidates are further refined by generating distinguishing test cases.

Beside the theoretical foundations and the algorithms we also discuss the results obtained from an empirical evaluation where we are able to show that distinguishing test cases improve diagnosis of spreadsheets substantially. In particular, results show that on average 3.1 distinguishing test cases are generated and 3.2 mutants are reported as possible fixes. On average, the generation of the mutants and distinguishing test cases requires 47.9 seconds in total, rendering the approach applicable as a real-time application. In future work, we will extend the toolset (i) by supporting more functionality of spreadsheets, and (ii) by integrating it into a spreadsheet framework.

Acknowledgement. The work described in this paper has been funded by the Austrian Science Fund (FWF) project DEbugging Of Spreadsheet programs (DEOS) under contract number I2144 and the Deutsche Forschungsgemeinschaft (DFG) under contract number JA 2095/4-1.

References

1. Abraham, R., Erwig, M.: GoalDebug: A spreadsheet debugger for end users. In: Proceedings of the 29th International Conference on Software Engineering ICSE 2007, pp. 251–260. IEEE Computer Society, Washington, DC, USA (2007)
2. Abraham, R., Erwig, M.: UCheck: a spreadsheet type checker for end users. J. Vis. Lang. Comput. **18**, 71–95 (2007)
3. Abreu, R., Hofer, B., Perez, A., Wotawa, F.: Using constraints to diagnose faulty spreadsheets. Softw. Qual. J. **23**(2), 297–322 (2015)
4. Ahmad, Y., Antoniu, T., Goldwater, S., Krishnamurthi, S.: A type system for statically detecting spreadsheet errors. In: 18th IEEE International Conference on Automated Software Engineering (ASE 2003), pp. 174–183. IEEE Computer Society (2003)

5. Ausserlechner, S., Fruhmann, S., Wieser, W., Hofer, B., Spork, R., Mühlbacher, C., Wotawa, F.: The right choice matters! SMT solving substantially improves model-based debugging of spreadsheets. In: 2013 13th International Conference on Quality Software (QSIC 2013). pp. 139–148 (2013)

6. Chadwick, D., Knight, B., Rajalingham, K.: Quality control in spreadsheets: a visual approach using color codings to reduce errors in formulae. Softw. Qual. Control **9**(2), 133–143 (2001)

7. de Moura, L., Bjørner, N.S.: Z3: an efficient SMT solver. In: Ramakrishnan, C.R., Rehof, J. (eds.) TACAS 2008. LNCS, vol. 4963, pp. 337–340. Springer, Heidelberg (2008)

8. Dechter, R.: Constraint Processing. Morgan Kaufmann, San Mateo (2003)

9. Halstead, M.H.: Elements of Software Science (Operating and programming systems series). Elsevier Science Inc., New York (1977)

10. Hofer, B., Perez, A., Abreu, R., Wotawa, F.: On the empirical evaluation of similarity coefficients for spreadsheets fault localization. In: Journal of Automated Software Engineering - Special Issue on Realizing Artificial Intelligence and Software Engineering Synergies, vol. 22(1), pp. 47–74. Springer, US (2015)

11. Hofer, B., Riboira, A., Wotawa, F., Abreu, R., Getzner, E.: On the empirical evaluation of fault localization techniques for spreadsheets. In: Cortellessa, V., Varró, D. (eds.) FASE 2013 (ETAPS 2013). LNCS, vol. 7793, pp. 68–82. Springer, Heidelberg (2013)

12. Hofer, B., Wotawa, F.: Mutation-based spreadsheet debugging. In: International workshop on program debugging (IWPD), - Supplemental Proceedings ISSRE 2013, pp. 132–137 (2013)

13. Jannach, D., Engler, U.: Toward model-based debugging of spreadsheet programs. In: Proceedings of the 9th Joint Conference on Knowledge-Based Software Engineering. JCKBSE 2010, pp. 252–264. Kaunas, Lithuania (2010)

14. Ko, A.J., Abraham, R., Beckwith, L., Blackwell, A., Burnett, M., Erwig, M., Scaffidi, C., Lawrance, J., Lieberman, H., Myers, B., Rosson, M.B., Rothermel, G., Shaw, M., Wiedenbeck, S.: The state of the art in end-user software engineering. ACM Comput. Surv. **43**(3), 21:1–21:4 (2011)

15. Liffiton, M.H., Sakallah, K.A.: Algorithms for computing minimal unsatisfiable subsets of constraints. J. Autom. Reasoning (JAR) **40**(1), 1–33 (2008)

16. Liffiton, M.H., Sakallah, K.A.: Generalizing core-guided max-SAT. In: Kullmann, O. (ed.) SAT 2009. LNCS, vol. 5584, pp. 481–494. Springer, Heidelberg (2009)

17. Nica, M., Nica, S., Wotawa, F.: On the use of mutations and testing for debugging. Software : practice & experience (2012). http://dx.doi.org/10.1002/spe.1142

18. Panko, R.R.: Applying code inspection to spreadsheet testing. J. Manag. Inf. Syst. **16**(2), 159–176 (1999)

19. Panko, R.R., Port, D.: End user computing: The dark matter (and dark energy) of corporate IT. In: Proceedings of the 45th Hawaii International Conference on Systems Science (HICSS-45 2012), pp. 4603–4612 (2012)

20. Reiter, R.: A theory of diagnosis from first principles. Artif. Intell. **32**(1), 57–95 (1987)

21. Rothermel, K.J., Cook, C.R., Burnett, M.M., Schonfeld, J., Green, T.R.G., Rothermel, G.: WYSIWYT testing in the spreadsheet paradigm: an empirical evaluation. In: Proceedings of the 22nd International Conference on Software engineering ICSE 2000, pp. 230–239. ACM, New York (2000)

22. Ruthruff, J., Creswick, E., Burnett, M., Cook, C., Prabhakararao, S., Fisher, II, M., Main, M.: End-user software visualizations for fault localization. In: Proceedings of the 2003 ACM Symposium on Software visualization (SoftVis 2003), pp. 123–132. ACM, New York (2003)

23. Weimer, W., Nguyen, T., Le Goues, C., Forrest, S.: Automatically finding patches using genetic programming. In: Proceedings of the 31st International Conference on Software Engineering ICSE 2009, pp. 364–374. IEEE Computer Society, Washington, DC (2009)

Novel Insights on Cross Project Fault Prediction Applied to Automotive Software

Harald Altinger[1]([✉]), Steffen Herbold[2], Jens Grabowski[2], and Franz Wotawa[3]

[1] Audi Electronics Venture GmbH, 85080 Gaimersheim, Germany
harald.altinger@audi.de
[2] Institute of Computer Science, University of Göttingen, 37077 Göttingen, Germany
{herbold,grabowski}@cs.uni-goettingen.de
[3] Institute for Software Technology, Graz University of Technology,
8010 Graz, Austria
wotawa@ist.tugraz.at

Abstract. Defect prediction is a powerful tool that greatly helps focusing quality assurance efforts during development. In the case of the availability of fault data from a particular context, there are different ways of using such fault predictions in practice. Companies like Google, Bell Labs and Cisco make use of fault prediction, whereas its use within automotive industry has not yet gained a lot of attraction, although, modern cars require a huge amount of software to operate. In this paper, we want to contribute the adoption of fault prediction techniques for automotive software projects. Hereby we rely on a publicly available data set comprising fault data from three automotive software projects. When learning a fault prediction model from the data of one particular project, we achieve a remarkably high and nearly perfect prediction performance for the same project. However, when applying a cross-project prediction we obtain rather poor results. These results are rather surprising, because of the fact that the underlying projects are as similar as two distinct projects can possibly be within a certain application context. Therefore we investigate the reasons behind this observation through correlation and factor analyses techniques. We further report the obtained findings and discuss the consequences for future applications of Cross-Project Fault Prediction (CPFP) in the domain of automotive software.

Keywords: Project fault prediction · Cross project fault prediction · Automotive · Principal component analysis

1 Introduction

A modern day premium car like the 2016s Audi Q7 contains up to 90 Electronic Control Unit (ECU)s, 11 different communication networks (Controller Area Network (CAN), FlexRay, etc.) and a wide range of Advanced Driver Assistance Systems (ADAS) that are all realized using software. An analysis carried out by Broy [4] states that software consumes up to 40 % of a cars development

© IFIP International Federation for Information Processing 2015
K. El-Fakih et al. (Eds.): ICTSS 2015, LNCS 9447, pp. 141–157, 2015.
DOI: 10.1007/978-3-319-25945-1_9

budget. Software used in cars has up to 10 million Lines Of Code (LOC). Assuring quality of software thus is a major challenge as its complexity is still rising and the currently used testing approaches like Hardware in the Loop (HiL) tests might not scale well. In the automotive industry software engineering follows the W-development process [15], where testing is a core part of every development stage. Predictions about the locations of faults would be a powerful tool to support this process. This paper uses metrics data obtained when carrying out projects for making fault predictions.

In this paper, we contribute to this goal of having tools for fault prediction in the automotive industry. In this work, we consider both the performance of prediction within the context of a project, i.e., fault predictions based on earlier revisions of a project, as well as cross-project predictions, i.e., fault predictions based data from other projects. Considering cross-project predictions is required because empirical data of a project is of course missing when starting the project. In our empirical analysis we focus on the question of whether a strict development process applied for safety and security relevant software modules actually supports fault prediction performance due to restrictive policies. The results obtained do not indicate that a strict development process has an influence on prediction performance. Hence, we also performed an in-depth analysis of possible reasons behind it and discuss this analysis in detail in this paper.

The main contributions of this paper are, an empirical study on within-project and CPFP for safety-critical automotive software as well as an in-depth analysis of the obtained results.

The remainder of this paper is structured as follows. We discuss related work in Sect. 2. Then we present our fault prediction study in Sect. 3. Afterwards, we perform an in-depth analysis on the causes behind the obtained prediction performance in Sect. 4. In addition we discuss threats to its validity in Sect. 5 and finally conclude the paper in Sect. 6.

2   Related Work

Altinger et al. [2] identified Matlab Simulink as the major development environment in the automotive industry, which is often combined with model-based testing and unit testing. In the testing stage there is an equal distribution between Model in the Loop (MiL), Software in the Loop (SiL) and HiL where more than 50 % of the developers are using white or grey box testing techniques. The applicability of Software Fault Prediction (SFP) techniques in such an automotive software development was analysed by Rakesh et al. [23]. They surveyed eight different methods and their best operation time along the life cycle as well as their required input data and their potential to enhance software quality. In comparison to Rakesh et al., the projects we consider in this paper follow a different development process. Our underlying process comprises at least 4 Releases. One represents an *interface freeze*, where external interfaces (CAN, Application Programming Interface (API), methods, etc.) need to be fixed and are not allowed to be changed anymore. *feature freeze*, where all functions need to be implemented, but might not run fully. They just need to be call-able from external functions. The last release prior to the shipment with the car to customers is *100 % Software* which means that it is the last delivery. After this point, there will be only bug fixes and parameter optimisations, but no feature enhancements.

2.1 Industrial Fault Prediction

SFP is still a very active research field where many datasets are available and studies have been performed. Since we focus on the industrial application of fault prediction in the automotive industry, we only discuss related work in the context of papers dealing with industrial applications of fault prediction methods. For surveys and benchmarks for fault prediction in general we refer the interested reader to, e.g., [6]. The available industrial reports are mainly from Bell labs reporting on their obtained experiences, e.g., Bell et al. [3], Ostrand et al. [21] and et al. [22]. There the authors report a high prediction performance of up to 80 % true positives using three different telecom software products which were developed at AT&T. The authors claim industrial developers benefit from their achieved performance. All reports benefit from a strict bug reporting policy. The underlying fault prediction approach is mainly based on recent changes to files. In contrast to this paper, we consider a machine learning based approach that relies on metrics that can be easily obtained from the software during development.

2.2 Cross-Project Fault Prediction

To overcome the lack of historical data in the early stages of a project's development CPFP uses data from other projects to train fault prediction models. Due to the heterogeneity between different projects, this is a difficult problem. Zimmermann et al. [29] performed a cross-project study on industrial code from Microsoft as well as popular open source software. They state that only 3.4 % of their analysed cross-project predictions achieve more than 0.75 recall, precision and f-measure. However, they demonstrated that whenever project factors are included in the selection of training data during the learning of a decision tree, the likelihood of good predictions can be improved.

Throughout the last years various approaches for improving fault predictions were proposed. In this work, we apply the k-nearest neighbour approach for data selection by Turhan et al. [26] and the normalization approaches by Watanabe et al. [27] and Nam et al. [20]. Other approaches that could be applied are, e.g., a data weighting technique by Ma et al. [18] or transformation of the data according to Camargo Cruz et al. [5]. Moreover, approaches based on the selection of appropriate projects for training, like proposed by He et al. [12] and Herbold [14] are not considered, because we only rely on a setting comprising two projects, where a further selection is obviously not possible.

3   Defect Prediction Case Study

In this section, we present a case study in which we tackle the following research question:

RQ1: Can CPFP be applied in projects using automatically generated code and restrictive coding standards like MISRA [25] which was developed for the same target platform?

This research question **RQ1** is answered by the evaluation of two hypotheses that we initially suspect to be true based on our experience obtained from previous research:

H1: Within-project fault prediction can be applied successfully to automatically generated code.
H2: CPFP is enabled by auto-generated code within a restrictive setting.

Our rational for **H1** is that there are many examples for successful fault predictions in a within-project setting reported in the literature (see, e.g., Catal et al. [6] for an overview). We expect that this is also true for the generated code.

Our rational for **H2** is that differences between metrics due to developer characteristics, etc. can be excluded. Moreover, we expect that the rules used by code generators lead to repetitive patterns in the generated source code. This, in turn, should lead to patterns in the metric values, which should lead to strong correlations between the metric values, even between projects.

Rational for **H2** is that differences between the project context are one of the conjectured greatest threats to CPFP. Zimmermann et al. [29] showed that with a simple decision tree based on context factors the performance of predictions can be greatly improved. In a more recent publication Zhang et al. [28] again demonstrated the power of using context factors. The context factors of the projects we consider are nearly identical. They were developed by the same company, using the same development process, with source code automatically generated with the same code generator following a strict coding standard. This removes a lot of project-specific and developer-specific noise from the data.

3.1   Evaluation Criteria

To evaluate the performance of the fault prediction models, we use the following metrics.

$$recall = \frac{tp}{tp + fn} \tag{1}$$

$$precision = \frac{tp}{tp + fp} \tag{2}$$

$$F\text{-}measure = 2 \cdot \frac{recall \cdot precision}{recall + precision} \tag{3}$$

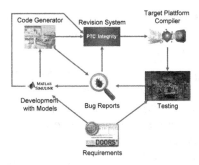

Fig. 1. Workflow during software development

In the above definition, tp, respectively tn are the number of true positive respectively negative predictions, fp, respectively fn are the number of false positive respectively negative predictions. The *recall* measures how many of the existing faults are found. The *precision* measures how many of the found results are actually faults. The *F-measure* is the harmonic mean between *precision* and *recall*. The *error* measures the overall rate of misclassification.

3.2   Data Description

We use the data from a publicity available dataset released by Altinger et al. [1]. The dataset contains fault data of three automotive projects for proprietary reasons simply refereed as A, K, and L. The size of the projects ranges from 10.000 LOC to 36.500 LOC. Two of the three projects are safety relevant, which means that the testing effort had been very high. A special attribute of the data is that the software was not developed by writing source code but by creating Matlab/Simulink models. The source code is then generated automatically using the dSpace TargetLink code generator that fulfils the MISRA [25] guidelines. The workflow during the software development cycle is visualized in Fig. 1. The revisions from all development tools have been analysed and tested. Therefore, the projects stay with the same software during their whole life cycle. As the three projects are from the same time scale, the versions and settings are identical.

Whereas the dataset contains three projects, we only consider the A and the K project in this paper. The reason for this is that the third project L has a very low fault rate, with only three unique faults detected during development. This fault rate is too low to be used in a machine learning approach for fault prediction.

3.3   Defect Prediction Models

In this paper, we use one classification model for within-project predictions and six classification models for cross-project predictions. With the first model, we look at the performance of within-project predictions for baseline comparison reasons. For the cross-project predictions, we predict the faults in the A using the data from K and the faults in K using the data from A. The classification models we use are the following:

- WP: a within-project fault prediction model. Since the data is ordered by time, we use the data from the oldest 50 % of revisions for training and the remaining 50 % of revisions for evaluation of predictions.
- KNN: cross-project prediction with the k-nearest neighbour approach for data selection introduced by Turhan et al. [26]. We use $k = 10$, which is the same as for the original study. This means, for every entity in the target project, we select the 10 closest entities in the training project for our training data.
- N1: cross-project prediction with min-max normalization [17] of the training and target data separately to the interval [0,1], i.e.,

$$\hat{m}_i(s) = \frac{m_i(s) - \min_{s' \in S} m_i(s')}{\max_{s' \in S} m_i(s') - \min_{s' \in S} m_i(s')}.$$

This approach for normalization is quite common and, e.g., used by [12–14,18,20,27].

- N2: cross-project prediction with z-score normalization [17], which transforms the training and the target data separately such that the mean value and the standard deviation to one, see e.g. Nam et al. [20], i.e.,

$$\hat{m}_i(s) = \frac{m_i(s) - mean(m_i(S))}{std(m_i(S))}.$$

- N4:[1] Cross-project prediction with z-score normalization of the training and target data, both based on the mean and standard deviation of the target data after Nam et al. [20], i.e.,

$$\hat{m}_i(s) = \frac{m_i(s) - mean(m_i(S^*))}{std(m_i(S^*))}.$$

- N5: cross-project prediction with normalization of data according to the mean standardization proposed by Watanabe et al. [27], i.e.,

$$\hat{m}_i(s) = \frac{m_i(s) \cdot mean(m_i(S^*))}{mean(m_i(S))}.$$

For the training of all classification models, we used under sampling [8] to treat the bias towards non-fault-prone classifications due to the small number of fault-prone entities in the data sets. As classifier, we used a Support Vector Machine (SVM) with a Radial Basis Function (RBF) kernel [24], one of the over-all best performing classifiers from the machine learning literature [10]. Please note that we did not use a cross-project model without normalization. The reasons for this are that we used a SVM as classifier and SVMs often perform poorly if no scaling or normalization is used [10].

---

[1] We use N4 instead of N3 to be consistent to the naming of Nam et al. [20].

3.4   Prediction Performance

In the following, we report the results obtained for fault prediction. Table 1 lists the values for recall, precision, and F-measure achieved with the prediction models. The first column contains the within-project predictions, the other columns the results for the cross-project predictions with the various transfer learning techniques.

Table 1. Results achieved with the various classification models on the data sets. Abbreviations see Sect. 3.3

		WP	KNN	N1	N2	N4	N5
Recall	A	0.59	-	-	-	-	-
	K → A	-	0.48	0.48	0.48	0.48	0.48
	K	0.89	-	-	-	-	-
	A → K	-	0.75	0.75	0.75	0.75	0.69
Precision	A	0.16	-	-	-	-	-
	K → A	-	0.19	0.19	0.19	0.19	0.18
	K	0.21	-	-	-	-	-
	A → K	-	0.20	0.17	0.17	0.17	0.24
F-measure	A	0.25	-	-	-	-	-
	K → A	-	0.28	0.28	0.28	0.28	0.27
	K	0.34	-	-	-	-	-
	A → K	-	0.32	0.27	0.27	0.27	0.36

For the within-project predictions, our results show a mediocre value of 0.59 for the project A and a very good recall of 0.89 for the project K. The precision is very low in both cases with 0.16 for A and 0.21 for K. Hence, the F-measure is low in both projects, i.e., 0.25 for A and 0.34 for K.

The cross-projects recall predictions is lower than for within-project predictions on both A and K. The value of recall is almost always 0.48 for A, and 0.75 for K with the exception of the prediction of K when using N5 normalization, where the recall is slightly worse with 0.69. In terms of precision, we observe a mixed picture. For project A, the precision of the cross-predictions are actually slightly better than the within-project predictions with a value of 0.19 for KNN, N1, N2, and N4 and 0.18 for N5. However, the difference is rather small with 0.03 and 0.02, respectively. For Project K, the precision of the within-project prediction is better than the KNN, N1, N2, and N4 model. KNN achieves a precision of 0.20 and N1, N2, and N4 a value of 0.17. The N5 model beats the within-project prediction with a value of 0.24, i.e., a small gain of 0.03. This gain in precision seems to be the reason for the slightly worse recall. This mixture of the results is also reflected by the F-measure. For project A, the F-measure of the cross-project predictions is slightly higher with a value of 0.28 for KNN, N1,

N2, and N4 and 0.27 for N5. This gain in F-measure is due to the slightly higher precision, which offsets the lower recall. For the project K, the F-measure for KNN, N1, N2, and N4 is lower than for the within-project model. Only N5 beats the within-project prediction slightly with a value of 0.36, i.e., a very small gain of 0.02 in comparison to the within-project prediction.

In summary: the N5 cross-project prediction model performs consistently best in terms of F-measure, but has a lower recall than the within-project predictions obtained. However, the precision of all models is quite low, i.e., less than 0.25 in all cases. Accordingly to the testing experts we consulted, finding 80 % of the fault-prone instances would still be a great enhancement during the testing stages, which means that such a low precision might be acceptable for the practical implementation and is comparable to statements by Ostrand et al. [21].

3.5 Hypotheses Evaluation

In this section, we discuss the consequences of the results obtained for fault prediction on the hypotheses **H1, H2** as well as on our underlying research question **RQ1**.

H1: Within-Project Fault Prediction Can be Applied Successfully to Automatically Generated Code. Our results show a good recall for within-project predictions, i.e., it is possible to find the faults, but the precision is rather low. However, according to the testing experts that were involved in the Projects A and K, predicting 80 % of the fault-prone instances would still be a great enhancement during the testing stages, which means that a low precision might be acceptable in practice. Due to the high recall, we find some support for this hypothesis, but further studies need to be performed to see if the low precision really is acceptable for the practitioners.

H2: CPFP is Enabled by Auto-generated Code Within a Restrictive Setting. Our results for the cross-project prediction are not much worse than for the within-project prediction, even though we note some drop in the recall. However, the F-measure of the N5 normalization is even better than for within-project prediction. Hence, we conclude that it also depends on the practitioners point of view, if the rather low precision is acceptable.

RQ1: Can CPFP be Applied in Projects Using Automatically Generated Code and Restrictive Coding Standards Like MISRA [25] That Was Developed for the Same Target Platform? Based on our findings, we conclude that further research in this direction is warranted but the overall performance is not as good as we initially expected. Further insights are required to improve the prediction models in the future to increase precision. Moreover, a test carried out in a practical setting, where testing experts evaluate the approach in a pilot project, would be very much helpful to evaluate the question of whether or not low values of precision are really acceptable.

4   Causes for the Obtained Prediction Performance

Our results show an overall surprisingly low prediction performance, especially in terms of precision. Due to the extremely high similarity between the projects A and K in terms of the development process and, additionally, the fact that the source code is automatically generated, which should further increase the similarities, we were expecting much better prediction results. Therefore, we further investigated in the following research questions.

RQ2: What are the use fault prediction models reasons to perform low?

To answer this question we perform an in-depth analysis. We postulate three hypothesis, which we believe should be true for good fault prediction models. Then, we evaluate whether these hypothesis are true for our data and, thereby, try to gain insights into why the precision of our predictions is low. The hypotheses are the following:

H3: Metric values are strongly correlated between software projects based on automatically generated code.
H4: The available software metrics carry information about the faults.
H5: The faulty regions in the training and test data are similar.

Our rational for **H3** is that differences between metrics due to developer characteristics, etc. can be excluded. Moreover, we expect that the rules of code generators lead to repetitive patterns within the generated source code. This, in turn, should lead to patterns within the metric values, which should lead to strong correlations between the metric values, even between projects. Strong correlations between software projects are a pre-requisite for good cross-project predictions and week correlations here might by a reasons for a lower prediction performance.

With **H4**, we simply state the underlying assumption of fault prediction models based on software metrics and machine learning: that the metrics actually contain information about the location of the faults. Similarly, with **H5**, we want to investigate a general assumption for machine learning: that the distributions of the training and test data are similar. If this is not the case, the prediction model is trained using a wrong distribution that in turn decreases the prediction performance, which is somehow comparable to He et al's [13] findings.

4.1   Correlation Analysis

From the Dataset, [1], one can see a strong correlation between the static code metrics LOC, Halstead (Volume (Hv), Difficultly (Hd) and Effort (He)) and number of functions (nfunctions). A similar strong correlation has been obtained between change metrics (LOC add and removed per commit), but only a weak correlation to the author. We used Kendall's τ [16] correlation analysis to investigate the influence of the selected attributes. See Table 2 for the results. In general there is a small correlation between bugs and all 11 metrics. LOC can be seen as the strongest correlation to bugs, but is still weak at 0.23. These results are in correlation with the attribute influence analysis in Table 3, where LOC is among the first influencing metric attributes to fault prediction.

Table 2. Kandals τ correlation analysis for metrics with bugs

		static source code attribute					change attribute				social attribute
		sloc	McCab	Hv	Hd	He	nfunctions	loc_add	loc_remove	commit_age	num_commits	author
bug	Project A	0.22	0.16	0.23	0.23	0.22	0.15	0.10	0.10	-0.12	-0.08	-0.10
	Project K	0.23	0.26	0.24	0.23	0.24	0.22	0.13	0.13	0.02	0.05	0.03

To see if the bug regions are correlated we selected all commits containing a fault and correlated their metric attributes with each other. In general there is a weak or small negative correlation between those two projects, which might be caused by different bug regions. Again the strongest correlation values are achieved by static source code metrics (LOC, Halstead, McCab).

Based on this one might conclude "within projects fault prediction" report on bad performance and "cross project fault prediction" will be impossible, at least based on the selected attribute metrics.

4.2   Information Gain

We analyzed the influence of 11 attributes using Information Gain. See Table 3 for the results, which delivers consistent values to the Kendall τ correlation analysis given in Table 2, where static source code attributes (LOC, number of functions, etc.) have got a higher correlation than change metrics (LOC_add, LOC_remove, ...). This ranking is in contrast to Graves et al. [11] or Meneely et al. [19] but similar to Curtis et al. [7]. This might be caused by the development method, as the code generator can be seen as the same author for the actual code files. Due to the fact that a code generator uses templates and the developer is limited to a finite set of blocks when designing the Matlab/Simulink Model, the code structure itself is very comparable among the methods. The influence of a developer's style is little, because every block will be generated in the same way.

4.3   Visual Analysis

In addition to the correlation analysis, we performed a visual analysis to determine possible reasons for prediction errors. To visualize the fault data, we use Principle Component Analysis (PCA) [9] to reduce the dimension of the data.

Table 3. ranked error types with explanation

Information Gain	Rank	Attribute	Explanation
0.16637	1	Hv	Halstead Volume
0.13540	2	McCabe	McCabe Cyclomatic Complexity
0.13505	3	Hd	Halstead Difficulty
0.12628	4	He	Halstead Effort
0.12303	5	sloc	Lines Of Code
0.05445	6	nfunctions	Number of Functions
0.03483	7	commit_age	Number of Days since last commit
0.02384	8	loc_add	LOC Added since last commit
0.02358	9	loc_remove	LOC Removed since last commit
0.00948	10	num_commits	Number of total commits to file
0	11	Author	Last commiting Author

PCA is a technique that orthogonally transforms into linearly uncorrelated variables, such that the first principle component has the largest possible variance and, thereby, explains as much of the variance in the data as possible. In our case, we can explain 89 %–92 % percent of the variance within the data by using just the first two principle components. This allows us to create two-dimensional scatter plots in which we can visually compare data.

In Fig. 2(a) and (b) we show the visual representation of the data of A and K used for the within-project evaluation. The training data are the oldest 50 % revisions in the data, the test data are the newest 50 %. We have three types of interesting areas in those figures.

1. Defects from the training data that are the same area as in the test data. These faults should be detected correctly.
2. Defects in the training data are located in a region in which no faults are present in the test data. These faults should lead to false positives and, therefore, decrease the precision.
3. Defects in the training data are not in the same area as faults in the test data. These faults are probably not detected by the classification model and lead to a decrease in recall.

The figures show that for the most part, we are in the first areas, where we find faults in both data sets. However, in both data sets there are also areas where there is no overlap. These lead to the drops in recall and precision. As the figures also show, there are many more non-fault-prone entities than fault-prone entities. This is the reasons for the low precision: even if only a relatively small area in the training data contains faults, where there are no faults in the test data, the precision drops drastically. Moreover, in the K project, there is also the problem that the area around the coordinates (0,0) is heavily populated by both fault-prone and non-fault-prone entities in both the training and test data.

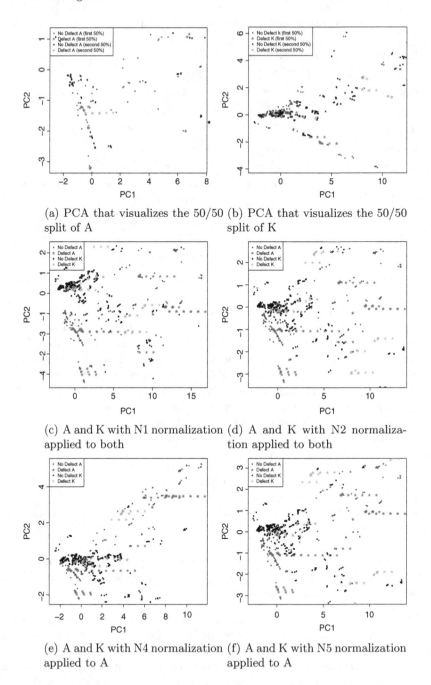

(a) PCA that visualizes the 50/50 (b) PCA that visualizes the 50/50
split of A   split of K

(c) A and K with N1 normalization (d) A and K with N2 normaliza-
applied to both   tion applied to both

(e) A and K with N4 normalization (f) A and K with N5 normalization
applied to A   applied to A

Fig. 2. Data visualization with PCA. The PCA is performed with all plotted data points, i.e., with the full data from A/K for the sub-figures (a) and (b) and with the data from both A and K for sub-figures (c)–(f). The first two principle components of the data explain between 89 %–92 % of the variance.

This leads to additional noise in the data and a further drop in the precision and recall. To further analyze these effects, we compare the training and test data of the cross-project predictions using the four normalization techniques N1, N2, N4 and N5 in Fig. 2(c)–(f). The areas of interest are similar.

1. Defects from the data of project A/K that are the same as in the other project. These faults should be detected correctly by the cross-project prediction.
2. Defects in the data of project A that are located in a region in which no faults are present in the project K. These faults should lead to false positives in the cross-project prediction $A \to K$ and, therefore, decrease the precision. Moreover, these faults are likely not detected in the cross-project prediction $K \to A$ and lead to a decrease in recall.
3. Defects in the data of project K that are located in a region in which no faults are present in the project A. These faults should lead to false positives in the cross-project prediction $K \to A$ and, therefore, decrease the precision. Moreover, these faults are likely not detected in the cross-project prediction $A \to K$ and lead to a decrease in recall.

As can be seen on all four plots, the faults between A and K are for the most part non-overlapping. Hence, we are for the most parts in the two "bad" areas of interest, which reduce the recall and precision. However, a closer look reveals that whereas the faulty areas themselves are not overlapping, the faults are still in somewhat similar areas in the data. For example, many faults of K are in all four plots close to the coordinates (0,0). On the Y-axis only very few instances of K are located below that cluster. Hence, fault predictors might assume the full area below those faults as fault-prone. Within that area many faulty instances of A are located, which then may be predicted correctly as fault prone. Such effects explain the still relatively good values for the recall. However, the plots also show that within the very same area below (0,0) many non-faulty instances of A are also located. They would all also be predicted as faulty, which explains the very low precision. In addition, we are interested in the general overlap between non-fault-prone instances of the two projects, i.e., how often the non-fault-prone are within the same area. The task of the normalization is exactly this: transform the non-faulty instances in such a way that they are within similar areas. We observe that the overlap depends on the normalization technique. With N1, i.e., simple min-max normalization, we see most instances of K in the top-left quadrant of the plot, whereas the instances of A are distributed scattered through the whole area of the plot. With the other normalization technique N2, N4, and N5, such a differentiation is not possible and the data seems to be more evenly distributed for both projects.

4.4   Hypothesis Evaluation

In this section, we discuss the results of the fault predictions, the hypotheses **H3–H5**, as well as our underlying research question **RQ2**.

H3: Metric Values Are Strongly Correlated Between Software Projects Based on Automatically Generated Code. Our correlation analysis performance shows a very weak correlation between the two projects A and K. Therefore, we do not find support for this hypothesis. This weak correlation is the possible source for the low precision and overall bad performance of the cross-project predictions.

H4: The Available Software Metrics Carry Information About the Faults. The correlation analysis shows that most of the metrics are weakly correlated with the fault information, with the exception of the commit age, for which we find almost no correlation. Additionally, we considered the information gain of the attributes in relation to the fault information. Here, we determined that about half of the metrics carry information about the faults, however, also only weak information. The other attributes carry almost no information about the faults. If we consider this together, this is another reason for low performance, but it also explains why the predictions did not fail completely, since we found weak correlations and mutual information between the metrics and the fault information.

H5: The Faulty Regions in the Training and Test Data Are Similar. Our PCA based visual analysis shows that the faulty regions are not overlapping as expected, but only to some degree. We consider this the main source of the problems with the precision. The transfer learning only helps to fix this to a minor degree.

RQ2: What Are the Reasons for the Low Performance of the Used Fault Prediction Models? In our analysis, we found that all three hypotheses we had are actually not well supported by our data. Hence, it is not surprising that we have trouble with the overall prediction performance. The reasons we determined are merely weak instead of strong correlations of the metrics between projects, weak correlation and low mutual information of the metrics and the fault information, and a bad overlapping of the faulty regions in the training and test data.

5   Threats to Validity

We identified several threats to the validity of our results. First of all, our results are restricted to a narrow setting within the automotive industry. It is unclear how this translates to other settings, which is a threat to the external validity of our results. Moreover, the templates used by the code generators may impact our study. Different templates, which might be part of a new major release on the code generator, maybe will change our findings. Additionally, we used only two data sets for our case study. Furthermore, both data sets contain only few errors. The results may change if projects have many errors.

6   Conclusion and Outlook

In this paper, we present a case study on fault prediction models in the context of software development in the automotive industry, which is based on projects comprising automatically generated code. In our study, we considered both the within-project and the cross-project setting. Our findings show that predicting faults is possible. However, the precision of the predictions is rather low. Due to this, we presented an in-depth analysis of possible reasons for this lack of precision. Our analysis shows that the correlation and mutual information between the software metrics and the bugs is rather weak. Moreover, the correlation between the projects is also worse then expected, as we show both with a correlation analysis as well as a visual analysis of the data.

Using these results as a starting point, we suggest multiple venues for future investigations. Since our findings regarding the metric correlation and mutual information are rather weak, we suspect that possibly using model-level metrics, instead of source code level metrics would lead to better results. Therefore, we plan to study the impact of using model-level metrics on the fault predictions. As part of this extension to model-level metrics, we also plan to investigate the influence of static code metrics, change metrics, and social metrics again. Most modern literature that considers the impact of social and change metrics is based on modern languages like Java, whereas we consider C code with restrictive coding conventions. It is unclear if the findings hold in this setting.

Acknowledgement. The authors would like to thank the project managers in charge of the analyzed projects in the data set for the long discussions and good insights they gave to development history, process and testing methods used during development and their rating of our achieved performance values on SFP.

References

1. Altinger, H., Siegl, S., Dajsuren, Y., Wotawa, F.: A novel industry grade dataset for fault prediction based on model-driven developed automotive embedded software. In: Proceedings of the 12th Working Conference on Mining Software Repositories (MSR). IEEE, Florence, Italy (2015)
2. Altinger, H., Wotawa, F., Schurius, M.: Testing methods used in the automotive industry: results from a survey. In: Proceedings of the 2014 Workshop on Joining AcadeMiA and Industry Contributions to Test Automation and Model-Based Testing (JAMAICA). ACM (2014)
3. Bell, R.M., Ostrand, T.J., Weyuker, E.J.: Looking for bugs in all the right places. In: Proceedings of the 2006 International Symposium on Software Testing and Analysis (ISSTA). ACM (2006)
4. Broy, M.: Challenges in automotive software engineering. In: Proceedings of the 28th International Conference on Software Engineering. ACM (2006). http://doi.acm.org/10.1145/1134285.1134292
5. Camargo Cruz, A.E., Ochimizu, K.: Towards logistic regression models for predicting fault-prone code across software projects. In: Proceedings of the 3rd International Symposium on Empirical Software Engineering and Measurement (ESEM). IEEE Computer Society (2009)
6. Catal, C., Diri, B.: A systematic review of software fault prediction studies. Expert Syst. Appl. **36**(4), 7346–7354 (2009)
7. Curtis, B., Sheppard, S.B., Milliman, P.: Third time charm: Stronger prediction of programmer performance by software complexity metrics. In: Proceedings of the 4th International Conference on Software Engineering (1979)

8. Drummond, C., Holte, R.C.: C4.5, class imbalance, and cost sensitivity: why under-sampling beats over-sampling. In: Workshop on Learning from Imbalanced Datasets II (2003)
9. Karl Pearson, F.R.S.: LIII. On lines and planes of closest fit to systems of points in space. Philos. Mag. Ser. 6 **2**(11), 559–572 (1901)
10. van Gestel, T., Suykens, J., Baesens, B., Viaene, S., Vanthienen, J., Dedene, G., de Moor, B., Vandewalle, J.: Benchmarking least squares support vector machine classifiers. Mach. Learn. **54**(1), 5–32 (2004)
11. Graves, T.L., Karr, A.F., Marron, J.S., Siy, H.: Predicting fault incidence using software change history. IEEE Trans. Softw. Eng. **26**(7), 653–661 (2000)
12. He, Z., Peters, F., Menzies, T., Yang, Y.: Learning from open-source projects: an empirical study on defect prediction. In: Proceedings of the 7th International Symposium on Empirical Software Engineering and Measurement (ESEM) (2013)
13. He, Z., Shu, F., Yang, Y., Li, M., Wang, Q.: An investigation on the feasibility of cross-project defect prediction. Autom. Softw. Eng. **19**(2), 167–199 (2012). http://dx.doi.org/10.1007/s10515-011-0090-3
14. Herbold, S.: Training data selection for cross-project defect prediction. In: Proceedings of the 9th International International Conference on Predictive Models in Software Engineering (PROMISE). ACM (2013)
15. Jin-Hua, L., Qiong, L., Jing, L.: The w-model for testing software product lines. In: International Symposium on Computer Science and Computational Technology (ISCSCT) (2008)
16. Kendall, M.G.: Rank correlation methods (1948)
17. Kotsiantis, S., Kanellopoulos, D., Pintelas, P.: Data preprocessing for supervised leaning. Int. J. Comput. Sci. **1**(2), 111–117 (2006)
18. Ma, Y., Luo, G., Zeng, X., Chen, A.: Transfer learning for cross-company software defect prediction. Inf. Softw. Technol. **54**(3), 248–256 (2012)
19. Meneely, A., Williams, L., Snipes, W., Osborne, J.: Predicting failures with developer networks and social network analysis. In: Proceedings of the 16th ACM SIG-SOFT International Symposium on Foundations of Software Engineering (FSE) (2008)
20. Nam, J., Pan, S.J., Kim, S.: Transfer defect learning. In: Proceedings of the 35th International International Conference on Software Engineering (ICSE) (2013)
21. Ostrand, T.J., Weyuker, E.J.: The distribution of faults in a large industrial software system. ACM SIGSOFT Softw. Eng. Notes **27**, 55–64 (2002)
22. Ostrand, T.J., Weyuker, E.J., Bell, R.M.: Predicting the location and number of faults in large software systems. IEEE Trans. Softw. Eng. **31**(4), 340–355 (2005)
23. Rana, R., Staron, M., Hansson, J., Nilsson, M.: Defect prediction over software life cycle in automotive domain. In: Proceedings of the Joint International Conference on Software Technologies (ICSOFT) (2014)
24. Schölkopf, B., Smola, A.J.: Learning with Kernels. MIT Press, Cambridge (2002)
25. The Motor Industry Software Reliability Association: MISRA-C:2004 - Guidelines for the use of the C language in critical systems, 2nd edn. MISRA, Warwickshire (2004)
26. Turhan, B., Menzies, T., Bener, A., Di Stefano, J.: On the relative value of cross-company and within-company data for defect prediction. Empirical Softw. Eng. **14**, 540–578 (2009)
27. Watanabe, S., Kaiya, H., Kaijiri, K.: Adapting a fault prediction model to allow inter language reuse. In: Proceedings of the 4th International International Workshop on Predictor Models in Software Engineering (PROMISE). ACM (2008)

28. Zhang, F., Mockus, A., Keivanloo, I., Zou, Y.: Towards building a universal defect prediction model. In: Proceedings of the 11th Working Conference on Mining Software Repositories (MSR) (2014)

29. Zimmermann, T., Nagappan, N., Gall, H., Giger, E., Murphy, B.: Cross-project defect prediction: a large scale experiment on data vs. domain vs. process. In: Proceedings of the the 7th Joint Meeting European Software Engineering Conference (ESEC) and the ACM SIGSOFT Symposium on the Foundations of Software Engineering (FSE) (2009)

Model and System Testing

Inferring Finite State Machines Without Reset Using State Identification Sequences

Roland Groz[1]($\boxtimes$), Adenilso Simao[2], Alexandre Petrenko[3], and Catherine Oriat[1]

[1] Université Grenoble Alpes, Saint-Martin-d'Hères, France
{Roland.Groz,Catherine.Oriat}@imag.fr
[2] Universidade de São Paulo, Saint-Martin-d'Hères, São Paulo, Brasil
adenilso@icmc.usp.br
[3] CRIM, Montréal, Canada
Alexandre.Petrenko@crim.ca

Abstract. Identifying the (finite state) control structure of a black box system from the traces observed in finite interaction is of great interest for many model-based activities, such as model-based testing or model-driven engineering. There are several inference methods, but all those methods assume that the system can be reset whenever necessary. In this paper, we address the issue of inferring a finite state machine (FSM) that cannot be reset; we propose a method, inspired by FSM-based testing generation methods. We assume classical testing hypotheses, namely that we are given a bound n on the number of states and a set W of characterizing sequences to distinguish states. To the best of our knowledge, this is the first model inference method that does not require resetting the system, and does not require an external oracle to decide on equivalence. The length of the test sequence is polynomial in n and the exponent depends on the cardinal $|W|$ of the characterization set.

Keywords: Finite state machines · Model inference · Testing

1 Introduction

For model-driven software engineering, model-based testing including, it is important to rely on models of the software artefacts. It is also essential that the models are up-to-date. In many contexts, however, such models are not available. In the last decade, interest has risen on methods to retrieve models from software artefacts, see, e.g., [1, 2, 4, 7, 10, 12, 17]. Depending on the context, goal and assumptions, various types of techniques have been considered for specification mining, reengineering or model inference. When source code is available, automated analysis of its structure can yield adequate models [5, 11].

Various algorithms have been proposed for inference of finite state machines. Such methods have been used to retrieve finite state behavioural models of black box components by testing them [16, 17]. Typically, such components could be accessed over a network, so that we do not even assume that the executable can be scrutinized: the system can only be observed at its interfaces [1]. This corresponds to a typical black

© IFIP International Federation for Information Processing 2015
K. El-Fakih et al. (Eds.): ICTSS 2015, LNCS 9447, pp. 161–177, 2015.
DOI: 10.1007/978-3-319-25945-1_10

box testing scenario, where the tester would send inputs to a system and observe its outputs. This scenario arises in many practical situations. For instance, a component has to be treated as a black box, when its internals cannot be available due to intellectual property constraints.

We assume that the System Under Test (SUT) can be modelled, at some level of abstraction on its inputs and outputs, as a Finite State Machine (FSM). FSM-based testing theory has shown that an FSM can be identified, i.e., the SUT can be tested to be proven equivalent to it, with the help of state identifying (distinguishing) sequences, constituting, e.g., a characterization set (W-set) of input sequences.

Existing inference algorithms assume that the black box can be reliably reset to its initial state. This makes the inference task somehow easier, because it is possible to start each new experiment from a known state, and explore progressively the neighbouring states. But there are cases where a black box cannot be reset, or where it is unsure that we can rely on it being restored to the same initial state. There are also cases where restarting the system completely might be very costly requiring a lot of time to reset the whole configuration (e.g., rebooting a machine, with possibly many software components to configure and reinitialize). Actually, our research was triggered by a case study from the SPaCIoS European project where we had to infer a software provided (as is common now) as a virtual machine. Although an i/o interaction in HTTP with it over the local network would require less than a millisecond, resetting the application would need more than a minute, around 10^5 more than an i/o.

In this paper, we propose an algorithm that can infer a black-box implementation without resetting it. This problem has similarities with classical testing methods, in particular the DS-method [6] and the W-method [18]. In classical testing methods, we are provided with a characterization set, and we derive a checking sequence or experiment that identifies a black box. The key difference is that classical testing methods start from a known specification machine, and just check whether the black box is equivalent (or conformant) to this specification. Therefore, those methods heavily rely on transfer sequences that make it possible to test a new state through a path known to transfer to the right state in the specification. In our context, since no specification is available, we cannot rely on known transfer sequences. Although the absence of reset had already been addressed by Hennie [6] and others in the case of a single distinguishing sequence, the task is made much harder in our context since we cannot return to a known state to compare the responses to a state of the specification. Moreover, we consider the case where the black box may not have a distinguishing sequence. This problem has been investigated in [6, 8, 13, 14], where a characterization set is used. It turns out that generating a checking sequence (without reset) from a known specification FSM with a characterization set is very costly, due to the fact that the sequences of this set have to be applied a number of times which is proportional to some exponential on the number of states in the specification [14]. Recent work [8, 13] has reduced the effort by some constant factor, which is a practical improvement; nonetheless, the complexity remains exponential.

As with other identification problems in FSM based testing, we rely on assumptions on the black box. First, we assume that an upper bound n on the number of states of the black box is known. Second, we are provided with a set W of input sequences that characterize the different states of the black box: each state produces a different set of output responses to these input sequences. Such a set could be derived from a previous version of the software or from domain-specific knowledge.

Rivest and Schapire [15] pioneered the inference of automata without reset, but their method was based on Angluin's L* algorithm [3] which assumes that an oracle can answer equivalence queries. In a typical software testing context, such an oracle cannot be provided. Our method does not require any equivalence query, and there is no oracle apart from the black box. In order to guarantee equivalence, we just assume we know an upper bound on the number of states, which is a much weaker assumption. Identifying states by their i/o responses to sequences of W is somehow similar to the set of suffixes in L* although we do not need suffix-closure contrary to L*.

Our method relies on a localizer, a procedure that can reliably bring the black box to the same state all over again to make sure that responses to all sequences from the W-set are observed from a single state. Therefore, it is possible to extend progressively the knowledge of the transitions starting from that state, while being sure that we actually come back to a known (previously learnt) state. This procedure is inspired by the construction of locating sequence used in [6, 14]. The algorithm uses the localizer to start from a known state, which becomes the first learnt state. Thus, it does not require the black box to be initially in a particular state. It then tries to characterize progressively the tail state reached after the application of the localizer by repeatedly applying the sequences from W. By doing so, it will often end up in unknown states, therefore the algorithm alternates between applications of sequences from W to get more knowledge and applications of the localizer to restart from some previously learnt state. The algorithm identifies a correct model in $O(p(f + p)\ 2^p\ n^{p+2})$ inputs, where n is the number of states of the machine, f is the size of the input set and p is the size of the W-set. Hence, the length of the identification sequence is polynomial in the number of states, although the exponent depends on the number of characterizing sequences.

The paper is organized as follows. Section 2 provides definitions and notations for our method. Section 3 describes the inference procedure, while Sect. 4 is dedicated to the localizer subroutine. Section 5 illustrates the algorithm on a small example. Proofs of termination and correctness, as well as an upper bound on complexity are in Sect. 6. Section 7 discusses assumptions and Sect. 8 concludes.

2 Definitions

2.1 Basic Definitions

A Finite State Machine is a <u>complete</u> deterministic Mealy machine. Formally, a Finite State Machine (FSM) M is a 6-tuple $(S, s_0, I, O, \delta, \lambda)$, where

- S is a finite set of states with the initial state s_0,
- I is a finite set of inputs, and O is a finite set of outputs,
- $\delta: S \times I \to S$ is a transition function, and
- $\lambda: S \times I \to O$ is an output function.

δ and λ are actually mappings, i.e., $dom(\delta) = dom(\lambda) = S \times I$ since we only consider complete machines. As M is deterministic, a tuple $(s, x) \in S \times I$ uniquely determines a *transition* of M. For simplicity we use (s, x) to denote the transition, thus omitting its output and final state. We extend the transition and output functions from input symbols to input sequences, including the empty sequence ε, as usual: $\delta(s, \varepsilon) = s$ and $\lambda(s, \varepsilon) = \varepsilon$, for $s \in S$; for $\alpha x \in I^+$, $\delta(s, \alpha x) = \delta(\delta(s, \alpha), x)$ and $\lambda(s, \alpha x) = \lambda(s, \alpha)\lambda(\delta(s, \alpha), x)$. An FSM M is said to be *strongly connected*, if for each pair of states $s, s' \in S$, there exists an input sequence $\alpha \in I^*$, such that $\delta(s, \alpha) = s'$; α is called a *transfer* sequence.

Two states $s, s' \in S$ are *distinguishable*, if there exists $\gamma \in I^*$, such that $\lambda(s, \gamma) \neq \lambda(s', \gamma)$. We say that γ distinguishes s and s'. Given a set $H \subseteq I^*$, states s and s' are *H-equivalent*, if $\lambda(s, \gamma) = \lambda(s', \gamma)$ for all $\gamma \in H$. Otherwise, i.e., if there exists $\gamma \in H$ such that $\lambda(s, \gamma) \neq \lambda(s', \gamma)$, the states are *H-distinguishable*. We define *H*-distinguishability and *H*-equivalence of machines as a corresponding relation between their initial states. An FSM M is *minimal*, if all states are pairwise distinguishable. In this paper, the machines are assumed to be <u>minimal</u> and <u>strongly connected</u>. A set of inputs W is a *characterization* set for an FSM M if each pair of states is W-distinguishable.

A sequence of input/output pairs $\alpha \in (IO)^*$ is a *trace*. Given traces α, β, and ω, such that $\omega = \alpha\beta$, we write $\omega \setminus \beta$, when we need to refer to the result of deleting the suffix β from the trace ω, resulting in trace α. The notation $\alpha \leq \omega$ is used to refer to a prefix α of the trace ω; $\omega{\downarrow}A$, where $A \subseteq I \cup O$, denotes the projection of ω to A, obtained by removing symbols that are not in A from the trace ω. Formally, $\varepsilon{\downarrow}A = \varepsilon$; if $x \in A$, then $(\alpha x){\downarrow}A = (\alpha{\downarrow}A)x$; if $x \notin A$, then $(\alpha x){\downarrow}A = (\alpha{\downarrow}A)$.

Given a machine $M = (S, s_0, I, O, \delta, \lambda)$ with a state s_i and an input sequence $\alpha \in I^*$, we use $tr_i(\alpha)$ to denote the trace from state s_i such that $tr_i(\alpha){\downarrow}I = \alpha$ and $tr_i(\alpha){\downarrow}O = \lambda(s_i, \alpha)$. Given a characterization set W, rather than naming or numbering states (such as "s_i"), we may refer to a state by its *state characterization* $Tr_i(W) = \{tr_i(w) \mid w \in W\}$. A state characterization Tr_i can be seen as a mapping q_i from W to $(IO)^*$ such that $q_i(w) = tr_i(w)$. The set of all mappings $Q = \{q_1, q_2, \ldots, q_n\}$ corresponds to the set of states of the machine. Namely, for $q \in Q$ and $s \in S$, we write $q \leftrightarrow s$ if $\forall w \in W, q(w){\downarrow}O = \lambda(s, w)$. Inferring an unknown FSM with the same characterization set, each mapping $q \in Q$ can then be considered as its state. In the sequel, we use B (instead of the general M) to refer to a black-box machine, P (instead of S) to refer to its states, whereas the inferred model (also called "conjecture", in line with L^*) will have states denoted by Q.

2.2   Definitions for the Inference Method

Let $B = (P, p_0, I, O, \delta, \lambda)$ denote an FSM modelling a given black-box (BB) with the characterization set W. As the BB cannot be reset, it is possible to observe only a single trace from it. We introduce the notion of *labelling* function $C: (IO)^* \rightarrow Q \cup \{\bot\}$, which maps each prefix of an observed trace to a state q of Q, if it can be inferred that the machine B will be in state p such that $q \leftrightarrow p$ after the observed trace; otherwise C maps the prefix to an unknown state, denoted $\bot$.

Let ω be an observed trace. A labelling C is *deterministic* for ω if the following property holds:

$$\text{For } \alpha, \alpha' \in (IO)*, \text{ such that } \alpha \leq \omega, \text{ and } \alpha' \leq \omega, \text{ if } C(\alpha) = C(\alpha') \neq \bot,$$

$$\text{then for any } \beta, \beta' \in (IO)*, \text{ such that } \alpha\beta \leq \omega, \alpha'\beta' \leq \omega \text{ and } \beta \downarrow I = \beta' \downarrow I,$$

$$\text{we have } \beta = \beta' \text{ and } C(\alpha\beta) = C(\alpha'\beta').$$

Obviously, a labelling should be deterministic. It should also be *consistent* with the state characterizations, i.e., the following property should also hold:

$$\text{For all } \alpha, \gamma \in (IO)* \text{ such that } \alpha\gamma \leq \omega, \text{ if } C(\alpha) = q \neq \perp \text{and} \gamma \downarrow I = w \in W,$$
$$\text{then } q(w) = \gamma.$$

We capture the notion of known (or inferred) state by stating that a labelling C should be revealing. Let $B = (P, p_0, I, O, \delta, \lambda)$, a labelling C is *revealing* w.r.t. B if, and only if $\forall \alpha \in (IO)^* (\exists p \in P \text{ s.t. } \forall p' \in P (\delta(p', \alpha \downarrow I)) = p) \Rightarrow \exists q \text{ s.t. } C(\alpha) = q \text{ and } q \leftrightarrow p$. In other words, this property forces C to be defined on any trace α that is "homing" [9], i.e., which leads unambiguously to a single state with a known state characterization in the FSM B, irrespective of the start state.

The labelling function and state characterizations are the main components of the proposed method. To ease the presentation and simplify the algorithm, we also introduce several auxiliary notations and definitions, derived from the labelling function.

A trace is *verified* if it is a subtrace of the observed trace ω and its start and end states are known (labelled by C). Each verified trace is the result of execution of several transitions between the known states of the FSM B. We define a set of tuples containing a verified trace together with its start and end states $V \subseteq Q \times (IO)^* \times Q$. Formally, $V = \{(q, \alpha, q') \mid \exists \sigma \alpha \leq \omega, C(\sigma) = q, C(\sigma\alpha) = q'\}$. Moreover, since we assume that C is deterministic, for all $(q, \alpha, q') \in V$, and all $\chi \leq \omega$, such that $C(\chi) = q$, we have $C(\chi\alpha) = q'$.

We will also use a subset of it to refer to single transitions, called *verified* transitions, and not to their sequences. Let $T \subseteq V$, $T = \{(q, xo, q') \mid x \in I, o \in O \text{ and } \exists \sigma xo \leq \omega, C(\sigma) = q, C(\sigma xo) = q'\}$ be the set of verified transitions. We will use as well the term of *input verified in state* when we do not need to refer to the end state of a verified transition. Thus $R = \{(q, x) \in Q \times I \mid \exists o \in O, q' \in Q, (q, xo, q') \in T\}$ is the set of inputs verified in corresponding states.

Moreover, since we will discover new states as the observed trace grows, we will have a set of known states associated with a current trace ω. Q_C denotes a set of states *discovered* by ω such that $q \in Q_C$ iff $C(\alpha) = q$, for some $\alpha \leq \omega$.

We shall be able to derive from ω a *complete* conjecture, i.e., the FSM B, when for all $q \in Q_C$, for all $x \in I$, $(q, x) \in R$.

We further assume that the set W is an ordered set of p sequences and use $tr(w_p)$ to denote a subtrace produced by the BB when the last sequence of W viz. w_p is applied.

Finally, $K \subseteq Q \times (IO)^+ \times (IO)^*$ is used to keep track of the applications of $w \in W$ in a state q followed by either a transition or a trace of a sequence from W. $(q, \alpha, \gamma) \in K$, if there exists a trace β, such that $\beta\alpha\gamma \leq \omega$, $C(\beta) = q$, $\alpha \downarrow I \in I \cup W$ and $\gamma \downarrow I \in W$.

3   Inference Procedure

A localizer procedure $L(\omega, W)$ is used to ensure that we continue learning transitions from states visited before. The localizer procedure, given a current trace ω, produces an updated trace ω', a set of traces $Tr(W)$, and the last appended trace $tr(w_p)$ to label the state which has produced it and is thus identified with $Tr(W)$. Recall that a state is defined by its answers to sequences from W, i.e., by $Tr(W)$. At the end of the localizer, we know the BB is in state $\delta(Tr(W), w_p)$, and the state reached after $\omega\backslash tr(w_p)$ can be labelled as $Tr(W)$.

Before defining the localizer, we present the main algorithm that calls it.

Inference procedure
Initialize: $K = R = V = \varnothing$
$(\omega, q_0, tr(w_p)) := L(\varepsilon, W)$ % Home into (or through) a known state
$C(\omega \backslash tr(w_p)) := q_0$
$Q_C := \{q_0\}$
while $\exists q' \in Q_C$ and $x' \in I$, such that $(q', x') \notin R$ **do**
    if $C(\omega) = q \neq \bot$, **then**   % If current state is known
                                     % move to unverified transition
        <u>Find</u> a shortest $\alpha = \alpha_1\alpha_2...\alpha_k$,
            s.t. for all i $(q_i, \alpha_i, q_{i+1}) \in V$, $q_1 = q$, and $x \in I$ s.t. $(q_{k+1}, x) \notin R$
        Apply $\alpha\downarrow I$, observe α
        $\omega := \omega\alpha$
        $\chi := \omega$
        Apply x, observe xo % observe transition
        $\sigma := xo$
        $\omega := \omega xo$
    else   % else use a previous known state
        <u>Find</u> the shortest γ, s.t. $C(\omega \backslash \gamma) \neq \bot$ % could be shorter than w_p
        $\chi := \omega \backslash \gamma$
        $\sigma := \gamma$
    end if
    $q := C(\chi)$ % here ω is unknown
    Choose $w \in W$, such that there is no $tr(w)$ s.t. $(q, \sigma, tr(w)) \in K$
    Apply w, observe $tr(w)$ % improve characterization of (q, σ)
    $\omega := \omega tr(w)$
    $K := K \cup \{(q, \sigma, tr(w))\}$
    if $\{w \in W \mid (q, \sigma, tr(w)) \in K\} = W$, **then**   % full characterization reached
        $C(\chi\sigma) := \{tr(w) \mid w \in W$ and $(q, \sigma, tr(w)) \in K\}$
        $Q_C := Q_C \cup \{C(\chi\sigma)\}$
        Update V, R, K and C
    end if
    if $C(\omega) = \bot$ **then**   % move to an identified state
        $(\omega, q', tr(w_p)) := L(\omega, W)$
        $C(\omega\backslash tr(w_p)) := q'$
        $Q_C := Q_C \cup \{q'\}$
        Update V, R, K and C
    end if
end while

Build the conjecture from Q_C and T.

The sets K, V (hence T) and R should be updated to reflect the changes in C. The update is done by applying the following rules as long as possible (fix point iterations with monotonic increase of the sets):

Rule 1   If $C(\beta) = q$, $C(\beta\alpha) = q'$, $\beta\alpha \leq \omega$, then $(q, \alpha, q') \in V$

Rule 2   If $C(\beta) = q$, $\beta\alpha \leq \omega$ and $(q, \alpha, q') \in V$ then $C(\beta\alpha) = q'$

Rule 3   If $(q, x, q') \in V$, for $x \in I$, then $(q, x) \in R$

Rule 4   If $C(\beta) = q$, $\beta\alpha\gamma \leq \omega$, $\alpha{\downarrow}I \in I \cup W$, $\gamma{\downarrow}I \in W$, then $(q, \alpha, \gamma) \in K$

Rule 5   If $\exists\alpha$ s.t. $\{w \in W \mid (q, \alpha, tr(w)) \in K\} = W$ then $\forall\beta\alpha \leq \omega$ s.t. $C(\beta) = q$, we have $C(\beta\alpha) = \{\gamma \mid (q, \alpha, \gamma) \in K\}$

Notice that although in this definition of updates we derive V and K sets to be consistent with their definitions, we do not need to add all elements to them. Typically, V is transitively closed, but we only need a transitive reduction of it. If $(q, \alpha, q') \in V$ and $(q', \beta, q'') \in V$ then in the implementation of the procedure we would not store $(q, \alpha\beta, q'')$ in V because we use V to find a shortest concatenation of sequences that would themselves be in V or to verify transitions (sequences of length 1).

4   Localizer Procedure

In our inference procedure, the main use of the localizer procedure is to ensure that when the BB is in an unknown state q, we can restart a test from a state q' of the BB for which we can be certain that we know all its traces for all sequences from the W-set, and thus we can identify state q' of the BB. Actually, we present a generalized procedure that can work with any set of sequences Z, where Z may not be a fully characterizing set, i.e., there could be non-equivalent states in the BB that are Z-equivalent. The localizer procedure will be defined recursively with increasing subsets Z of W.

For the design of this localizer procedure, we extend an idea that had already been investigated by Hennie [6]. The key idea is that since the number of states is finite and bounded by n, by repeatedly applying a given input sequence α we can observe at most n different output sequences. This implies that in the state reached applying n times α the BB must have reached a cycle, coming to one of the states visited after some α^i. But we do not know which one because different states could still have the same output response to α. The length of the cycle is itself bounded by n. As the proof will show, it is enough to repeat α another $n - 1$ times (so $2n - 1$ in total) in the worst case to identify the cycle and be able to know what would be the response from the BB to the $2n$-th application and all subsequent applications of α.

This means that after $2n - 1$ applications of α, we are in a state p and we can apply another input sequence β, and be sure that we know the response of p to both α and β. If $\{\alpha, \beta\}$ is a W-set, we can continue a test from a state p that has been fully characterized, or at least from $\delta(p, \beta)$ which is a well-defined state. Jumping to more than two sequences is a bit more elaborate, but it is ensured by the recursive definition of the localizer. Actually, we build embedded cycles.

We illustrate the above discussion on the example in Fig. 1.

This 3-state machine has no distinguishing sequence. However, states can be fully characterized by their traces for sequences from the set $W = \{a, b\}$. Suppose we start

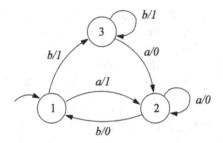

Fig. 1. An FSM to be inferred.

our experiment when the machine is in state 1 by sending an input a. We shall get an output 1. The localizer will repeatedly apply the input sequence a. The second and third outputs will be 0. Since we know the machine has no more than 3 states, after 3 applications of a, the fourth application will elicit an output which must be one of those previously seen, 0 or 1. In this case, it will be a 0. Now, since the last 3 outputs were 0s, we can be sure that the fifth application of a would elicit a 0. We can now apply a b, and we get 0 as output, since we were trapped in state 2. We know that just before applying the b, we were in a state that answers 0 to both a and b. Since we assume W to be a fully characterizing set, the state is distinguishable from all others. We shall call it the state $\{a0, b0\}$, which corresponds to state 2 in the example.

Note that at the end of the localizer procedure we are not in the state p that has been fully characterized, but past it: in the example of Fig. 1 we are in state 1 instead of 2, and more generally with $W = \{\alpha, \beta\}$ we are actually in $\delta(p, \beta)$. This will also be the case for our generalized localizer: at the end of the procedure, the BB will be in a state that follows the application of the last input sequence w_k of the Z set, and the state characterized with the set Z will be the state reached just before applying the last w_k sequence. This is not an issue because our inference procedure handles this situation. Note that this means that the sequence built by the localizer is not a homing sequence [9], although it could easily be adapted to provide a kind of homing sequence, modulo the fact that the states are initially unknown, as we discover state characterization while applying the localizer. To make a homing sequence, we would just have to add an empty sequence ε as the last sequence w_{k+1} of Z.

The localizer procedure is formulated for fixed alphabets I and O, and an assumed bound on the number of states in the black box n. The procedure uses a given sequence ω that has already been observed from the BB and has left it in an unknown state, and given a non-empty ordered set Z of input sequences. It returns an updated ω' trace (ω concatenated with the new inputs applied by the localizer and observed outputs), the set of traces for Z that can be confirmed as the traces of the state p reached just before the last w_k sequence of Z, and the trace suffix observed from the state p.

Localizer procedure
Signature $L: ((IO)^* \times (I^*)^+) \rightarrow ((IO)^* \times 2^{(IO)^*} \times (IO)^*)$

procedure $L(\omega, Z)$
if $|Z| = 1$, i.e., $Z = (w)$ **then**
    Apply w, observe $tr(w)$
    $\omega := \omega tr(w)$
    return $(\omega, \{tr(w)\}, tr(w))$
else let $Z = (w_1, \dots, w_k)$, $(w_1, \dots, w_{k-2}, w_{k-1}) = Z_1$, $(w_1, \dots, w_{k-2}, w_k) = Z_2$
    for i **from** 0 **to** $2n - 2$ **do**
        $(\omega', Tr(Z_1), \tau_i) := L(\omega, Z_1)$ % τ_i is $tr(w_{k-1})$
        $\omega := \omega'$
    end for
    Find greatest j, $0 \leq j \leq n - 1$ s.t. for all $m \in [0, n - 2]$ $\tau_{j+m} = \tau_{n+m}$
    $(\omega', Tr(Z_2), tr(w_k)) := L(\omega, Z_2)$
    return $(\omega', Tr(Z_2) \cup \{\tau_{j+n-1}\}, tr(w_k))$
end if

Note that if $k = 2$, the list $w_1, \dots, w_{k-2}$ is empty, hence $Z_1 = (w_1)$ and $Z_2 = (w_2)$.

In the **for** loop, we repeatedly apply the same localizer sequence $L(\omega, Z_1)$. We store in an array τ_i the trace observed for the last element of Z_1, i.e., $tr(w_{k-1})$. After the n-th application, we must have reached a cycle, where τ_{n+1} must be equal to some previous τ_i. But it could be equal to several τ_i therefore we must continue another $n - 1$ times to ensure that we have completed the cycle. In any case, after $2n - 1$ applications, even if the length of the cycle is unknown, since $\tau_{j+n-2} = \tau_{n+n-2}$ is in the cycle, applying w_{k-1} instead of w_k would have produced τ_{j+n-1}. Now we know what would be the answer of the state to w_{k-1} and we can apply w_k instead.

We illustrate the localizer procedure on our example in Fig. 1. We start from initial state 1, with $\omega = \varepsilon$ and $Z = (a, b)$. We have $Z_1 = (a)$ and $Z_2 = (b)$. Since the **for** loop is executed $2n - 1 = 5$ times, we apply $w_1 = a$ to BB 5 times and reach the 5th step of the trace. We get the trace $a1a0a0a0a0$, with $\tau_0 = a1$, $\tau_1 = a0$, $\tau_2 = a0$, $\tau_3 = a0$ and $\tau_4 = a0$. At this point, we recognize the cycle $\tau_2 = \tau_3$ and $\tau_3 = \tau_4$ ($j = 2$) and we know that if we apply a, we would get 0. Subsequently we apply $w_2 = b$ and get 0.

We identify the state $q_0 = \{a0, b0\}$ The result of the localizer procedure is thus $(a1a0a0a0a0b0, q_0 = \{a0, b0\}, b0)$.

The input sequence used by the localizer is a fixed sequence. In our small example, it is a^5b. For a machine with at most n states and $W = \{w_1, w_2\}$, the input sequence is $w_1^{2n-1}w_2$; with $W = \{w_1, w_2, w_3\}$, it becomes $(w_1^{2n-1}w_2)^{2n-1}(w_1^{2n-1}w_3)$, and with $W = \{w_1, w_2, w_3, w_4\}$, it becomes $[(w_1^{2n-1}w_2)^{2n-1}(w_1^{2n-1}w_3)]^{2n-1}(w_1^{2n-1}w_2)^{2n-1}(w_1^{2n-1}w_4)$ and so on.

5 Example of FSM Inference

We now illustrate the proposed method on the example in Fig. 1. As illustrated above, applying the localizer procedure allows us to identify a first state of the machine: $C(\omega \setminus b0) = q_0 = \{a0, b0\}$. Thus, the prefix obtained in the 5th step is labelled by q_0. C is updated in the third line of the inference procedure.

We then enter the main **while** loop in the inference procedure. As the last state of ω (6th step in the trace) is not yet labelled we proceed to the else part of the first **if** statement. Then $\gamma = b0$, $\chi = a1a0a0a0a0$ and $\sigma = b0$.

After the first **if** statement, $q = q_0$, K is empty, and we choose $w = a$. We apply a, observe $a1$ and arrive at the 7th step. We get $K = \{(q_0, b0, a1)\}$, $V = R = \varnothing$.

$$1 \xrightarrow{a/1} 2 \xrightarrow{a/0} 2 \xrightarrow{a/0} 2 \xrightarrow{a/0} 2 \xrightarrow{a/0} 2 \xrightarrow{b/0} 1 \xrightarrow{a/1} 2$$
$$_0 \qquad _1 \qquad _2 \qquad _3 \qquad _4 \qquad _5 \qquad _6 \qquad _7$$
$$q0=\{a0,b0\}$$

Since the condition of the second **if** statement is false, we proceed with the third **if** statement, which is true. We apply again the localizer procedure, and label the state after $a0a0a0a0a0$ (12th step) with q_0: $C(12) = q_0$. We then restart the **while** loop.

We enter the **else** part of the **if** statement, with $\gamma = \sigma = b0$. Then $q = q_0$, and we choose $w = b$. We apply b, observe $b1$ and arrive at the 14th step. We get $K = \{(q_0, b0, a1), (q_0, b0, b1)\}$.

The condition of the second **if** statement is now true, we have thus identified a new state $q_1 = \{a1, b1\}$ and $C(13) = q_1$. Then $V = \{(q_0, b0, q_1)\}$, $R = \{(q_0, b)\}$ and $C(6) = q_1$. Thus $K = \{(q_0, b0, a1), (q_0, b0, b1), (q_1, a1, a0)\}$.

$$2 \xrightarrow{a/0} 2 \xrightarrow{a/0} 2 \xrightarrow{a/0} 2 \xrightarrow{a/0} 2 \xrightarrow{a/0} 2 \xrightarrow{b/0} 1 \xrightarrow{b/1} 3$$
$$_7 \qquad _8 \qquad _9 \qquad _{10} \qquad _{11} \qquad _{12} \qquad _{13} \qquad _{14}$$
$$q0 \quad q1=\{a1,b1\}$$

We now execute the third **if** statement: we apply the localizer procedure and arrive at the 20th step. $C(19) = q_0$ and $C(20) = q_1$. K is unchanged. We then restart the **while** loop. Since the last (20th) step is now labelled, we enter the **then** part of the first **if** statement. $\alpha = \varepsilon$ and we choose $x = a$. We apply a, observe $a1$ and arrive at step 21. We have $\sigma = a1$. Now $q = q_1$, and we choose $w = b$. We apply b, observe $b0$ and arrive at step 22. We update $K = \{(q_0, b0, a1), (q_0, b0, b1), (q_1, a1, a0), (q_1, a1, b0)\}$.

Since the condition of the second **if** statement is true, we identify $C(21) = q_0 = \{a0, b0\}$. We update V, R, C and K: $V = \{(q_0, b0, q_1), (q_1, a1, q_0)\}$, $R = \{(q_0, b), (q_1, a)\}$, $C(7) = q_0$, $C(22) = q_1$, $K = \{(q_0, b0, a1), (q_0, b0, b1), (q_1, a1, a0), (q_1, a1, b0), (q_0, a0, a0), (q_1, b1, a0)\}$. The trace at the last step (22) is labelled, and the condition of the third **if** statement is false.

$$3 \xrightarrow{a/0} 2 \xrightarrow{a/0} 2 \xrightarrow{a/0} 2 \xrightarrow{a/0} 2 \xrightarrow{a/0} 2 \xrightarrow{b/0} 1 \xrightarrow{a/1} 2 \xrightarrow{b/0} 1$$

| 14 | 15 | 16 | 17 | 18 | 19 | 20 | 21 | 22 |

$q0$ $q1$ $q0$

We then restart the **while** loop, which allows us to identify a new state $q_2 = \{a0, b1\}$ and label $C(23) = q_2$. We apply the localizer procedure and arrive at step 30. $C(29) = q_0$, $C(30) = q_1$. At this point, $V = \{(q_0, b0, q_1), (q_1, a1, q_0), (q_1, b1, q_2), (q_2, b1a0a0a0a0a0, q_0)\}$, $K = \{(q_0, b0, a1), (q_0, b0, b1), (q_1, a1, a0), (q_1, a1, b0), (q_0, a0, a0), (q_1, b1, a0), (q_1, b1, b1), (q_2, b1, a0)\}$, $R = \{(q_0, b), (q_1, a), (q_1, b)\}$ and $C(14) = q_2$.

$$2 \xrightarrow{b/1} 3 \xrightarrow{b/1} 3 \xrightarrow{a/0} 2 \xrightarrow{a/0} 2 \xrightarrow{a/0} 2 \xrightarrow{a/0} 2 \xrightarrow{a/0} 2 \xrightarrow{b/0} 1$$

| 22 | 23 | 24 | 25 | 26 | 27 | 28 | 29 | 30 |

$q1$ $q2$ $q0$ $q1$

We restart the **while** loop. As the last step (30) is labelled, we enter the **then** part of the first **if** statement. As all transitions from q_1 are now known, we must apply a transfer sequence to move to an unverified transition. We choose to go to q_0 with $\alpha = a1$ and $x = a$. We apply a, observe $a1$, apply a again, observe $a0$ and arrive at step 32. $\sigma = a0$.

We choose $w = b$, apply b, observe $b0$, arrive at step 33 and add $(q_0, a0, b0)$ to K. The condition of the second **if** statement is true, we have $C(32) = q_0$ and we add $(q_0, a0, q_0)$ to V. Now $R = \{(q_0, b), (q_1, a), (q_1, b), (q_0, a)\}$, $C(7) = C(7) = \ldots = C(11) = q_0$, $C(33) = q_1$.

After applying the **while** loop two more times, we obtain the trace below, with $V = \{(q_0, b0, q_1), (q_1, a1, q_0), (q_1, b1, q_2), (q_0, a0, q_0), (q_2, a0, q_0), (q_2, b1, q_2)\}$ and $R = \{(q_0, b), (q_1, a), (q_1, b), (q_0, a), (q_2, a), (q_2, b)\}$. All transitions are known and $C(38) = q_2$.

$$1 \xrightarrow{a/1} 2 \xrightarrow{a/0} 2 \xrightarrow{b/0} 1 \xrightarrow{b/1} 3 \xrightarrow{a/0} 2 \xrightarrow{b/0} 1 \xrightarrow{b/1} 3 \xrightarrow{b/1} 3$$

| 30 | 31 | 32 | 33 | 34 | 35 | 36 | 37 | 38 |

$q1$ $q0$ $q0$ $q1$ $q2$ $q0$ $q1$ $q2$ $q2$

We now exit from the **while** loop and V gives us the inferred finite state machine, which is isomorphic to the FSM in Fig. 1.

6 Proofs and Complexity

6.1 Proof of Localizer

The key theorem for our approach states that the localizer will ensure that the BB reached (before the application of the last sequence from W) a state that can be labelled with the mapping returned by the localizer.

Theorem 1. When $Z = W$, from any starting state, the localizer will return (ω', X, β) such that $C(\omega' \setminus \beta) = X$ and $X \downarrow I = W$.

To prove this theorem, we first introduce notations and two lemmas.

Let IL be the input projection of a trace added by a localizer $L(\omega, Z)$, $Z = (w_1, \ldots, w_k)$ returning ω' as the first element, i.e., $\omega' \downarrow I = \omega \downarrow I = IL(w_1, \ldots, w_k)$. We denote $P = IL \setminus w_k$, thus, $IL(w_1, \ldots, w_k) = P(w_1, \ldots, w_{k-1}) w_k$.

Lemma 1. For all $k \geq 1$, we have that $P(w_1, \ldots, w_k) = [P(w_1, \ldots, w_{k-1}) w_k]^{2n-1} P(w_1, \ldots, w_{k-1})$.

Proof. This lemma is proved by induction from $k = 1$ for P, accordingly we start with $IL(w_1, w_2)$. In the loop, $Z_1 = (w_1)$ and $Z_2 = (w_2)$ hence we apply w_1^{2n-1} then w_2. So $IL(w_1, w_2) = w_1^{2n-1}w_2$, $P(w_1) = w_1^{2n-1}$ and $P(w_1, w_0)$ is an empty sequence by definition of IL. Thus indeed $P(w_1) = [P(w_1, w_0) w_1]^{2n-1} P(w_1, w_0)$.

Assuming it is true for some $k \geq 1$, then by definition of P we have:
$IL(w_1, \ldots, w_{k+2}) = P(w_1, \ldots, w_{k+1}) w_{k+2}$.

And by the structure of the localizer, we have:
$IL(w_1, \ldots, w_{k+2}) = IL(w_1, \ldots, w_{k+1})^{2n-1} IL(w_1, \ldots, w_k, w_{k+2}) = ([P(w_1, \ldots, w_k)w_{k+1}]^{2n-1} P(w_1, \ldots, w_k)w_{k+2}$.

Using the induction hypothesis, we get:
$P(w_1, \ldots, w_{k+1}) = = ([P(w_1, \ldots, w_k)w_{k+1}]^{2n-1} P(w_1, \ldots, w_k)$. QED.

Lemma 2. Let ω' be a trace returned by the localizer for $Z = (w_1, \ldots, w_k)$ and $B = (S, s_0, I, O, \delta, \lambda)$, then for all $w \in Z$, $\lambda(s, w) = tr(w) \downarrow O$, where $s = \delta(s_0, \omega' \setminus tr(w_k) \downarrow I)$.

Proof. We prove this by induction on $|Z|$.

For $|Z| = 1$, $tr(w)$ is the β just observed on applying w at the end of ω which was $\omega' \setminus \beta$; thus $\lambda(s, w) = \beta \downarrow O = tr(w) \downarrow O$.

Let us assume the property holds for $|Z| = k - 1 \geq 1$. Since Z_2 has $k - 1$ elements, we already have for all $w \in Z_2$, $\lambda(s, w) = tr(w) \downarrow O$ (see how s is defined in Lemma 2). The only thing which we have to prove is that $\lambda(s, w_{k-1}) = tr(w_{k-1}) \downarrow O = \tau_{j+n-1} \downarrow O$. Actually, $(\omega' \setminus tr(w_k)) \downarrow I = (\omega \downarrow I).P(w_1, \ldots, w_{k-1})$ by definition of P. Let us denote $M = P(w_1, \ldots, w_{k-2})$, and $q = \delta(s_0, \omega \downarrow I)$. Using Lemma 1, we have $s = \delta(q, P(w_1, \ldots, w_{k-1})) = \delta(q, [Mw_{k-1}]^{2n-1}M) = \delta(q, M[w_{k-1}M]^{2n-1})$. Let $q_i = \delta(q, M[w_{k-1}M]^i)$, and $\lambda_i = \lambda(q_i, w_{k-1})$ for $i \in [0, 2n - 1]$. Note that $s = q_{2n-1}$ and according to the notations of the algorithm, for all $i \in [0, 2n - 2]$ $\lambda_i = \tau_i \downarrow O$. Since there are at most n distinct states, and we repeat the sequence $w_{k-1}M$, q_n must be equal to one of the $q_{j'}$ for some $j' < n$. Then, for all $m \in [0, n - 1]$, $\lambda_{j'+m} = \lambda_{n+m}$. Hence there is at least one such j, as required by the algorithm.

- If $q_n = q_p$ for some $p > 0$, then the length of the cycle is $n - 1$ at most and for any $j < n$ such that for all $m \in [0, n - 2]$, $\lambda_{j+m} = \lambda_{n+m}$ then we have: $\lambda_{j+n-1} = \lambda_{n+n-1} = \lambda(s, w_{k-1})$.
- If the greatest j is 0, this means there is no cycle of output of length less than n, then $q_n = q$, $q_n = q_0$ and $s = q_{2n-1} = q_{n-1}$ and $\lambda(s, w_{k-1}) = \lambda_{j+n-1}$ since $j = 0$.
- So in both cases we have $\lambda(s, w_{k-1}) = \lambda_{j+n-1} = \tau_{j+n-1} \downarrow O$.

QED.

It may be worth mentioning that taking the largest j means we identify the shortest cycle of outputs. The cycle of states entered by the implementation will have a length that is divisible by $n-j$: with the notation of the proof, $n - j$ divides $n - j'$.

We can now proceed to the proof of the Theorem 1. Recall that we denote states of the BB by their $Tr(W)$.

Actually, in all cases, $Tr(X)\downarrow I = Z$. This directly follows from the recursive definition: it holds for a singleton, and when we compute Tr for $(w_1, \ldots, w_k)$ we produce a set of traces that adds some $tr(w_{k-1})$ thus the set of traces is computed on $Z_2 = (w_1, \ldots, w_{k-2}, w_k)$. If $Z = W$ then by Lemma 2, the definition of C and the fact that C is revealing, we have $C(\omega' \setminus tr(w_k)) = X$ and $X\downarrow I = W$. QED.

6.2 Proof of the Method

To prove the correctness of the method we need to demonstrate that the mappings correspond to the states of the BB. We will use the following theorem.

Theorem 2. If $q \in Q_C$ then $\exists p \in P$ such that $q \leftrightarrow p$.

This theorem follows from the definitions of C and Q_C. The proof of the method itself (captured by Theorem 3) proceeds in several steps following the structure of the algorithm. In particular we must prove that all the steps that rely on an existence ("find", "choose") are well defined and will find an element, and we show that the algorithm increases monotonically the set of known states and transitions, and terminates when a conjecture can be built which is equivalent to the FSM $B = (P, p_0, I, O, \delta, \lambda)$.

1. On every entry in the **while** loop, either we are in a known state, i.e. the BB is in a state p such that $C(\omega) = q \leftrightarrow p$ or we are at the end of a localizer, i.e., $C(\omega \setminus tr(w_p))$ is defined (a known state). This is trivial on the first entry in the loop, since we just applied the localizer and did not move in the BB. And at the end of a cycle in the loop, we reach either after the case $C(\omega) = \bot$, in which case we reapply the localizer and are again at the end of it, or $C(\omega)$ is defined.

2. Find a shortest α: since we entered the while loop, we know that $\exists q' \in Q_\omega$ and $x \in I$, such that $(q', x) \notin R$. Moreover, we are in a state q. Then either $\exists x' \in I$, such that $(q, x') \notin R$, and we just have to pick $\alpha = \varepsilon$; or we know all successors of q. In that case, we build the connected graph reachable from q through verified transitions: if one of them has an unverified transition, we pick the one closest to q, i.e., that yields the shortest α. Otherwise, this would imply that there is a $q' \in Q_C$ such that there is a prefix $\exists \sigma \le \omega$, $C(\sigma) = q'$ which would be distinct from all the successor states of q that constitute a strongly connected component. Since all successor states and this state q' are all paired (through the $\leftrightarrow$ relation) to states of the BB (by Theorem 2), this would contradict the assumption that the BB is strongly connected.

3. "Else find the shortest γ". In this else branch, we are in the case where $C(\omega) = \bot$. The existence of γ follows from 1: $\gamma = w_p$ in this case.

4. "Choose w": this comes one line after the "end if". If we followed the "else" branch, state $C(\chi\sigma) \notin dom(C)$ and there is a w for which $(q, \sigma, tr(w)) \notin K$. If we followed the "then" branch, then $(q_{k+1}, x) \notin R$ and $\sigma := xo$ and by definition of R, we again have a w.

5. Progress: each loop iteration adds an element to K (by the structure of the loop), either at the end of a transition (xo) or at the end of a localizer.

6. Termination: there is a finite number of transitions in the BB (hence in the set Q_C by Theorem 2), each one is followed by a finite number of traces from the (finite)

set W. Hence the potential number of elements in K is finite, and the process will terminate.

7. Building the conjecture: based on Theorem 2, we can build a conjecture that is isomorphic to the BB by connecting all the transitions of R when the algorithm terminates.

Theorem 3. The inference procedure terminates and yields a conjecture that is isomorphic to the minimal FSM modelling the BB.

6.3   Complexity

As in all testing procedures, interacting with the system under test contributes mostly to the cost. Therefore we analyse the worst case complexity as the length (number of inputs) of the test sequence created by the procedure. The key element is the length of the localizer. Let L be the length of $L(\omega, W)$ and $|w_i|$ the length of an element of W. As in the notations of the algorithm, $p = |W|$ is the number of elements of the characterization set, n is the number of states, and f is the number of inputs (fan-out). Thus, L can be computed as follows.

$$L = \big(((|w_1|) \times (2n - 1) + |w_2|) \times (2n - 1) + \ldots + |w_{p-1}|\big)$$
$$\times (2n - 1) + \big((|w_1|)\ldots \times (2n - 1) + |w_{p-2}|\big) + |w_p|.$$

$O(L) = |w1|\ (2n{-}1)p$ since we can assume that for any i, we have $|wi| < $ n: it is known that in a complete FSM with n states, any two states can be distinguished by a sequence of length no more than n. Thus, the length of the localizer is polynomial in n and exponential in p.

We apply the localizer at most once for each execution of the loop. The loop itself adds at least one element to K, thus the number of iterations of the loop is $n(f + p)$ p. Within the loop, the extension to ω would be $U = \mathbf{max}(|\alpha| + 1 + |w|, |\gamma| + |w|)$. $|\gamma| + |w|$ is bounded by $2n$, and $|\alpha|$ is bounded by n^2. Then the overall complexity would be $L + n$ $(f + p)p\ (L + U)$ bounded by $(n(f + p)p + 1)(L + n^2 + n + 1)$. As a coarse bound, we have $(n(f + p)p + 1)(n(2n - 1)^p + n^2 + n + 1)$ which is $O(p(f + p)\ 2^p n^{p+2})$, again polynomial in n and exponential in p.

Of course, this is a coarse upper bound for a worst-case complexity, and it is unsure it could be reached or even approached. As can be seen from the example, as soon as states and transitions are added to Q and V, the number of uses of the localizer decreases. Given the structure of the localizer, the sequences in W would be ordered by increasing length. And the localizer could be shortened because we may recognize cycles before reaching $2n - 1$ iterations.

Our experiments with hundreds of randomly generated machines show that for $n = 15, f = 10$, inference is achieved in around 10^4 steps for $p = 2$ (around 7000 when $|w_1| = 1$, and around 15000 when $|w_1| = 2$), i.e., around 500 times (3 orders of magnitude) less than the theoretical bound. To put this in perspective, we had initially tried classical inference methods [12, 16] on web applications, where a reset would typically take more than 1 min (restarting a virtual machine and restoring data configuration), whereas interacting with it over a local network would take around 1 ms per I/O pair. In such typical contexts, an inference sequence of length 10^5 would require no more time than a single reset.

7 Discussion

Our method assumes we know an upper bound n on the number of states of the BB and a characterization set W for it. We now discuss the impact of these assumptions. First let us remark that the localizer does not assume that W is characterizing. It can work with any set Z and just ensures that we characterize a state reached w.r.t. Z-equivalence [12]. However, an incorrect value for n could disrupt the localizer.

Actually, if either n or W is wrong (i.e., the assumptions for the BB are not satisfied), then two cases can occur:

1. The inference procedure runs to the end, but produces an FSM that is not isomorphic to a model of the BB.
2. The inference procedure detects an inconsistency (or fails to converge).

In the first case, we can either consider that the inference procedure provides a model that is approximate, and consistent with all observations: it will have produced an unrefined model of the BB that may be enough for the intended use of the model. Alternatively, we could now use the inferred model to check whether the BB conforms to this model, by some method of conformance testing, e.g., randomly walking through the model until we find a discrepancy or conclude on some level of confidence for the approximated model.

In the second case, let us first consider the case where n was an incorrect bound (too low), and this impacts the localizer. The only problem that can occur there is in the line "find the greatest j". We may fail to recognize a cycle in $2n - 1$ iterations. This can be easily addressed: first, we would continue iterating the **for** loop until we spot such an output cycle; then, we increase the value of n accordingly; at this point, we restart the whole inference procedure, because we cannot trust the previous equivalence of states.

Let us now consider the case where W would not be characterizing. This will not create any problem in the localizer, but in the main procedure. When we reapply a verified sequence α to go to a given state q_{k+1} or when we reapply an input x we may get a different output. This implies that the sequence we just applied distinguishes two states that we thought were equivalent. That sequence, or a part of it (up to the first divergence) could be added to W.

This can also be related to the initial assumption about W. The main issue is about how a characterizing set for a black box can be known. One possibility could be that we had such a set for a previous version of an implementation, and we take it as input of the method when we need to infer an updated implementation. It may also be possible to formulate domain-specific heuristics to identify candidate characterization sets.

8 Conclusion

We have presented a method that can infer a model of a non-resettable black box FSM for which we know an upper bound n on the number of states and a characterizing set W. The method is polynomial in n; the degree of the polynomial is bounded by the cardinality of W. It has now been implemented, and we are investigating its effectiveness under various settings. We are in particular interested in assessing the average complexity for various cases of characterization sets.

It might also be interesting to see how the algorithm proposed here could benefit from the improvements that have been proposed in the related problem of conformance testing for non-resettable machines. As mentioned in several parts of the paper, the algorithm lends itself to optimizations that could reduce the length of the sequence of inputs. In particular, the number of iterations in the localizer could be reduced when short cycles are recognized.

Another direction for research is on relaxing the assumptions, and providing adaptive heuristics. One direction could be to work towards inference of quotients [12].

Acknowledgments. The authors acknowledge the work of Laurent Anadon, an intern from Ecole Polytechnique with whom we started this problem on the DS case. The implementation of the algorithm was carried out by Nicolas Brémond, an intern from Enseirb-Matmeca. A. Simao had financial support of Brazilian Funding Agencies, FAPESP and CNPq. A. Petrenko acknowledges financial support of NSERC via Discovery grant RGPIN/194381-2012.

References

1. Aarts, F., Jonsson, B., Uijen, J.: Generating models of infinite-state communication protocols using regular inference with abstraction. In: Petrenko, A., Simão, A., Maldonado, J.C. (eds.) ICTSS 2010. LNCS, vol. 6435, pp. 188–204. Springer, Heidelberg (2010)
2. Ammons, G., Bodik, R., Larus, J.: Mining specifications. In: POPL 2002, pp. 4–16 (2002)
3. Angluin, D.: Learning regular sets from queries and counterexamples. Inf. Comput. **2**, 87–106 (1987)
4. Bertolino, A., Inverardi, P., Pelliccione, P., Tivoli, M.: Automatic synthesis of behavior protocols for composable web-services. In: ESEC/FSE 2009, pp. 141–150 (2009)
5. Corbett, J.C., Dwyer, M.B., Hatcliff, J., Laubach, S., Pasareanu, C.S., Robby, Zheng, H.: Bandera: extracting finite-state models from Java source code. In: 22nd ICSE, pp. 439–448 (2000)
6. Hennie, F.C.: Fault-detecting experiments for sequential circuits. In: Proceedings of Fifth Annual Symposium On Circuit Theory and Logical Design, pp. 95–110 (1965)
7. Irfan, M.N., Oriat, C., Groz, R.: Angluin style finite state machine inference with non-optimal counterexamples. In: Workshop on Model Inference In Testing 2010, ISSTA, 11–19 (2010)
8. Jourdan, G.V., Ural, H., Yenigün, H.: Reduced checking sequences using unreliable reset. Inf. Process. Lett. **115**(5), 532–535 (2015)
9. Lee, D., Yannakakis, M.: Principles and methods of testing finite state machines - a survey. Proc. IEEE **84**, 1090–1123 (1996)

10. Meinke, K.: CGE: a sequential learning algorithm for Mealy automata. In: Sempere, J.M., García, P. (eds.) ICGI 2010. LNCS, vol. 6339, pp. 148–162. Springer, Heidelberg (2010)
11. Mihancea, P.F., Minea, M.: jModex: model extraction for verifying security properties of web applications. In: CSMR-WCRE, pp. 450–453 (2014)
12. Petrenko, A., Li, K., Groz, R., Hossen, K., Oriat, C.: Inferring approximated models for systems engineering. In: HASE 2014, pp 249–253 (2014)
13. Porto, F.R., Endo, A.T., Simao, A.: Generation of checking sequences using identification sets. In: Groves, L., Sun, J. (eds.) ICFEM 2013. LNCS, vol. 8144, pp. 115–130. Springer, Heidelberg (2013)
14. Rezaki, A., Ural, H.: Construction of checking sequences based on characterization sets. Comput. Commun. **18**(12), 911–920 (1995)
15. Rivest, R.L., Schapire, R.E.: Inference of finite automata using homing sequences. In: Hanson, S.J., Remmele, W., Rivest, R.L. (eds.) Machine Learning: From Theory to Applications. LNCS, vol. 661, pp. 51–73. Springer, Heidelberg (1993)
16. Shahbaz, M., Groz, R.: Inferring Mealy machines. In: Cavalcanti, A., Dams, D.R. (eds.) FM 2009. LNCS, vol. 5850, pp. 207–222. Springer, Heidelberg (2009)
17. Steffen, B., Howar, F., Merten, M.: Introduction to active automata learning from a practical perspective. In: Bernardo, M., Issarny, V. (eds.) SFM 2011. LNCS, vol. 6659, pp. 256–296. Springer, Heidelberg (2011)
18. Vasilevskii, M.P.: Failure diagnosis of automata. Cybernetics **9**, 653–665 (1973)

mu2: A Refactoring-Based Mutation Testing Framework for Erlang

Ramsay Taylor[✉] and John Derrick

Department of Computer Science, The University of Sheffield, Sheffield, UK
r.g.taylor@sheffield.ac.uk

Abstract. We present a mutation testing framework for the Erlang functional programming language. Mutation testing evaluates a test set by mutating the original System Under Test (SUT) and measuring the test set's ability to detect the change. Designing mutation operators can be difficult, since they must modify the original program in a way that is both semantically significant, and a realistic simulation of a potential fault (either a fault with the system in its real context, or a common programmer error). The principal contribution of this work is the *mu2* framework, which leverages the Wrangler refactoring API to allow users to specify their own mutation operators. The framework makes it possible to quickly and clearly define mutation operators that can have complex and subtle effects on the SUT. This allows users to define domain-specific operators that can simulate faults that are of particular relevance to their project, rather than relying on standard operators. The mutation testing framework was evaluated in an industrial setting and compared to code coverage test adequacy metrics. It was found to be a valuable compliment to code coverage techniques, since it was able to uncover additional testing limitations that could not be easily identified by coverage alone.

1 Introduction

Testing is a vital component of any software development process, and often accounts for a large portion of the development effort. The purpose of testing is to provide assurance that the software functions correctly. However, as software projects expand, the size and complexity of the test sets also expand. This can create a new requirement to provide assurance of the "correct functioning" of the test set, i.e. that the test set is adequately assessing the software functionality.

Although measures such as code coverage provide some information about a test set's scope, they may not provide an accurate measure of a test set's ability to detect faults [8]. Mutation testing [10] provides an alternative approach, which has been shown to be able to identify limitations of test sets that could not be identified even with advanced coverage metrics such as MC/DC [4]. Mutation testing is a testing methodology which inserts deliberate faults into the System Under Test (SUT) to generate *mutants* of the program. The test set to be evaluated is run on each of these mutants. Since the tests were designed to evaluate the operation of the correct program they should report failure when

© IFIP International Federation for Information Processing 2015
K. El-Fakih et al. (Eds.): ICTSS 2015, LNCS 9447, pp. 178–193, 2015.
DOI: 10.1007/978-3-319-25945-1_11

run on the mutant. The mutation testing terminology is that the tests "kill" the mutants. Those mutants that are not killed are either *semantically equivalent* to the original program — that is, although they will have undergone a syntactic change, they will have identical behaviour to the original — or they identify a class of fault that the test set is not adequately identifying. The percentage of mutants killed provides a numeric metric for the effectiveness of the test set.

Mutation testing has been applied successfully to various imperative languages, such as Java, C, and Ada [4,7,11,14]. Simple, random changes to the syntax of the source files can produce many thousands of mutants easily, but a very high proportion will simply not compile, and many more will be semantically equivalent. An improvement over simple mutation testing is provided by first parsing the source file and then applying mutation operators to the parsed form — changing the semantics of the program directly — before re-rendering the program to a source code file.

It is not practical to seed every possible fault into a program and measure a test set's ability to detect these, so it is important that the mutants generated are in some way representative of a broader class of system faults. In this case a test set's ability to identify a particular deliberate fault provides good evidence that the test set is well written with respect to this class of fault or this particular section of the system. This provides some assurance that it would also identify other faults if they were present. Given this, it is important that the faults that are seeded in the mutants are representative of faults that are either likely or significant to the system under test. Consequently, while some general mutation operators are useful and provide a baseline measure of the quality of a test set, a principle objective of this work was to allow the development of domain-specific mutation operators for particular use cases. Specifically, we provide:

- A framework that allows the rapid development of semantically-rich mutation operators for specific domains
- Integration of mutation testing with the Erlang ecosystem and automation of a mutation testing workflow for Erlang modules
- An evaluation of the mutation testing framework with an industrial partner that demonstrates mutations testing's value, but also how it can be used as a *compliment* to other test adequacy metrics

The paper is structured as follows: Sect. 2 contains some background on Erlang and mutation testing. It also describes the process of applying mutation testing to the kinds of test suites common in Erlang. Section 3 describes the *mu2* framework that implements and automates that application of mutation testing to Erlang. Section 4 details our refactoring-based system for defining mutation operators that allows semantically rich operators to be developed rapidly. Section 5 documents the evaluation study carried out with Interoud Innovation. Finally, Sect. 6 concludes.

2   Background

2.1   Erlang

Erlang [1,2,15] is a programming language originally developed at Ericsson for use in their telecoms infrastructure products. It is now available as open source software, and used in a wide variety of companies both large and small. As a language it is declarative and uses several components of the functional programming paradigm, such as pattern matching and extensive use of recursion.

```
-module(abiftest).
-export([dv/2]).

dv(A,B) ->
    if (A == 0) and (B > 4) ->
            B;
       true ->
            B / A
    end.
```

Fig. 1. The *abiftest* erlang module

An Erlang module contains a number of functions, each of which is defined by a series of patterns starting with a name, a set of parameters, the arrow symbol ->, the function definition, and ends with a full stop. For example, the abiftest module in Fig. 1 contains just one function, dv, which takes two numbers A and B and divides B by A unless some conditions hold. Functions can have multiple patterns, with separate patterns separated by semicolons and the final pattern terminated with a full stop. The same syntax extends to internal decisions, such as the if statement in Fig. 1, or case statements that match structural patterns over values. Patterns are matched in order with the first matching pattern being applied — hence the if statement having true as the final pattern, since this will always match and so functions like an else or otherwise in other languages.

Variable names begin with capital letters or the underscore character (e.g. Var, _S), whilst lower case letters indicate an "atom" value (conceptually a user defined keyword, e.g. lock, unlock). Tuples are contained in curly brackets ({lock, S}), lists in square brackets ([a,b,c]). Strings are treated as lists but can be presented in double quotation marks. Erlang is an interpreted language and so the failure of the interpreter to find a matching pattern for a particular function application is reported at runtime. There is an exception throwing model for error handling, which allows pattern matching over the types of exceptions caught.

Erlang also features a process-oriented distributed programming model that uses asynchronous communication channels. Messages sent from one process to another accumulate in the receiver's message queue. The receive construct allows the process to pattern match over the incoming messages. The first message is compared to the patterns and, if it matches any one, then the relevant code is executed. In the event that the first message in the queue does not match any of the patterns in the current `receive` construct, then the second message in the queue is compared, and so on until a message matches. In this way it is possible for an Erlang process to skip some messages and handle particular message patterns with higher or lower priority. In the event that no message matches the current patterns the process with block until either a message arrives that does match, or a time limit (specified with the `timeout` pattern) is reached.

There is a large range of testing frameworks and support for Erlang. Conventional unit testing is often carried out with the Eunit [5] framework, but there is considerable use made of more advanced test generation and property-based testing using the Erlang QuickCheck system [3].

2.2   Mutation Testing

The objectives of any test adequacy metric are:

- Give a general quality metric for the test set
- Identify specific weaknesses of the test set
- Give constructive feedback that guides a user to improve the test set and address the weaknesses

Mutation testing — first described in [10] — seeks to evaluate test sets by simulating faults in a software system and measuring the test set's ability to identify the faults. Standard mutation testing makes a modification to the software's source code to produce a 'mutant'. The mutant code is compiled and then tested using the test suite. If the mutant fails the test suite, such a mutant is referred to as 'killed', if not then it is 'alive'. Where a mutant remains alive it must be inspected to determine whether the mutation actually produced a functional change. In some cases the mutations to the source code have no effect on the semantics - changing the name of an unused variable, for example.

For a non-trivial program, it is not realistic to explore all possible mutations. This is why one would usually focus on those that seem 'representative' of the defects a program may contain. For example, a typical hypothesis here is of a 'competent programmer' who may introduce an occasional error (such as in a form of a comparison operator the wrong way around). In this case, a good test suite is the one that kills all single-comparison mutants.

For example, consider the simple test set given in Fig. 2, which tests the *abiftest* module from Fig. 1. The *abiftest* module passes all these tests, however, it contains a defect that is not identified by this test set. Specifically: the `dv` function can produce a divide by zero error if it is called in such a way that the first `if` decision is false but A contains the value 0. Because the decision is a conjunction this can be triggered by a test in which A is equal to 0, but B is less than 5. This is not covered by any of these test cases.

Mutation testing assumes that all tests pass for the original source file. For the test results produced for each mutant, if any of the tests has failed then

```
-module(abiftest_tests).

-include_lib("eunit/include/eunit.hrl").

zero_test() ->
        ?assert(abiftest:dv(5,0) == 0.0).
one_test() ->
        ?assert(abiftest:dv(1,5) == 5.0).
two_test() ->
        ?assert(abiftest:dv(2,5) == 2.5).
two_twos_test() ->
        ?assert(abiftest:dv(2,2) == 1.0).
five_test() ->
        ?assert(abiftest:dv(5,5) == 1.0).
```

Fig. 2. A test set for *abiftest*

the test suite was able to identify the change. This is referred to as *killing* the mutant. If all the tests pass, then the change was not detected and the mutant remains *alive*. The count of *killed* vs *alive* mutants gives a numerical assessment of the fault identification power of the test suite, which meets the requirement for a general quality metric.

Reviewing the specific mutants that remained alive can give much more detailed information about the weaknesses of the test set. That a particular change went unnoticed by the test set implies that the section of the program is not adequately tested. This is the primary reason why the *mu2* framework produces separate mutant files with only one mutation in each file, since this allows clear identification of the specific change that was not detected. This detail about each undetected mutation provides the required identification of specific weaknesses of the test set, and the fact that it is tied directly to the code provides immediate guidance on the areas of the testing to improve.

3   The *mu2* Framework

Overview. We have developed the *mu2* framework to automate and simplify the process described in Sect. 2.2, but also to allow the definition of domain-specific mutation operators in an efficient way.

To support mutation testing the source file of the program is parsed and analysed, and possible mutations identified. Each mutant is produced by applying one mutation operator to one point in the program. This allows the mutation testing results to identify and characterise specific weaknesses of the test suite in both particular areas of the program and particular styles of fault. To make the mutation testing efficient it is preferable to first identify all the possible mutations, and then select mutations from the list to produce mutants, thus preventing the creation of multiple mutants with identical mutations.

Mutation operators are defined as a triple that includes a name, a function to identify applicable parts of the program, and a function to apply the change. The detailed structure of mutation operators is covered in Sect. 4. By automating the application of mutation operators and the generation and collation of mutants, *mu2* allows a user to concentrate their efforts on developing innovative and rich mutation operators that reflect the specific faults they want to simulate, and against which they want to evaluate their test suite.

Mutant Generation. The *mu2* tool[1] takes as input an Erlang source file and a set of mutation operators. The source file is parsed and all of the possible applications of each of the mutation operators are enumerated. Mutants are then generated by selecting from the possible applications and producing a new Erlang source file with the mutation applied and a header comment added to describe the type and location of the mutation. The result is a folder containing as many mutant files as requested — up to the number of possible mutation applications. The test suite can then be run against each of these modules and the pass or fail status recorded.

The *mu2* module provides the *generate* function to produce mutants. It can take parameters to specify a particular subset of available operators, or a limited number of mutants, but in its simplest form it takes the source file and an output folder:

```
Eshell V6.0  (abort with ^G)
1> mu2:generate("abiftest.erl","mutants").
Checking applicability of plus_to_minus, 98 more to try...
The current file under checking is:
"abiftest.erl"
Checking applicability of plus_to_mul, 97 more to try...
The current file under checking is:
"abiftest.erl"
[...]
Applying gt_to_lt at {{5,22},{5,26}}...
Renaming to "abiftest_gt_to_le_5_22_5_26"
Writing "mutants/abiftest_gt_to_le_5_22_5_26.erl"...
Applying eq_to_le at {{5,9},{5,14}}...
Renaming to "abiftest_eq_to_le_5_9_5_14"
Writing "mutants/abiftest_eq_to_le_5_9_5_14.erl"...
[...]
```

This produces a series of files in the output folder, each names according to the original module name, the mutation operator applied, and the line and character position of the application.

The mutant *abiftest_gt_to_le_5_22_5_26* is shown in Fig. 3, next to the original source file. The name represents that it is built from the *abiftest* module by

---

[1] The *mu2* Erlang mutation testing framework is available at: https://github.com/ramsay-t/mu2.

```
-module(abiftest).                      -module(abiftest_gt_to_le_5_22_5_26).
-export([dv/2]).                        -export([dv/2]).

dv(A,B) ->                              dv(A,B) ->
    if (A == 0) and (B > 4) ->              if  (A == 0) and (B =< 4) ->
          B;                                      B;
       true ->                                 true ->
          B / A                                   B / A
    end.                                    end.
```

Fig. 3. The application of the gt_to_le operator to abiftest.erl

applying the *gt_to_le* operator (replacing a "greater than" operator with a "less than or equals" operator) at line 5, characters 22 through 26.

```
-module(abiftest).                      -module(abiftest_eq_to_le_5_9_5_14).
-export([dv/2]).                        -export([dv/2]).

dv(A,B) ->                              dv(A,B) ->
    if (A == 0) and (B > 4) ->              if  (A =< 0) and (B > 4) ->
          B;                                      B;
       true ->                                 true ->
          B / A                                   B / A
    end.                                    end.
```

Fig. 4. The application of the eq_to_le operator to abiftest.erl

In a similar fashion, Fig. 4 shows the application of the *eq_to_le* operator, replacing an equals operator with a "less than or equals" operator.

Test Set Evaluation. The exact process of evaluating the original test set against each mutant may vary between projects if there are substantial requirements for the testing environment. However, the *mu2* framework includes some support functions to evaluate a test set against mutants. The *test* function takes a source folder, module name, mutant folder name, and a test function. It then takes each of the mutants in turn and moves them into the source folder, refactors the mutant name to the original module name, then compiles the module and runs the tests with the mutant in place of the original module.

```
32> Res = mu2:test(".",abiftest,"mutants",fun abiftest_tests:test/0).
Testing "mutants/abiftest_and_to_or_5_9_5_26.erl"
Renaming to "abiftest"
Writing "./abiftest.erl"...
Loading "./abiftest.erl"
abiftest_tests: two_test...*failed*
```

```
[...]
[{"abiftest_and_to_or_5_9_5_26.erl",error},
 {"abiftest_and_to_xor_5_9_5_26.erl",error},
 {"abiftest_div_to_minus_6_16_6_20.erl",error},
 {"abiftest_div_to_mul_6_16_6_20.erl",error},
 {"abiftest_div_to_plus_6_16_6_20.erl",error},
 {"abiftest_div_to_rem_6_16_6_20.erl",error},
 {"abiftest_eq_to_ge_5_9_5_14.erl",error},
 {"abiftest_eq_to_gt_5_9_5_14.erl",error},
 {"abiftest_eq_to_le_5_9_5_14.erl",ok},
 {"abiftest_eq_to_lt_5_9_5_14.erl",ok},
 {"abiftest_eq_to_ne_5_9_5_14.erl",error},
 {"abiftest_eq_to_nte_5_9_5_14.erl",error},
 {"abiftest_eq_to_te_5_9_5_14.erl",ok},
 {"abiftest_exchange_if_guard_5_5_7_7.erl",error},
 {"abiftest_exchange_if_pattern_5_5_7_7.erl",error},
 {"abiftest_gt_to_eq_5_22_5_26.erl",ok},
 {"abiftest_gt_to_ge_5_22_5_26.erl",ok},
 {"abiftest_gt_to_le_5_22_5_26.erl",ok},
 {"abiftest_gt_to_lt_5_22_5_26.erl",ok},
 {"abiftest_gt_to_ne_5_22_5_26.erl",ok},
 {"abiftest_gt_to_nte_5_22_5_26.erl",ok},
 {"abiftest_gt_to_te_5_22_5_26.erl",ok},
 {"abiftest_remove_last_if_5_5_7_7.erl",error},
 {"abiftest_swap_if_order_5_5_7_7.erl",ok},
 {"abiftest_true_to_false_6_8_6_11.erl",error}]
```

The final result is a collation of mutant names and the atom *ok* or *error* to indicate the success or failure of the test set. Converting this into a simple killed/alive ratio is simple, but the retention of the mutant names allows the user to trace any mutants that survive and identify the weakness in the test set. In this simple example 11 of the 25 mutants were not killed. Of these only one can be considered semantically equivalent: replacing the == operator with the type-specific =:= is irrelevant, since it would not be meaningful for the function to behave differently with 0.0 than with 0.

However, all of the remaining tests highlight the weakness in the test set — namely that it does not adequately explore the combinations of ways of satisfying and falsifying the condition over A and B. The majority of surviving mutants have modified the condition $B > 4$ on line 5, characters 22 to 26. Although this condition is exercised, it is only exercised in a limited range of settings (it is only falsified when the other part of the decision is also falsified).

The addition of this test identifies that error in the original code (and, incidentally, achieves full MC/DC coverage of the system as discussed in [16]):

```
div_zero_test() ->
        ?assert(abiftest:dv(0,2) == 2.0).
```

This succinctly demonstrates the way the *mu2* framework meets the test adequacy metric requirements from Sect. 2.2. The mutation *score* of 11/25 is a general quality metric for the test set, and can be expressed as a percentage with the test set killing only 56 % of mutants. This may not be directly comparable to other test adequacy metrics, but gives a similar intuition about the quality of the test suite that a 56 % coverage score would do.

That the surviving mutants were predominantly located on line 5, characters 22 to 26 identified not only that decision point as the weakly tested element, but also identified the specific condition that was inadequately tested. Mutation testing is not limited to decision points, as collection of surviving mutants on any other program element (e.g. an output or a calculation) would provide similar evidence that the specific element was inadequately tested. Additionally, the mutants give some guidance on producing new tests, since it highlights some examples that should be distinguished – e.g. if $B > 4$ and $B < 4$ are not distinguished then clearly the system should be tested with values of B both greater and less than 4 (and, perhaps, B equal to 4).

4   Operator Definitions

Practical mutation testing requires that changes be made to the source program's parsed form rather than its source code. Erlang has many libraries in the standard installation that support the parsing of Erlang programs to an abstract syntax tree, but modifications to these trees can be complicated to specify and difficult to understand. The mutation operators that are used in this work can require quite subtle semantic changes that would be particularly complicated to specify in terms of standard syntax tree alterations.

To provide a more succinct and readable interface this work leverages the Wrangler refactoring system [13]. Wrangler is a refactoring system that presents an emacs interface, but it also contains a programatically accessible API. The Wrangler API allows refactorings to be specified in an elegant template format.

In general, *refactoring* is a process that changes a program's source code structure in a consistent way. Common refactorings include: renaming a variable everywhere it is used, extracting blocks of repeated code into a new function, or moving code between levels in a class hierarchy. In order to support such changes, refactoring tools require a rich understanding of the semantics of the target language (e.g. to understand scoping issues when renaming variables). Consequently, the Wrangler refactoring system provides an ideal platform on which to build the mutation operators required for Erlang mutation testing.

The template format of the Wrangler refactoring API uses a series of macros to specify code transformations. The ?RULE macro defines a rule with three components: a pattern of Erlang code to match, a programatic transformation on that code, and a programatic guard statement to limit the application of the rule. Several different macros define the traversal of the abstract syntax tree; the ?FULL_TD_TP macro traverses all nodes in the tree. As an example, a function to convert addition to subtraction at a specific program location is shown in Fig. 5.

However, this requires an understanding of the Wrangler system, and it requires the application of multiple Wrangler macros. To speed up the development of mutation operators and allow users to focus on interesting semantic

```
plus_to_minus(File, Loc) ->
                ?FULL_TD_TP([?RULE(?T("X@ + Y@"),
                    ?TO_AST("X@ - Y@"),
                    api_refac:start_end_loc(_This@)==Loc)],
                [File]).
```

Fig. 5. The Wrangler API code to convert addition to subtraction

```
{plus_to_minus,
?MUTATION_MATCH("X@ + Y@"),
?MUTATION_EXCHANGE("X@ + Y@", "X@ - Y@")}
```

Fig. 6. The *mu2* plus_to_minus operator definition

operations the *mu2* framework provides a simplified definition structure. A *mu2* mutation operator is a triple containing a name that will be used to identify the change, a function to identify applicable locations, and a function to alter the code. The *mu2* framework also provides several macros to implement common operations.

Figure 6 shows the same replacement of addition with subtraction but as a *mu2* operator. The ?MUTATION_MATCH macro provides a simple way to express a location identifier function that simply matches a template, and the ?MUTATION_EXCHANGE macro is for mutations that are simple rearrangements or syntax modifications that do not alter the meta-variables.

The significant power of the Wrangler API comes from the ability to perform arbitrary operations on the syntax tree as part of the refactoring operation. The meta-variables in the Wrangler patterns allow the syntax components to be manipulated easily. For example, Fig. 7 shows a refactoring to re-order the patterns in a case statement, using the Pats@@@, Guards@@@, and Body@@@ meta variables that contain lists of the syntax components for the case statement.

```
{swap_case_order,
     ?MUTATION_RESTRICT("case Expr@ of Pats@@@ when Guards@@@ -> Body@@@ end",
 is_valid_pattern_set(Pats@@@)
),
     ?MUTATION("case Expr@ of Pats@@@ when Guards@@@ -> Body@@@ end",
begin
    A = random:uniform(length(Pats@@@)),
    B = random_not_n(length(Pats@@@), A),
    NewPats@@@ = swap(Pats@@@, A, B),
    NewGuards@@@ = swap(Guards@@@, A, B),
    NewBody@@@ = swap(Body@@@, A, B),
    ?TO_AST("case Expr@ of NewPats@@@ when NewGuards@@@ -> NewBody@@@ end")
end)}
```

Fig. 7. The *mu2* swap_case_order operator

The ?MUTATION_RESTRICT macro creates a location identifier that matches a pattern but also evaluates a boolean function over the metavariables (in this example is simply calls another function to check that the list of patterns is valid). The general ?MUTATION macro produces a modification function that matches a pattern and then performs an arbitrary function over the meta-variables. This function must return a Wrangler Abstract Syntax Tree, but this is simplified by the ?TO_AST macro that can build an AST from a template, which can reference newly constructed meta-variables.

5   Evaluation

The *mu2* framework was built as part of the EU funded PROWESS project[2] (Property-based testing of web services). As part of the project the tool was evaluated in an industrial context, and we briefly explain here the evaluation and its results.

5.1   Research Questions

As discussed in Sect. 2.2, a test adequacy metric must produce both a rigorous assessment and measure of the quality of a test set, and useful feedback to guide a test developer to improve the test set. A simple measure of the *rigour* of an adequacy metric is the number of tests required — assuming that the test set developers don't produce spurious or overly-repetitive tests. The requirement for *useful guidance* is more difficult to measure.

Testing methodologies are often measured using code coverage as a test adequacy metric (e.g. [6]). Several coverage metrics are available for Erlang, including basic line coverage metric provided by the *cover* tool that is included in the standard Erlang library, and MC/DC analysis provided by the *Smother* tool [16]. These have the advantage of requiring less time and effort to apply, since they only require the test suite to be run once, rather than once per mutant. However, [4] showed that — for the imperative languages C and Ada — mutation testing was not only able to provide equivalent levels of quality assurance, but also provide complimentary information and guidance to the test developers.

Consequently, the *mu2* framework is evaluated in comparison to these metrics to demonstrate that it provides similar complimentary benefits in a functional programming language. Specifically we choose the following research questions as the basis for our evaluation:

1. Does mutation testing require more tests than other test adequacy metrics (e.g. coverage) to achieve a maximal score?
2. Do test sets with high mutation scores also achieve high coverage scores, or are they testing different system behaviours?
3. How much longer does it take to perform mutation testing on realistic Erlang modules than testing to maximise coverage?
4. How useful is the feedback provided by mutation testing compared to other metrics?

---

[2] http://www.prowessproject.eu/.

5.2 Evaluation Results

The PROWESS project partner Interoud Innovation[3] evaluated the *mu2* framework by applying the procedure above. They did not develop any domain-specific operators and used the simple arithmetic and structural operators that are included by default with he framework.

The evaluation itself consisted of an iterative process. The participant developers first measured the coverage and mutation score of their current tests set and then used feedback from the coverage tools and mutation testing tool to improve their test set. The feedback - either uncovered sections or code, or un-killed mutants - should prompt the developers to write new tests. Alternatively, particular execution sequences or mutants may be presented but impossible to cover and can be discarded. The augmented test set can be re-run and new feedback generated. This processes was repeated until there were no uncovered sections of code, no un-killed mutants, until all that remains was identified as impossible, or until the developers judged the remaining items not significant.

This produces a collection of test sets, each produced using feedback from a different metric. The original test set is referred to as T, then the test set developed using *cover* is TC, that produced from *Smother* is TS, and that produced from *mu2* is TM. As well as comparing the improvement made in their own metric, the final test sets were each evaluated using all of the metrics. The numerical results for the metric are presented in tabular form below, followed by a description of each of the test sets.

	Original test set (T)	Cover based test set (TC)	Smother based test set (TS)	Mu2 based test set (TM)
Coverage(C)	31.17% (77/247 lines)	69.23% (171/247 lines)	53.44% (132/247 lines)	49.79% (123/247 lines)
Coverage(S)	47.99%	73.16%	69.84%	64.17%
Coverage(M)	16.86% (14/83 killed)	49.39% (41/83 killed)	74.69% (62/83 killed)	80.72% (67/83 killed)

Original test set (*T*)

– The original test set contains 4 QuickCheck properties and 81 Eunit tests.

Cover based test set (*TC*)

– This test set has been developed with the aim of improving line coverage using the Cover tool. It adds 67 Eunit tests to the original test set (4 QuickCheck properties and 148 Eunit tests).

---

[3] http://www.interoud.com/.

- That this test set achieves a higher percentage MC/DC (*Smother*) score than the test set explicitly designed to achieve a high MC/DC score demonstrates a problem with representing MC/DC scores numerically. Since the developers of TC were aiming to simply execute all lines at least once, this test set executes more lines than TS, resulting in a large number of partially explored decisions. Meanwhile, the developers of TS thoroughly explored the decisions that they considered important, and ignored some that they considered less significant. However, that means that TS leaves a number of decisions completely unexplored, and these contribute multiple MC/DC elements to the percentage since they may contain multiple subcomponents with multiple potential evaluations.

Smother based test set (TS)

- This test set adds 64 Eunit tests to the original test set (4 QuickCheck properties and 145 Eunit tests).
- This development took approximately 20 hours, although part of that time was needed to find and fix the bug noted below. This development was also finished before reaching the maximum reachable MC/DC coverage since it was considered more than reasonable coverage.

Mutation based test set (TM)

- This test set has been developed with the aim of improving mutation coverage using the *mu2* tool. It adds 15 Eunit tests to the original test set (4 QuickCheck properties and 96 Eunit tests).
- This development took approximately 8 hours and tests were added for almost every mutant. Only 16 of the 83 mutants remained alive:
  - 7 of them were not killed because the mutations were semantically equivalent to the original code (e.g. reordering completely specified case clauses or changing =:= to == when comparing atoms).
  - 7 of them were not killed because the mutation can never be executed. This is the case when the mutation is applied in an internal function with controlled input, so that it is impossible from the tests to cause the input that would make the test fail. In one example the mutant changed an equal comparison by a less than comparison but there is no way of passing a value $<$ normal into the function parameter, because a previous clause would have match for any other allowed value. This is related to the impossible conditions required by Smother, but statically determining the limitations on variable values is a complex problem.
  - 2 of them were not killed because tests to kill them would be too difficult to implement and not useful.

5.3 Developer Feedback

The Interoud developers provided some subjective comments about the usefulness of the different strategies used to generate test cases, summarised here:

Cover.

- Interoud developers think it may be easier to generate tests focusing on lines of code but it produces worse tests than other metrics.

Smother.

- The test set developed for Smother was the most difficult to develop by the Interoud developers. Getting complete coverage in clause based functions is hard because it is likely that some unexpected input (i.e. values of different types or forbidden values, mostly on internal functions) is not covered. Interoud only developed tests using Eunit, but using QuickCheck should have made it easy to check all condition combinations.
- About MC/DC coverage, Interoud developers think it is more useful than line coverage, as it focuses on important lines of code.

mu2

- The mutant based test set is very specific, which makes it more time consuming to apply. Interoud developers created tests for this pilot study that aimed to kill mutants in the most isolated way. Since several mutations are different changes to operators in the same condition, some of these tests kill several mutants.
- Interoud developers think that the *mu2* tool is slow generating mutants, although this was not a problem since mutants were generated only once for all developed test sets.
- Regarding mutation coverage, it was the easiest to develop test for and, although they tend to be too specific, they can be refactored later.
- The default set of mutation operators was only of limited value, but Interoud developers think that the investment of time needed to develop more advanced operators would be worthwhile.

5.4   Evaluation Conclusions

As expected, the test set developed using only line coverage feedback (TC) did not achieve high scores in MC/DC or Mutation assessment. The Smother based test set (TS) and the *mu2* based test set (TM) achieved commendable performance when measured by each other's metric, but there were clearly some areas of difference that represent complementary value — features that are best identified with one metric or the other.

It is significant that although the time taken to generate mutants was mentioned as a weakness of the mutation testing approach, the overall time taken to develop the mutation based test set was considerably shorter. The developers report that the mutants provided the most clear and direct feedback as to what feature was not being executed and how to write a relevant test, although there was some concern that these tests were then too narrowly targeted.

6   Conclusions

This work has produced a framework for applying mutation testing to Erlang programs, and that supports a powerful refactoring based system for defining domain-specific mutation operators. The industrial evaluation of the *mu2* framework demonstrated that it was not only valuable as a test adequacy framework in itself, but that it provided complimentary information to MC/DC analysis of the same system.

Although at the start of this work there was no published mutation testing framework for any functional programming language, the recently released *MuCheck* [12] is a mutation testing environment for Haskell, designed to work with Haskell Quick Check. MuCheck provides conventional mutation operators for list operations and for reordering pattern in pattern matching. The authors make a similar observation in Haskell about the impact of mutations on recursive functions and how this can cause divergent behaviour.

The authors of [9] proposed an approach to automatically generating tests that uses mutation testing to identify areas and types of fault that were of interest. By generating and optimising test sets to kill mutants they expect to create test sets more likely to identify real faults in systems. Because both the mutant generation and test set generation is automated this can be run on a large scale if resources are available. Erlang QuickCheck supports *feature based testing* that allows test generation to be targeted at specific "features". This could be used in conjunction with *mu2* mutants to apply this approach to Erlang.

The *mu2* framework has been released as an open-source project on GitHub.

References

1. Armstrong, J.: Erlang. Commun. ACM **53**(9), 68–75 (2010)
2. Armstrong, J., Virding, R., Wikström, C., Williams, M.: Concurrent Programming in ERLANG. Prentice Hall, Hertfordshire (1996)
3. Arts, T., Hughes, J., Johansson, J., Wiger, U.T.: Testing telecoms software with quviq QuickCheck. In: Feeley, M., Trinder, P.W. (eds.) Proceedings of the 2006 ACM SIGPLAN Workshop on Erlang, pp. 2–10. ACM (2006)
4. Baker, R., Habli, I.: An empirical evaluation of mutation testing for improving the test quality of safety-critical software. IEEE Trans. Softw. Eng. **39**(6), 787–805 (2013)
5. Carlsson, R., Rémond, M.: EUnit: a lightweight unit testing framework for Erlang. In: Proceedings of the 2006 ACM SIGPLAN Workshop on Erlang, pp. 1–1. ACM (2006)
6. Fraser, G., Arcuri, A.: Whole test suite generation. IEEE Trans. Softw. Eng. **39**(2), 276–291 (2013)
7. Fraser, G., Arcuri, A.: Achieving scalable mutation-based generation of whole test suites. Empirical Softw. Eng. **20**(3), 783–812 (2014)
8. Fraser, G., Walkinshaw, N.: Behaviourally Adequate Software Testing. In: Proceedings of the Fifth International Conference on Software Testing, Verification and Validation (ICST) (2012)

9. Fraser, G., Zeller, A.: Mutation-driven generation of unit tests and oracles. IEEE Trans. Softw. Eng. **38**(2), 278–292 (2012)
10. Hamlet, R.G.: Testing programs with the aid of a compiler. IEEE Trans. Softw. Eng. **3**, 279–290 (1977)
11. Harman, M., Jia, Y., Langdon, W.B.: Strong higher order mutation-based test data generation. In: Proceedings of the 19th ACM SIGSOFT Symposium and the 13th European Conference on Foundations of Software Engineering, pp. 212–222. ACM (2011)
12. Le, D., Alipour, M.A., Gopinath, R., Groce, A.: MuCheck: an extensible tool for mutation testing of Haskell programs. In: Proceedings of the 2014 International Symposium on Software Testing and Analysis, ISSTA 2014, pp. 429–432. ACM (2014)
13. Li, H., Thompson, S.: A user-extensible refactoring tool for Erlang programs. Technical report, University of Kent (2011)
14. Reales Mateo, P., Polo Usaola, M., Offutt, J.: Mutation at the multi-class and system levels. Sci. Comput. Program. **78**(4), 364–387 (2013)
15. Ryder, B.G., Hailpern, B. (eds.) HOPL III: Proceedings of the Third ACM SIGPLAN Conference on History of Programming Languages. ACM (2007)
16. Taylor, R.G., Derrick, J.: Smother - an MC/DC analysis tool for Erlang. In: Proceedings of the Fourteenth ACM SIGPLAN workshop on Erlang. ACM (2015, to appear)

A Survey on Testing for Cyber Physical System

Sara Abbaspour Asadollah[1]([✉]), Rafia Inam[2],
and Hans Hansson[1]

[1] Mälardalen University, Västerås, Sweden
{sara.abbaspour,hans.hansson}@mdh.se
[2] Ericsson AB, Kista, Sweden
rafia.inam@ericsson.com

Abstract. Cyber Physical Systems (CPS) bridge the cyber-world of computing and communications with the physical world and require development of secure and reliable software. It asserts a big challenge not only on testing and verifying the correctness of all physical and cyber components of such big systems, but also on integration of these components. This paper develops a categorization of multiple levels of testing required to test CPS and makes a comparison of these levels with the levels of software testing based on the V-model. It presents a detailed state-of-the-art survey on the testing approaches performed on the CPS. Further, it provides challenges in CPS testing.

Keywords: Testing · Cyber physical systems · Survey

1 Introduction

Cyber Physical System (CPS) is one type of complex engineering systems, which is based on the integration of physical, computation and communication parts. The operation of this type of systems needs to be controlled, coordinated, monitored and integrated by a computing and communication core which is integrated in the physical environment. Examples of CPS with different functionality can be found in diverse areas, such as health care, smart transportations, data centers, smart buildings, smart homes, power grids and safety support system. The most important issues within these systems are dependability, efficiency, and security.

A CPS typically consists of *physical and cyber* spaces, with various sensors and actuators, as graphically shown in Fig. 1. These spaces integrate computation and physical processes, and are interconnected by a network layer for exchange of data between these two spaces.

Testing and verifying the correctness of all physical and cyber components of such complex CPS poses a big challenge. It may contain hardware and software testing, computation and communicational testing, extra-functional testing for each component individually, besides integration, and system testing to test the complete system. Despite the well-established concept of CPS, relatively little work has been performed on testing methods for CPS.

© IFIP International Federation for Information Processing 2015
K. El-Fakih et al. (Eds.): ICTSS 2015, LNCS 9447, pp. 194–207, 2015.
DOI: 10.1007/978-3-319-25945-1_12

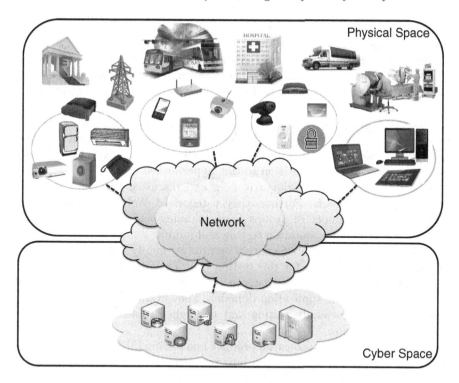

Fig. 1. Cyber physical system components

Contributions: This paper presents (1) multiple levels of testing required to test a complete CPS, and makes a comparison of these levels with the levels of testing based on the V-model; (2) a state-of-the-art survey on different testing methods performed on the CPS; and (3) challenges in CPS testing.

Outline: Section 2 presents related work. Section 3 presents different levels of CPS testing. Section 4 investigates state-of-the-art methods for testing CPS, Sect. 5 outlines some challenges in testing the CPS and Sect. 6 concludes the paper.

2   Related Work

Testing is an essential activity in engineering and it is widely used in industry in order to guarantee the quality of any type of system. Bertolino [4] has organized the outstanding research challenges for software testing into a consistent roadmap.

There are many studies performed on testing for different SW development methods [5,11,14,16] (like web services, cloud, software product lines), and testing software development process [24]. However, to the best of our knowledge, this paper is the first study to explore the different CPS testing types and performing a state-of-the-art survey on it.

Koray, et al. performed a survey of software testing of cloud-based systems and classified related literature according to research activities performed in the cloud-based testing area [11]. They also identified and clarified the terminologies, the gaps and open issues.

Bozkurt et al., presented a survey on testing Web service by classifying the testing types and techniques [5]. They also categorized the previous work undertaken on web service testing based on some functional testing techniques. Another survey on web application testing is performed by Li, et al. [16]. They reviewed the recent Web testing advances and discussed the employed techniques, targets and goals. Further, they categorized Web application testing techniques into a number of groups (e.g., scanning and crawling techniques, search-based techniques, mutation testing and more).

Tevanlinna, et al., presented a survey on product family testing and described methodology and processes for this testing [24]. They emphasized the use of a careful planned testing process that can be easily adapted and used for product families in different application domains. They evaluated the current state-of-the-art in product family testing and highlight problems that need to be addressed in the future.

A survey framework on software product line testing (SPL) is defined in [14]. Lee, et al., divided the SPL testing into two separate test engineering activities: (1) domain testing and (2) application testing. In domain testing assets (test plans, test cases, and test scenarios) are used as inputs to application testing. They believe that in the normal case, complete products are not obtained during domain engineering sine domain engineering focuses on core asset development. Therefore, in most cases domain system testing can only be conducted in a limited way. By testing core assets in domain testing the application testing can focus on the application specific parts, which were not covered in domain testing. They explained that SPL testing has a W-shape lifecycle, which is typically called, extended V-model and formed by two overlapping V-models. They explored the software product line testing approaches by defining a reference SPL testing processes and identifying their key research perspectives which were related to testing field.

Research on using monitors for testing purpose has mostly focused on monitors for software that is neither real-time nor distributed. Only a few studies have addressed monitoring real-time or distributed systems, which characterized safety-critical systems such as flight-critical systems for aircraft and spacecraft. A survey on monitors to test distributed real-time systems [7].

Abbaspour et al. classified concurrency bugs based on the observable properties for multicore applications [1]. They address that such a taxonomy can help testers and debuggers to understand the causes of concurrency bugs and to avoid introducing them. Classification helps them to make appropriate decisions when they encounter problems. It can serve as a structure in which the current body of knowledge can be arranged, thereby allowing for identification of gaps in this knowledge by easing the debugging process, and help users heuristics for more precise detection tools.

Gupta, et al. compare different approaches towards design and verification of energy sustainable computing for CPS [8]. They address that a perfect way to perform verification is either through experimentation on actual deployment of a CPS or through accurate simulation of the system. Simulation based verification is widely used since the resources required to build experimental test-bed may not be affordable. Both simulation and experimentation can also be used to characterize various functions. Moreover, in many CPS, verification is required at the design time without real deployment. The early design time verification has two advantages: it avoids creating real test-scenarios putting lives at risk; and it provides a way to guarantee and certify the CPS behavior.

3   CPS Testing

In this section we present different levels of testing required to check and verify CPS, and then compares these levels with the testing types of the V-model.

3.1   Levels of CPS Testing

As explained in Sect. 1 a variety of testing types may be used in testing the different components of a CPS.

Hardware Testing: Hardware testing consists of testing hardware components of CPS, including tests of each component's functionality based on the system requirements. The most common and important variables in evaluating and testing hardware such as desktops, laptops, printers, PDAs and other important hardware that are used in the CPS are memory size, speed, storage capacity, spindle size, I/O interfaces (ports), synchronization capabilities, expandability and similar.

There is another issue in checking the hardware functionality, which is hardware verification. Hardware verification tests the hardware under specific conditions, checking that the hardware follows the local environment requirements conditions, confirming to the applicable quality assurance measures and more. Thus, hardware testing is typically more structured and detailed than hardware verification. There are some similarities between software and hardware testing. Hardware testing has fewer steps and does not usually undergo a pilot project.

Structural and Computation Testing: Structural testing is normally based on the detailed design and not on the required functions of the program. However, for computation testing the tester (or developer) uses the structure of the program and chose paths that are used to recognize domains. Computation testing is one form of structural testing, which focuses on the computational part of software.

Extra-Functional Properties Testing (EFP Testing): Multiple parts of a CPS are often embedded systems executing real-time software. For such a system it is required to guarantee both (1) function correctness and (2) non-functional or extra-functional correctness. Extra-functional properties are closely related to the inherent interaction with the system environment. Examples of such properties may be temperature, power consumption, and timing [21, 26].

Network Testing: Communication and network testing are other important issues in a CPS testing. The aim of this testing is to check and verify the protocols used in a communication flow among multiple devices and users. Besides, the actual measurement and recording of a networks, state of operation during a period of time is called network testing. In network testing the tester is assisted for verifying, controlling or comparing the performance by recording the current state of network operation.

Integration Testing: Combining the individual software modules in a group and testing the grouped module is called integration testing. It is a phase of software testing and prepares the system for the next phase of testing which is system testing. The errors, that appear because of combining different units are detected in this phase. In other words, any inconsistency between integrated software units or integrated software units and hardware can be discovered by integration testing [19].

System Testing: Finally, hardware system testing or software system testing is related to test a complete integrated system when all units in a system are integrated to fulfil the overall requirements of the system [19]. The purpose of this testing is not just testing the design of the system, but to also test and verify the behavior and the assumed expectations of the user.

3.2 Comparison of Testing Levels of CPS with the Traditional V-Model

Comparing to the testing levels presented in a typical V-model [19] which are performed to verify only software, the levels of CPS testing have to verify software, hardware, network and the integration of all these components to work as a single system.

In the V-model, unit testing represents code level or unit level testing, e.g. a single program module. It verifies the smallest functional code when isolated from the rest of the codes. For CPS, as shown in Fig. 2, the unit testing is performed at the hardware and software levels separately, to independently test the functionality of both hardware and software. Further, the network testing is important to verify the network operations and communication flow, which is not an integral/separate part of the testing levels in the V-model.

Integration testing verifies that different independent units can be integrated together and that they communicate correctly. Thus, the network testing is performed at both, unit and integration testing levels. In CPS testing it covers a bigger umbrella by encapsulating the integration of software components as well as the integration of hardware components, as compared to the traditional integration testing that refers to the integration of software components only.

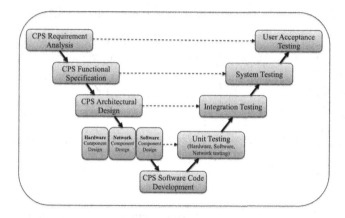

Fig. 2. Life cycle model for CPS

System testing verifies the whole application for its functionality, interdependency and communication. In the V-model, it usually consist of only a software part while in CPS, it encapsulates hardware, software, and network parts. User Acceptance testing is performed in a user environment and verifies that system is ready to use and meets user's requirement, and is relevant for CPS and V-model testing.

4 State-of-the-Art Survey

This section categorizes the SOTA survey based on the testing types described in the preceding section.

The string that we have used to search articles in Google scholar is ((cyber physical system) OR (medical systems) OR (real-time systems) OR (robot software) OR (vehicle software) OR (hybrid control system) OR (embedded system)) AND ((testing) OR (validating) OR (evaluating)). Based on the search string, we found totally 59 papers. We considered the most relevant and recent papers w.r.t. testing, and short-listed 16 papers, which are summarised in Table 1 and are explained below.

We see from Table 1 that most considered studies focus on System testing. There are a few studies on Hardware and Network testing. Further, we see that only *Real-time hybrid structural testing* [10,25] performs all six levels of CPS testing.

4.1 Hardware Testing

L. C. Silva, et al., present a model-based architecture for validating/verifying the Medical CPS [22]. Their architecture includes components representing models for medical devices and a model for the patient. The architecture can help developers/testers to generate test cases by validating these models.

Table 1. Relation between state of the art and testing types

CPS Testing Level / State of the Art	[1]	[2]	[3]	[6]	[7]	[9]	[10]	[12]	[13]	[15]	[17]	[18]	[22]	[23]	[25]	[27]	Total
Hardware testing						✓					✓		✓		✓	✓	5
Structural testing		✓				✓		✓	✓	✓	✓	✓	✓		✓	✓	10
EFP testing		✓	✓	✓		✓		✓				✓			✓	✓	8
Network testing	✓				✓	✓					✓				✓		5
Integration testing	✓					✓					✓				✓		4
System testing	✓	✓		✓	✓	✓	✓	✓		✓	✓	✓			✓	✓	12

Zhang, et al., address the challenges of generating test cases for CPS from Formal models [27]. They generate test cases from formal specifications by applying differential dynamic logic (DL). Differential DL is a logic for specifying and verifying hybrid systems. They translate the test cases, which are generated from formal specification into a model in Modelica language. Modelica is sometimes called a hardware description language that allows the user to specify mathematical models of complex physical systems, thus this testing approach can be applied to perform hardware testing.

Lim, et al. propose a hierarchical test model and automated test framework for robot software components of Robot Technology Component (RTC), which was combined with hardware module [17]. The proposed hierarchical testing procedure model included three levels of testing: unit testing, integration testing and system testing. Here the unit testing corresponds to the hardware testing. Hardware module is considered as a basic unit for hierarchical testing for robotic software component.

Real-time hybrid structural testing [10, 25] is identified as a grand challenge for CPS and includes all six levels of testing. The physical test specimen in *Real-time hybrid structural testing* of Huang et al.'s experimental setup is composed of a small steel compression spring, which is used to represent the bending stiffness of an actual column in a portal frame structure, thus performing hardware tests [10]. Tidwell et al. present an initial work on a Cyber-physical Instrument for Real-time hybrid Structural Testing (CIRST). It targets to provide a highly configurable architecture for integrating computers and physical components, thus performing hardware tests [25].

4.2 Structural and Computation Testing

Conformance test using timed automata is another famous approach to perform structural testing and to test properties of the real-time system [6, 13, 18]. In this method, a conformance test algorithm is provided which constructs a set of test cases. The final output of the test method is either a Yes if the implementation conforms to its specification, or No when the implementation fails to conform to the specification because it fails a particular experiment.

Zhang, et al., generate test cases for CPS from Formal models by applying differential dynamic logic (DL) for testing in [27].

Badban, et al., present algorithms and techniques for automated test case and test data generation to test hybrid controlled cyber-physical systems [3].

A model-based architecture is used to test the Medical CPS [22]. A controlled experiment is performed to verify the behavior of components designed for the proposed architecture. The experiment analyzes the interaction among components. The most important concern in the Medical system is the patient's safety. Thus, the architecture focuses on the aspect that developers can test their applications without putting any risk on compromising the security of patients. Moreover, the data privacy is maintained, while keeping the generated data statistically compatible with real data.

Lee, et al., present embedded system software testing using a Service Oriented Architecture (SOA) method [15]. They present a mobile service testing process using test case specification. They conclude that service interoperability test process can extend the application testing to develop cost efficient and optimized mobile services. They analyze mobile application requirement, write service specification, optimize the design, and provide extended use case specification.

Srivastava and Kim develop variable length genetic algorithms to optimize software testing [23]. Genetic search algorithms are used to find critical path clusters in software code, and consequently, based on their identification they present a technique for optimizing testing and report preliminary results. Exhaustive software testing is intractable for even medium sized software. Therefore, they present a more selective approach to testing by focusing on those parts that are most error-prone and critical so that these paths can be tested first. The efficiency of testing is increased as their technique focuses on the most critical paths. Additionally, authors address that by applying generic algorithms they made an undependable technique from any specific problem and it can be of tremendous importance for users.

Lim, et al. perform structural testing within their hierarchical test model and automated test framework for robotics software by testing a series of operations for software component, which were specified in the document of software component requirement [17].

Structural testing is an integral part to test *real-time hybrid structural testing* [10,25]. Huang et al. perform structural testing using a case study of several fundamental interlocking challenges in developing and evaluating CPS [10].

4.3   EFP Testing

Goodloe and Pike check the real-time properties of distributed hard real-time systems using an online *monitor* [7]. They claim that testing and formal verification are not sufficient to demonstrate the reliability of real-time systems, and advocate online monitoring as a promising technique for making safety-critical real-time distributed systems more reliable. Online monitors execute as a separate process, check conformance to a specification or property at runtime and can change the system direction into a known state if it deviates from its given specification, thus are better suited for safety-critical real-time system, like space shuttle and aircraft systems.

Badban, et al., present automated test case generation techniques that are applicable for testing the hybrid controlled embedded real-time systems like in avionics and railway [3].

As said in the previous section, *Conformance test* using timed automata is another approach to test properties of the real-time system. A new testing framework for real-time systems based on partially observable, non-deterministic timed automata and a formal conformance is proposed in [13]. The framework allows users to define the interface between the tester and the system under test (SUT) as well as assumptions on the environment of SUT via suitable model. The algorithms are provided in online or offline mode that generate analog clock or digital clock tests. Authors present coverage criteria to reduce the number of generated tests. The system is validated using a prototype test generation tool and two different case studies. Another study on automated derivation of functional test cases for real-time systems is proposed in [18]. A method for semiautomatic derivation of test cases is presented using formal specifications coded in TRIO language in order to fill a critical gap in the field of rigorous verification. The method is applied to several real-life case studies with industrial partners. The method discovers subtle errors that remained uncovered by human inspection and by using more-traditional techniques. Finally, authors also compare TRIO with the TRIO+ language. Another work based on the conformance test method using networks of timed automata is presented in [6]. Based on a testable model for real-time timed transition systems (TTTS) the author introduces fault hypotheses and a conformance test generation algorithm that constructs a set of test cases from a TTTS. The test view detects information on a particular set of tests, such as: the selection of relevant events to be observed, the mapping between implementation and specification events, the granularity of the observer's clock, a partition of test events into inputs and outputs. After selecting different test views, the tester can control the number of tests required: more detailed tests can be used for critical test purposes, and less detailed tests elsewhere. The authors claim that this method can reduce the number of test cases and can produce the effective use of features such as persistent variables. Moreover, testers can use independent test methods to check that assumptions made are reasonable and that users can easily define have their experiments in Uppaal specifications and different test views. Since complete test suites are expensive, authors believe this method is a proper way to reduce the cost when just critical parts of the system are tested by complete conformance test methods.

Zhang, et al., generate test cases from formal models. Modelica language is also used for the purpose of computer simulation of dynamic systems where behavior evolves as a function of time, thus it can be used to test timing properties [27].

Real-time systems are always tested extensively for the timing behaviour, like deadline misses etc. Thus, EFP testing is covered in *real-time hybrid structural testing* [10,25]. To examine the source of the deadline misses, Huang et al. measure the time for reading sensor data, writing actuator commands and other numerical computations [10]. Tidwell et al. claim that their testing method has broad impacts on both civil engineering and real-time computing and that it can enable real-time testing of a wide range of civil infrastructures and provide a CPS for the study and evaluation of real-time middleware [25].

4.4   Network Testing

A penetration testing policy is used by F. Alisherov and F. Sattarova [2] in order to test services and bring conformity between penetration testers and clients of the penetration test. It is a traditional testing method in which a tester send data to and from a secure system and then analyze the security measures of the system using a packet sniffer. This testing method falls under network testing since the data is sent to and from the system.

Lim, et al. [17] propose an automated test framework for robot software components in which the wireless communication station connects test-bed system to the main PC of robot test engine. Since they propose the wireless communication station in their framework they may use some technique(s) to test the communication. However this is not explained completely in the paper.

Real-time hybrid structural testing includes network testing [10,25]. Structural testing is typically based on data-flow, therefore, researchers explore the lower level details on testing the communication between ports (over network, local or shared memory).

He, et al. propose a cyber physical test bed (CPT) in order to visualize the environment of the wireless access and localize the body sensor networks (BSN) [9]. They design an analog channel emulator for Ultra Wide Brand (UWB) technologies. In order to verify their approach and to showcase the application of the CPT they accomplish some case studies. They evaluate the performance of data transmission inside the human body and TOA-based indoor localization. The results of case studies reveal the best performance of the indoor tracking system in the non-multipath condition. They also find the influence of the wooden wall and the metallic chamber in data transmission.

4.5   Integration Testing

F. Alisherov and F. Sattarova tested the integration and security of a CPS in [2] using penetration testing technique.

The second level of hierarchical testing procedure model is integration testing which is performed after unit testing for validation of hardware module [17]. The interoperability of hardware modules and software components was checked by performing integration testing while the robot hardware API was tested for performance index of functionality by using test cases.

Testing the integration of components in big distributed real-time CPS is very important and performed for *Real-time hybrid structural testing* [10,25]. Huang et al. test some of the components alone and visualize other components' behavior. They also perform integration testing by checking the synchronization among components [10]. Tidwell et al. perform integration testing using CRIST to test highly configurable architecture for integrating computers and physical components and provide a system for supporting real-time operations in distributed hybrid testing [25].

4.6   System Testing

Kane, et al., use system testing on a prototype vehicle design using a passive external runtime monitor to detect violations of high-level critical properties [12]. They limit the scope of testing in two respects: (1) by describing and testing only critical properties instead of complete behavior of system and (2) by providing approximate bounds to safety instead of specifying exact safety invariants. The method is applied on an automotive domain. Automotive networks periodically broadcast system state message. The simulation-based monitor reads the log file generated by the vehicle's CAN broadcast network, and verifies whether the execution trace satisfies the targeted properties or not.

Goodloe and Pike focus on testing system-level properties of a distributed real-time systems using online monitors [7]. *Conformance test* method [6,13,18] is performed on the complete integrated system, thus we categorize this method under system testing. Testing a Medical CPS includes detailed testing of hardware, structural and computations, and of complete system to ensure the patient's safety.

Modelica is a physical modeling language that allows tools to generate efficient simulation code automatically to facilitate exchange of models, and simulation specifications to test a simulation of complete cyber-physical system [27].

A classification of the concurrency bugs based on the observable properties is presented by Abbaspur et al. [1]. They categorized concurrency bug properties for concurrent and multicore application, that will help in system testing.

As described previously, the penetration testing is used to test the system's security measures [2], thus it falls under the system testing category.

The third level of hierarchical testing procedure model is system testing [17]. In their approach, the test cases are derived using black box testing techniques. The performance index of functionality includes completeness of function realization, correctness of data, compatibility of data and etc. Testing techniques of boundary value analysis, equal partitioning testing and state transition testing are used for system testing of robot software component.

The complete system is tested in real or using simulations for *Real-time hybrid structural testing* [10,25].

5   Challenges in Testing the CPS

The confluence of cyber and physical spaces of CPS technologies leads to new opportunities and subsequently some challenges in testing the system. Some of these challenges are summarized as follows:

- One of the essential challenges in validation, verification and certification of CPS is the current gap between formal methods and testing [20]. Thus compositional verification and testing methods that explore the heterogeneous nature of CPS models are necessary.
- Multiple parts of a CPS are often embedded systems with a real-time software executing. A real-time system requires to guarantee both (1) function correctness and (2) non-functional or extra -functional correctness. Extra-functional properties are closely related to the inherent interaction with the system environment. Examples of such properties may be temperature, power consumption, and timing [21,26]. Testing both functional and specially non-functional correctness in such systems is a challenge.
- The assertion of the correctness in designing and implementing CPS is another challenges. Correctness does not only encompass algorithmic and functional aspects but also extra-functional properties that are closely related to the inherent interaction with the system environment.
- Creating an automated or semi-automated method to evaluate the results of system testing is a limitation in CPS testing.
- To test run-time monitoring of real systems, the abstract model technique is used. In this technique, the real system is mapped to an abstract model. The runtime state information to perform monitoring is provided by this abstract model. However, abstract models will not be sufficient and it makes challenges on real system testing time.
- Defining the boundaries of the test landscape by environment is a challenge in testing the CPS. For instance, capturing physical limitations of devices or bounding the frequency of periodic inputs. Thus, system usually tested for the inputs specified, while it is necessary to also test for any inputs outside those ranges.
- The CPS which are related to electric power grid testing for power consumption has specific challenge since it requires ingrained measurements.
- The nature of some CPS are related to real-time, therefore testing the system with multiple time scales of interacting, distributed and control might be a challenge.
- Many CPS will highly interface with users. These CPS must be user-friendly to their many non-technical users. There are challenges in designing and testing these systems. For instance, testing a distance system for daily medical checks with couple of sensors and controls for old people or people with disabilities is a challenging task. Thus, testing the user-friendly property of this type of systems is a challenge.
- From real-time systems perspective the CPS research not only encounters the adaptation of components technologies and network systems, but also concerns using physical and logical properties (like physical laws, safety, security,

robustness, verification, energy and resource) [21]. Accordingly, compositional verification and testing methods should be adapted for the heterogeneous CPS models. To make a secure CPS with mentioned properties more work is required towards developing new verification and validation techniques. One approach could be bridge formal methods and testing approaches [20].

6   Discussion and Conclusion

This paper surveyed a number of past and recent efforts in CPS testing and verification and/or validation method. Several research groups have had ongoing efforts in the area for over a decade and have produced impressive tools. Consequently, there is a solid foundation of research in complete testing which can cover all phase of testing lifecycle of an application. Yet, little research to date has focused on testing and validation for CPS within health care, smart transportation, power grids and safety support, where suitable testing method can arguably have profound impact in preventing costly and possibly fatal system failures. Compositional verification and testing methods should be adapted for the heterogeneous CPS models. To make a secure CPS, more work is required towards developing new verification and validation techniques specifically targeting security vulnerabilities. Also, the use of formal methods in combination with testing, e.g. in the form of mode-based testing, has potential and should be further explored. Moreover, in the development of new CPS new mathematical foundation will be defined, therefore a variety of questions need to be resolved at different phases of software testing to trigger and ease the integration of the physical and cyber worlds.

Creating an automated or semi-automated method to evaluate the results of system testing is a challenge in CPS testing that also deserves attention.

Acknowledgments. This research is supported by Swedish Foundation for Strategic Research (SSF) via the SYNOPSIS Project.

References

1. Abbaspour A.S., Hansson, H., Sundmark, D., Eldh, S.: Towards classification of concurrency bugs based on observable properties. In: Workshop on Complex faUlts and Failures in LargE Software Systems (COUFLESS) (2015)
2. Alisherov, F., Sattarova, F.: Methodology for penetration testing. Int. J. Grid Distrib. Comput. **2**(2), 43–50 (2009). Citeseer
3. Badban, B., Fränzle, M., Peleska, J., Teige, T.: Test automation for hybrid systems. In: Workshop on Software Quality Assurance, pp. 14–21, ACM (2006)
4. Bertolino, A.: Software testing research: achievements, challenges, dreams. In: Future of Software Engineering, pp. 85–103 (2007)
5. Bozkurt, M., Harman, M., Hassoun, Y.: Testing web services: a survey. Department of Computer Science, King's College London, Technical report TR-10-01 (2010)
6. Cardell-Oliver, R.: Conformance tests for real-time systems with timed automata specifications. Form. Asp. Comput. **12**(5), 350–371 (2000)

7. Goodloe, A.E., Pike, L.: Monitoring distributed real-time systems: a survey and future directions. Technical report, NASA Langley Research Center (2010)
8. Gupta, S.K.S., Mukherjee, T., Varsamopoulos, G., Banerjee, A.: Research directions in energy-sustainable cyberphysical systems. Sustain. Comput. Inf. Syst. **1**(1), 57–74 (2011)
9. He, J., Geng, Y., Wan, Y., Li, S., Pahlavan, K.: A cyber physical test-bed for virtualization of RF access environment for body sensor network. IEEE Sens. J. **13**(10), 3826–3836 (2013)
10. Huang, H.M., Tidwell, T., Gill, C., Lu, C., Gao, X., Dyke, S.: Cyber-physical systems for real-time hybrid structural testing: a case study. In: 1st International Conference on Cyber-Physical Systems, pp. 69–78, ACM (2010)
11. Incki, K., Ar, I., Sözer, H.: A survey of software testing in the cloud. In: Software Security and Reliability Companion (SERE-C), pp. 18–23 (2012)
12. Kane, A., Fuhrman, T., Koopman, P.: Monitor based oracles for cyber-physical system testing. In: Dependable Systems and Networks (2014)
13. Krichen, M., Tripakis, S.: Conformance testing for real-time systems. Form. Methods Syst. Des. **34**(3), 238–304 (2009)
14. Lee, J., Kang, S., Lee, D.: A survey on software product line testing. In: Proceedings of the 16th International Software Product Line Conference, vol. 1, pp. 31–40. SPLC 2012, ACM, New York, NY, USA (2012)
15. Lee, M.H., Yoo, C.J., Jang, O.B.: Embedded system software testing based on SOA for mobile service. J. Adv. Sci. Technol. **1**(1), 55–64 (2008)
16. Li, Y.F., Das, P.K., Dowe, D.L.: Two decades of web application testing–a survey of recent advances. Inf. Syst. **43**, 20–54 (2014)
17. Lim, J.H., Song, S.H., Son, J.R., Kuc, T.Y., Park, H.S., Kim, H.S.: An automated test method for robot platform and its components. Int. J. Softw. Eng. Its Appl. **4**(3), 9–18 (2010)
18. Mandrioli, D., Morasca, S., Morzenti, A.: Generating test cases for real-time systems from logic specifications. Trans. Comput. Syst. **13**(4), 365–398 (1995)
19. Mathur, S., Malik, S.: Advancements in the V-Model. Int. J. Comput. Appl. **1**(12), 29–34 (2010)
20. Rajkumar, R.R., Lee, I., Sha, L., Stankovic, J.: Cyber-physical systems: the next computing revolution. In: 47th Design Automation Conference, pp. 731–736 (2010)
21. Sha, L., Gopalakrishnan, S., Liu, X., Wang, Q.: Cyber-physical systems: a new frontier. In: IEEE International Conference on Sensor Networks, Ubiquitous and Trustworthy Computing 2008, SUTC 2008, pp. 1–9 (2008)
22. Silva, L.C., Perkusich, M., Bublitz, F.M., Almeida, H.O., Perkusich, A.: A model-based architecture for testing medical cyber-physical systems. In: 29th Annual ACM Symposium on Applied Computing, pp. 25–30, New York, NY, USA (2014)
23. Srivastava, P.R., Kim, T-h: Application of genetic algorithm in software testing. J. Softw. Eng. Its Appl. **3**(4), 87–96 (2009)
24. Tevanlinna, A., Taina, J., Kauppinen, R.: Product family testing: a survey. SIGSOFT Softw. Eng. Notes **29**(2), 12–12 (2004)
25. Tidwell, T., Gao, X., Huang, H.M., Lu, C., Dyke, S., Gill, C.: Towards configurable real-time hybrid structural testing: a cyber-physical system approach. In: ISORC, pp. 37–44 (2009)
26. Woehrle, M., Lampka, K., Thiele, L.: Conformance testing for cyber-physical systems. ACM Trans. Embed. Comput. Syst. **11**(4), 84 (2012)
27. Zhang, L., He, J., Yu, W.: Test case generation from formal models of cyber physical system. J. Hybrid Inf. Technol. **6**(3), 15 (2013)

Real-Time Systems

Test-Data Generation for Testing Parallel Real-Time Systems

Muhammad Waqar Aziz$^{(\boxtimes)}$ and Syed Abdul Baqi Shah

Science and Technology Unit, Umm Al-Qura University,
Makkah, Kingdom of Saudi Arabia
{mwaziz,sashah}@uqu.edu.sa

Abstract. The Worst-Case Execution Time (WCET) of real-time systems is mainly influenced by the program design, its execution environment and the input data. To cover the last factor in the context of WCET estimation, the objective of this work is to generate the test-data that maximize the execution times of the parallel real-time systems. In this paper, a test-data generation technique is proposed that uses Genetic Algorithms to automatically generate the input data, to be used for testing of parallel real-time systems. The proposed technique was applied to a parallel embedded application – *Stringsearch*. The result was an analysis that took as input the parallel program and generated the test-data that cause maximal execution times. The generated test-data showed improvements by exercising long execution times in comparison to randomly generated input data.

Keywords: Test-data generation · Genetic Algorithm · Real-time systems · Measurement-based analysis · Worst-case execution time analysis · End-to-end testing

1 Introduction

With the wide use of multicore processors in desktop computers and embedded systems, and the growing demands of high performance real-time applications, it is expected that multicore processors will be increasingly used in real-time systems [26]. The deployment of real-time applications on multicore platforms with tens or hundreds of cores may become a reality very soon [3]. This demands special methods and techniques for the design and testing of future multicore embedded real-time systems, where the previous research mostly assumes sequential code running on single-core platforms.

The fundamental property to guarantee the performance of a real-time system is its Worst-Case Execution Time (WCET) testing. The worst-case bounds can be derived either by using static timing analysis [11], or by measuring the programs execution time on a given hardware or simulator using a set of inputs [24]. The static timing analysis methods applied on hardware and software models of the system are very difficult to apply for parallel systems. For instance,

© IFIP International Federation for Information Processing 2015
K. El-Fakih et al. (Eds.): ICTSS 2015, LNCS 9447, pp. 211–223, 2015.
DOI: 10.1007/978-3-319-25945-1_13

the inter-thread interferences among shared resources, e.g., L2 caches are hard to analyze statically [26]. In contrast, measurement-based methods can be used for better estimating the execution time of parallel systems and therefore are widely used in the industry.

The problem of WCET testing is to find the test-data that causes execution of the longest path of the program, and thus causes the longest execution time. But to do so, a complete test with all possible inputs, generally cannot be carried out. Similarly, exhausting all the possible program paths, for a given input, is usually infeasible. To handle these problems, evolutionary testing can be utilized that automatically searches the test-data to estimate the WCET. For instance, if searching the worst-case inputs from the set of all possible inputs is considered as an optimization problem, Genetic Algorithms (GA) [1] can be utilized to automatically search the required test-data.

The current research efforts of WCET analysis for multicore systems are focused on performance enhancing hardware features [12,15,19], and application [4,16,18] or programming level [9,27,28]. However, there is lack of research in test-data generation for WCET estimation of parallel real-time systems executing on multicore architectures. To fill this gap, this work proposes a Search-Based Software Engineering (SBSE) technique to generate test-data for testing parallel real-time systems. The proposed technique uses GA to sub-optimally evolve the worst-case inputs, with the objective to find those inputs that will cause the program to take longest execution time.

The proposed technique is applied by measuring the end-to-end execution time of the *ParMiBench* benchmark suite [14]. *ParMiBench* is an open source parallel version of a subset of *MiBench* benchmark suite [10] – many of whose benchmarks appear to be suitable candidates for WCET analysis [7]. *ParMiBench* benchmark suite, actually designed to evaluate the performance of embedded multi-core systems, is implemented using C language and POSIX threads to achieve parallelism and supports Unix/Linux based platforms [14]. The end-to-end time was measured by gathering the execution traces of the parallel program using the Gem5 simulator [2].

This article is organized as follows. Section 2 explains the methodology followed in this work. Section 3 describes the method to approach the problem of test-data generation along with the details of the actions performed. Section 4 reports the experimental setup and the results obtained from the experiment. The evaluation of this work is provided in Sect. 5. Section 6 describes related work in measurement-based WCET analysis for parallel real-time systems. Section 7 contains concluding remarks and directions for future work.

2   Methodology

The *ParMiBench* benchmark suite, used in this work, is a set of embedded parallel benchmarks from various domains of the embedded applications which include, control and automation, networks, offices, and security. However, we have selected the *Stringsearch* benchmark from the suite that is related to searching a *token* (strings stored in a *pattern file*) from a *text file*, due to the following reasons:

- In this work, the benchmarks are seen as a black box that consumes input and generates timing information. However, for the testing process to be effective and the testing results to be meaningful, we need benchmarks with a rich input space.
- the current Gem5 framework forces to execute the benchmarks from within a disk image in the full system mode. This requires the benchmarks to have input parameters that can be easily fed, e.g., via command line.

In the initial experiment, the simulation was executed with the existing data set of *Stringsearch* benchmark. However, the initial experiment revealed that the text and pattern files in the existing data set consist of repeated contents. Consequently, any new pattern file generated, with tokens picked up randomly from the text file, had tokens that exist in every line of the file regardless of which line they have been picked. Thus, the existing data set of the benchmark was inappropriate to allow evolutionary testing, as the data set should not contain duplicate values. Therefore, a new text file with dissimilar tokens was generated that consists of 102400 random characters (file size ≈ 100 KB), and a pattern file containing 64 tokens each of five characters length. The token length was kept fixed (i.e., five characters, similar to the given benchmark) to observe the execution time variations unassociated with the input length. Additionally, fixed size inputs allow the easy alignment of parts during crossover operation.

In this work, Gem5 architecture simulator was used to measure the end-to-end execution time of the parallel benchmark. Gem5 was selected as it provides full-system simulation to execute a program in the operating system environment, with support of several commercial Instruction Set Architectures (just as ARM, ALPHA). To get the execution traces of our interest, we performed some tweaking to the simulator. We applied a Kernel patch and made some custom modifications to the simulator to get the execution traces of the benchmark[1]. These traces were then used to calculate the end-to-end execution time of the benchmark. Instead of manual calculation, the end-to-end execution time was calculated automatically by a Java application.

3   Proposed Test-Data Generation Technique

The technique proposed in this work for test-data generation, is based on SBSE approach, namely GA. GA mimics the process of natural selection and chooses the best from one generation to produce the next generation and attempts to reach the solution much faster than otherwise. The steps of the proposed test-data generation technique, as depicted in Fig. 1, are described is below:

---

[1] Interested readers can visit our technical report for more configuration details, http://bit.ly/1JqheNS.

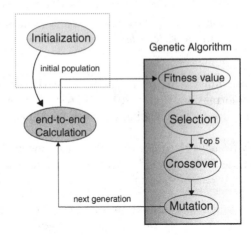

Fig. 1. GA based test-data generation technique proposed for parallel real-time systems

3.1 Define the Initial Population

For applying GA, an initial population of individuals need to be defined which is evolved across a number of generations. Individuals are usually random guesses to the solution of a problem. Care should be given to maintain diversity in the population so that premature convergence towards a sub-optimal solution can be prevented. For instance, in case of *Stringsearch*, a good candidate for the best individual produced by the GA in the last generation is the input to the program where all tokens to be searched do not exist in the text file.

To achieve this, an intuition-based selection was made to start from a point where 50 % of tokens exist in the text and 50 % do not. An initial population of one hundred pattern files, to be used in GA, was generated using the following ways:

(a) By randomly picking up tokens from this newly generated text file
(b) By randomly generating totally new tokens

Consequently, each file contained a set of tokens gathered from a mixture of 50 % randomly generated tokens and 50 % tokens picked up from the text. Thus, the chances of each token within a pattern file are equally likely to be in the text or not, making it a fair distribution to start with.

To conclude, there are $(n*k)/2$ tokens that exist in the text, and are randomly distributed among the total $n*k$ tokens in n files (considering n pattern files, each having k patterns). This allows to give the 50-50 found/not found distribution without making individuals in the population biased. This set of one hundred pattern files collectively formed the genetic representation of the solution domain. Thus, the initial population in this experiment consists of one hundred chromosomes and 64 genes of each chromosome, in GA terminology.

3.2   End-to-End Time Calculation

In this work, it is proposed to use the end-to-end execution time of parallel program as *fitness function*. The end-to-end time was calculated from the traces obtained from the Gem5 simulator by executing the parallel application. Each trace was generated by detecting the starting and ending points of a thread execution. A Java application was written to automatically calculate the end-to-end time from the obtained execution traces. In the initialization phase, the end-to-end time was calculated for all the 100 files present in the initial population. The simulation was run one hundred times to generate one hundred traces, i.e., one time for each pattern file. However, in all the other iterations it was calculated for the new individuals of the next generation only.

3.3   Applying Genetic Algorithm

GA uses the concept of natural evolution to reach the desired solution from a given huge search space. The main idea of using GA, in this work, is to execute the program with sets of inputs throughout a number of generations. The process starts with generating k random vectors initially (first generation) and obtain their timing information. Then, the generated k random inputs with the timing information are used to produce the next k inputs (second generation). This process is repeated for n generations. The details of the steps of GA as followed in the proposed technique are given below.

1. **Calculate the Fitness Value**

   The fitness of the individuals is a problem-dependent value that specifies the goodness of an individual in solving the problem at hand. The selection of an individual for the next generation depends on its fitness value, i.e., each individual in the population is evaluated by calculating its fitness. The fitness value is used to select the best of any generation to 'mate' them in order to produce the new generation.

   As already mentioned, the end-to-end time is considered as a fitness value, in this work. Thus, the longer the end-to-end time, the higher would be the fitness. The fitness value is generated in GA through fitness function. It means that calculating the fitness function requires the execution of the program to produce traces. The time taken by *Stringsearch* to execute each pattern file was considered as the fitness value of that pattern file. The use of GA is suppose to search the inputs with higher fitness values in each generation. In this way, the program execution using GA would lead towards inputs having larger fitness values.

   It is worth mentioning here that cache hits or misses, thread conflicts or any other parameters were not considered to evaluate the fitness. Because considering these parameters is a huge research in its own and requires more effort and time. In addition, Gem5 simulator does not provide much information about these parameters which can be useful at this level.

2. Select the Individuals

A selection strategy is applied to the individuals of a population in a given generation to decide which ones are allowed to proceed to the next generation. To make a rank based selection, the individual need to be sorted based on their fitness values. It is proposed to select only five individuals, as selecting more individuals would take more time in the remaining steps and also in calculating their fitness in next generation.

In this experiment, the pattern files were sorted based on their fitness values. The top five pattern files were selected as chromosomes for the next generation. Top five files were selected because selecting 50 files, for instance, will be a big enough number as it will make 100 files for the next generation which will take too long to calculate their fitness.

3. Crossover

The evolution of the population involves the exchange of genetic material between the individuals through crossover operation. Traditionally, this is achieved by choosing a point along two bit strings at random and swapping the tails. To produce new files, a crossover was made amongst the top five selected pattern files, by merging two lists of tokens picked up from randomly selected pattern files. This crossover resulted in ten new chromosomes. In crossover, one part of a file was concatenated with another part of the second file, where the size of selected parts may not be the same, e.g., 2 tokens picked from one file were concatenated with 62 tokens from the other file. This selection is based on cutting one chromosome at a random location and concatenating it with the remaining part of the second chromosome cut at the same location.

4. Mutation

The evolution of the population also involves the alteration of the genetic material of a single individual through mutation operation. Mutation is achieved by picking a bit at random and flipping its value. Mutation was applied to the results of crossover to produce and further improve the next generation. It was done by randomly picking a token from a pattern file and replacing its any letter with another random character. This process was repeated until the desired percentage of mutation was achieved. In this way, the next generation of 10 chromosomes was produced.

The above process was repeated for a set of ten chromosomes, which was reproduced after each generation. The evolution continues until a good-enough individual that solves the problem adequately is found, or until a maximum number of generations is reached. Opting for the latter case, the whole process was repeated for 50 generations, as the probability of improving over several generations is high.

With the above modeled parameters, a Java application was developed that implemented GA in the experiment. The implementation used the given pattern files composed of tokens without converting them into binary strings. This simplified the complex problem of coding and decoding of inputs for this specific case.

4   Experimentation

4.1   Experimental Setup

The Gem5 configurations, as used in this experiment, included four cores of ARM detailed architecture as specified by Gem5 (ARMv7-A ISA based) with default size of L2 cache (2 MB) and 256 MB of Memory. The disk image contained ARM embedded Linux (AEL) as the guest operating system for the simulator. We used Gem5 to run the simulations and execute benchmarks for collecting the kernel level thread traces and computing the end-to-end times. We had Xeon processor with twelve logical cores and enough memory (48 GB) available in our machine to accommodate multiple instances of simulator running in parallel.

4.2   Experimental Results

To observe the effects of applying GA using visual representation, graphs of the calculated end-to-end times were plotted for each generation. In each graph, the length of the execution time is represented on the vertical axis in terms of CPU ticks, whereas the ten pattern files of each generation are represented horizontally. For example, in first generation the highest and the lowest values were found as 59843433000 and 59603617500 ticks for 4th and 8th pattern files respectively, as shown in Fig. 2(a). Some other results produced during fifty generations are depicted in the remaining parts of Fig. 2.

From the plotted graphs, i.e., the measured end-to-end times, it is observed that by using GA an overall improvement can be achieved in the fitness values corresponding to the pattern files. For instance, in first and third generations (Fig. 2(a) and (b)) there are only three pattern files which caused the program to execute for a period longer than 5.98e+10 ticks. In comparison, the number of pattern files, which execute longer than this number of ticks, is increased to eight pattern files in 25th generation and nine pattern files in 50th generation (Fig. 2(c) and (d)). This increase in the number of input files after applying several generations shows that the inputs are taking longer time. This is a clear indication that the proposed technique has improved the inputs, i.e., those inputs are generated that cause the longest time to execute.

Table 1 shows the WCET measured during the experiments in different generations for five character length input token. A threshold value of 5.98e+10 was defined to analyze the improvement in the inputs over all generations. The number of files taking greater or equal time than the threshold value was counted, as represented by Above (Th.5.98) column in Table 1.

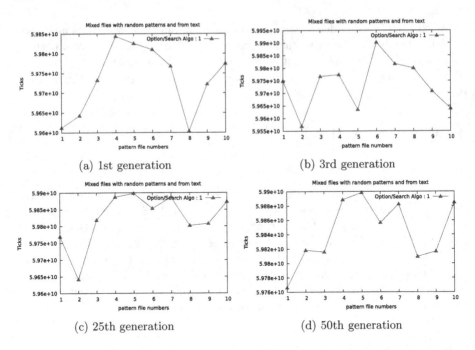

Fig. 2. End-to-End times (fitness values) in different generations for the pattern files with five characters long tokens

An increasing number of input files above the threshold can be observed, in Table 1, except for 30th generation. This is due to the very nature of GA where results can degrade even after reaching to an improved position. However, an overall improvement is achieved across 50 generations.

5   Evaluation

In order to evaluate the scalability of the proposed technique, the experiment was repeated with other input files as given with the benchmark. To this end, the complete process was re-performed for tokens with a length of 10 characters; compared to the original experiment where five characters input token was used. Some of the graphs, representing different generations produced using 10 characters length are depicted in Fig. 3. The WCET measured for input tokens of 10 characters length are displayed in Table 2. The threshold value, in this case, was defined as 5.9e+10 with the same purpose of analyzing the inputs over all generations.

From Table 2, it can be observed that the number of input files increased with the number of generations. Although the number of files slightly increased and decreased due to GA, an overall steady increase in the number of files was observed after 50th generations.

Table 1. Measured WCET across different generations for 5 characters length token

Input token size	Generation no	WCET	Above (Th.5.98)
5 characters	1	59843433000	3
	10	59878900000	5
	20	59895367000	8
	30	59898941500	6
	40	59896569500	7
	50	59898461000	9

6 Related Work and Discussion

Most of WCET-analysis research is performed for sequential software and single-core hardware. Recently, research on WCET analysis of sequential code on multi-core processors has been a main focus. The work that has been done in this area so far can be divided into two parts (1) static hardware modeling for WCET analysis on multi-core architectures [8,25,26,29], and (2) design of analyzable multi-core computers that favor timing predictability over performance [6,17,20,21]. In relation to this work, research on parallel applications running on multi-core architectures is very limited. For instance, Rochange et al. [19] highlights the problem of analyzing the timing behavior of non-sequential

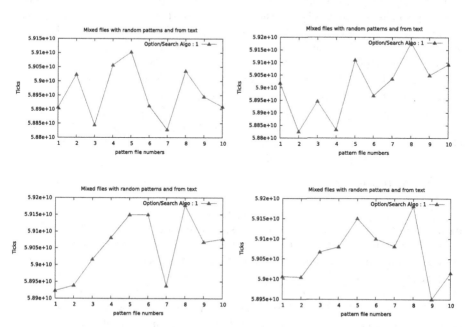

Fig. 3. End-to-End times (fitness values) in different generations for the pattern files with ten character long tokens

Table 2. Measured WCET across different generations for 10 characters length token

Input token size	Generation no	WCET	Above (Th.5.90)
10 characters	1	59102869500	4
	10	59134277000	5
	20	59097647500	6
	30	59100034000	6
	40	59181076000	7
	50	59181090000	9

software on a multi-core architecture. They report a manual analysis of a parallel application, which determines the synchronization and communication between its executing threads.

In contrast, we have used GA to heuristically search the input from a huge search space of tokens that would cause the program to execute for the longest period of time. It was observed that the execution time of the search tends to decrease with the increase in size of the input text (see e.g., WCET of 5 and 10 characters). In general, the proposed technique is applicable to any parallel real-time system where optimization is needed. This further requires that the system under consideration can be genetically represented and has a fitness function for its evaluation. However, the proposed technique should be complemented with static timing analysis if *safety* is required, i.e., to ensure that the obtained results are close to the actual WCET of the considered system.

Evolutionary search (more specifically GA) has been employed in the literature [5,13,22] to find long execution times of real-time programs. Although, research on using GA for testing real-time systems dates back to 90s [23], it has not been used for WCET analysis of parallel programs running on multi-core hardware, to the best of our knowledge. The fitness function used in this work considered the end-to-end time for the execution of a program as the fitness value. This consideration has helped us to produce good enough results by using GA that maximized the fitness value.

7   Conclusion

In this paper, a measurement-based technique is proposed for automatic test-data generation for parallel real-time systems running on a multicore architecture. The technique uses Genetic Algorithm to generate test data that maximize the execution times of the parallel application. It evolves input vectors that cause long execution times of the program using evolutionary testing. The results of the experiment showed a significant improvement in the execution times of input files after applying the proposed technique. Thus, the aim of producing large execution times, which are either the WCET or close to it, was achieved.

In the future, we aim to use a real-life, real-time application to evaluate our work. In case of publicly-unavailability of such applications, the method can be tested with other benchmarks of *ParMiBench*. Moreover, the static timing analysis is planned to be performed to evaluate the safeness and tightness of the proposed technique. Although, the end-to-end time is considered as an output to the fitness function, it is also planned to consider a richer multi-objective fitness function in future that might include thread conflicts, cache misses/hits and cache sizes.

Acknowledgments. This research is funded by the program of strategic technologies of the National Science, Technology, and Innovation plan in Saudi Arabia (Grant No. 11-INF1705-10). We acknowledge KACST (King Abdulaziz City for Science and Technology) for funding this research and STU (Science and Technology Unit), Umm Al-Qura University, Makkah for providing necessary support.

References

1. Berg, C., Engblom, J., Wilhelm, R.: Requirements for and design of a processor with predictable timing. In: Design of Systems with Predictable Behaviour (2004)
2. Binkert, N., Beckmann, B., Black, G., Reinhardt, S.K., Saidi, A., Basu, A., Hestness, J., Hower, D.R., Krishna, T., Sardashti, S., et al.: The gem5 simulator. ACM SIGARCH Comput. Archit. News **39**(2), 1–7 (2011)
3. Calandrino, J.M., Anderson, J.H., Baumberger, D.P.: A hybrid real-time scheduling approach for large-scale multicore platforms. In: 19th Euromicro Conference on Real-Time Systems, 2007, ECRTS 2007, pp. 247–258, IEEE (2007)
4. Ding, Y., Zhang, W.: Multicore-aware code co-positioning to reduce wcet on dual-core processors with shared instruction caches. JCSE **6**(1), 12–25 (2012)
5. Gross, H.G.: An evaluation of dynamic, optimisation-based worst-case execution time analysis. In: Proceedings of the International Conference on Information Technology: Prospects and Challenges in the 21st Century, Kathmandu, Nepal (2003)
6. Guan, N., Stigge, M., Yi, W., Yu, G.: Cache-aware scheduling and analysis for multicores. In: Proceedings of the Seventh ACM International Conference on Embedded Software, pp. 245–254, ACM (2009)
7. Gustafsson, J., Betts, A., Ermedahl, A., Lisper, B.: The mälardalen wcet benchmarks: past, present and future. In: OASIcs-OpenAccess Series in Informatics, vol. 15, Schloss Dagstuhl-Leibniz-Zentrum fuer Informatik (2010)
8. Gustavsson, A., Ermedahl, A., Lisper, B., Pettersson, P.: Towards wcet analysis of multicore architectures using uppaal. In: OASIcs-OpenAccess Series in Informatics, vol. 15, Schloss Dagstuhl-Leibniz-Zentrum fuer Informatik (2010)
9. Gustavsson, A., Gustafsson, J., Lisper, B.: Toward static timing analysis of parallel software. In: OASIcs-OpenAccess Series in Informatics, vol. 23, Schloss Dagstuhl-Leibniz-Zentrum fuer Informatik (2012)
10. Guthaus, M.R., Ringenberg, J.S., Ernst, D., Austin, T.M., Mudge, T., Brown, R.B.: Mibench: a free, commercially representative embedded benchmark suite. In: 2001 IEEE International Workshop on Workload Characterization 2001, WWC-4, pp. 3–14, IEEE (2001)
11. Heckmann, R., Ferdinand, C.: Worst-case execution time prediction by static program analysis. In: 18th International Parallel and Distributed Processing Symposium (IPDPS 2004), pp. 26–30, IEEE Computer Society (2004)

12. Kästner, D., Schlickling, M., Pister, M., Cullmann, C., Gebhard, G., Heckmann, R., Ferdinand, C.: Meeting real-time requirements with multi-core processors. In: Ortmeier, F., Daniel, P. (eds.) SAFECOMP Workshops 2012. LNCS, vol. 7613, pp. 117–131. Springer, Heidelberg (2012)

13. Khan, U., Bate, I.: Wcet analysis of modern processors using multi-criteria optimisation. In: 2009 1st International Symposium on Search Based Software Engineering, pp. 103–112, IEEE (2009)

14. Liang, Y., Iqbal, S.M.Z.: OpenMPBench-an open-source benchmark for multiprocessor based embedded systems. Ph.D. thesis, Master thesis report MCS-2010: 02, School of Computing, Blekinge Institute of Technology, Sweden (2010)

15. Liang, Y., Ding, H., Mitra, T., Roychoudhury, A., Li, Y., Suhendra, V.: Timing analysis of concurrent programs running on shared cache multi-cores. Real-Time Syst. 48(6), 638–680 (2012)

16. Ozaktas, H., Rochange, C., Sainrat, P.: Automatic wcet analysis of real-time parallel applications. In: OASIcs-OpenAccess Series in Informatics, vol. 30, Schloss Dagstuhl-Leibniz-Zentrum fuer Informatik (2013)

17. Pitter, C., Schoeberl, M.: A real-time java chip-multiprocessor. ACM Trans. Embed. Comput. Syst. (TECS) 10(1), 9 (2010)

18. Potop-Butucaru, D., Puaut, I., et al.: Integrated worst-case response time evaluation of multicore non-preemptive applications (2013)

19. Rochange, C., Bonenfant, A., Sainrat, P., Gerdes, M., Wolf, J., Ungerer, T., Petrov, Z., Mikulu, F.: Wcet analysis of a parallel 3D multigrid solver executed on the merasa multi-core. In: OASIcs-OpenAccess Series in Informatics, vol. 15, Schloss Dagstuhl-Leibniz-Zentrum fuer Informatik (2010)

20. Rosen, J., Andrei, A., Eles, P., Peng, Z.: Bus access optimization for predictable implementation of real-time applications on multiprocessor systems-on-chip. In: 28th IEEE International Real-Time Systems Symposium 2007, RTSS 2007, pp. 49–60, IEEE (2007)

21. Supercomputing, B.: Merasa: multicore execution of hard real-time applications supporting analyzability (2010)

22. Wegener, J., Mueller, F.: A comparison of static analysis and evolutionary testing for the verification of timing constraints. Real-Time Syst. 21(3), 241–268 (2001)

23. Wegener, J., Sthamer, H., Jones, B.F., Eyres, D.E.: Testing real-time systems using genetic algorithms. Softw. Qual. J. 6(2), 127–135 (1997)

24. Wilhelm, R., Engblom, J., Ermedahl, A., Holsti, N., Thesing, S., Whalley, D., Bernat, G., Ferdinand, C., Heckmann, R., Mitra, T., et al.: The worst-case execution-time problem–overview of methods and survey of tools. ACM Trans. Embed. Comput. Syst. (TECS) 7(3), 36 (2008)

25. Wu, L., Zhang, W.: Bounding worst-case execution time for multicore processors through model checking. In: Proceedings of 16th IEEE Real-Time and Embedded Technology and Applications Symposium (RTAS 2010), Work-in-Progress Session, pp. 17–20 (2010)

26. Yan, J., Zhang, W.: Wcet analysis for multi-core processors with shared l2 instruction caches. In: IEEE Real-Time and Embedded Technology and Applications Symposium 2008, RTAS 2008, pp. 80–89, IEEE (2008)

27. Yip, E., Roop, P.S., Biglari-Abhari, M.: Predictable parallel programming using PRET-C. Faculty of Engineering, University of Auckland (2010)

28. Yip, E., Roop, P.S., Biglari-Abhari, M., Girault, A.: Programming and timing analysis of parallel programs on multicores. In: 2013 13th International Conference on Application of Concurrency to System Design (ACSD), pp. 160–169, IEEE (2013)
29. Zhang, W., Yan, J.: Accurately estimating worst-case execution time for multi-core processors with shared direct-mapped instruction caches. In: 15th IEEE International Conference on Embedded and Real-Time Computing Systems and Applications 2009, RTCSA 2009, pp. 455–463, IEEE (2009)

Selective Test Generation Approach for Testing Dynamic Behavioral Adaptations

Mariam Lahami[1]([✉]), Moez Krichen[1,2], Hajer Barhoumi[1],
and Mohamed Jmaiel[1,3]

[1] ReDCAD Research Laboratory, National School of Engineering of Sfax,
University of Sfax, B.P. 1173, Sfax, Tunisia
{mariam.lahami,hajer.barhoumi}@redcad.org
[2] Faculty of Computer Science and Information Technology,
Al-Baha University, Al Bahah, Kingdom of Saudi Arabia
moez.krichen@redcad.org
[3] Research Center for Computer Science,
Multimedia and Digital Data Processing of Sfax,
B.P. 275, 3021 Sfax, Sakiet Ezzit, Tunisia
mohamed.jmaiel@enis.rnu.tn

Abstract. This paper presents a model-based black-box testing approach for dynamically adaptive systems. Behavioral models of such systems are formally specified using timed automata. With the aim of obtaining the new test suite and avoiding its regeneration in a cost effective manner, we propose a selective test generation approach. The latter comprises essentially three modules: (1) a model differencing module that detects similarities and differences between the initial and the evolved behavioral models, (2) an old test classification module that identifies reusable and retestable tests from the old test suite, and finally (3) a test generation module that generates new tests covering new behaviors and adapts old tests that failed during animation. To show its efficiency, the proposed technique is illustrated through the Toast application and compared to the classical Regenerate All and Retest All approaches.

1 Introduction

Due to increasingly rapid changes in the context, goals, and user requirements of recent critical software systems, there is a demand to perform automatically validation tasks at runtime to ensure firstly that existing functionalities have not been affected by dynamic changes. Secondly, it is essential to verify that new requirements are fulfilled by the new version of the system.

One of the emerging and promising techniques for testing a software is the Model Based Testing (MBT) approach. Instead of writing hundred of test cases manually, the test designer defines an abstract model of the System Under Test (SUT) and then MBT tool generates automatically a set of test cases from the model. MBT methods have recently gained increased attention because maintaining and adapting test cases can be facilitated and also automated [17].

Another technique widely used for testing an evolving software system is the Regression Testing. Most research and tools perform usually white box regression

© IFIP International Federation for Information Processing 2015
K. El-Fakih et al. (Eds.): ICTSS 2015, LNCS 9447, pp. 224–239, 2015.
DOI: 10.1007/978-3-319-25945-1_14

testing at design time [7,16]. Up to our best knowledge, there is a trend to merge these two techniques to build approaches and tools for black/gray box regression testing, known as specification-based regression approaches [4,15]. The majority of those potential solutions use UML diagrams to model SUT behaviors and deal mainly with selecting test cases from existing test suites specified before modifications. This is not sufficient because new tests have to be generated and thus stored test suites need to be updated [5,6].

Following this direction, we provide a selective test generation approach called TestGenApp, that reduces the cost of adapting and maintaining test suites covering either modified or newly added behaviors at runtime. Our proposal ensures that tests cases continue to be consistent and fault revealing even if the SUT evolves dynamically. It avoids the regeneration of the full test suite by covering only affected parts of the behavioral model. The latter was specified using UPPAAL Timed Automata formalism. The well-establish tool UPPAAL Cover is customized to generate effectively new abstract tests and to adapt failed ones. To do so, we reuse its expressive approach to specify coverage criteria, called Observer Automata. To show its efficiency, the proposed technique is illustrated through the Toast dynamic application [13] and compared to the classical Regenerate All and Retest All approaches.

The rest of this paper is organized as follows. Section 2 provides background material for understanding the research problem. Subsequently, the selective test generation approach is outlined in Sect. 3. Afterward, its application to the Toast application is highlighted in Sect. 4. Section 5 draws comparison with related work in the context of selective regression testing. Finally, in Sect. 6, we conclude with a summary of paper contributions, and we identify potential areas of future research.

2 Background

This section provides background material on testing evolvable systems, formal modeling as timed automata, coverage criteria and automata observers.

2.1 Testing Evolvable Systems

One of the well-known technique used to check the correctness of software after modification is *Regression Testing*. As quoted from [8], it "attempts to validate modified software and ensure that no new errors are introduced into previously tested code". This technique guarantees that the modified software is still working according to its specification and it is maintaining its level of reliability. It is commonly applied during development phase and not at runtime. Leung et al. [12] present two types of regression testing. In the progressive regression testing, the SUT specification can be modified by reflecting some enhancements or some new requirements added in the SUT. In the corrective regression testing, only the SUT code is modified by altering some instructions in the program whereas

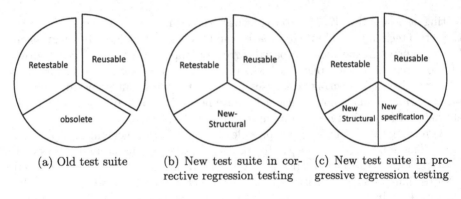

(a) Old test suite   (b) New test suite in cor-   (c) New test suite in pro-
                      rective regression testing   gressive regression testing

Fig. 1. Test classification

the specification does not change. For the above defined types, Leung et al. illustrate the same test case classification of the old test suite into three categories (see Fig. 1a):

- Reusable tests: valid tests that cover the unmodified parts of the SUT.
- Retestable tests: still valid tests that cover modified parts of the SUT.
- Obsolete tests: invalid tests that cover deleted parts of the SUT.

After modifications, new tests can be classified into two classes (see Fig. 1b and c):

- New specification tests: include new test cases generated from the modified parts of the specification.
- New structural tests: include structural-based test cases that test altered program instructions.

   Contrary to regression testing, *runtime testing* is emerging as a novel solution for the validation of dynamically evolvable systems. It is defined in Brenner et al. [3] as an online testing method that is carried out on the final execution environment of a system when the system or a part of it is operational. It can be performed either at deployment-time or at service-time. The deployment-time testing serves to validate and verify the assembled system in its runtime environment while it is deployed for the first time. For systems whose architecture remains constant after initial installation, there is obviously no need to retest the system when it has been placed in- service. On the contrary, if the execution environment or the system behavior or its architecture has been changed, service-time testing will be a necessity to verify and validate the new system in the new situation.

   In this work, we merge findings on both specification-based regression testing and runtime testing with the aim of conceiving a runtime model-based testing approach. The latter is applied in a cost effective manner whenever the SUT behavior evolves dynamically.

2.2   Formal Modeling Using UPPAAL

UPPAAL is a well-established model-checking tool charged with verifying a given model w.r.t. a formally expressed requirement specification. It uses a popular and widespread formalism for specifying critical and real-time systems, called Timed Automata (TA). Indeed, a system is modeled as a network of timed automata, called processes. A timed automaton is an extended finite-state machine equipped with a set of clock-variables that track the progress of time and that can guard when transitions are allowed. In this work, we adopt the particular UPPAAL style of timed automata. As they have proven their expressiveness and convenience, behavioral models of both initial system and the evolved system are expressed using the formal notation bellow:

Definition of Timed Automaton

Let $\mathcal{C}$ be a set of valued variables called clocks, and $\mathcal{A} = \mathcal{I} \cup \mathcal{O} \cup \{\tau\}$ with $\mathcal{I}$ a set of input actions, $\mathcal{O}$ a set of output actions (denoted a? and a!), and the non-synchronizing action (denoted τ). Let $\mathcal{G}(\mathcal{C})$ denote the set of guards on clocks being conjunctions of constraints of the form $c \bowtie n$, and let $\mathcal{U}(\mathcal{C})$ denote the set of updates of clocks corresponding to sequences of statements of the form $c := n$, where $c \in \mathcal{C}$, $n \in \mathbf{N}$, and $\bowtie \in \{\leqslant, \leq, =, \geq, \geqslant\}$. A timed automaton over $(\mathcal{A}, \mathcal{C})$ is a quadruple (L, l_0, I, E), where:

- L is a set of locations, $l_0 \in L$ is an initial location.
- $I : L \longmapsto \mathcal{G}(\mathcal{C})$ a function that assigns to each location an invariant.
- E is a set of edges such that $E \subseteq L \times \mathcal{G}(\mathcal{C}) \times \mathcal{A}_\tau \times \mathcal{U}(\mathcal{C}) \times L$

We shall write $l \xrightarrow{g,\alpha,u} l'$ when $\langle l, g, \alpha, u, l' \rangle \in E$.

Due to space limitations, the semantics of TA as well as the semantics of a network of TA have not been presented in this paper. Moreover, it is worthy to note that UPPAAL modeling language extends timed automata with additional features such as integer variables, urgent locations, and committed locations, etc. For more details, readers can refer to [2].

It is worthy to note that several restrictions have to be fulfilled in this work by each timed automaton in the SUT behavioral specification. They have to be deterministic input enabled output urgent timed automata (DIEOU-TA). For short these restrictions means that: (i) Two transitions with the same label lead to the same state, (ii) no delay can be done when an input is enabled, (iii) when an output is enabled, no input, output, or delay is permitted [10]. Moreover, we assume that the test specification is given as a closed network of TA that can be partitioned into one network of TA modeling the SUT behavior, and one modeling its environment behavior (ENV). Note here that the tester replaces the environment and controls the SUT via a distinguished set of observable input and output actions.

2.3   Automata Observer for Specifying Coverage Criteria

A coverage criterion is a specification of items such as locations and edges to be traversed or visited by the timed automaton. An example of a coverage criterion

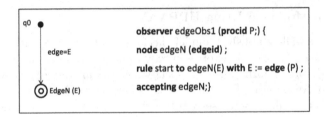

Fig. 2. Edge coverage observer presented in both textual and graphical notations.

is *edge coverage* which means that a test case should traverse all edges of a given timed automaton. An item to be traversed or visited is called a coverage item and can be modeled by an observer. The latter observes the execution of a timed automaton and accepts when the coverage item is covered by the trace.

As depicted in Fig. 2, an observer automaton can be presented either in graphical or textual notations. It is made of locations and edges. Locations are labeled with a name and optional variables, and edges are labeled with predicates. Two special types of locations are identified: the initial location denoted with a black filled circle, and the accepting location denoted with a double circle. In addition, an observer can only have one initial location but can reach several accepting locations. Formally, an observer automaton is a quadruple (Q, q_0, Q_f, B) where:

- Q is a finite set of observer locations.
- q_0 is the initial observer location.
- $Q_f \subset Q$ is a set of accepting observer locations.
- B is a set of edges such $q \xrightarrow{b} q'$ where b is a predicate based on attributes of timed automata as variables, edges, locations, etc.

We believe that the use of the observer language simplifies the expression of coverage criteria as it can be used to specify and combine the most popular ones such as "all edges", "all locations", "all-definition use-pairs"[9], etc. In our context, this formalism is used to express our own coverage criteria: covering new items and adapted ones.

3   Selective Test Generation Approach

The proposed selective test generation approach, called TestGenApp, is built upon three modules as outlined in Fig. 3. Each one is introduced in the following subsections.

3.1   Model Differencing Module

Model differencing technique is used to detect similarities and differences between the original model M and the evolved M' taken as inputs. It generates as output a colored M_{diff} that highlights changed and unchanged elements. Added locations and transitions are marked in Red, modified locations

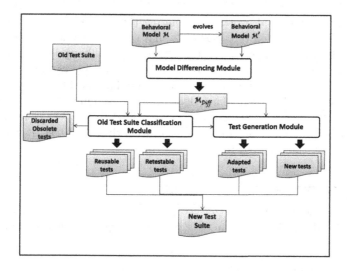

Fig. 3. TestGenApp: selective test generation approach.

and transitions are marked in Yellow, finally unchanged locations and transitions are marked in Green. The colored model includes a new variable called *col* initially equal to 1. This variable is updated in response to the performed modification. If target and source locations or transition labels (guard, update, synchronization) are newly added and then colored in Red, the *col* variable associated with this transition is multiplied by zero (i.e., $col := col * 0$). Similarly, if transition labels, source or target location are colored in Yellow, the *col* variable is multiplied by two (i.e., $col := col * 2$). Otherwise, transition labels, target and source location are unchanged and so the *col* variable is multiplied by one (i.e., $col := col * 1$).

Several kinds of changes are taken into account in this work. First of all, we support clock modification, location addition/removal and transition addition/removal. Moreover, state modification is considered by changing state invariant or changing the incoming and the outgoing transitions. Finally, transition modification is also handled by changing guard, synchronization and update fields. It is worthy to note that we support elementary as well as complex modifications.

3.2 Old Test Suite Classification Module

Based on the test classification proposed by Leung et al. [12], the old test suite issued from the original model $\mathcal{M}$ is divided into reusable, retestable and obsolete tests. Tests that traverse inchanged parts (locations and transitions marked as green) on the $\mathcal{M}_{diff}$ model are classified as *reusable tests*. Tests that cover at least a removed state or removed transition are classified as *obsolete tests* and will be automatically discarded from the new test suite.

We extend Leung et al. work by animating the remaining set of tests. First, we obtain valid tests called *retestabe tests* that cover the same coverage items in the new model and traverse the same paths with possibly updated clock values. Second, some failed tests are also detected. Generally, they cannot be animated on the new model because they may traverse altered paths. Thus, they need to be adapted by regenerating them. The Algorithm 1 is used in this test classification step. To do so, a new variable called $ColY$ is added to the $\mathcal{M}_{diff}$ model and it is used to mark the new reachable transition with the failed test. It will be used later to generate the adapted test.

Algorithm 1. Test Classification Algorithm

Input: Old test traces $\mathcal{TR}$
    A network of Timed Automata TA_{diff} highlighting unchanged and changed elements.
Output: Reusable tests T_{Ru}.
    Retestable tests T_{Rt}.

1: **BEGIN**
2: **for** each trace in $\mathcal{TR}$ **do**
3:    $coveredItemsList=$ get_CoveredItems(trace)
4:    **if** (VerifColorGreen($coveredItemsList$)= true) **then**
5:      $trace \in T_{Ru}$
6:    **else**
7:      **if** (isAnimated($trace,TA_{diff}$)=true) **then**
8:        $trace \in T_{Rt}$
9:      **else**
10:        $trace$ needs to be adapted
11:        the new reachable $transition.setUpdate(ColY := 1)$
12:      **end if**
13:    **end if**
14: **end for**
15: **END**

3.3   Test Generation Module

The used test generation technique is based on model checking. The main idea is to formulate the test generation problem as a reachability problem that can be solved with the model checker tool UPPAAL [2]. However, instead of using model annotations and reachability properties to express coverage criteria, the observer language is used.

In this direction, we reuse the finding of Hessel et al. [9] by exploiting its extension of UPPAAL namely UPPAAL CO$\sqrt{}$ER[1]. This tool takes as inputs a model, an observer and a configuration file. The model is specified as a network of

---

[1] http://user.it.uu.se/~hessel/CoVer/index.php.

```
observer obs (procid P;varid col;varid colY;) {

node edgeN (edgeid, varid) ;

node edgeA(edgeid,varid) ;

rule start to edgeA(K,colY) with K:=edge(P),eval(colY)==1;

rule start to edgeN(E, col) with E:=edge(P),eval(col)==0 ;

accepting edgeN,edgeA;}
```

Fig. 4. Covering new and adapted tests with automata observers

UPPAAL timed automata (.xml) that comprises a SUT part and an environment part. The observer (.obs) expresses the coverage criterion that guides the model exploration during test case generation. The configuration file (.cfg) describes mainly the interactions between the system part and the environment part in terms of input/output signals. It may also specify the variables that should be passed as parameters in these signals. As output, it produces a test suite containing a set of timed traces (.xml).

Our test generation module is built upon these well-elaborated tools. The key idea here is to use UPPAAL CO$\sqrt{}$ER and its generic and formal specification language for coverage criteria to generate new tests and adapted ones.

As depicted in Fig. 4, we express our own observer that covers only new behaviors and adapts modified ones. Observer parameters are denoted with capital letters. The parameters can refer in the model to variables, edges, locations, variable valuations, etc. In this example, we use the E parameter for an edge. The observer collects all different edges from the parameter process P. $edge(E)$ is a predicate which evaluates to true if the observer monitors edge E of the timed automaton. The evaluation of the col variable to zero indicates that the current edge is marked as new edge. The rule *rule start to edgeN(E, col) with E:=edge(P),eval(col)==0;* formalizes this new edge coverage criterion. A test sequence satisfies this coverage criterion if when executed on the model it traverses at least on edge where the col variable is updated to zero. Similarly, if the variable *colY* is evaluated to one as outlined in the rule *rule start to edgeA(K,colY) with K:=edge(P),eval(colY)==1;* this means that the current edge is marked as modified edge. Thus, the monitored edge can be taken as accepted covered item by the new generated test sequence.

4   Application to the Toast Case Study

In this section, we describe the application of the presented technique on a case study in the telematics and fleet management domain called Toast [13]. For this aim, our prototype has been implemented in Java language. We have used the UPPAAL model checker, version 4.1.18 for modeling the SUT specification with timed automata and for checking that the developed models are deadlock free. Regarding the test generation, UPPAAL CO$\sqrt{}$ER version 1.4 is adopted.

4.1   Toast Description

Toast is an OSGi[2] application used to demonstrate a wide range of EclipseRT technologies. It provides means to manage and to interact with devices installable in a vehicle. For the sake of simplicity, the studied scenario covers the case of emergency notification. The vehicle comprises two devices: an Airbag and a GPS. If the airbag deploys, an Emergency Monitor is notified. In this case, the monitor queries the GPS for the vehicle heading, latitude, longitude and speed (see Fig. 5). The three components in the Toast initial configuration can be modeled by the three UPPAAL timed automata as shown in Fig. 6. In the beginning, timing constraints are omitted and we focus mainly on synchronization of inputs and outputs signals between components.

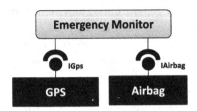

Fig. 5. Initial toast architecture.

When the airbag is deployed (i.e., this internal action is modeled with an empty label from location _0 to location _1), the Airbag component sends a message (via the action em) to the Emergency Monitor and waits for an acknowledge (an emAck action). In case of a negative replay (modeled by action emNoAck), the Airbag sends the emergency message again. Afterwards, the Emergency Monitor interacts with the GPS to get vehicle's latitude, longitude, heading and speed. To allow the system to come back to its initial state, the Airbag is undeployed (this internal action is modeled with an empty label from location _5 to location _6). Similarly, it sends a corresponding message to the Emergency Monitor. Notice that the Emergency Monitor depends on both GPS and Airbag but GPS and Airbag are independent of one another. Also, it can only communicate with the GPS component.

4.2   Dynamic Toast Evolution

Starting from the basic configuration introduced in the subsection below, new components and features can be installed at run-time during system operation. To prove the feasibility of our approach and its efficiency in reducing the test generation cost, five cases of behavioral adaptations are studied as illustrated in Table 1.

---

[2] Open Services Gateway initiative.

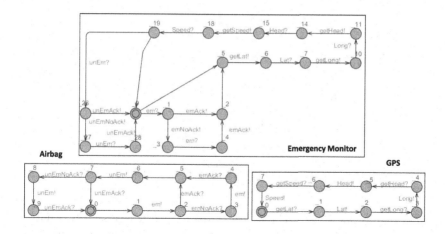

Fig. 6. Behavioral models of the initial configuration.

Table 1. Several studied toast evolutions.

Case study evolutions	Kind of the evolution	Templates	States	Transitions
Case 0:Initial toast configuration	——	GPS	8	8
		Airbag	10	12
		Emergency	17	21
Case 1:Case 0 with updated GPS behavior	Complex (updating transition labels)	GPS	8	8
		Airbag	10	12
		Emergency	17	21
Case 2: Case 0 with errors in data transmission	Complex (adding states and transitions)	GPS	16	20
		Airbag	10	12
		Emergency	25	33
Case 3: Case 0 with timing constraints	Complex (adding transitions)	GPS	8	12
		Airbag	10	12
		Emergency	17	25
Case 4: Case 2 with Back End Server	Complex (adding templates)	GPS	16	20
		Airbag	10	12
		Emergency	29	38
		Back End	4	5
Case 5: Case 4 with timing constraints	Complex (adding and updating transitions)	GPS	16	28
		Airbag	10	12
		Emergency	29	46
		Back End	4	5

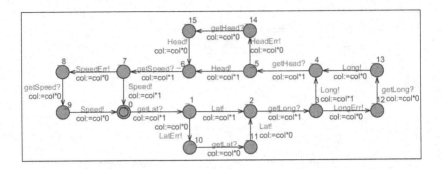

Fig. 7. The GPS_{diff} model in case 2.

Case 1: The initial Toast architecture is maintained whereas GPS behavior is changed with sending bearing[3] measure instead of heading measure to the Emergency Monitor. In the new version of the GPS model, getHead? and Head! transition labels are replaced with getBearing? and Bearing! transition labels. Such modification is propagated to the Emergency Monitor model, as well. Notice that for each modified transition the *col* variable is updated with $col := col * 2$.

Case 2: The initial GPS behavior is improved with taking into account errors during data emission to the Emergency Monitor. To handle such problem, the new version of the GPS component sends vehicle information again in case of error occurrence. Such modification introduces new states and transitions both in GPS and Emergency Monitor models.

Due to space constraints, Fig. 7 depicts only the generated GPS model by the model differencing module. It points out that for each new transition the *col* variable is updated with $col := col * 0$ and for each unchanged transition this variable is updated with $col := col * 1$.

Case 3: The initial GPS behavioral model is enhanced with timing constraints. In fact, we assume that the new GPS version sends each requested vehicle information in lapse of time that does not exceed *Tprocessing* which is equal to 4 time units. In this case, different transitions are updated and others new transitions are added to both Emergency Monitor and GPS automata. Figure 8 illustrates modifications made on the GPS component. As mentioned before, the *col* variable is updated in response to modifications made on the SUT model.

Case 4: The Toast architecture is evolved while including the new Back End component [1]. The latter is responsible with collecting information from the

---

[3] Bearing is the direction from the vehicle location to the destination point given in degree from the north whereas the heading is a direction toward which a vehicle is (or should be) moving.

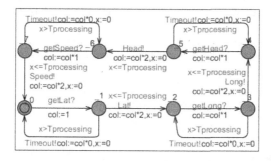

Fig. 8. The GPS_{diff} model in case 3.

Emergency Monitor. It is a server running entirely on a separate computer and it listens for the client to report emergencies. The new architecture is outlined in Fig. 9a. The overall toast behavior is changed and a new template for the Back End component is introduced as shown in Fig. 9b.

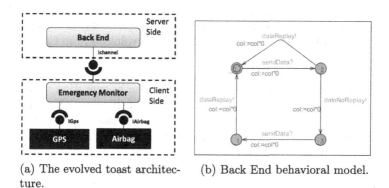

(a) The evolved toast architec-   (b) Back End behavioral model.
ture.

Fig. 9. The addition of Back End template in the toast specification (Case 4).

The main idea is to establish the correctness of the evolved Toast application in a cost effective manner. This can be done by avoiding the regeneration of the full test suite and applying our TestGenApp technique as discussed in the next subsection.

4.3   Selective Test Generation with TestGenApp

As mentioned before, UPPAAL CO√ER is used to generate diagnostic traces. From each diagnostic trace, a test sequence that is an alternating sequence of concrete delay actions and observable actions, may be obtained simply by projecting the trace to the environment model, while removing invisible transitions, and summing adjacent delay actions [9]. The same tool is used to generate test

Table 2. Comparison between Regenerate All, Retest All and TestGenApp strategies.

Case study evolutions	Regenerate All	Retest All		TestGenApp			
		Old	New	Reusable	New	Retestable	Adapted
From Case 0 to Case 1	2 traces	2	0	1	0	0	1
From Case 0 to Case 2	6 traces	2	4	2	4	0	0
From Case 0 to Case 3	6 traces	2	4	0	4	2	0
From Case 2 to Case 4	6 traces	6	2	4	2	0	0
From Case 3 to Case 5	11 traces	6	5	6	5	0	0
From Case 4 to Case 5	11 traces	6	8	0	8	3	0

cases when dynamic evolutions take place. An example of the obtained test sequence for case 0 is highlighted in the following:

em! emAck? getLat? Lat! getLong? Long! getHead? Head! getSpeed? Speed! unEm! unNoEmAck? unEm!

Compared to the Regenerate All technique, our proposal reduces the number of generated traces as shown in Table 2. For instance, instead of generating the full test suite (6 traces here) when the Toast evolves from Case 2 to Case 4, only 2 traces are newly generated and 4 traces are still valid and cover unimpacted parts of the model by the evolution. Similarly, the evolution from Case 0 to Case 2 requires the generation of 4 tests and the selection of 2 retestable tests from the old test suite.

Concerning the Retest All strategy, it consists in re-executing all tests from the old test suite and generates tests for uncovered behaviors. The main limitation of this approach is that it possibly re-executes obsolete tests. As outlined in Table 2, when the Toast evolves from Case 0 to Case 1, the two old traces are re-executed by this approach whereas one of them is failed and requires to be adapted.

To conclude, our proposal reduces the cost of test generation and gives an important information about the obtained tests and which parts of the SUT they cover.

5 Related Work

There has been a spate of interest in how to reestablish confidence in modified software systems. As one of the key method to improve software quality and dependability, selective regression testing has been widely used. Three kinds of approaches are identified in this research area: code-based regression testing [7,16], model based regression testing [4–6,15] and software architecture based regression testing [14]. In the first class, Granja et al. [7] discuss two techniques of code-based regression testing. The first one deals with identifying program modifications and selecting attributes required for regression testing. Based on dataflow analysis, the second technique uses the obtained required elements to select retestable tests. According to the metrics defined in Rothermel et al. [16], authors show that their proposal has a good precision, a high generality but requires further work to attain inclusiveness and efficiency. Contrarily to these approaches, our work deals with model based regression testing. Such method has the main advantage to handle test selection and test generation on a higher abstraction level.

In the second class, we introduce the work of Brian et al. [4] that present a UML-based regression test selection strategy. By supporting changes in actions of sequence diagrams and in variables, operations, relationships and classes, the proposed change analysis approach automatically classifies tests on obsolete, reusable and retestable tests. In the same direction, the approach cited in [6] deals with minimizing the impact of test case evolution by avoiding the regeneration of full test suites and focusing only on generating the new or the updated ones. A point in favor this work is the improvement of test classification based on code analysis proposed by [12]. In fact, authors enable more precise test status definition based on model dependence analysis. Notably, retestable tests are animated on the model and can be classified as updated, adapted, unimpacted, re-executed, outdated or failed tests. Conversely to our approach, these approaches are based on UML as a semi formal description language to model system behaviors (namely class, object and statechart diagrams). Analyzing such various diagrams to identify modification impact can be seen as a tedious task. Such problem has been resolved by Pilskalns et al. [15]. They present a regression testing approach based on an integrated model called Object Method Directed Acyclic Graph (OMDAG) built from class diagrams, sequence diagrams and OCL expressions. They consider when a path in the OMDAG changes it affects one or more test cases associated to the path and they classify changes as NEWSET, MODSET and DELSET. Based on Extended Finite State Machine (EFSM) models, [5] proposes a safe regression technique relying on dependence analysis, as well. It supports three types of elementary modifications of the machine (addition, deletion, modification of a transition). Similarly, our approach takes into account such kinds of transition modifications and improves them by considering also addition, deletion and modification of a state. Another point in favor our approach is the support of either elementary or composite modifications.

In the third class, Muccini et al. [14] propose an effective approach called SARTE: SA-based regression testing. The authors apply regression testing at both code and architecture levels whenever the system architecture or its implementation evolve. First , they test the conformance of a modified implementation to a given software architecture. Second, they test the implementation conformance to the new software architecture. SA specifications are modeled using Labeled Transition Systems (LTS). Similar to our proposal, authors utilize a SAdiff algorithm which compares the behavioral models of both architectures and returns differences between them. This technique was used to identify tests to rerun covering the affected paths. This work differs from our in two major ways. First, our approach deals with model-based black box regression testing. Thus, we assume that code is not available and we consider that any modification done at the code source level is reflected at/in the behavioral model of the SUT. Second, our focus is mainly on dynamic behavioral adaptations, structural modifications are studied in previous work [11].

6   Conclusion

This paper described a selective test generation approach for critical and dynamically adaptive systems formally modeled as Timed Automta. First of all, a model differencing technique was applied to detect similarities and differences between initial and evolved behavioral models. Moreover, we presented a simple and flexible technique for specifying coverage criteria using observer automata with parameters. This technique was adopted to generate in a cost effective manner new tests and adapt modified ones. The use of UPPAAL as a well-established model checker and its extension for test generation UPPAAL CO√ER makes our approach more consistent and sound.

Its application to the Toast architecture shows the efficiency of TestGenApp in reducing the cost of test generation especially when model scale increases. The comparison of our solution with the Regenerate All and the Retest All strategies highlighted such efficiency.

As future work, we investigate efforts in improving our methodology and applying it to more complex and real systems. Also, we aim to conceive several transformations rules for the mapping of the obtained abstract test suites to executable TTCN-3[4] test suites.

References

1. De Angelis, F., Di Berardini, M.R., Muccini, H., Polini, A.: CASSANDRA: an online failure prediction strategy for dynamically evolving systems. In: Merz, S., Pang, J. (eds.) ICFEM 2014. LNCS, vol. 8829, pp. 107–122. Springer, Heidelberg (2014)
2. Behrmann, G., David, A., Larsen, K.G.: A tutorial on UPPAAL. In: Bernardo, M., Corradini, F. (eds.) SFM-RT 2004. LNCS, vol. 3185, pp. 200–236. Springer, Heidelberg (2004)
3. Brenner, D., Atkinson, C., Malaka, R., Merdes, M., Paech, B., Suliman, D.: Reducing verification effort in component-based software engineering through built-in testing. Inf. Syst. Front. 9(2–3), 151–162 (2007)
4. Briand, L.C., Labiche, Y., He, S.: Automating regression test selection based on UML designs. Inf. Softw. Technol. 51(1), 16–30 (2009). http://dx.doi.org/10.1016/j.infsof.2008.09.010
5. Chen, Y., Probert, R.L., Ural, H.: Model-based regression test suite generation using dependence analysis. In: Proceedings of the 3rd International Workshop on Advances in Model-based Testing, A-MOST 2007, pp. 54–62. ACM, New York (2007). http://doi.acm.org/10.1145/1291535.1291541

---

[4] Testing and Test Control Notation.

6. Fourneret, E., Bouquet, F., Dadeau, F., Debricon, S.: Selective test generation method for evolving critical systems. In: Proceedings of the 2011 IEEE Fourth International Conference on Software Testing, Verification and Validation Workshops, ICSTW 2011, pp. 125–134. IEEE Computer Society, Washington (2011). http://dx.doi.org/10.1109/ICSTW.2011.95

7. Granja, I., Jino, M.: Techniques for regression testing: selecting test case sets tailored to possibly modified functionalities. In: Proceedings of the Third European Conference on Software Maintenance and Reengineering, CSMR 1999, p. 2. IEEE Computer Society, Washington (1999). http://dl.acm.org/citation.cfm?id=794202. 795237

8. Harrold, M.J.: Testing: a roadmap. In: Proceedings of the Conference on the Future of Software Engineering, ICSE 2000, pp. 61–72. ACM, New York (2000). http:// doi.acm.org/10.1145/336512.336532

9. Hessel, A., Larsen, K.G., Mikucionis, M., Nielsen, B., Pettersson, P., Skou, A.: Testing real-time systems using UPPAAL. In: Hierons, R.M., Bowen, J.P., Harman, M. (eds.) FORTEST. LNCS, vol. 4949, pp. 77–117. Springer, Heidelberg (2008)

10. Hessel, A., Larsen, K.G., Nielsen, B., Pettersson, P., Skou, A.: Time-optimal real-time test case generation using UPPAAL. In: Petrenko, A., Ulrich, A. (eds.) FATES 2003. LNCS, vol. 2931, pp. 114–130. Springer, Heidelberg (2004)

11. Lahami, M., Krichen, M., Jmaiel, M.: Runtime testing framework for improving quality in dynamic service-based systems. In: Bianculli, D., Guinea, S., Hallé, S., Polini, A. (eds.) Proceedings of the 2nd International Workshop on Quality Assurance for Service-based Applications, QASBA 2013, in conjunction with ISSTA 2013, July 15, 2013, pp. 17–24. ACM, Lugano (2013). http://doi.acm.org/10.1145/ 2489300.2489335

12. Leung, H., White, L.: Insights into regression testing [software testing]. In: 1989 Proceedings Conference on Software Maintenance, pp. 60–69 (1989)

13. McAffer, J., VanderLei, P., Archer, S.: OSGi and Equinox: Creating Highly Modular Java Systems. Addison-Wesley, Upper Saddle River (2010)

14. Muccini, H., Dias, M.S., Richardson, D.J.: Software architecture-based regression testing. J. Syst. Softw. **79**(10), 1379–1396 (2006). http://dx.doi.org/10.1016/j.jss.2006.02.059

15. Pilskalns, O., Uyan, G., Andrews, A.: Regression testing uml designs. In: Proceedings of the 22nd IEEE International Conference on Software Maintenance, ICSM 2006, pp. 254–264. IEEE Computer Society, Washington (2006). http://dx.doi.org/10.1109/ICSM.2006.53

16. Rothermel, G., Harrold, M.: Analyzing regression test selection techniques. IEEE Trans. Softw. Eng. **22**(8), 529–551 (1996)

17. Utting, M., Legeard, B.: Practical Model-Based Testing: A Tools Approach. Morgan Kaufmann Publishers Inc., San Francisco (2006)

Short Papers

Heuristics for Deriving Adaptive Homing and Distinguishing Sequences for Nondeterministic Finite State Machines

Natalia Kushik[1,2(⊠)] and Hüsnü Yenigün[3]

[1] Tomsk State University, Tomsk, Russia
ngkushik@gmail.com
[2] Telecom SudParis, Evry, France
[3] Sabanci University, Istanbul, Turkey
yenigun@sabanciuniv.edu

Abstract. Distinguishing Sequences (DS) and Homing Sequences (HS) are used for state identification purposes in Finite State Machine (FSM) based testing. For deterministic FSMs, DS and HS related problems are well studied, for both preset and adaptive cases. There are also recent algorithms for checking the existence and constructing Adaptive DS and Adaptive HS for nondeterministic FSMs. However, most of the related problems are proven to be PSPACE-complete, while the worst case height of Adaptive DS and HS is known to be exponential. Therefore, novel heuristics and FSM classes where they can be applied need to be provided for effective derivation of such sequences. In this paper, we present a work in progress on the minimization of Adaptive DS and Adaptive HS for nondeterministic FSMs.

Keywords: Nondeterministic finite state machines · Adaptive homing sequence · Adaptive distinguishing sequence · Novel heuristics

1 Introduction

Distinguishing Sequences (DS) and Homing Sequences (HS) are used for state iden-tification purposes in Finite State Machine (FSM) based testing [1–3]. A DS identifies the initial state of the FSM under investigation, while an HS is used to identify the final state after the sequence has been applied. A sequence is *adaptive* if the next input to be applied to an FSM under investigation is chosen based on the previously observed outputs, and the sequence is *preset* if the outputs need to be observed only after the entire sequence applied. The methods to derive preset/adaptive HS/DS are well elab-orated for complete and deterministic FSMs [3–5]. Even though the length of most of these sequences is polynomial w.r.t. the number of FSM states, the current complexity of digital systems and software makes it almost impossible to derive a complete deterministic behavior of the system integrated into the overall software and/or hard-ware environment. Moreover, current specifications of telecommunication protocols and other digital systems include an optionality of output responses under the same

K. El-Fakih et al. (Eds.): ICTSS 2015, LNCS 9447, pp. 243–248, 2015.
DOI: 10.1007/978-3-319-25945-1_15

queries. That is the reason why researchers turn their attention towards special FSM types, and in particular, nondeterministic FSMs.

A method for deriving a DS for two states of an observable nondeterministic FSM has been proposed in [6], where the length of this sequence is shown to be exponential for nondeterministic FSMs. The upper bound on the length of an HS for an observable nondeterministic FSM is shown to be exponential as well, and this upper bound is reachable [7]. As for adaptive experiments for nondeterministic FSMs, it has been shown that the length of a shortest adaptive DS for two states of an observable non-deterministic FSM with n states is at most $n(n - 1)/2$ [8]. Whenever such an adaptive sequence is derived to distinguish $m > 2$ states of an observable nondeterministic FSM, the length of this sequence grows exponentially [9]. The problem of checking the existence of a preset DS is known to be PSPACE-complete even for complete *deterministic* FSMs [3]. The latter means one cannot directly apply these techniques to effectively derive test sequences against FSM specifications. That is the reason why a number of heuristics to decrease such complexity have been proposed. In particular, various heuristic methods to construct reduced adaptive DS for complete deterministic FSMs have been proposed in [10]. However, it has been also proven that constructing a minimal adaptive DS for complete deterministic FSMs is an NP-hard problem [11]. Therefore, novel heuristics need to be provided for effective derivation of adaptive HS and adaptive DS for nondeterministic FSMs.

In this paper, we focus on two techniques for deriving adaptive DS and adaptive HS for nondeterministic FSMs. In particular, we present a class of nondeterministic FSMs for which it is possible to construct an adaptive DS without using any nondeterministic transitions. We also argue how existing adaptive DS minimization approaches can be used for such nondeterministic FSMs. As for adaptive HS, we address a method proposed in [9] that constructs an adaptive HS for an observable nondeterministic FSM when each state pair is adaptively homing. We discuss how this method can be improved so that the resulting adaptive HS can be shorter. Therefore, the main contributions of this work in progress are two novel heuristics for effective derivation of adaptive DSs for nondeterministic FSMs and adaptive HSs for observable nondeterministic FSMs.

The paper is organized as follows. Section 2 contains preliminaries. A heuristic method for effective adaptive DS derivation for nondeterministic FSMs is given in Sect. 3 while Sect. 4 presents an approach for minimizing adaptive HS for observable nondeterministic FSMs. Section 5 concludes the paper.

2 Preliminaries

In this paper, we focus on minimizing adaptive HS and DS for nondeterministic FSMs. As usual, an *FSM* S is a 4-tuple (S, I, O, h_S), where **S** is a finite set of states; I and O are finite non-empty disjoint sets of inputs and outputs, respectively; $h_S \subseteq S \times I \times O \times S$ is a *transition relation*, where a 4-tuple $(s, i, o, s') \in h_S$ is a *transition*. An FSM is *complete* if for each pair $(s, i) \in S \times I$ there exists $(o, s') \in O \times S$ such that $(s, i, o, s') \in h_S$. Otherwise it is called *partially specified*. If for some pair $(s, i) \in S \times I$, there exist two transitions $(s, i, o_1, s_1), (s, i, o_2, s_2) \in h_S$, such that $o_1 \neq o_2$ or $s_1 \neq s_2$ then **s** is called *nondeterministic*. For a nondeterministic FSM the nondeterminism is *observable* if each input/output pair *i/o* uniquely identifies the successor of each FSM state (if it exists). Given a state *s* of **s** and an input/output sequence α/β, the α/β-*successor* of state *s* is the set of all states that are reached from *s* via an application of α when an output reaction β is produced. Note that for an observable FSM **s**, the cardinality of the α/β-*successor* of state *s* is at most one for any input/output sequence α/β.

A sequence α is a *distinguishing* (*homing*) sequence (DS/HS) for the FSM **S** if after applying α and observing output reaction β one can uniquely conclude about the initial (final/current) state of **S**. The length of preset DS and HS is exponential for nondeterministic FSMs, however sometimes this length can be shorter when adaptivity is used. An adaptive DS/HS can be represented as a tree or as a specific acyclic single-input output-complete FSM that are called test cases [3, 12].

A number of methods for deriving adaptive DS and HS for nondeterministic FSMs have been proposed (see, for example [9]). However, the length of the corresponding sequence in general case remains exponential and thus, novel heuristics need to be provided for minimizing the length of such sequences.

3   Nondeterministic FSMs with a Deterministic Adaptive DS

For a complete deterministic FSM with n states, it is known that $n(n - 1)/2$ is the tight upper bound for the height of an adaptive DS [3]. However, for nondeterministic FSMs, the height of an adaptive DS is exponential in general. In this section, we present a class of nondeterministic FSMs for which the height of an adaptive DS is at most $2n^2 - n - 1$ and existing algorithms of adaptive DS minimization can be readily applied.

A transition $(s, i, o', s') \in h_S$ is a *deterministic transition* if for any transition $(s, i, o'', s'') \in h_S$ we have $o''= o'$ and $s''= s'$. For a given FSM **S**, we define *the deterministic projection* $\mathbf{S}^d$ of **S** as follows. $\mathbf{S}^d$ and **S** have the same set **S** of states. For a transition $(s, i, o', s') \in h_S$, $(s, i, o', s') \in h^d{}_S$, if and only if (s, i, o', s') is a deterministic transition in **S**. I^d and O^d consist of the inputs and outputs used in the transitions in $h^d{}_S$. Intuitively, $\mathbf{S}^d$ is the same FSM as **S** where the deterministic transitions are preserved but all other transitions are removed. Hence, $\mathbf{S}^d$ is a deterministic FSM by definition. It is easy to see that an adaptive DS for $\mathbf{S}^d$ can be directly used as an adaptive DS for **S** as well, and it will be a *deterministic adaptive DS* in the sense that only the deterministic transitions are used throughout the application of the adaptive DS in **S**. In the lucky case that $\mathbf{S}^d$ is a complete deterministic FSM, the existence check and the adaptive DS construction algorithms given in [3] can be directly applied. However, in general, $\mathbf{S}^d$ is a partially specified deterministic FSM. Moreover, in the worst case the transition relation of $\mathbf{S}^d$ can be empty, and in this case, the question of existence of an ADS for **S** remains open.

Although there usually is a complexity jump for the algorithms when one considers partially specified FSMs, this is not the case for the problems related to adaptive DS. In [13] a polynomial time algorithm is provided to check if a partially specified FSM has an adaptive DS or not. In this paper, we adapt this algorithm for efficient derivation of an ADS for a nondeterministic FSM that requires a partial deterministic projection.

We also improve the upper bound on the length of such ADS compared to the one given in [13]. In fact, the approach given in [13] is based on constructing a complete deterministic FSM $C(\mathbf{S}^d)$ from a given partially specified deterministic FSM $\mathbf{S}^d$ such that there exists an adaptive DS with the height H for $C(\mathbf{S}^d)$ iff there exists an adaptive DS with height $H - 1$ for $C(\mathbf{S}^d)$. The number of states in $C(\mathbf{S}^d)$ is $2n$, where n is the number of states in $\mathbf{S}^d$. Therefore, it is possible to check if there exists an adaptive DS for $\mathbf{S}^d$ (and hence a deterministic ADS for $\mathbf{S}$) in $O(pn\lg n)$ time [3], where p is the cardinality of I^d.

If there exists an adaptive DS for $C(\mathbf{S}^d)$, one can then use the LY algorithm (the adaptive DS construction algorithm given in [3]) to construct an adaptive DS. Although [13] provides an upper bound of $\pi^2 n^2/3$ for the height H of the adaptive DS constructed for $C(\mathbf{S}^d)$, using the result in [14], the LY algorithm actually constructs an adaptive DS with the height at most $H = 2n^2 - n$ for $C(\mathbf{S}^d)$. Therefore, the height of the adaptive DS for $\mathbf{S}^d$ is at most $H - 1 = 2n^2 - n - 1$.

Note that the LY algorithm does not aim for the minimization of the adaptive DS it constructs. However, there exist heuristics for the minimization of adaptive DSs with respect to different metrics (e.g. height, total external path length, etc.) for complete deterministic FSMs [10]. Since $C(\mathbf{S}^d)$ is a complete deterministic FSM, one can directly use these heuristics in order to construct minimized adaptive DSs for $C(\mathbf{S}^d)$, and hence for the nondeterministic FSM $\mathbf{S}$. Note that $\mathbf{S}$ can be nonobservable as well.

4   Minimizing Adaptive HS for Nondeterministic FSMs

In this section, we discuss how to optimize the procedure for deriving an adaptive HS for an observable FSM $\mathbf{S}$. The procedure is taken from [9] while the complexity of the related problem is given in [15]. The homing test case derivation strategy is based on the condition that each state pair of $\mathbf{S}$ is adaptively homing. In other words, there exists a homing test case for $\mathbf{S}$ if there exists an adaptive homing sequence for each subset $\{s_i, s_j\} \subseteq S$ of states of the observable nondeterministic FSM $\mathbf{S}$. A test case $\mathbf{P}_{i,j}$ is a *homing test case* for the subset $\{s_i, s_j\} \subseteq S$ of states if for every input/output sequence α/β defined in $\mathbf{P}_{i,j}$, the α/β-successor of the subset $\{s_i, s_j\} \subseteq S$ has at most one state.

If there exists a homing test case for the FSM $\mathbf{S}$ then the set S is a *homing set* and the test case $\mathbf{P}$ is a *homing test case for the set* S or the test case $\mathbf{P}$ *homes* states of the set S. Otherwise, the set S is not homing. The homing test case for the set $S = \{s_1,.., s_n\}$ is derived iteratively. As mentioned above, $\mathbf{P}_{i,j}$ is a homing test case for the subset (pair) $\{s_i, s_j\} \subseteq S$ of FSM states. The procedure starts with a homing test case $\mathbf{P}_{1,2}$ for the set $\{s_1, s_2\}$, then state s_3 is added to the subset $\{s_1, s_2\} \subseteq S$. Each input/output sequence α/β that is defined in the test case $\mathbf{P}_{1,2}$ is applied at state s_3. If the sequence α/β is defined at state s_3, then the deadlock state q in the test case $\mathbf{P}_{1,2}$ is replaced with a test case $\mathbf{P}_{q,z}$, where q is the α/β-successor of state pair $\{s_1, s_2\}$, while z is the α/β-successor of state s_3. All the input/output sequences α/β' that are defined at state s_3 but not defined in the test case $\mathbf{P}_{1,2}$ are also included into the test case $\mathbf{P}_{1,2,3}$. Proceeding in this way by iteratively adding the remaining states $s_4, s_5, ..., s_n$, the test case $\mathbf{P}_{1,2,...,n}$ is derived.

We note that there exist various homing test cases $\mathbf{P}_{i,j}$ for the same state pair $\{s_i, s_j\} \subseteq S$. Therefore, the first optimization step can be to consider a somehow optimal test case $P_{i,j}$ that is chosen for the first state pair and for those test cases $P_{q,z}$ that are appended iteratively, when $P_{1,2,...,n}$ is being derived. On the other hand, the length of the resulting test case can significantly depend on the choice of state s_j that is added to the test case $P_{1,2,...,j-1}$. Thus, the second optimization criterion can be on an optimal choice of the next state s_j when the test case $P_{1,2,...,j-1}$ is already constructed. We further discuss how these two ideas can be taken into account to effectively derive a test case $P_{1,2,...,n}$. We mention that when optimizing the length of the corresponding adaptive HS, represented as a test case, we focus on optimizing not only the height of the corresponding tree but also the number of transitions in the acyclic FSM.

The first type of heuristics is related to making an optimal choice between possible initial state pairs $\{s_i, s_j\} \subseteq S$, $i < j$, as well as defining the best homing test case $P_{i,j}$ for this pair. As it is shown in [9], the length of the overall homing test case $P_{1,2,...,n}$ significantly depends even on the first input to be included into the test case $P_{1,2}$. As the test case $P_{1,2,...,j}$ is defined based on the test case $P_{1,2,...,j-1}$, the height/the number of transitions of it significantly depends on the number of sequences that are defined in the test case $P_{1,2,...,j-1}$ and in state s_j that will be added to the root of the corresponding successor tree. That is the reason why we suggest to choose a pair $\{s_i, s_j\} \subseteq S$ to start with in such a way that its homing test case $P_{i,j}$ is a homing test case for some other state pairs. It is naturally to assume that the more state pairs are 'covered' by a homing test case $P_{i,j}$, the better is the resulting test case $P_{1,2,...,n}$. Therefore, we suggest to choose the first state pair $\{s_i, s_j\} \subseteq S$, $i < j$, such that there exists a homing test case P for this pair that homes as much state pairs in S as possible.

The idea behind the second optimization step is the same as in the previous case. In particular, we suggest choosing the next state s_j to be added to a test case $P_{1,2,...,j-1}$ in such a way that the number of input/output sequences that are defined in $P_{1,2,...,j-1}$ and are not defined at state s_j would be minimal. This fact can help to reduce the number of homing test cases $P_{q,z}$ that have to be appended at each state z, where z is the α/β-successor of state s_j, and q is the α/β-successor of the set $\{s_1, ..., s_{j-1}\}$. Moreover, as for each pair of states $\{q, z\}$ there can exist various adaptive homing test cases, the best choice of the test case $P_{q,z}$ can affect the overall height / transition number of the test case $P_{1,2,...,n}$. Therefore, it is also necessary to consider which test case $P_{q,z}$ should be chosen for an intermediate state pair $\{q, z\} \subseteq S$.

We mention that both optimization steps for deriving an adaptive homing test case $P_{1,2,...,n}$ need to be thoroughly estimated. On one hand, theoretical investigation on FSM classes that have shorter adaptive HS need to be elaborated, and on the other, experimental evaluation on the efficiency of proposed heuristics needs to be performed.

5   Conclusion

In this paper, we proposed two heuristic methods for optimizing the size of adaptive DS and adaptive HS for nondeterministic FSMs. The topic of such optimization is always motivated by the fact that the length of such sequences is exponential for nondeterministic FSMs. Moreover, related decision problems on the existence of such sequences even for the preset case are known to be PSPACE-complete. We note that this current work in progress only presents the ideas behind optimization criteria and optimization techniques to achieve shorter resulting trees for adaptive DS or HS. As a future work, we plan to perform experimental evaluation over machines of various types (random, protocol specifications, etc.) to estimate the efficiency of the proposed techniques.

Acknowledgments. The authors gratefully acknowledge Prof. N. Yevtushenko for interesting discussions.

This work is partially supported by RFBR Grant# 15-58-46013 CT_a and TÜBİTAK Grant# 114E921.

References

1. Dorofeeva, R., El-Fakih, K., Maag, S., Cavalli, A.R., Yevtushenko, N.: FSM-based conformance testing methods: a survey annotated with experimental evaluation. Inf. Softw. Technol. 52, 1286–1297 (2010)
2. Gill, A.: State-identification experiments in finite automata. Inf. Control 4, 132–154 (1961)
3. Lee, D., Yannakakis, M.: Testing finite-state machines: state identification and verification. IEEE Trans. Comput. 43(3), 306–320 (1994)
4. Kohavi, Z.: Switching and Finite Automata Theory. McGraw-Hill, New York (1978)
5. Moore, E.F.: Gedanken-experiments on sequential machines. In: Automata Studies (Annals of Mathematical Studies no.1), pp. 129–153. Princeton University Press (1956)
6. Spitsyna, N., El-Fakih, K., Yevtushenko, N.: Studying the separability relation between finite state machines. Softw. Test. Verification Reliab. 17(4), 227–241 (2007)
7. Kushik, N., Yevtushenko, N.: On the length of homing sequences for nondeterministic finite state machines. In: Proceedings of CIAA 2013, pp. 220–231 (2013)
8. Alur, R. Courcoubetis, C., Yannakakis, M.: Distinguishing tests for nondeterministic and probabilistic machines. In: Proceedings of the 27th ACM Symposium on Theory of Computing, pp. 363-372 (1995)
9. Kushik, N., El-Fakih, K., Yevtushenko, N., Cavalli, A.R.: On adaptive experiments for nondeterministic finite state machines. Softw. Tools Technol. Transf. (2014). doi:10.1007/s10009-014-0357-7
10. Türker, U.C., Ünlüyurt, T., Yenigün, H.: Lookahead-based approaches for minimizing adaptive distinguishing sequences. In: Merayo, M.G., de Oca, E.M. (eds.) ICTSS 2014. LNCS, vol. 8763, pp. 32–47. Springer, Heidelberg (2014)
11. Türker, U.C., Yenigün, H.: Hardness and inapproximability of minimizing adaptive distinguishing sequences. Formal Meth. Syst. Des. 44(3), 264–294 (2014)
12. Petrenko, A., Yevtushenko, N.: Conformance tests as checking experiments for partial nondeterministic FSM. In: Grieskamp, W., Weise, C. (eds.) FATES 2005. LNCS, vol. 3997, pp. 118–133. Springer, Heidelberg (2005)
13. Hierons, R.M., Türker, U.C.: Distinguishing sequences for partially specified FSMs. In: Badger, J.M., Rozier, K.Y. (eds.) NFM 2014. LNCS, vol. 8430, pp. 62–76. Springer, Heidelberg (2014)
14. Sokolovskii, M.N.: Diagnostic experiments with automata. Cybern. Syst. Anal. 7, 988–994 (1971)
15. Kushik, N., Yevtushenko, N.: Adaptive Homing is in P. In: Proceedings of MBT 2015, pp. 73–78 (2015)

Genetic Algorithm Application for Enhancing State-Sensitivity Partitioning

Ammar Mohammed Sultan, Salmi Baharom$^{(\boxtimes)}$,
Abdul Azim Abd Ghani, Jamilah Din, and Hazura Zulzalil

Software Engineering and Information System Department,
Faculty of Computer Science and Information Technology,
Universiti Putra Malaysia, 43400 Serdang, Selangor, Malaysia
ammar.alsultan@hotmail.com,
{salmi,azim,jamilahd,hazura}@upm.edu.my

Abstract. Software testing is the most crucial phase in software development life cycle which intends to find faults as much as possible. Test case generation leads the research in software testing. So, many techniques were proposed for the sake of automating the test case generation process. State sensitivity partitioning is a technique that partitions the entire states of a module. The generated test cases are composed of sequences of events. However, there is an infinite set of sequences with no upper bound on the length of a sequence. Thus, a lengthy test sequence might be encountered with redundant data states, which will increase the size of test suite and, consequently, the process of testing will be ineffective. Therefore, there is a need to optimize those test cases generated by SSP. GA has been identified as the most common potential technique among several optimization techniques. Thus, GA is investigated to integrate it with the existing SSP. This paper addresses the issue on deriving the fitness function for optimizing the sequence of events produced by SSP.

Keywords: Genetic Algorithm (GA) · State-Sensitivity partitioning (SSP) · Test case · Sequence of events · Data state

1 Introduction

Amongst software development life cycle (SDLC) phases, software testing is the most crucial one [1]. It intends to execute the software and find faults as much as possible. Generally, test case generation dominates the research in software testing while other research areas include test execution and test oracles. Hence, a number of techniques were proposed for improving the effectiveness and efficiency of faults detection. State-sensitivity portioning (SSP) is one of them [2–4].

SSP employs Parnas formal specifications in order to test a module that consists of one or more access programs, which share the same data structure. The output depends on the event triggered, input parameters, conditions and actions. Thus, test data for a module might consist of event sequences (or test sequences) rather than a single event. For the sake of avoiding the exhaustive testing of a module's entire states, SSP partitions the entire states according to their sensitiveness toward events, conditions and

© IFIP International Federation for Information Processing 2015
K. El-Fakih et al. (Eds.): ICTSS 2015, LNCS 9447, pp. 249–256, 2015.
DOI: 10.1007/978-3-319-25945-1_16

actions. Test sequences are selected manually based on all-transitions coverage crite-rion. However, the sequence of events can be very lengthy and might contain redundant data states, which makes the testing expensive and relatively ineffective.

In the literature, many optimization techniques have been suggested. One technique is search techniques [5, 6] and, among them, genetic algorithm (GA) has been iden-tified as the most common for generating test cases [7]. The success stories of GA inspired us to adopt GA in our work. Similar to other search techniques, the adoption of GA requires the derivation of fitness function [8]. Thus, this paper describes the on-going research that addresses the issue of deriving a fitness function in order to search within the population of states produced by SSP sequence of events. The remainder of this paper is organized as follows: an overview of SSP is presented in the next section; followed by a general overview on GA. Next, the fitness function application in SSP is being described followed by a case study. Finally, the last section summarizes the paper along with the conclusion.

2 State-Sensitivity Partitioning (SSP)

A module may consist of one or more access programs that share the same data structure. Its behavior is depending on the event triggered, the value of input param-eters and conditions. Consequently, generating test cases for such a module might involve a large number of data states, which grows exponentially in terms of the number of program variables. For example, approximately 10^{20} tests (2^{32} X 2^{32}) have to be performed in order to test the correctness of two variables A and B of 32 bit integers, as in [9]. Hence, it would take more than 30,000 years of testing with the assumption of performing 10^8 tests per second. Therefore, it is impossible to explore the space of entire states with limited time resources and memories.

SSP is a test case generation technique for modules [2–4]. The states are partitioned based on state's sensitivity towards events, conditions (pre-conditions) and actions (post-conditions). The goal is to group all states that behave similarly towards access-programs (events), conditions and actions (either sensitive or insensitive) together.

SSP has six sequential steps, which are: (i) identifying sensitive access programs, (ii) partitioning states into equivalence classes, (iii) constructing a state transition model, (iv) selecting test cases based on all-transition coverage criteria, (v) adding the insensitive events to the end of each selected test case and (vi) applying boundary value analysis (BVA) technique in order to select the input parameters. Nonetheless, each test case from the fourth step must be represented by at least one sequence of events. The SSP sequence of events has to be selected randomly as long as it follows the specified conditions of the constructed state transition model in step three (3). Below is an example.

2.1 Example

In order to grasp the idea of SSP, let's consider the example of circular queue. Circular queue has three access programs, which are: add(), remove(), and front(). The former two access programs are sensitive as they modify the data states during their execution while the latter is insensitive as it does not modify the data states. According to SSP, the entire data states are partitioned into equivalence classes based on the number of identified sensitive access programs. So, the circular queue has four possible partitions. In the third step, a state transition model is constructed as in Fig. 1.

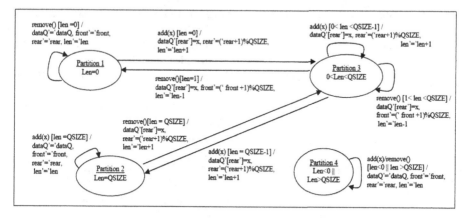

Fig. 1. State transition model for circular queue

Once the state transition diagram is constructed, all-transitions coverage criteria will be used for selecting test cases. Table 1 lists the ten test cases obtained from the state transition model. Each test case will be represented by at least one sequence of events. Then, the insensitive events is going to be added to the end of the sequence. Lastly, the BVA technique is applied in order to determine the value of input parameter. With the assumption that maximum length of the circular queue is five, here are some examples of test sequences produced by SSP.

TC1:	_.add(1).front()
TC2:	_.remove().front()
TC3:	_.add(1).add(−1).remove().add(1295644148).add(−1295644148).front()
TC4:	_.add(0).add(Integer.Max_value).add(Integer.Min_value).add(1).add(−1).front()

As the SSP sequence of events is selected randomly, any sequence follows the conditions specified by the state transition model is valid. For example, a sequence of events for adding an item to a full queue might include adding twenty items; removing eighteen items, adding fifty more, removing fifty two, adding ten more, removing ten, adding one more and checking the result. Hence, the sequence of events might be lengthy and contain redundant data states. The lengthy sequence with redundant states makes testing expensive and ineffective. Also, there is a redundancy occurs between two or more test sequences (i.e. sequence of events), where a test sequence is subset from other sequence(s). Therefore, there is a need to optimize the test suites through removing redundant data states. Among the available techniques, search techniques are the most common for obtaining optimized test suites.

Table 1. The test cases for circularqueue program

#	P	Event	Pre-condition	Post-condition
1.	1	**Add**	len = 0	dataQ'[rear'] = x, rear' = ('rear + 1)%QSIZE, len'='len + 1
2.	1	**Remove**	len = 0	dataQ'='dataQ, front'='front, rear'='rear, len' = 'len
3.	2	**Add**	len = QSIZE	dataQ'='dataQ, front'='front, rear'='rear, len' = 'len
4.	2	**Remove**	len = QSIZE	dataQ'[rear'] = x, front' = ('front + 1)% QSIZE, len'='len−1
5.	3	**Add**	0 < len < QSIZE − 1	dataQ'[rear'] = x, rear' = ('rear + 1)%QSIZE, len'='len + 1
6.	3	**Add**	len = QSIZE − 1	dataQ'[rear'] = x, rear' = ('rear + 1)%QSIZE, len'='len + 1
7.	3	**Remove**	1 < len < QSIZE	dataQ'[rear'] = x, front' = ('front + 1)% QSIZE, len'='len−1
8.	3	**Remove**	len = 1	dataQ'[rear'] = x, front' = ('front + 1)% QSIZE, len'='len−1
9.	4	**Add**	len < 0 && len > QSIZE	dataQ'='dataQ, front'='front, rear'='rear, len' = 'len
10.	4	**Remove**	len < 0 && len > QSIZE	dataQ'='dataQ, front'='front, rear'='rear, len' = 'len

3   Genetic Algorithm (GA)

The applications of search techniques in the domain of software testing grew dramatically as they save efforts and times. For test cases generation, GA is the most common amongst all search techniques. It is a population based metaheuristic technique that follows the theory of natural evolution by Darwin. In GA, the optimal solutions evolved through applying reproduction and selection operations on populations over successive generations [10]. The typical GA consists of five repetitive steps that continue till the stopping criteria is met. The stopping criteria is either finding an optimum solution or reaching the maximum number of iterations. The GA steps are: (1) random initialization of population that contains candidate solutions. Each solution is represented as a chromosome or sequence of variables [11]; (2) evaluation of new candidate solutions, if the stopping criteria is not met; (3) selection of promising candidate solutions based on fitness function. Fitness function is used for evaluating the solution in terms of its ability to solve the problem; (4) crossover; and (5) mutation.

GA performs search in parallel, which leads to fast calculations. Consequently, software testing leads the GA applications compared with other SDLC phases. This includes different disciplines such as test cases generation [7, 12], test cases prioritization within test suites [13], and test suites reductions [11].

However, prior to apply GA for optimizing the test cases, there is a need to derive the fitness function. Besides, the invocation of each event in the sequence may lead to different states. Therefore, there is a need to grasp the changes of states and search within for good solutions to be used in GA next iterations. In the next section, the derivation of fitness function is described.

4 Fitness Function Application in SSP

Fitness function plays an important role in guiding the search within a population of solutions. It judges whether a potential solution presents a good candidate and, hence, has to be used in GA next iterations. The fitness function comes from existing software metrics followed by several refinements according to the results [8].

Anyhow, SSP sequences of events produced a group of states which are unique and redundant states. In order to optimize SSP, we aim to remove the redundant states. There are two types of redundancies: (1) redundancy in test case level and (2) redundancy in test suite level. Therefore, the calculation of fitness function has to take both types into consideration. We introduce two score namely test case states minimization (TCSM) and test suite states minimization (TSSM). The fitness function is:

$$\text{Fitness} = \text{TCSM} + \text{TSSM} \tag{1}$$

4.1 Test Cases States Minimization (TCSM)

TCSM aims to remove redundant states on the test case level, such as the states encountered when trying to add to after reaching the maximum in circular queue or removing when there is no item to be removed. In order to calculate TCSM, there is a need to differentiate between unique and redundant states per sequence of events. A score of TCSM is calculated based on the following equation:

$$\text{TCSM} = \text{USC} + \text{RSC} \tag{2}$$

where USC is the unique states score per sequence of events and RSC is the redundant states score per sequence of events. Let A be a set of unique states in a sequence of events. The calculations for USC is shown in the following equation:

$$USC = \sum_{i=1}^{|A|} \left[\frac{A}{MAX} \right]_i = \frac{1}{MAX} + \frac{1}{MAX} + \dots + \frac{1}{MAX} \tag{3}$$

where |A| is the cardinality for set A, which counts the number of unique states in the sequence of events and MAX is the maximum number of items that can be added to the data structure. For the calculation of RSC, let B be the set of redundant states in a sequence of events where $B \subseteq A$ and $B \cap A = B$. The calculation for RSC as follows:

$$RSC = \sum_{i=1}^{|B|} \left[\frac{-B}{MAX} \right]_i = -\frac{1}{MAX} - \frac{1}{MAX} - \dots - \frac{1}{MAX} \tag{4}$$

where $|B|$ is the cardinality for set B, which counts the number of redundant states per sequence of events. Obviously, the score of TCSM can produce a negative value, which indicates that the sequence is unlikely to be in the GA next generations.

4.2 Test Suites States Minimization (TSSM)

TSSM focuses on removing redundancies between sequences of events in the test suites. This is due to the fact that some sequences of events are subsets from others. So, for a set $C = \{tc_1, tc_2 \ldots tc_n\}$ of test cases (tc), the TSSM is calculated as follows:

$$TSSM = \frac{TCO}{|C|} \tag{5}$$

where $|C|$ is the cardinality for set C, which counts the number of test cases in the population and TCO is a test case occurrence, which counts the occurrences of a specific sequence within the suite. In order to calculate TCO, every sequence (test case) is considered as an individual set such as: $\{tc_1\}, \{tc_2\}, \{tc_n\}$. If k is the counter for counting the occurrence of similar test cases, the sets are compared as follows:

$$\forall tc_{n-1} \subseteq tc_n; \ k = k + 1; \tag{6}$$

5   Case Study

Assume that the following test suite is produced from the SSP technique based on the circular queue example.

TC1:	_.add(1).front()
TC2:	_.remove().front()
TC3:	_.add(1).add(−1).remove().add(1295644148).add(−1295644148).add(0).add(1).add(−1).front()
TC4:	_.add(0).add(Integer.Max_value).add(Integer.Min_value).add(1).add(−1).front()
TC5:	_.remove().remove().front()

To get the fitness, Eq. (1) will be used. However, the values may be greater than or equal to one. So, there is a need to use the average fitness as follows:

$$Average\,Fitness = \frac{Fitness}{Total\,Fitness} \tag{7}$$

where Total Fitness is the summation of all fitness values in the population. Table 2 shows the fitness along with the average fitness for the population above.

The results show that test cases with events close to the maximum number of items that can be added to the data structure. Hence, TC3 got the highest value followed by

Table 2. The fitness values

ID	SC	TSM	Fitness	Average fitness
TC1	0.2	0.4	0.6	0.15
TC2	0.2	0.4	0.6	0.15
TC3	1.2	0.2	1.4	0.35
TC4	1	0.2	1.2	0.3
TC5	0	0.2	0.2	0.05
TOTAL		4	1	

TC4. Besides, the test cases with redundant events, such as TC5, obtain the lowest value.

6 Conclusion

The integration of SSP and GA is promising in order to optimize sequence of events. Prior to any application, there is a need to derive a fitness function that guides the search for solutions within a population. This is a part of an on-going research which aims to enhance the effectiveness of test case generation technique for testing a module with internal memory. We believe that the adoption of GA can improve the effectiveness of SSP to overcome the redundancy issues in SSP and consequently will produce optimized test cases.

References

1. Pressman, R.S.: Software Engineering: A Practitioner's Approach. McGraw-Hill Higher Education, New York (2010)
2. Baharom, S., Shukur, Z.: Module documentation based testing using Grey-Box approach. In: ITSim 2008. International Symposium on Information Technology, 2008 (2008)
3. Baharom, S., Shukur, Z.: State-Sensitivity Partitioning technique for module documentation-based testing. In: Business Transformation through Innovation and Knowledge Management an Academic Perspective. Istanbul, Turkey (2010)
4. Baharom, S., Shukur, Z.: An experimental assessment of module documentation-based testing. Inf. Softw. Technol. 53(7), 747–760 (2011)
5. Alsmadi, I., et al.: Effective generation of test cases using genetic algorithms and optimization theory. J. Commun. Comput. 7(11), 72–82 (2010)
6. Kulkarni, N.J., et al.: Test case optimization using artificial bee colony algorithm. In: Abraham, A., Mauri, J.L., Buford, J.F., Suzuki, J., Thampi, S.M. (eds.) Advances in Computing and Communications. Communications in Computer and Information Science, vol. 192, pp. 570–579. Springer, Heidelberg (2011)
7. Ali, S., et al.: A systematic review of the application and empirical investigation of search-based test case generation. IEEE Trans. Softw. Eng. 36(6), 742–762 (2010)
8. Harman, M., McMinn, P., de Souza, J.T., Yoo, S.: Search based software engineering: techniques, taxonomy, tutorial. In: Meyer, B., Nordio, M. (eds.) Empirical Software Engineering and Verification. LNCS, vol. 7007, pp. 1–59. Springer, Heidelberg (2012)

9. Gannon, J.D., Purtilo, J., Zelkowitz, M.V.: Software Specification: A Comparison of Formal Methods. Ablex Publishing Company, Norwood (1994)
10. Holland, J.H.: Adaptation in Natural and Artificial Systems: An Introductory Analysis with Applications to Biology, Control, and Artificial Intelligence. University of Michigan, Ann Arbor (1975)
11. Li, Z., Harman, M., Hierons, R.M.: Search algorithms for regression test case prioritization. IEEE Trans. Softw. Eng. 33(4), 225–237 (2007)
12. McMinn, P.: Search-based software test data generation: a survey. Softw. Test. Verification Reliab. 14(2), 105–156 (2004)
13. Conrad, A.P., Roos, R.S., Kapfhammer, G.M.: Empirically studying the role of selection operators duringsearch-based test suite prioritization. ACM (2010)

A Negative Input Space Complexity Metric as Selection Criterion for Fuzz Testing

Martin A. Schneider$^{(\boxtimes)}$, Marc-Florian Wendland, and Andreas Hoffmann

Fraunhofer FOKUS, Kaiserin-Augusta-Allee 31, 10589 Berlin, Germany
martin.schneider@fokus.fraunhofer.de

Abstract. Fuzz testing is an established technique in order to find zero-day-vulnerabilities by stimulating a system under test with invalid or unexpected input data. However, fuzzing techniques still generate far more test cases than can be executed. Therefore, different kinds of risk-based testing approaches are used for test case identification, selection and prioritization. In contrast to many approaches that require manual risk analysis, such as fault tree analysis, failure mode and effect analysis, and the CORAS method, we propose an automated approach that takes advantage of an already shown correlation between interface complexity and error proneness. Since fuzzing is a negative testing approach, we propose a complexity metric for the negative input space that measures the boundaries of the negative input space of primitive types and complex data types. Based on this metric, the assumed most error prone interfaces are selected and used as a starting point for fuzz test case generation. This paper presents work in progress.

Keywords: Security testing · Risk-based testing · Fuzz testing · Security metrics

1 Introduction

Today's system are getting more and more complex, becoming systems of systems, such as Cyber-Physical Systems and Internet of Things. This has several implications, in particular with respect to the security point of view. Security relevant vulnerabilities are found and exploited nearly everywhere and have an impact of 3 trillion dollars on the economy [2]. As systems grow and getting more complex, the risk for security-relevant faults is also increasing. This is true for several reasons: complex systems such as Cyber-Physical Systems are a heterogeneous network of sensors, actuators and components that process sensor data and control the actuators. Different transport mechanisms and processing algorithms, e.g. HTTP and SQL, may also lead to vulnerabilities. Complex interfaces, data types and dependencies between different fields of complex data types as well as between different parts of an interface are exacerbating such problems.

Fuzz testing is a technique that tests for faulty input validation mechanism of a system under test (SUT) and their effects if invalid input data is not recognized

© IFIP International Federation for Information Processing 2015
K. El-Fakih et al. (Eds.): ICTSS 2015, LNCS 9447, pp. 257–262, 2015.
DOI: 10.1007/978-3-319-25945-1_17

and rejected but processed by the SUT. Input validation mechanisms determine whether a given value is valid or not in terms of a specification. They specify the boundaries of the input space for valid data. The complement of the input space of valid data is the negative input space comprising all invalid values. We suppose that the more boundaries have to be checked for given data, the higher is the risk of a faulty implementation of the corresponding validation mechanisms.

The rest of this paper is organized as follows: Sect. 2 presents related work with respect to metrics for vulnerabilities that supports our hypothesis. Section 3 describes the different elements our metric is composed of. Since we propose to use this metric as a selection criterion for fuzz testing, we describe in Sect. 4 how this could be achieved. Section 5 presents first results from the MIDAS project and Sect. 6 concludes with an outlook.

2   Related Work

There are several investigations on complexity of code and its error proneness. This includes vulnerabilities as well. Corresponding metrics can be distinguished whether they are based on source code, code changes or interfaces.

Shin et al. [7] employed a combination of different code complexity, code churn, and developer metrics in order to predict vulnerabilities and vulnerable source code files, built prediction models using logistic regression and showed their prediction capabilities on the Mozilla Firefox web browser and the Linux kernel. Their goal was to reduce the effort for code inspection and testing.

Chowdhury and Zulkernine [6] presented a framework for vulnerability prediction based on complexity, coupling, and cohesion metrics applied to source code. They built vulnerability predictors employing C4.5, random forest, logistic regression, and naive-Bayes classifier. A vulnerability prediction accuracy of 74 % has been achieved by this approach.

Cataldo et al. [5] showed that there is not only a correlation between source code based metrics and vulnerabilities but also between interface complexity and error proneness. Since he considered only errors that occurred for systems in the field, this correlation is not only of statistical but also of practical significance. Cataldo employed the metrics interface size and operation argument complexity that were used by Bandi et al. [3]. Operation argument complexity was dependent of the type of the operation's arguments. A constant value is assigned to each type, e.g. 0 is assigned to Boolean, 2 to Real, and 6 to Record, Struct, and Objects. The operation argument complexity is determined by the sum of the complexity of each argument's type [3]. The interface size is defined the product of the number of parameters and the sum of their sizes (operation argument complexity).

3   Negative Input Space Complexity

The works of Cataldo [5] and Bandi [3] form the basis for a negative input space complexity suitable for security testing. In contrast to Shin [7] and Chowdhury [6], the metrics used by Cataldo do not require access to source code but only to the interfaces while preserving a correlation to the error proneness. Thus, this correlation is appropriate for black box approaches. Therefore, we call such metrics black box metrics.

We aim at using black box metrics in order to assess the risk for a vulnerability within an implementation of an interface. Since there is a correlation between interface complexity, operation argument complexity and error proneness, we suppose this correlation holds true for security-relevant errors as well.

We would like to exploit the supposed correlation for prioritization of security test cases generated by using data fuzzing techniques and to select types as a starting point for fuzzing. Data fuzzing techniques inject invalid or unexpected input data to a system under test in order to reveal security-relevant implementation flaws based on missing or faulty input validation mechanisms [4]. Semi-valid input data is generated to test each input validation mechanism separately in order to ensure that each constraint that must be hold by valid input data is correctly implemented. Our presumption is: The more constraints apply for an input date of a certain type, the higher is the chance that one of these validation mechanism is faulty.

The negative input space of a certain type is determined by the boundaries of the positive input space comprising all valid values. The boundaries between the positive and negative input space is specified by the constraint a valid input data has to respect. Therefore, the negative input space metric is expressed with respect to these constraints.

Hypothesis: A high negative input space complexity is an indicator for a higher risk of a faulty implementation of an input validation mechanism.

However, given the fact that there is a faulty implementation of an input validation mechanism, there may be two cases. On one hand, the validation mechanism is too loose, i.e. an actually invalid input date is considered to be valid. Such a situation may pose a security-relevant fault, i.e. a vulnerability. On the other hand, the validation mechanism may be too strict and reject actual valid values assuming that they are invalid. This may constitute a functional error. Whilst the focus of this work is on the first case, it may also have an impact on assessing the functionality of a system considering the second case.

Since our metric is based on the constraints for valid input data, we have to carefully investigate the different kinds and the structure of them and how they may be assessed by the metrics.

Basically, we can distinguish two kinds of separations between valid and invalid input data: static and dynamic boundaries. A static boundary is defined by an expression that does not contain any variable despite that one whose value shall be decided whether it is valid or not. Considering $x > 5$ as a constraint for valid values. x is the variable whose valid range is defined to be all values greater than 5. Obviously, such a constraint is quite easily implemented and there is only very little chance for a faulty implementation of a corresponding input validation mechanism. However, considering as input type a string, there may be a lot of such constraints that has to be tested in order to decide whether a given value is valid leading to a higher risk of a faulty validation mechanism.

In contrast, a dynamic boundary depends on other variables, e.g. parts of a given input data, in order to determine if a provided data is valid. Considering a calendar date, the lower boundary of the day value is static, i.e. $day > 0$, while its upper boundary is dynamic because it depends on the month:

$(day < 29 \wedge month = 2) \vee$
$(day < 31 \wedge (month = 4 \vee month = 6 \vee month = 9 \vee month = 11)) \vee$
$(day < 32 \wedge (month = 1 \vee month = 3 \vee month = 5 \vee month = 7 \vee$
$month = 8 \vee month = 10 \vee month = 12))$

This boundary is dynamic, i.e. it is a different value depending on the value of another variable, the month. The implementation of an appropriate input validation mechanism is more error prone than one of a static boundary because another variable has to be evaluated. Obviously, the above-noted expression is not correct because leap years are not yet considered. Considering leap years increases the complexity of the expression because additional logical clauses have to be added that take the year variable into account. On the whole, the validity of the day number depends on two other variables (month and year) and on a complex expression that specifies four boundaries (28, 29, 30, and 31 may be the upper boundary of a valid day number).

Until now, the metric shall take into account the following aspects: whether a boundary is static or dynamic, the number of different boundaries, and on how many variables a dynamic boundary depends on.

The complexity of the expression for a boundary does also have an impact on the complexity and may increase the error proneness of the implementation. The complexity of the boundary expression can be measured using the corresponding abstract syntax tree that depends on its height. This is the fourth aspect that shall influence the metrics. A first approximation of the metric is defined as follows:

$$|b_{stat}| + \sum_{i=1}^{|b_{dyn}|} |vars_i| \cdot height_{AST} \tag{1}$$

where $|b_{stat}|$ denotes the number of static boundaries, i.e. boundaries that do not depend on any other variable as for instance $day > 0$,

$|b_{dyn}|$ denotes the number of dynamic boundaries, i.e. boundaries that do depend on other variables, e.g. 28, 29, 30, and 31 for a day,

$|vars_i|$ denotes the number of variables on which a dynamic boundary depends, e.g. 2 for the day its dynamic boundaries that depends on month and year,

$height_{AST}$ denotes the height of the abstract syntax tree of the expression of a dynamic boundary, e.g. 1 for the expression $(day < 29 \wedge month = 2)$, and 2 for the expression $(day < 31 \wedge (month = 4 \vee month = 6 \vee month = 9 \vee month = 11))$.

The correct implementation of an input validation mechanism for a static boundary is rather easy to implement, we set it to one, resulting in a complexity that depends on the number of static boundaries $|b_{stat}|$. For each dynamic boundary, we determine its complexity by the number of variables it depends on ($|vars_i|$) and the complexity of its expression in terms of the height of the expression's abstract syntax tree ($height_{AST}$). We use the sum of the complexity of all boundaries as metric of the negative input space complexity.

4   Using the Metric as Selection Criterion for Fuzz Testing

The metric described above presents an approach to assess the proneness of the implementation of an interface for being faulty in terms of input validation and thus, for potential vulnerabilities. The easiest way to use this metric is to perform a prioritization of testing efforts based on decreasing metric score. Of much more interest would be to find a threshold of the complexity metric beyond the most implementations, e.g. 80 percent, are faulty. Of course, this threshold may depend on other factors such as the programming language. Another aspect would be whether the interface size by Bandi et al. [3] is still of statistical significance when being based on the presented metric.

5   Examples from the MIDAS Project

Within the MIDAS European research project [1], we are currently building a test platform on the cloud for testing of service-oriented architectures. As part of this project, we are implementing different fuzzing techniques in addition to the metric presented above. Our joint input model is a Domain Specific Language (DSL) based on Unified Modeling Language (UML) and UML Testing Profile (UTP) which already provides mechanics for defining fuzzing operators for test cases.

Within the project, we are working together with industrial partners. One is from the logistics domains. Its web services are implementing the Global Standards One (GS1) Logistics Interoperability Model (LIM)[1]. It provides a large number of different types specified using XML schema.

We parsed the type specifications and their constraints and calculated a few complexity scores depicted in Table 1. The first type String80Type is a simple string with a length restriction of at least one character and at most 80. The calculated score is determined by the number of boundaries, in this example 2, one for the lower bound and one for the upper bound. The remaining two types are of interest because the type validity is specified by a regular expression. In order to determine their complexity score, we resolve predefined character classes and evaluate the different number of character ranges as well as quantifiers. The difference between the two types GIAIType and GRAIType results from the predefined character range \d that comprises many more than the Arabic digits and thus, are constituting an interesting starting point for fuzz testing.

---

[1] http://www.gs1.org/lim.

Table 1. Complexity Score Examples from GS1 LIM

Type name	Expression	Complexity score
String80Type	$length \geq 1 \wedge length \leq 80$	2
GIAIType	[-!"&'()*+,./0-9:;<=>?A–Z_a–z]4,30	27
GRAIType	\d{14}[-!"&'()*+,./0-9:;<=>?A–Z_a–z]4,30	102

6 Outlook

Within the MIDAS project, we will validate the metrics using our pilots from the Logistics domain and the Healthcare domain, using HL7-based web services and thus, a complex type system as well. We will adjust the metric based on our experiences and are considering also different aspects, such as the different number of constraint types, e.g. regular expressions and simple constraints, e.g. the length constraints. Investigating a threshold beyond that components, interfaces, and types shall be selected for fuzzing testing is a second task of importance. A comparison with other metric-based vulnerability prediction frameworks described in Sect. 2 can be achieved by applying the metric to the Mozilla Firefox web browser.

Acknowledgments. This work was partially funded by the EU FP7 projects MIDAS (no. 318786) and RASEN (no. 316853).

References

1. EC FP7 MIDAS Project, FP7-316853 (2012–2015). www.midas-project.eu
2. Risk and responsibility in a hyperconnected world. Technical report, World Economic Forum/McKinsey (2014)
3. Bandi, R., Vaishnavi, V., Turk, D.: Predicting maintenance performance using object-oriented design complexity metrics. IEEE Trans. Softw. Eng. **29**(1), 77–87 (2003)
4. Bekrar, S., Bekrar, C., Groz, R., Mounier, L.: Finding software vulnerabilities by smart fuzzing. In: IEEE Fourth International Conference on Software Testing, Verification and Validation (ICST) 2011, pp. 427–430 (March 2011)
5. Cataldo, M., Souza, C.R.B.D., Bentolila, D.L., Mir, T.C., Nambiar, S.: The impact of interface complexity on failures: an empirical analysis and implications for tool design (2010)
6. Chowdhury, I., Zulkernine, M.: Using complexity, coupling, and cohesion metrics as early indicators of vulnerabilities. J. Syst. Archit.- Embed. Syst. Des. **57**(3), 294–313 (2011). http://dx.doi.org/10.1016/j.sysarc.2010.06.003
7. Shin, Y., Meneely, A., Williams, L., Osborne, J.: Evaluating complexity, code churn, and developer activity metrics as indicators of software vulnerabilities. IEEE Trans. Softw. Eng. **37**(6), 772–787 (2011)

A Practical Evaluation Method of Network Traffic Load for Capacity Planning

Takeshi Kitahara$^{(\boxtimes)}$, Shuichi Nawata, Masaki Suzuki,
Norihiro Fukumoto, and Shigehiro Ano

KDDI R&D Laboratories Inc., 2-1-15 Ohara, Fujimino-shi, Saitama, Japan
kitahara@kddilabs.jp

Abstract. Communications network operators are supposed to provide high quality network service at low cost. Operators always monitor the amount of traffic and decide equipment investment when the amount exceeds a certain threshold considering trade-offs between link capacity and its utilization. To find the proper threshold efficiently, this paper proposes a practical threshold definition method which consists of fine grained data collection and computer simulation. We evaluate the proposed method using commercial traffic data-set. The results show the proper timing for the equipment investment.

Keywords: Capacity planning · Traffic monitoring · Traffic load testing · Queuing simulation

1 Introduction

The largest mission for communications network operator is to provide high-quality network service at low cost, but there always exists trade-off between quality and cost. To ensure quality of network service, it is crucial to keep traffic load of the link below a certain threshold level and to upgrade the link capacity immediately after the load exceeds the threshold. From the viewpoint of the capital expenditure, on the other hand, this threshold value should be set to high so that traffic can be accommodated into the link as much as possible. Thus finding the appropriate threshold value is the main effort for capacity planning.

Traffic load is typically observed with a monitoring tool such as MRTG [1] (Multi Router Traffic Grapher) in terms of average volume during several minutes, because watching traffic load with finer granularity requires computing resources. Considering practical use, the threshold mentioned above should be represented as the ratio of average traffic volume in minutes to the original link capacity. For example, the threshold would be 80 % if five-minute average of 800 Mbit/s is the maximum load for a certain GbE (Gigabit Ethernet) link so as not to degrade quality. However, averaging through minutes masks information about burstiness of traffic on each link. In the case of bursty traffic where the difference between the instantaneous peak and several-minute average is large, probability of packet loss would be high compared to the case of traffic where such the difference is small even though average loads in minutes are equivalent. Thus capacity for links with bursty traffic should be upgraded earlier than links with not-bursty traffic. A lot of past work addressed characterizing traffic

© IFIP International Federation for Information Processing 2015
K. El-Fakih et al. (Eds.): ICTSS 2015, LNCS 9447, pp. 263–268, 2015.
DOI: 10.1007/978-3-319-25945-1_18

burstiness [2–6], but there are no generalized models which can be applied to individual network operating and/or planning task because network structure, network usage, and applications on network are quite diverse nowadays.

For the purpose of obtaining an appropriate threshold of upgrading capacity for each link, we propose a practical method to evaluate traffic load considering its burstiness while satisfying the target level of packet loss ratio. Furthermore, we also evaluate this method using commercial traffic data-set in an operator's network.

2   Proposed Method

There are two challenges to be addressed in this study. One is to comprehend the burstiness about the traffic on the target link and the other is to calculate the threshold for upgrading capacity considering burstiness. Thus the proposed method consists of (1) collecting data about inter-packet arrival time and packet size for several minutes on the target link and (2) evaluating the burstiness of the collected data and to calculate the threshold value using computer simulation.

(1)   Data collection

Burstiness of traffic cannot be estimated from five-minute average load where operators usually observe. To show that, we select four data-sets which were observed at two different points and on two different dates. Figure 1 shows the data-sets. They are hereinafter referred to as Data 1, Data 2, Data 3 and Data 4. All data-sets describe traffic load on Link A or Link B in terms of bit/s for five minutes. Note that X-axes of all figures indicate 0 to 300 s. Each of Link A and Link B belongs to different commercial network. Traffic load during five minutes of Data 1 and Data 3 are nearly equal to that of Data 2 and Data 4, respectively. The normalized five-minute volumes of Data 1 through Data 4 are 1.003, 1.000, 1.210 and 1.223, respectively. Note that Y-axes of all figures are in the same scale. We also show three kinds of granularity of each data-set, which are one-millisecond, one-second and five-minutes. For evaluation of burstiness, the proposed method obtains packet-by-packet data. Note that this is only for deciding the threshold and observing fine grained data is not required for daily operation.

(2)   Computer simulation

The simulation solves the least required link capacity under the given conditions regarding target packet loss ratio and buffer size when traffic pattern is provided as input. The input data in this study is time-series data describing a pair of inter-arrival time and length of each packet, which are extracted from Data 1 through Data 4. The size of each input data for the simulation ranges from around 70 Mbytes to 130 Mbytes. The least required capacity corresponds to the value of the threshold discussed so far. The notations of R, B, X, m and p are output rate from the queue, buffer size, input traffic to the queue, input mean rate to the queue and target packet loss ratio, respectively. In the simulation, an event will be processed each time the packet #n ($n = 1, \ldots,$ N) arrives at the queue. Note that X consists of N packets. We define t_n, l_n and $Q[n]$ as the time when the packet #n arrives, the length of the packet #n and the queue length at the time t_n, respectively. Figure 2 represents the relationship among the notations.

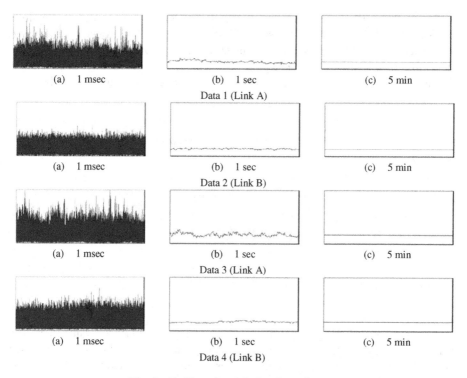

Fig. 1. Traffic volume during five minutes

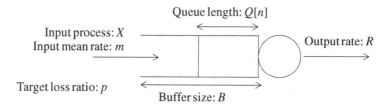

Fig. 2. Notations of the simulation.

According to Eq. (1), $Q[n]$ will be updated each time n is increased, which means a packet arrives at the queue. This process will continue until n reaches N.

$$Q_{tmp} = Q[n-1] - R \cdot (t_n - t_{n-1}) \ (n = 1, 2, \ldots, N)$$

$$Q[n] = \begin{cases} Q_{tmp} + l_n & (if \ Q_{tmp} + l_n < B) \\ Q_{tmp} & (otherwise) \end{cases} \qquad (1)$$

$$N_{loss} = \begin{cases} N_{loss} & (if \ Q_{tmp} + l_n < B) \\ N_{loss} + 1 & (otherwise) \end{cases}$$

where N_{loss} describes the number of packet losses during the simulation. Figure 3 shows an example of queuing process. In this example, packet #n enters into the queue but packet #($n + 1$) is dropped. To calculate the least required capacity meeting the packet loss ratio p, the following steps are performed. Such the capacity is denoted as C_{opt} and we employ a bisection method to find the value of C_{opt} for this study.

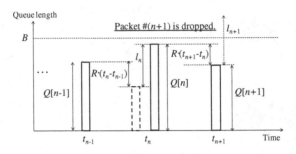

Fig. 3. Example of simulation process.

Step 1

Determine p and B based on the operation policy. Calculate the value of m of a data-set X we focus on. Determine C_{low} and C_{high} for initial values of R. We used $C_{low} = m$ and $C_{high} = 10\ m$ as the initial values, respectively. In addition, dC should be determined as the terminal condition. In this simulation, we employ 100 kbit/s as the value of dC.

Step 2

Perform the queuing simulation based on Eq. (1) in the both cases of C_{low} and C_{high}. The values of N_{loss} for both cases are obtained through the simulation. Note that the simulation will be terminated, if N_{loss} exceeds $p \cdot N$ during the simulation.

Step 3

Update C_{low} and C_{high} by using a bisection method [6]. If $N_{loss}/N > p$, C_{low} is set to $(C_{low} + C_{high})/2$. In the same manner, if $N_{loss}/N < p$, C_{high} is set to $(C_{low} + C_{high})/2$. Figure 4 shows the conceptual diagram of the bisection method for this simulation.

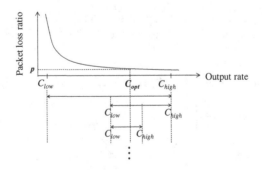

Fig. 4. Bisection method for the simulation.

Step 4

Repeat Step 3 until $C_{high} - C_{low} < dC$. Then the value obtained is C_{opt}. We define ρ as m/C_{opt}, which is the key indicator for capacity planning. This is because the value of ρ represents maximum allowable ratio of traffic load to meet the target quality for the link.

3 Simulation Result and Discussion

Figure 5 shows the result of the simulation using Data 1 through Data 4. In the simulation, buffer size B for each simulation is set to m multiplied by 1 and 10 ms. This implies that maximum delay of the buffer is around 1 or 10 ms. We observe the significant difference regarding ρ between Data 1 and Data 2 although the values m are nearly equivalent as mentioned before. This is also applied to between Data 3 and Data 4. Since each of Data 1 and Data 3 is bursty compared to each of Data 2 and Data 4 respectively as intuitively confirmed in Fig. 1, the difference of ρ is found to depend on the burstiness of the traffic. Furthermore ρ of Data 1 is quite close to that of Data 3 and this relationship is applied to between Data 2 and Data 4. This suggests that the degree of the burstiness should be dependent on the link we observed. In other words, average volume do not have a large impact on the value of ρ. In addition, we confirm the target packet loss ratio has a considerable impact to the value of ρ. This targeting is left to a policy of the trade-off between quality and investment. To make a right decision for operators, the obtained values of ρ are quite beneficial. Furthermore, computing time required to obtain the results is important from the practical viewpoint. In this simulation, it takes about 10 to 20 min to complete a simulation to obtain one value of ρ corresponding to one point in Fig. 5.

There are not purely theoretical methods to calculate the value of ρ, because ρ is determined by quite many factors. The possible factors affecting ρ are the number of nodes where the traffic goes through, services and applications generating traffic, customers where the network is targeted for, and so on. This paper, however, does not focus on these factors because these factors themselves are not so important from the viewpoint of practical capacity planning. The largest interest for practitioners is *"when do I need to increase the capacity?"*. The answer is when the observed mean rate

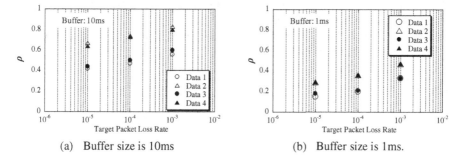

(a) Buffer size is 10ms   (b) Buffer size is 1ms.

Fig. 5. Simulation results regarding maximum allowable ratio of traffic load ρ.

reaches original link capacity C multiplied by ρ. Since the mean rate is able to be predicted using conventional techniques of time-series analysis, the appropriate timing for enhancement of capacity can be easily estimated. If a practitioner collects some datasets on a certain link and calculates ρ corresponding to each dataset, the lowest value of ρ should be applied to the link against the unexpected excessive load while it depends on operator's policy. Note that we assume that the value of ρ of the future, which is the time when total traffic volume increases, should not be significantly changed. Figure 5 supports this assumption.

4 Conclusion

While research related to burstiness of traffic have been studied in these twenty years, network operators might still rely on their experienced knowledge. Since real traffic is quite diverse, there are no generalized models which can apply to all kinds of traffic. Thus we were eager to fill the gap between research and practice. This paper proposed a practical evaluation method for network capacity planning. We applied the proposed method to commercial traffic data which were observed at two different points and on two different dates. Since the proposed method is quite specific and concrete, network operators can easily apply this method to their work. We believe the contribution of this paper helps them to improve quality of their work.

References

1. Shipway, S.: Using MRTG with RRDtool and Routers2, Cheshire Cat Computing (2010)
2. Leland, W.E., et al.: On the self-similar nature of ethernet traffic (extended version). IEEE/ACM Trans. on Netw. 2(1), 1–15 (1994)
3. Taqqu, M.S., et al.: Proof of a fundamental result in self-similar traffic modeling. ACM SIGCOMM Comput. Commun. Rev. 27(2), 5–23 (1997)
4. Erramilli, A., et al.: Experimental queuing analysis with long-range dependent packet traffic. IEEE/ACM Trans. on Netw. 4(2), 226–244 (1996)
5. Kandula, S., et al.: The nature of data center traffic: measurements & analysis. In: Proceedings of the 9th ACM SIGCOMM Conference on Internet Measurement Conference (IMC 2009) (2009)
6. Benson, T., et al.: Understanding data center traffic characteristic. ACM SIGCOMM Comput. Commun. Rev. 40(1), 92–99 (2010)
7. Burden, R.L., Faires, J.D.: 2.1 The bisection algorithm. In: Numerical Analysis. PWS Publishers, Englewood Cliffs (1985)

Author Index

Printed in the United States
By Bookmasters